Financial Stability, Systems and Regulation

Ever since the 2007–8 global financial crisis and its aftermath, Hyman Minsky's theory has never been more relevant.

Throughout his career, Jan Kregel has called attention to Minsky's contributions to understanding the evolution of financial systems, the development of financial fragility and instability, and designing the financial structure necessary to support the capital development of the economy. Building on Minsky, Kregel developed a framework to analyze how different financial structures develop financial fragility over time. Rather than characterizing financial systems as market-based or bank-based, Kregel argued that it is necessary to distinguish between the risks that are carried on the balance sheets of banks and other financial institutions. This volume, brought together by Felipe C. Rezende, highlights these major contributions from Kregel through a collection of his influential papers from various journals and conferences.

Kregel's approach provides a strong theoretical background to understand the making and unfolding of the crisis and helps us to draw policy implications to improve financial stability, and suggest an alternative financial structure for a market economy. In this book, his knowledge is consolidated and the ideas he puts forward offer a path for future developments in economics which will be of great interest to those studying and researching in the fields of economics and finance.

Jan Kregel is Director of Research at the Levy Economics Institute of Bard College, USA. He is also Director of the Levy Institute Master's Program in Economic Theory and Policy, and Head of the Institute's Monetary Policy and Financial Structure program. In addition, he holds the position of Professor of Development Finance at Tallinn University of Technology, Estonia. In 2011, he was elected to the Accademia Nazionale dei Lincei, also known as the Lincean Academy, and he is a life fellow of the Royal Economic Society (UK) and an elected member of the Società Italiana degli Economisti.

Felipe C. Rezende is an Associate Professor of Economics and Finance, and Director of the finance program at Bard College, USA. He previously taught at Hobart and William Smith Colleges (2010–17) and the University of Missouri–Kansas City (2009) and is a regular columnist in American and Brazilian newspapers.

Routledge Critical Studies in Finance and Stability

Edited by Jan Toporowski

School of Oriental and African Studies, University of London, UK

The 2007–8 Banking Crash has induced a major and wide-ranging discussion on the subject of financial (in)stability and a need to re-evaluate theory and policy. The response of policy-makers to the crisis has been to refocus fiscal and monetary policy on financial stabilization and reconstruction. However, this has been done with only vague ideas of bank recapitalization and "Keynesian" reflation aroused by the exigencies of the crisis, rather than the application of any systematic theory or theories of financial instability.

Routledge Critical Studies in Finance and Stability covers a range of issues in the area of finance including instability, systemic failure, financial macroeconomics in the vein of Hyman P. Minsky, Ben Bernanke and Mark Gertler, central bank operations, financial regulation, developing countries and financial crises, new portfolio theory and New International Monetary and Financial Architecture.

For more information about this series, please visit www.routledge.com/series/RCSFS

Financial Stability, Systems and Regulation

Jan Kregel

Edited by Felipe C. Rezende

Routledge
Taylor & Francis Group

LONDON AND NEW YORK

First published 2019
by Routledge
2 Park Square, Milton Park, Abingdon, Oxon OX14 4RN

and by Routledge
52 Vanderbilt Avenue, New York, NY 10017, USA

First issued in paperback 2020

Routledge is an imprint of the Taylor & Francis Group, an informa business

© 2019 Jan Kregel and Felipe C. Rezende

British Library Cataloguing-in-Publication Data
A catalogue record for this book is available from the British Library

Library of Congress Cataloging-in-Publication Data
Names: Kregel, Jan, author. | Rezende, Felipe C., 1981– editor.
Title: Financial stability, systems and regulation / by Jan Kregel ;
    edited by Felipe C. Rezende.
Description: 1 Edition. | New York : Routledge, 2019. | Series: Routledge critical
    studies in finance and stability | Includes bibliographical references and index.
Identifiers: LCCN 2018019892 (print) | LCCN 2018020906 (ebook) |
    ISBN 9781315438290 (Ebook) | ISBN 9781138218130 (hardback : alk. paper)
Subjects: LCSH: International finance. | Financial services industry—State
    supervision. | Universal banks. | Monetary policy.
Classification: LCC HG3881 (ebook) | LCC HG3881 .K74 2019 (print) |
    DDC 332/.042—dc23
LC record available at https://lccn.loc.gov/2018019892

ISBN 13: 978-0-367-58632-4 (pbk)
ISBN 13: 978-1-138-21813-0 (hbk)

Typeset in Bembo
by Apex CoVantage, LLC

Contents

Preface

The essays in this collection represent the application of an economic tradition which seems to have been lost in modern academic economics dealing with macroeconomics and money. My own introduction to these subjects was motivated by Paul Davidson's insistence that Keynes's *General Theory* could only be understood as an expression of monetary theory. This would not have been a particularly novel position in the 1930s, but in the 1960s under the compromise of the neoclassical synthesis and the onslaught of the Monetarist counter-revolution it was indeed novel. But my own realization of this approach came through early study of the *Treatise on Money* which despite its title was less an analysis of what was then considered monetary theory and more a theory of business cycles and a description of financial markets. For example, it is only by understanding Keynes's use of normal backwardation in forward markets discussed in the *Treatise* that one can appreciate that the *General Theory* was not the application of Marshallian partial equilibrium to the economy as whole in the short period.

Acquaintance with the *Treatise* and prior work also provides a clear understanding of why the charge that the money supply is exogenous in the *General Theory* completely misunderstands Keynes approach to money, as well as that of most all of his business cycle contemporaries in England and on the continent. For anyone who bothers to follow up this literature from Schumpeter onwards can find it very clearly stated that the entrepreneur's decision to produce requires the decision to issue liabilities which the banking system validates through the creation of its own liabilities which serve as means of payment. In more modern jargon, "loans create deposits" was simply the expression of these economists' knowledge of the actual operation of the financial system. Indeed most of them were actively involved in the sophisticated financial markets of the pre-14–18 war financial system and the disruptions that followed. Had modern post-Keynesian monetary debate started from this point, there would never have been a need for horizontalists versus verticalists, or an endogenous versus exogenous debate. It was not a question of theory, it was a question of how financial markets function. Starting from this point would also have saved a great deal of misrepresentation concerning the constraints on the economy. Again, from Schumpeter onwards it was taken at given that since there was no limit to the acceptance of business liabilities by the banking system, there could be no limit on expenditures, other than the banks' willingness to lend and the ability of the business firms to meet the service on their liabilities. In modern jargon, "savings cannot limit investment." These two points were the building blocks of business cycles, and they put paid to any idea that you could split economic analysis into real and money terms: no veil was possible in this approach, it made no sense. But the interpretation of this fact did generate a sharp policy split for on the one hand it was possible to argue that government could spend as much as it needed to reach full employment without diverting limited private savings, while on the other it was possible to make a strong case to limit lending so as to make the system behave as if investment was limited by savings.

With these sorts of rudimentary ideas about money and macroeconomics I arrived in Cambridge with the idea of putting monetary factors into what came to be called the post-Keynesian tradition of growth and distribution. I was quickly abused of that idea and reframed things in terms of the *General Theory* being about the Marshallian short period, and thus in need of an equivalent Marshallian long period. Although Joan Robinson and Nicholas Kaldor were financially sophisticated, they really never seemed to follow what seemed to me to be Keynes' modus operandi – from financial markets to economic theory. It was first to the Marshall and then we will come back and fit in the money and finance.

It was at this time that I was ripe for an encounter with Hy Minsky who kept insisting that Keynes was a business cycle theorist steeped in financial markets wisdom as he was – which was historically correct. It is telling that he spent most of his time on a Cambridge sabbatical reading the *Treatise* in order to produce his book John Maynard Keynes which is about the *General Theory*. But the *General Theory* was not a book about business cycles, but about underemployment equilibrium. This caused no end of disputation between Minsky and Davidson who looked on money the key to Keynes explanation of equilibrium and Minsky's idea that it would produce endless expansions and contractions that would require an active approach to financial regulation as well as economic policies. Indeed, Minsky's whole approach was built on the idea that even if you managed to produce economic policies – it was then called fine-tuning and gained traction under Kennedy and the New Frontier – that produced stability, this would surreptitiously create financing structures which would become increasingly fragile and lead eventually to crisis. No stabilization policy without regulatory policy, and even then, the best you could do would be to dampen the natural instability of the capitalist system based on the simple premise that ownership or control of capital assets was gained by issuing liabilities, which were held as assets of financial institutions and which had to be validated by the earnings of those capital assets. If they were insufficient, as eventually they always would be, then the system would naturally skirt crisis. It was the role of regulation to try to limit the fragility of the financial structure.

On this basis I went on to provide an explication of the *General Theory* solely in terms of financial market instruments, which Geoff Harcourt has baptized the "College Bursar's" version of the book. These essays, in contrast, simply apply this way of thinking about a sophisticated financial economic system that I absorbed from these mentors. If there is anything in this collection that would be considered more than a simple elaboration or application of their work, it is in the section on international and developmental implications. It is often noted that the *General Theory* did not make express reference to international trade and payments, although they were at the center of the *Treatise* and Keynes spent most of his life on these issues. While Minsky was very focused on US institutions and conditions, he did leave clear markers on how he might have expanded his approach to more global considerations. Given current economic and political difficulties that have emerged from the global integration of production and finance they are perhaps the most pertinent guides to how this approach should develop.

Acknowledgments

We would like to thank Wiley for permission to reproduce the following paper:

Kregel, J.A., "Market Form and Financial Performance," *Economic Notes*, Vol. 24, No. 3, 1995, pp. 485–504.

We would like to thank the Levy Economics Institute of Bard College for permission to reproduce the following papers:

Kregel, J.A., "Managing the Impact of Volatility in International Capital Markets in an Uncertain World," (April 24, 2009). Levy Economics Institute Working Paper No. 558.

Kregel, J.A., "The Natural Instability of Financial Markets," (December 2007). Levy Economics Institute Working Paper No. 523.

Kregel, J.A., "Yes, 'It' Did Happen Again – A Minsky Crisis Happened in Asia," Working Paper No. 234, Jerome Levy Economics Institute.

Kregel, J.A., "The Brazilian Crisis: From Inertial Inflation to Financial Fragility," Working Paper No. 294, Jeromy Levy Economics Institute.

Kregel, J.A., "Emerging Markets and the International Financial Architecture: A Blueprint for Reform (February 11, 2015)," Working Papers Series No. 833, Levy Economics Institute.

Kregel, J.A., "Using Minsky to Simplify Financial Regulation," Levy Economics Institute Research Report, April 2012.

Kregel, J. "Minsky and Dynamic Macroprudential Regulation" "Minsky and Dynamic Macroprudential Regulation," Public Policy Brief Archive ppb_131, Levy Economics Institute.

We would like to thank Moneta e Credito for permission to reproduce the following paper:

Kregel, J.A., "Universal Banking, US Banking Reform and Financial Competition in the EEC," *Banca Nazionale del Lavoro Quarterly Review*, No. 182, September, 1992, pp. 231–54 (in Italian, No. 179, pp. 289–314).

We would like to thank Palgrave Macmillan for permission to reproduce the following papers:

Kregel, J.A., "Financial Liberalization and Domestic Policy Space: Theory and Practice With Reference to Latin America," in Arestis, P. and Paula, L. F. (eds.), *Financial Liberalization and Economic Performance in Emerging Countries*. London: Palgrave Macmillan, 2008.
Kregel, J.A., "Currency Stabilization Through Full Employment: Can EMU Combine Price Stability With Employment and Income Growth?" *Eastern Economic Journal*, 1999, 25(1), 35–47.

We would like to thank the Einaudi Institute for Economics and Finance for permission to reproduce the following paper:

Kregel, J., "The Past and Future of Banks," Quaderni di Ricerche 21 (Einaudi, 1998).

We would like to thank Taylor & Francis for permission to reproduce the following papers:

Kregel, J.A., "Some Considerations on the Causes of Structural Change in Financial Markets," *Journal of Economic Issues*, September, 1992, pp. 733–47.
Kregel, J.A., "Margins of Safety and Weight of the Argument in Generating Financial Fragility," *Journal of Economic Issues*, June, 1997, pp. 543–8.

Part I

The evolution of financial systems

1   The past and future of banks[1]

Introduction

The trend decline in the share of financial assets intermediated on bank balance sheets has caused concern for the survival of banking. First noticed in the 1920s in the United States (cf. Currie, 1934), the problem reappeared some 30 years later (cf. Goldsmith, 1958) and after another 30-some years is again today cause for concern.[2] The phenomenon has also been observed in a wide range of countries including the UK and France (cf. Goldsmith, 1969). However, the decline of French banking, which occurred during the 1970s and 1980s, now seems to have been reversed, and the decline seems to have abated in a number of other countries, including the US. As yet, there has been little evidence in Germany, although it is widely predicted to occur as a response to the creation of the European Economic and Monetary Union (EMU) in Europe in 1999.

There is some dispute concerning the proper measure of the activity of banks in the economy and just exactly what these measures show. A commonly used benchmark is banks' share of assets held by all financial institutions. In the US this share has fallen from around 50% in the 1950s to around 25% in the 1990s. The figure was as high as 70% in the mid-19th century and over 60% in 1900 (cf. Goldsmith, 1958, 1969). On the other hand, measures of bank loans as a percentage of GDP show a rise from around 20% in the 1950s to over 30% in the 1990s and a rise in total bank assets as a proportion of GDP from 40% to 50% over the same period (cf. Boyd and Gertler, 1994). For the UK, the share of banks in total liabilities of financial intermediaries has fallen from over 60% in 1913 to under 30% in the 1990s (Kaufman and Mote, 1994, p. 8). Further, there are difficulties in defining appropriate measures for banks' activity (cf. Kaufman and Mote, 1994, pp. 4–5) as well as in defining what should be classified as a bank.

A number of major countries, such as the US, Italy, France, and Japan, emerged from the war with "segmented" banking systems in which legal restrictions limited the activities permitted to deposit-taking banks. These regulations created a legal and functional separation between "commercial" banks and "non-bank" financial institutions. The basic distinction was to restrict commercial banks' investments to short- and medium-term lending, whereas non-banks were forbidden from issuing short-term demand or sight deposits.

In contrast, countries such as Germany and the UK maintained their pre-war systems of bank regulation, which placed virtually no limitation on banks' assets or liabilities. France eventually introduced this type of banking regulation in 1984, while the US is still debating reform that will abolish the existing separation of commercial and investment banking. European Community banking laws now allow banks the right of establishment under the regulatory regime operating in their home country. This has meant that most countries have revised their banking laws to allow their domestic banks the same freedom of operation granted to banks in France, Germany, and the UK. This is the case of Italy, which has recently changed its banking legislation to allow what has come to be called "universal" banking. The US is the only country that has retained full segmentation, although with an increasing number of exceptions to the prevailing legislation. Under "Section 20" exemptions, specially authorized, highly capitalized banks were allowed to earn up to 5% of the income from special affiliated institutions undertaking activities normally excluded under prevailing US legislation. The limitation on earnings was increased to 10% and, in 1997, to 25%. Japan, whose post-war banking laws were patterned after those in the US, is also in the process of removing restrictions on bank activity.

It has been suggested that the change in the position of banks in the financing of business and household borrowing represents a process of financial disintermediation in which the number of intermediary agents involved in financial transactions is reduced. In particular, transactions take place directly between original contracting counterparties in the market rather than being arranged by banks acting as intermediaries.

Although changes are clearly taking place in the activities of banks, it is not clear that there has been a decrease in bank intermediation. For example, an increasing proportion of the demand deposits lost by commercial banks have been shifted to investment and mutual funds of various types that invest by lending to firms that were formerly borrowing funds from the commercial banks. Rather than a process of disintermediation, it is the form of bank intermediation that appears to have changed. In countries such as France, Italy, and even to some extent in the US, where banks have been permitted to extend their activities, their overall participation in the process of intermediation does not seem to have changed substantially. On the other hand, if banks are forbidden from organizing and participating in extended activities such as the sale and management of trust and investment funds, then it seems clear that the overall level of bank intermediation will fall. This has been the case of the commercial banks in the US operating without the Section 20 exemption.

This suggests that the "crisis" in banking is primarily a crisis relating to a particular definition of bank, the "commercial" bank, rather than financial institutions as a whole. Further, this suggests that it is primarily a crisis of American commercial banks, although banks in other countries are facing difficulties of a different nature. To the extent that banks are granted greater leeway to enter activities that had previously been forbidden to them by post-war regulations, their share in the intermediation of financial assets should not be expected to change substantially.

To evaluate the importance of this crisis in banking, it is thus necessary to evaluate the importance of the particular banking form, the "commercial bank," to the operation of the economy. To this end, Section 2 identifies two basic or "ideal" forms of bank, which seem to lie at the origins of the history of banking. Section 3 discusses the ways in which these two forms tended to merge the two diverse types of activity and the action of regulators to limit this integration. Section 4 attempts to discover the origin of modern commercial banks in the interaction between this tendency for banks to merge the two ideal forms of activity and the regulators attempts to keep them separate. It also seeks the reasons for the dominant presence of commercial banks, in particular in countries such as the US. Section 5 discusses the cause of the difficulties of commercial banks and the importance of these difficulties for the economy. As France has made a transition from a segmented system to a universal bank system, Section 6 investigates the way the French government responded to the similar difficulties facing French commercial banks in the post-war period and the impact of its new banking laws. The final section concludes that the difficulties facing commercial banks will not have dire consequences for the financing of the economy, although it is quite likely that the banking form that replaces commercial banks will have consequences for the stability of the banking system and thus on the performance of the economy as a whole. Whether banks, and the banking system, become more unstable depends on the prudential supervision and regulatory structures introduced that will determine the new form of banks and banking structure.

Two views of what banks do

The basic reason for modern economists' interest in banks is the idea that the rate of inflation is influenced by the growth of the supply of money. If banks are involved in the creation of the money supply, then control of banks must be an integral part of anti-inflation policy. As a result attention has been concentrated on the question of whether bank credit is money.

This approach denies money an impact on the operation of the real economy; it is a "veil" that must be pierced to discover the actual operation of the economic system. If this is the case, even if bank credit is money, banks are only of peripheral interest, for their ability to create credit will have no impact on the real system. This is a question of the difference between what Schumpeter called "real analysis" and "monetary analysis." But, even monetary analysis is only concerned to show that pure barter exchange and "the expression of the quantities of commodities and services and of exchange ratios between them" (Schumpeter, 1954, p. 278) are not sufficient for an understanding of the operation of the real economic system. Thus money is only considered important because it has a direct effect on the barter exchange process. The impact of money on the real economy is the result of its use as a means of exchange and is of importance because its use in exchange is capable of disturbing the "real" barter exchange ratios.

From this point of view, banks are of importance only if the creation of bank credit can influence real exchange ratios, that is, in Hayek's terminology, if money is not neutral. However, if bank credit is just a substitute for "money," then banks remain largely irrelevant, even under "monetary analysis," because the creation of money is outside their control. Thus, in either approach, the importance of banks turns on whether their credit is considered as "money." These questions were debated in the Bullionist Controversy over the resumption of specie payments after the 1797 Bank of England suspension of payment of its credit notes. Half a century later, the Banking and Currency Schools revisited the question. On this occasion the point under discussion had shifted to the substitution for banknotes for a new kind of bank credit, the transferable or chequeable deposit.

The joint-stock banks that were opened in London could not issue notes because this privilege was reserved to the Bank of England. There was, however, no restriction to prevent them from granting credits in the form of deposits subject to cheque. Because the framers of the Bank Act of 1844 thought that they had legislated the full substitution of banknotes and gold, the appearance of a new form of bank credit, the chequeable deposit, raised the question of whether or not deposits could be treated as equivalent to banknotes.

Given economists' obsession with the relation between money and prices, it is not surprising that these discussions are based on bank credit as a substitute for specie as a means of payment. However, there is another reason why banks may be of importance to the operation of the economy and which historically precedes the issue of notes. Indeed, it was only late in the history of banking, around the middle of the 19th century, that banks came to be primarily associated with their creation of means of exchange represented by the issue of circulating credits or "banknotes." The issue of notes as the main source of bank liabilities is a relatively new invention, given important impetus by the formation and ultimate success of the Bank of England. Before that time concentration was on the relation between banks and economic development. Indeed, banks were generally considered as quasi-alchemical institutions, capable of magically turning lead into gold by providing the capital required to promote economic development independently of the availability of real resources.

What is a bank?

Sir John Clapham, in his classic history of the Bank of England, observes that the note

> issue was the last of the classical banking functions to evolve spontaneously in England, and it was England's main contribution to the evolution of European banking. Deposit in some form or another, if only in the form of leaving your valuables with a man whom you trust who has a strong room, is very ancient; money lending perhaps more ancient still. Discount, the

purchase of bills of exchange, goes back to the 12th century in Europe and was well-known in England in the later Middle Ages. But the combination of all these functions in one pair of hands, which constituted modern banking, and the supplementing of deposit by use of the "write-off" from one account to another, and of the cheque for making payments to anyone, only took place finally in England between 1630 and 1670

(Clapham, 1945, I, p. 5)

Clapham's four banking functions may be summarized under the headings of *Income, Safety, Convenience, and Issue*. *Income* relates to bank investments such as lending and discounting, covering the purchases of both the liabilities of private individuals, as well as liabilities of the public sector. He notes that "[a] banking system is so closely associated with public borrowing and with what is the oldest and most jealously guarded function of the state, the issue of money, that governments can seldom afford to leave it entirely unlicensed and uncontrolled" (Clapham, 1945, I, p. 2). The *Issue* function is considered the most recent, first developed by the Bank of Sweden (1661) but suspended after only three years. The Bank of England in 1694 was among the first banks to have issued notes redeemable by the bearer rather than by the original creditor.

It is the *Issue* function that has attracted the attention of economists, overshadowing the *Income* function, which is largely overlooked in the analysis of the impact of banks on the economy. In simplified terms, this emphasis on the role of money as a means of payment has tended to concentrate attention on the liability side of the bank balance sheet at the expense of the asset side, which represents bank investments. Although assets must always equal liabilities, it should be obvious that the successful operation of any firm, whether it be a manufacturer or a bank, will depend on how the structure of its entire balance sheet contributes to the generation of net profits.

Clapham notes that the real novelty of the Bank of England was that its balance sheet was composed of government debt as its major income-earning asset and by notes payable to bearer as its major liability. Eventually, discounts were added to its assets, and a wider variety of note liabilities were issued, but it is this combination of long-term government debt financed by the issue of short-term circulating notes that is the distinguishing feature of the Bank. However, if the major innovation in banking in the 17th century was the issue of circulating bearer instruments, then the major function of banks before this date must have been independent of the creation of notes or deposits as substitutes for money.

Perusal of the available historical record[3] appears to support this supposition, for institutions defined as "banks" have been known to operate in some form or other in Italy at least since Roman times. During this period the operations carried out by institutions functioning under the name "bank" have covered wide combinations of assets and liabilities. Because there have been continuous innovations in both assets and liabilities and their combinations, what in any period has been called a "bank" has experienced periods of crisis that have usually provoked changes in structure and methods of operation. Some of these crises have been caused by dysfunction in the balance sheet combinations of the banks themselves. Others have arisen because of competition from financial institutions employing alternative balance sheet compositions. Banks, in some form or other have nonetheless survived at the center of the financial system despite challenges from other intermediaries.

Income: capital *banks*

Before the modern emphasis on note issue, banks were generally considered as necessary for the provision of capital for economic development. Indeed, the justification advanced in support of the creation of most early banks was that they would benefit general economic well-being by increasing wealth. This position was given a logical explanation and academic respectability by Schumpeter in his famous *Theory of Economic Development.* It is the credit creation aspect of banks that in Schumpeter's view, allows entrepreneurs with new, more profitable techniques of production and organization to appropriate resources from other, less efficient methods and users and break into the market.

The historical evolution of this aspect of banking is perhaps most easily understood by tracing the origins of the word "bank." It is generally believed that the English word "bank" is derived from the Italian "banco," which is thought to derive from the bench or long table used by money changers to conduct their business in the public markets of the early Italian city states (a probable confusion with the now more common "panca").

The similarity between the two words is misleading and most probably mistaken. Rather, the historical evidence suggests that the origin of the English "bank" comes from the German "banck." This is the German equivalent of the Italian "monte," which means a "mound" or a "store" where things are kept for future use.[4] In the case of banks, it is obviously money, as in a "mucchio di denaro," which today would be called "capitale." Originally, however, it was not restricted to stores of money. The modern English equivalent would be "fund," which is the name used in England for the public debts of the English sovereign.

The primary historical reference[5] is the 1171 decision of the Grand Council of Venice to impose a forced loan on Venetian citizens to finance a punitive expedition against the Eastern Emperor Manuel who had mistreated Venetian merchants. This loan was referred to colloquially as the "Monte." It eventually came to be known as the "Monte Vecchio" as the Grand Council followed with additional demands for funds in the form of the "Monte Nuovo" and then the "Monte Nuovissimo."

The Venetian citizen was compensated for the monies contributed to the Monte through receipt of a "credit," which took the form of a loan or stock certificate accruing annual interest. Presumably the expectation was that the war would produce sufficient spoils to repay the forced loan and the accumulated interest. The monte was managed by a group of commissioners, the Camera degli Imprestiti, who were responsible for the payment of interest to the holders of the certificates and kept books recording the transfer of the credit certificates between citizens. Because the loan was not repayable on demand of the lender, its value could only be realized by means of a private contract of sale or exchange to another Venetian citizen. Thus, the first Venetian "banck," or monte, created to finance Venetian war expenditure, also produced the first secondary market in which the certificates could be exchanged. As such, the government debt also served as means of payment: "From being convenient and valuable as an investment readily obtained, and as readily disposed of, it became, by a natural process a medium of payment in transactions of commerce" (Colwell, 1859, p. 292). In 1423 a decree was issued requiring all bills of exchange to be paid through the bank.

As the German "banck" was re-transliterated into Italian as "banco," it became synonymous with "monte" and thus came into common usage to signify a particular public loan issue. Today, just as investors talk about the price and conditions of a particular government bond issue, say the 8% Republic of Italy maturity 2000, Venetians would talk in the same way about the performance of a particular banco or monte, such as the Monte Nuovissimo. As noted, this same usage is found in the 18th-century English expression of "being in the funds," which means to have loaned money to the government against the issue of public debt.

This Venetian innovation for financing public expenditure spread quickly, and the practice was soon adopted by other Italian city states. Florence organized its first monte in 1336 to finance its war with Pisa; another followed in 1344. The loans of public creditors ("compere") of Genoa were reorganized on the same principles in the 14th century and probably circulated as means of payment. This system was again reorganized to produce the Casa di San Giorgio in 1407.

Remnants of this traditions are still present in some modern Italian financial institutions that are called "monte" rather than "banco" or the modern preference for the feminine "banca" (recall the affinity to "panca"). All of these represent descendants and adaptations of the Venetian method of forming a financial institution on the basis of a "monte" or "fund" – a pile of money.

A major innovation on the method of forced public subscription adopted in Venice was to make the public contribution of money to the funds voluntary. For example, charitable subscription of money in exchange for the issue of credits or certificates formed the basis for the Montes Pietatis or Monte di Pietà, which were organized by the Church to lend to the poor while respecting the prohibition of usury. This is a system that began in the 15th century (Orsingher, 1967, p. 77, suggests the first was in Orvieto in 1463) and spread throughout northern Italy. They were later replaced by Monte dei Pegni, which lent against personal property to individuals unable to gain access to banks. As noted, the "banck" or "fund" was not necessarily limited to money and could be composed of physical goods pledged to the institutions, such as the Monte Frumentari, formed from stocks of grain that could be lent to members.

The best-known modern survivor of the capital bank is the *Monte non vacabile de' Paschi della Città e Stato di Siena*, created in 1642. The original "monte" was produced from the grant by the Grand Duke Ferdinand II of the right to receive the future pasturage payments for the grazing lands ("paschi") in the maremme di Grosetto around Siena. This amounted to 10,000 scudi per annum. Capitalized at 5% it allowed the "monte" to sell shares in the income from the pasturage (the "luoghi di monte") to the Sienese citizenry. This produced the 200,000 scudi that formed the "pile of money" or capital of the bank, which was used as the basis for loans to merchants and farmers and the discounting of exchange bills. Just as in the Venetian Monte, the "luoghi di monte" could not be redeemed (they were "non vacabile"). However, they could be transferred or exchanged between individual holders at the discretion of the monte. They were generally accepted, not because of the stability of the monte's portfolio of investments but because they had a solid source of revenue flowing from the capital base represented by the right to the income from pasturage.[6] It was the bank's capital that produced the income that supported the value of the bank's shares. Equally, when the monte started to issue notes, they were accepted on the same support of an assured flow of future income.

As Clapham points out, a "monte" would not today be recognized as a bank because it resembles what would now be called a public debt agency. However, it represents the most important principle associated with banking before the Bank of England: the capitalization and sale of anticipated future income flows. This was the "magical" property first associated with banks, the alchemy that turned the future into the present, expectation into reality. In the case of the Monte Vecchio, this was the expected war booty and, in the case of the Monte dei Paschi, an expected flow of future pasturage payments. The anticipated incomes that were capitalized to form the "monte" of the bank's capital were not always this certain and secure.

A slightly different approach to this principle is found in the creation of the Bank of England as a vehicle for the intermediation of government debt. This was made necessary because of the lack of confidence in the "full faith and credit" of the British sovereign. The 1694 Tunnage Act[7] was introduced to raise £1,500,000 to meet the expenses of the war. Of that sum £1,200,000, representing about 2.5% of GNP (a quarter of which was to be paid in ready cash on subscription), was to be borrowed through the sale of government debt certificates bearing 8% interest. In addition to the interest, the lenders were to be granted a Royal Charter incorporating them for ten years as a joint-stock venture to be called "The Governor and Compania of the Bank of England." The Bank was to receive £4,000 in management fees for the sale of the debt.

As Clapham points out, the original Charter of the Bank made no explicit provision for the issue of notes. Clause 28 of the act, joined to the original bill as a separate schedule, makes reference to "Bills obligatory and of credit under the Seale of the Corporation" and makes these "sealed notes" assignable by endorsement. The Bank quickly started to issue them, along with cashier's notes, paying 2^d % per day, in an amount equivalent to the government debt it had agreed to acquire in exchange for the Bank Charter. Some of these notes were then used by the members of the Compania to complete their initial subscription for shares. Clapham (1945, I, p. 20, p. 305) also notes that the "bonds" of "subscribers," a sort of over-the-counter personal IOU, were also accepted in lieu of the stipulated cash payments. In fact, they represented bank advances to shareholders. As a result it is impossible to discover how much hard specie the government actually received from the Bank, but it was certainly less than a quarter of the sum stipulated in the act. The balance was financed by the credit created by the bank itself.

Thus, from its foundation the Bank had pledged to pay specie to the government that was more than its actually paid-in capital. To engage in any other operations, the Bank had to seek funds by borrowing through the issue of its own notes. The charter granted limited liability for the Bank's indebtedness up to the limit of its capital. This placed a restriction on the issue of notes that it fought, unsuccessfully, to remove. Instead, it created different types of "note" that were issued in addition to the "sealed" bill. It was also aided by the fact that an increasing number of its notes were returned to be held as deposits, allowing them to be reissued. The provision of *Security* and *Convenience* by the Bank thus worked in favor of the *Issue* function noted by Clapham. The important point, however, was that the issue of notes facilitated the Bank's use of its own credit to create its capital. Indeed, it allowed its owners meet their commitments by lending them the credit that they transferred to the sovereign.

The success of the Bank of England brought the first glimpses of banking alchemy, and the British landed gentry quickly proposed that a land bank be founded to issue notes against the "capital" of their property in land. The proposal was to give landowners notes in exchange for the "deposit" of a freehold on their estates. Indeed, the proposal was more solid than that which had created the Bank of England. Unfortunately, the formal conditions provided that a sum in notes of £8,000 would be given for an estate with an income of £150 per annum. However, at that time the "fee simple" or freehold title to land was being exchanged for 20 years' purchase. This meant a market valuation for such a £150 estate of a little less than £3,000, or a 5% per annum return. The proposal would have meant that the land bank would have lent nearly three times the market value of an estate or, alternatively, that it would receive a return of 2%, when rates were around three times higher and the government was paying 8%. Perhaps not surprisingly, the plan was approved by Parliament, but it was not subscribed, and the land bank never got off the ground. It is, however, representative of the way in which the combination of *Income* and *Issue* in the same institution could become dangerously explosive without express limits on the proportions between note issue and paid-in bank capital.

The alchemy of banking was taken to its extreme limit in the United States, where the first banks capitalized themselves without any income earning capital assets. They issued equity shares, which did not have to be paid immediately or could be bought in the market on a "time bargain," that is, on 100% margin. The bank would then lend to the purchasers of the shares against the collateral of the same shares.

The process was little different for the first Bank of the United States, formed under legislation passed in 1791. A joint venture with both private and government shareholders, the initial proposal provided that the Bank should lend the US government the $2 million for its share of the capital. Direct lending by the new Bank to create its own capital was considered inappropriate, and a more surreptitious route had to be found. The government debt commissioners had already borrowed money in the Netherlands under the 1790 "Act making provision for the Debt of the United States" (the act is partially reprinted in Dunbar, 1969, p. 10ff). The US government thus drew bills of exchange on the commissioners and presented them to the Bank of the United States for discount. The funds received provided the finance for the government share of the Bank's capital. To meet the bills when they came due, the US government issued $2 million in new debt, which was used to secure a loan in the form of the same $2 million of bills originally discounted by the Bank. The bills were thus returned to the commissioners before the maturity of the bills and any specie had been transferred (cf. Bray, 1967, p. 123).

The government bonds, which had been authorized in the original 1790 act, paid 6% over ten years, starting in 1793 (Dunbar, op. cit., p. 12). Both private and foreign investors were allowed to use this same debt issue to meet up to three-quarters of their subscription of the Bank's capital. Thus no less than three-fourths of the $8 million of the Bank's capital shares purchased by the private sector was met by the issue of government bonds. At the end of the complicated financing for the government portion, the Bank had acquired another $2 million of government debt. Only 20% of the Bank's capital was thus paid in specie, and Hammond (1967, p. 123) estimates that it never raised more than $400,000 in specie. All this for a bank whose regulations forbid purchase of public securities, although it could lend in limited amounts to the government and against real estate.

The idea of a national bank was a perennial point of contention between the individual states and the Federal government. Many supporters of states' rights believed that it was illegal because there was no explicit provision for the granting of bank charters by the Federal government in the US Constitution. Bank charters were not, however, forbidden to the states (although they were precluded from incurring indebtedness through the issue of notes, currency, bills, or other forms of debt instrument), and State governments soon came to look upon the chartering of banks as a means for promoting their economic development: "State legislatures resorted to the practice of granting banking privileges to railroad and canal companies, to gas and water works, to turnpike and power companies, and other similar enterprises to enable them to secure the necessary funds by issuing paper money" (Madeleine, 1943, pp. 66–7). These banks were chartered with the "usual banking powers," which implied a note issue of two or three times their capital, but "very little specie was ever paid in. Each institution simply created its capital in much the same way as it created the money it loaned to its patrons" (ibid., p. 70).[8]

The State of Kentucky incorporated its own bank in 1806 and was forced to suspend cash payments in 1819 as the result of the Bank of the United States presenting the Kentucky bank's notes for payment in specie. In 1818 and 1819

Kentucky chartered 40 new private banks. The Constitution of the State of Illinois expressly provided for a "Bank of the State," which was established in 1821 with a capital of $300,000, produced in the traditional fashion by a simple bookkeeping entry without the contribution of any specie or other real resource. The charter made no provision for repayment of notes in specie, and it followed good US practice in lending primarily to its officers to allow them to buy the bank's stock. In 1820 the State of Kentucky returned to the scene, creating the Bank of the Commonwealth of Kentucky with funds raised from the sale of public lands.

Thus both the Federal and State governments applied the principle that they could support their own development plans by creating banks, usually with a loan from the bank representing payment for the bank stock or by discounting the potential owners' stock notes and accepting the bank's cheque in payment for its own capital.

> Then comes the time for paying the second, third, or fourth installment. The Bank makes a call on the stockholders. Some of them hypothecate their stock, that is, pledge it to the Bank and with the means obtained from the Bank itself pay in their proportion. Others have obtained the means by discounts of accommodation notes, without any hypothecation of stock. Some few pay in real money: but they generally pay in the notes of the Bank itself, or of similar institutions. It is by this kind of hocus–pocus that Bank capitals are formed. After the first installment is paid, the Bank by its own operations, facilitates the paying of others. . . . Thus, Bank capitals are formed by exchanging one kind of promises to pay for another kind of promises to pay. This mode of forming Bank capitals, with the stock notes of subscribers, is not peculiar to the banks of the second and third order. The Banks of the most approved standing have formed their capitals in the same way.
> (William M. Gouge, p. 25: quoted in Robertson, 1964, pp. 162–3)

This is the system that in the US, replaced the Italian "monte" and the British Royal Charter. It is little wonder that banks came to be seen an magical institutions that could use alchemy to produce wealth out of nothing by the technique of using bank credit to create the equity in a bank. In the absence of a benefactor, such as Ferdinand II in Siena, US banks simply loaned to their founders the funds they used to purchase the bank's stock and provide its capital.

On the continent, the capitalization of income–earning assets was also the basis for Crédit Mobilier and Société Générale, formed in France and Belgium at the middle of the 19th century. These banks served as the pattern for the German Effektenbanken or Kreditbanken and the Italian industrial banks. The French proposals in fact went beyond simple industrial financing and proposed a sort of central bank for industry that would oversee the industrialization of the country by arranging associations and mergers rather than by wasteful competition. Another suggestion was for a bank that would hold shares in all industry and finance these holdings by selling its shares to the public. Today it would be considered a sort of "sector" index fund (cf. Confalonieri, 1974–6, I, pp. 252–8). In both France and Germany these banks were also soon to expand their activities to the issue of means of payment.

A good example of this process is Crédit Lyonnais (it is also a good example of an institution with no historical memory!). Formed in 1863, it attempted to combine the activities of the London deposit bankers, serving the local community as a sort of clearinghouse while at the same time servicing the financing needs of local industrial lending in the manner introduced by Crédit Mobilier. However, purely local industrial lending meant excessive exposure to individual enterprises, and as the result of the losses in the Fuchsine chemical-mineral complex, the bank nearly went bankrupt. This led not only to its decision to diversify geographically, first at the national and then at the international level, but the bank management eventually recognized that a choice had to be made between deposit banking and industrial banking. By 1874 it had decided in favor of the former: "Ce n'est pas notre métier d'être des entrepreneurs, mais de prêter aux entrepreneurs en leur laissant les risques . . . Nous sommes des banquiers, et pas d'autres chose . . . on ne peut prêter qu'aux riches" (quoted in Confalonieri, 1974–6, I, p. 360). Although the bank did not cease its industrial operations, it downgraded and segregated them from what it considered its main business: "Etendre sa cliéntele, développer ses affaires de banque, chercher des sources des bénéfices permanents dans les commissions et des différences d'intérêts, créer des elements de profit indépendants des affaires exceptionnelles qui font souvent défaut, donner ainsi aux dividendes une grande régularité, tel a toujours été le programme du Crédit Lyonnais" (op. cit., p. 361). The "affaires exceptionnelles qui font souvent défaut" refers to the industrial financing activities that the bank now referred to as "exceptional" business with respect to its "ordinary" business, which is outlined in the quotation from the 1882 report to stockholders and is summarized as "l'escompte du papier de commerce et des crédits à ouvrir aux négociants" (ibid). The bank management quickly recognized the liquidity risks involved in industrial lending, and as a result of its decision to minimize this business introduced "le règle au Crédit Lyonnais de maintenir toujours sous formes des ressources immédiatement disponibles les montant complet de dépots à vue et des comptes créanciers" (ibid., p. 363). These resources were defined as "l'encaisse . . . le portefeuille d'effets de commerce . . . les reports échéant tous les quinze jours ou tous les mois." Its investments in industry were strictly limited to its paid capital base. This example shows that bankers very quickly recognized the difficulties of combining income and issue or capital and money banking and were able to introduce appropriate risk management techniques in the form of the matching of maturities of assets and liabilities. Crédit Lyonnais is thus the first of what might be called the deposit banks or what in the US were to become commercial banks. The successful operation dates from the beginning of the 1880s, which is precisely the same period when the German Effektenbanks were being formed but on the basis of industrial lending without deposit issue or note issue.

The original German joint-stock Effektenbanks were founded at the middle of the century (cf. Emden, n.d., p. 200ff), but they only came to play a dominant role in the industrial development of Germany in 1871, when the flow of French reparations provided investment funds and a liberalization of company law made it possible to form companies without government approval. The change in company law also allowed joint-stock banks to be formed without restriction (cf. Born, 1983, p. 82ff). The formation, usually by groups of private banks, of the best known of today's "universal banks" date from this period. Whereas Dresdner (1872) was founded on the basis for providing industrial financing, Deutsche (1870) departed from the simple launching and financing of new enterprises that had characterized the activity of the pre-war Kreditbanks and emphasized foreign trade financing and deposit taking (cf. Whale, 1930).

Although the first of these banks sought the right to issue notes, this was denied to them. They were thus limited to raising capital on a joint-stock basis and investing it in forming new industrial enterprises. The banks took an active interest in management until the new firm was on sufficiently solid footing to be sold to the public through the issue and sale of shares. The bank would usually arrange for a direct subscription for the shares at a fixed offer price, with subsequent admission and quotation on an official exchange or by means of an initial admission and listing on an official exchange, with sales taking place through the bank acting as broker at market prices. It was also possible for the shares to be sold by private placement either to the bank's clients or to other banking firms.

As part of their services these banks provided "Kontokorrent" services (cf. Whale, 1930, p. 36ff), which usually outlasted the equity stake in a company or might be independent of it. This was not a bank deposit or current account, but more like a revolving line of creditor an overdraft account, in which debit and credit balances attracted interest and account balances were drawn at fixed, usually half-yearly intervals. Firms used these accounts for working balances, but more importantly they could be used to finance capital expenditures in anticipation of raising funds from the capital market, usually using the services of the same bank. Thus, a Kreditbank that had floated the shares of a company that it had financed would continue to provide short-term working capital for the firm as well as financing fixed investment expenditures that it would later fund in the capital market. This funding would also be accomplished by what would now be called a bought deal, purchasing the new issue in toto and then floating it in the market in one of the three ways previously mentioned.

Thus the basic activity of the 19th century joint-stock Effektenbank was investment of its shareholders capital selectively in new companies, acting more as active venture capitalists than as industrial holding companies with more or less permanent interests in particular companies. These investments were not considered as permanent or long-term relationships but underwriting operations, with the investment lasting only long enough to capitalize the value of the firm through sale to the general public. This is what Clapham (1936, p. 390ff) has called the "age of company promotion." Additional income was generated through the development of Kontokorrent services, which also generated underwriting income when the accounts were cleared by the issue of securities.

These early banks did not initially borrow short term from the public by issuing notes or by taking deposits.

These banks were eventually able to undertake such activity as they absorbed failing note-issuing banks and as they offered deposit services that were initially not subject to the same regulations. These banks thus quickly merged the *Income* and *Issue* functions. Their expansion was so rapid that by 1910, there were only eight dominant banks: the big "D" banks, Deutsche, Dresdner, Diskontogesell-schaft, Darmstädter, plus Schaffhausen, Berliner Handelsgesellschaft, Commerzbank, and Nationalbank für Deutschland.

All of these examples are of banks that in one way or another were initially founded on the basis of capitalizing the expected future flows from an income-earning asset. The income from the asset produced funds that the bank used to operate in discounting or lending. As Clapham observed, and as the historical experience demonstrates, note issue is not necessary for the success of this type of bank.

However, note issue did emerge in the case of the Bank of England, primarily because the Bank did not raise the full value of its assets. Indeed, given its proportion of GNP, this would have been improbable. It thus had to provide credit to its shareholders to meet the capital subscription; it was also obvious that it should carry on its own discounting and lending business in terms of its own credit instruments: Bank of England notes. The Bank of England also differed in that its income-earning assets were government bonds based on the tax-raising power of the sovereign – a far less than certain prospect.

In the US this process is carried to the extreme in which there are no longer any income-earning capital assets: the banks capitalize expected future income – of the bank! The notes that are issued are the equivalent to the junk bonds of the 1980s. In Germany, the Effektenbanks did not initially engage in note issue but did start to offer deposit business (aside from the Kontokorrent) quite quickly. As noted, the founder of one of the first Effektenbanks sought the right to issue notes but was denied. Deutsch bank, on the other hand, which originally concentrated on trade financing, started out with the intention of raising funds from taking deposits.

The typical bank of this class would thus start its life with the acquisition of an asset with expected earnings potential, which it would capitalize through the sale of shares. If the shares were not fully paid, it would create credit to fill the balance. Income was generated by the earnings and appreciation of the value of the original asset. In the German case the shareholders' funds often came first and were then invested in forming or acquiring young companies. Accruing earnings could then be used for the short-term banking business done with the companies through the Kontokorrent. The income was represented by the capital gain on the sale of the companies into the market and from the interest on Kontokorrent services. There was no need for short-term borrowing or note issue, although these banks were quick to introduce these functions.

However, when the capitalization of the bank's assets was less than complete, as was the case for the Bank of England, or it is the bank itself that is the asset that is being capitalized, as was the case for the Bank of the United States and most state banks, borrowing through the issue of notes or the sale of deposits became necessary for the bank to fund its asset acquisition and to produce income.

In the case of the state banks formed in the United States, where there were no assets and no capitalized value, the issue of other short-term liabilities was imperative. The only asset possessed by these banks were their charters, which were capitalized by the sale of shares to investors who used them as collateral for borrowing from the bank and that created the bank's assets. The banks thus had liabilities composed of the shares issued and assets composed of loans made against those shares, which it held as collateral. The assets generated no income, and there was no prospect of income because there were no capital funds available to produce net interest income. Short-term borrowing to fund income-earning assets was thus vital for the survival of the bank. These banks could not survive without issuing short-term liabilities, whether notes or deposits. Thus it was the creation of capital banks without capital that brought about the necessity of issuing short-term liabilities to fund investments and the typical liquidity risks associated with maturity mismatching that is now the basis of bank management. However, initially bankers did not foresee the difficulties involved in the operation of banks on the principle of borrowing short and lending long.

Convenience and security: giro banks

The "capital" bank formed to generate *Income* did not provide the aspects of banking, which Clapham called "*Convenience* and *Security*." *Security* was not only to provide a safe, sure store for wealth but also to provide a safe and convenient means of making payment. The earliest providers of *Security* were money changers and goldsmiths. Money changers have existed at least since Greek and Roman times. Their function was to convert the types of stamped or minted metal coins that were in general circulation into local currency or to convert them into "ideal" units of account at rates determined by the assayed metal content of the circulating coins. They are reputed to have thrown coins down on their "banco di prova" to test the quality of the metal, providing the alternative explanation of the term "bank" to that already given. A money changer often provided transfer services, holding customers' balances, which could be paid by transfer to the credit of third parties. They were also called money "scriveners" because they kept written records of the transfers between clients of the coins held on their books. But, they did not issue any counter liability or receipt similar to a banknote for the money held in their safekeeping.

Because trade dominated medieval economies, there was another aspect of security in addition to the need to exchange different types of metallic coin. Coin often had to be sent over long distances through territory without the benefit of government or the rule of law. Precious metals were easy prey for bandits who frequented isolated mountain passes or desert trails. The foreign exchange bill developed as a response to this problem of safety of means of payment. It was specialization in this instrument that allowed the British trading or "counting houses" to transform themselves from merchants dealing in commodities throughout the empire into "merchant bankers" transferring funds internationally via bills of exchange. Because they had flows of goods and counterflows of payments that did not always balance, they discovered that they could sell their transactions imbalances and payment services to third parties by accepting coin against the issue of a bill of exchange, or a credit, which they guaranteed to repay, either on presentation to themselves or to their agents or representatives abroad. In the latter case the bill was denominated in foreign money and was a foreign exchange bill, traded in the market for "foreign exchange" bills.

Not only were bills much easier to transport, but they offered almost total safety because they could not be negotiated even if stolen by bandits, and were sent in multiples so that loss in transit would not interrupt payment. They were also certain and secure because each endorser of a bill became sequentially responsible for payment. Thus a bill with three "names" endorsing it to another party carried the guaranteed for payment of all three, should the drawer of the bill default. Many modern national banks required that the bills they accepted for discount from private banks carry three good names, indicating that they were without risk.

Because the bills were drawn against flows of real goods and subject to repayment on presentation to the issuer, usually at a predetermined date, they were also short-term self-liquidating paper. The effective international means of payment from medieval times thus was not gold but bills of exchange. The discount of bills of exchange represented one of the major investments of excess funds for banks formed on capital, such as the Monte dei Paschi and the Bank of England, because of their safety due to multiple endorsement and their relatively short term to maturity. Discounting did not require either the issue of notes or the creation of deposits; it could be done by advancing specie and thus represented a temporary investment of earnings for a bank that did not issue notes or take deposits.

Similar attempts to provide a replacement for the physical use of gold coin in internal transactions led to the activities of the money scriveners, previously mentioned. Soon private bankers offered transfer services. Venetian private banks developed the use of a slip ("contado di banco"), which confirmed a client's deposit. They took the form of a promise by the banker to repay the sum deposited, or a verbatim extract from banker's records, showing the particulars of the transaction. These slips eventually began to circulate, and by the 14th century, they could be used to effectuate payment. Their value was discounted from the face amount according to the reliability of the banker. The "contado" represent the forerunner of the banknote and the deposit subject to cheque (cf. Orsingher, 1967, p. 75).

It was seldom the case that a banker set up in the payments business from scratch. Usually he was someone with a commercial reputation who extended his activities to deal in money. Although the funds received on deposit were seldom invested in other assets, it was common for private bankers to employ them in their own businesses, at this time primarily the purchase and resale of commodities. This was the case of nearly all of the Venetian private bankers. By the middle of the 16th century, 96 of 109 private banks organized in Venice had failed (Orsingher, 1967, p. 75). The characteristic difference of these banks relative to the Monte is that they had very little capital or that the capital was tied up in commerce and thus subject to occasionally sharp fluctuations in earnings.

This is really very little different from the experience of the state banks in the US, mentioned previously, that were founded as subsidiaries of businesses or development companies formed without a capital base. Due to the instability of these "private" banks, public authorities eventually required them to provide a "security" deposit, either in the form of specie or of public debt as an assurance of their ability to return customer deposits. This is an early form of what became the obligatory minimum reserve against deposits.

In Venice, legislation was introduced periodically throughout the Middle Ages to require bankers to make cash payments against deposits and to forbid them using deposited funds to finance their own trading in merchandise. It had little effect, and in 1584 the Venetian Senate took the extreme step of passing an act to ban private bankers. The authorities recognized that these private bankers were responding to an unfulfilled demand for a sure means of both domestic and international payments. They thus sought to provide for public banks offering secure means of payments.

Given the diversity of the different types and fineness of circulating coin, there was always a question of what fineness of coin or type of coin would be accepted in payment of a debt. This was especially important for bills of exchange, which were often written in imaginary units of account such as the ecu de marc, the fiorino, and so on (cf. Einaudi's 1953 discussion of "Imaginary Money") and paid by book clearing or transfer. Publicly regulated banking institutions were expressly created to resolve the problem of a safe means of payment and certainty over the value of the means of payment.

These banks, called deposit or giro banks, represent the second major form of banking institution. In 1587 Venice made provision for a publicly regulated bank, entirely independent of the "monte," which eventually produced the Bank of Rialto and the Banco del Giro. The Bank of Amsterdam was founded in Holland in 1609 and the Bank of Hamburg in 1619. Similar banks were founded in Nuremburg in 1621, and the Bank of Stockholm, the antecedent of the Sverige Riksbank, founded in 1608, issued receipts that circulated throughout Sweden as means of payment. These banks were founded on the basis of what came to be called the "Currency Principle" in the monetary debates in Britain in the 19th century, which led to the 1844 Banking Act. According to the Currency Principle, the circulating currency represents a receipt for coin deposited in the giro bank; because it is just a sign or substitute for the coin on deposit, it cannot be considered as an addition to the monetary circulation. The first public giro banks were thus pure clearinghouses, the equivalent of "money scriveners" that did not issue notes or make loans.

By the fact that these banks did not make investments in trade or in investment securities, they eliminated the problems that had plagued private merchant bankers. They were, in principle, simply clearing systems set up to make payments via account transfers. Nonetheless, these banks facilitated the use of exchange bills through the creation of a commonly accepted unit of account, the Florin and Mark Banco, which is the origin of "Moneta di Banco" or "bank money," (now central bank money or high powered money) of fixed value in terms of precious metals in which bills could be written and which provided the clearing mechanism for the book settlements in this unit. The importance of this function was already recognized by Adam Smith in the *Wealth of Nations*. All credit that was advanced was private credit, financed through the merchant trading houses; it was not the asset of the bank borrowed with a bank liability.

Unfortunately, having been created and regulated by governments, the giro banks were not exempt from the financing needs of their creators, and all of these giro banks eventually failed because they were forced (usually in utmost secrecy) to lend the specie deposited with them to support government expenditure projects. This was the case of the Bank of Amsterdam, which was used by the city government as a source of funding. The Bank of Stockholm, which had become the bank of issue, filed for bankruptcy in 1776 and repaid only 50% of the value of its notes.

These giro or deposit banks represent the antithesis of the Capital Banks, for they do not capitalize any assets and have no investments. They simply provide clearing or transfer services for an external payments mechanism founded on the bill of exchange. For example, all bills in excess of 600 Hfl were required to be drawn and paid in bank money of the Bank of Amsterdam. This meant that anyone doing business with Holland had to keep an account at the Bank.

Although not initially permitted, from 1683 the Bank made advances against deposits of coin via issue of a deposit receipt in bank money. These eventually began to circulate. The same was the case of the Bank of Sweden (cf. Orsingher, 1967, p. 24), whose receipts took the form of notes because in principle these pieces of paper were simply representations of specie on deposit in the bank and could be presented for payment.[9] However, there were restrictions on conversion represented by storage and other transactions costs, and bank money usually ran at a premium of as much as 5% in the case of Amsterdam, providing an economic incentive to use in-bank transfers. The entire income of the giro bank resulted from the charges for its clearing services. The goal of such banks was primarily *Safety* and *Convenience*, not *Income* or *Issue*. They were purely fee-based banks. Ironically, it was the safety and convenience aspects of the giro banks that were used by proponents of the creation of the Bank of England, although they were only adopted when the sovereign recognized the advantages of a capital bank in raising funds.

The pure deposit or giro public bank thus represents the response to the difficulties encountered by the private, non-capitalized, note-issuing banks – a response that was not entirely successful because these banks were all eventually drawn to note issue and investment of depositors' funds in the absence of their own capital. There were other responses. As seen, the problem of non-capital banks was particularly grave in the US, which proved a fertile proving ground for alternative approaches to bank safety mechanisms.

Imposing bank safety

One of the reasons that the Bank of the United States got into political difficulty was its attempt to act as a regulator of the security of state banks. Because of its good record on paying on its notes, it always had credit balances with the state-chartered banks. Despite its inauspicious start borrowing its capital base, by the time its charter was up for renewal, it held around $15 million in gold, a sum equal to the entire specie holdings of the state banks. If it felt a bank was not operating prudently, it would present that bank's notes for payment in specie, forcing the bank to restrict its note issue or to suspend payment. As a result of what was considered federal interference, several states attempted to retaliate by levying a tax on the notes of the Bank of the United States. The Supreme Court decision that rendered such taxes unconstitutional also resolved the issue of the right of the Federal government to operations compatible with the goals of the Constitution but not explicitly contained therein, such as the federal chartering of banks and printing money.

The decision did not, however, eliminate the right of individual states to establish or license banks. Nor did it prohibit state-chartered banks from lending to state governments via the issue of notes that could circulate as means of payment. Given their experience of continual suspension of payment on notes by state-chartered banks, some of the states tried to create stability by limiting bank formation through restrictions on the issue of bank charters. It was the failure of these restrictions on bank charters that eventually led to the era of "free bank chartering" and even greater instability. Most of these expedients to impose safety and stability were adaptations of the clearinghouse principle used by the giro banks.

The "Suffolk System" was first introduced by the New England Bank and then by the Suffolk Bank, both large Boston banks. A bank that kept low or zero reserves against notes and had virtually no capital had an interest in having its notes circulate as far away from the bank as possible to reduce the probability of their being presented for payment. A number of New England banks thus opened in the countryside as far from the commercial center of Boston as possible. A bank in the backwoods of Maine did not have to worry about excessive note issue if all its notes were lent to people doing business in Boston. Some banks even set up agents in Boston, lending at rates below those of the Boston banks. The inconvenience of the long journey to the bank's home office to redeem the notes was too great, and these country banknotes usually traded at a discount to their face value of as much as 5%, irrespective of the evaluation of the quality of the bank itself.

Given the inconvenience of redemption, Boston banks would not accept these notes – a prudent policy but one that meant that their own notes were presented much more frequently, requiring them to hold more specie reserves to meet them. It also meant that the Boston banknote circulation was dominated by the country banks' notes.

To counter this competition the Boston banks could have accepted the notes and accumulated them with the intention of presenting them for payment. An alternative, which took the name of the Suffolk System (cf. Robertson, 1955, pp. 140–2) was to offer to the country banks the possibility of redeeming their notes at the prevailing market discount if they would hold deposits exclusively with the Boston bank or to hold a permanent deposit of $5,000. Any bank that refused would be faced with mass redemption. In 1824 the Suffolk Bank joined with six other Boston banks to create a fund of $300,000 for the purpose of the purchase and presentation of the notes of non-participating banks. By 1925 the discount on country banknotes had disappeared, and they circulated at par but with the effect of greatly increasing the reserves held by the country banks through the reduction in their note issue. Eventually, the system emerged as a full-fledged clearinghouse in which notes were traded at par and surplus and deficit positions were created against all the banks in the region. A clearing deficit required payment in specie to the clearinghouse and a reduction in its note issue. A bank that was thought to be in weak condition would thus find its clearing balance deteriorating, causing it to take remedial action or go out of business.

New York State attempted to remedy its state banks' lack of capital by setting up a deposit insurance fund (one-half of 1% of deposits paid annually until it reached 3% of capital) in the Safety Fund Act of 1829.[10] The fund was to be used to meet any debts of a failed bank that remained after liquidation of assets. The fund was to be invested and any income returned to the banks as dividends. The act also made provision for periodic, rigorous examination every four months by three bank commissioners. All new banks and banks renewing charters had to become members, and more than 100 banks eventually came under the act.

Any bank chartered under the New York Safety Fund Act that refused to redeem its notes in specie was to be summarily closed and dissolved. Because most banks could not meet the requirement and had already announced suspension of payment as a result of the panic caused by the policies of the Second Bank of the United States of calling in loans, the law had to be suspended, and other means for guaranteeing the safety of bank deposits were sought. In the period after the Panic, the contributions to the Fund were not sufficient to cover bank losses, and the Fund came up nearly $1 million short and had to be supported by State government funds.

In response to the failure of the Safety Fund Act, New York State undertook a complete reform of its banking legislation and in 1838 introduced additional legislation that became the basis for free bank chartering. Although it retained the Safety Fund, it required banks to deposit securities (US government bonds and New York and other approved state bonds) with the state comptroller in exchange for the right to issue banknotes of an equivalent value. Half of the notes issued by the bank could be backed by real estate mortgage lending against less than half the value of the property. In addition banks had to meet minimum capital requirements. If a note less than $1,000 were refused, the comptroller on request could sell enough deposited securities to pay it. The law also included provision for a specie reserve of 12.5% of deposits, but this was repealed after a year and a half. This legislation was the origin of free banking.

Restriction on the number of banks by limiting charters had generally been viewed as a means of preventing over issue of notes and insuring the convertibility and thus the safety of the notes issued. The basic justification for free banking was that the conditions required to carry on banking business, in particular the stiff reserve conditions, should be so onerous that "banking would lose all its attraction except to the honest, the economical and the persevering; it would have no surplus profits to tempt the needy and the speculative, nor any cover for bankruptcy to allure the unprincipled" (Professor John Mc Vickar, quoted in Madeleine, 1943, p. 159). There would then be no need to restrict or regulate entry.

The first free banking act to be introduced was in Michigan, although the discussions in New York preceded it. It provided for a reserve deposit of securities with the State government of 100% of notes issued. This is, of course, the formal equivalent of imposing the purchase of income-earning capital on the bank. It was quickly contested in the courts by the banks and declared unconstitutional. By 1860, 18 of the 33 states had introduced free banking laws, most with severe reserve requirements backing note issue.

One of the most interesting alternatives seeking security of note issue reflects the approach that would eventually be applied in Germany. The Forstall System introduced in Louisiana in 1842 was based on the principle that banks serve primarily to provide means of payment and thus should limit their investments to short-term, self-liquidating assets. Banks were required to separate their "deadweight" loans, defined as longer-term credits secured by stocks or mortgages, from "liquid" loans against assets maturing in less than 90 days. They could increase deadweight lending only if their note and deposit (only Massachusetts and Louisiana had limitations on deposits) liabilities were secured by one-third in specie and two-thirds in paper liquidating in less than 90 days. This has the same effect of having a separate income bank and issue bank within the same entity (cf. Robertson, 1955, p. 152). The result is a system similar to that eventually adopted by Crédit Lyonnais.

Despite all these precautions, free banking did not produce the desired or promised *Convenience* and *Security* of note issue banking. The banks that were formed under free banking laws, especially in the Northeast and Middle West, became known as "wildcat" banks. The performance of the free banking laws of individual states was varied. In Massachusetts only two banks failed, and no note holders lost any money, but in New York some 30 banks failed in the five years after 1839 despite the increase in bank inspections. In Indiana 51 banks failed in the five years after 1851. The worst case was Michigan, where bank examiners are reputed to have been presented the same box of gold as representing the backing for the note issue in every bank they visited. Two years after the introduction of free banking in Michigan in 1837 all 40 banks opened had failed. Evidently there were limits to the velocity of circulation of the box of gold! A further unforeseen difficulty was that even when the required amounts of securities were deposited as reserves, they were of doubtful value and proved completely inadequate to rescue the failing banks.

Despite the growing concern for the regulation of banks, by the time of the Civil War, there were some 1,500 banks issuing more than 9,000 different types of banknotes (the Federal government had been out of the banking business since the Charter of the Second Bank of the United States lapsed in 1836 and was on a pure specie payment system from 1840). Counterfeiting became rampant, and all notes circulated at a discount from face value (cf. Robertson, 1955, p. 153ff).

When the Federal government decided that it should become involved in bank regulation again, it was thus clear that the two areas that needed correction were in providing unification of the note issue and insuring the sufficiency of reserves held against redemption of outstanding notes. The impetus behind the return of the Federal government to banking legislation was the Civil War, which was extremely difficult to finance on a pure specie basis. To economize on gold stocks, the "Union" (i.e., the Northern "United" States remaining after the secession of the Southern "Confederated" States) Treasury first issued "demand notes," which were not legal tender but were convertible on demand into gold. The shortage of gold in the Treasury soon led to suspension of convertibility, and the rest of the war was financed on the basis of the "Legal Tender Act of 1862," which provided for the issue of "United States Notes," popularly called "greenbacks," based on only the faith and credit of the government.[11] The US dollar today is known by the name of this first currency note issued directly by the US government, not by a Federally chartered government bank.

The greenback issue quickly proved insufficient to meet the rising war expenditures. Faced with increasing difficulty in borrowing, Treasury Secretary Salmon Chase decided to copy the experience of the states and to compete with them by introducing a form of federal "free banking" in the Union. In the same year as the formation of Crédit Lyonnais, 1863, the "National Bank Act" (revised in 1864) was introduced in the US. Patterned after the New York State legislation of 1838, it permitted (Section 5) any group of five persons to form a "National Banking Association," provided it met minimum conditions, the most onerous of which was bank capital of $100,000 ($200,000 for cities with more than 50,000 inhabitants), half of which has to be paid in. To solve the problem of the quality of reserves and to provide a preferential system of borrowing (Section 16), interest-bearing government bonds of not less than $30,000 and not less than one-third (subsequently one-fourth) of the capital of the bank had to be deposited with the US Treasury in exchange for the right to issue National Bank Notes of an amount equal to 90% of the market value of the deposited US government debt, not to exceed 90% of the par value or of the bank's total capital. The banks retained the right to receive interest on the bonds if they met the conditions of the act. The National Bank Notes were to be redeemable in legal tender but were legal in payment of all debts except interest on the public debt and customs charges.

The number of national banks grew slowly because the National Bank Notes had to compete with the notes of the state banks which had been the only banknotes in circulation since the demise of the Bank of the United States. Against the more than 1,500 state banks, only 638 national banks had been formed by the end of 1864. This was because the reserve requirements against notes of most states were much less onerous and thus permitted a greater note issue, making the operation of state-chartered banks more profitable. This competition was eliminated by a March 1865 act that placed a 10% tax on notes of the state banks paid out by any bank, state or national, after July 1, 1866; in 1866 the tax was extended to any use of state-chartered banks' notes in payment. This soon drove state banks' notes out of circulation and gave national banks an effective monopoly on the issue of banknotes. By the end of 1865 there were more than 1,500 national banks. At the end of the Civil War, the opening of banks in the South brought the National Bank Note issue to the maximum limit of $300,000.

"Commercial" banks emerge from the National Bank Act

The act was administered by the office of the Comptroller of the Currency established within the Treasury Department. The Comptroller had the responsibilities of national bank regulator and was to provide for regular bank examinations. Banks were required to submit statements of financial condition on the call of the Comptroller (still known today as call reports). To deal with the problem of reserves, it created 17 "named cities" (later called "reserve cities") whose banks were designated "approved associations" suitable for the "redemption" of notes. Banks located in the reserve cities were required to hold a 25% reserve on notes and deposits, half of which could be kept with approved "reserve agent" (banks in New York that were required to hold 25% cash reserves). All other banks were required to hold 15% reserves against their notes and deposits, 60% of which could be held in "approved associations" in any "named city." The remainder had to be kept as cash in the bank's vault. After 1873 reserves were required only against deposits. A 5% redemption fund deposit at the Treasury, which counted as reserves against deposits, had to be kept against notes outstanding.

National banks were forbidden from investing in real estate (Section 28) and could not lend against or invest in the bank's own stock (Section 35), but would otherwise have (Section 5) all "incidental powers necessary to carry on the business of banking, by discounting, receiving deposits, lending money on personal security, buying and selling exchange, coin and bullion, and issuing and circulating notes" subject to the provision that not more than 10% of their capital could be lent to a single borrower (Section 29). The business of banking was originally interpreted to include underwriting and investing in securities. Note the similarities with the ordinary business activities specified by the management of Crédit Lyonnais in the same period.

To control note issue the Comptroller declared that interest could not be paid on National Bank Notes and that they could not be used as collateral for loans of lawful money. Because deposits were quickly becoming a substitute for notes in this period, the rulings were also extended to prohibit interest on bank deposits. This is the same limitation on deposit interest that would be introduced in the 1933 banking legislation.

Although the act did not contain any instruction on bank branching, to prevent re-emergence of the problems that had been encountered in the era of state free banking via free branching, the Comptroller ruled in 1864 that branching was forbidden. However, to encourage state banks to convert to national status, they were allowed to keep any branches they possessed. This is the origin of restricted branching determined by state, rather than federal, legislation.

Much like the private London banks faced with the competition of Bank of England notes in Britain, the state banks countered by offering loans to their clients in the form of deposit accounts subject to cheque. The substitution of notes by deposits that had already started in the larger cities even before the Civil War thus proved to be a competitive substitute for the new National Bank Notes. By the end of the Civil War, the circulating notes used as means of payment had been reduced to the issue of federal greenbacks and National Bank Notes (and an issue of fractional notes in denominations of less than one dollar due to a lack of silver), and by 1870 deposits had largely displaced them in terms of importance in both city and country banks.[12] The problem of the plethora of state banknotes had been eliminated as much by the natural process of bank deposits replacing banknotes[13] as from the strength of the new national banking system. Indeed, the increased use of deposits greatly reduced the attractiveness of a national charter. It was also reduced by the Section 26 requirement that banks make good any decline in the value of the government bonds deposited as backing for their notes issued. This tended to make National Bank Notes less attractive when interest rates fell, as they did after 1873, and bond prices went to a premium. Banks were attracted by the possibility of retiring notes to take profits on their holdings, while high bond prices made National Bank Notes a more expensive form of lending than deposits. The process was reversed when interest rates rose, as they did in the late 1880s (cf. Barnett, 1911, pp. 225ff, Robertson, 1964, p. 316). In addition, state banks had less onerous reserve and capital requirements as well as being allowed real estate investments. They also benefitted from the increased attention of adequate regulation of deposit banking by state banking commissions, which increased their credibility. After about 1875 the move to national charters was reversed, and banks started to return to the less rigorous state charter. This ushered in a period of regulatory competition between the states and the Federal government.

Neither the greenback nor the National Bank Note was originally convertible into gold. Both were initially rigidly fixed in amount, although National Bank Notes could be redeemed and withdrawn from circulation. Subsequent legislation forbid this, but it still remained the case that the note circulation could only be increased if the bank increased its capital. National Bank Notes were thus ill-suited to respond to the frequent liquidity crises, such as those due to the failures of the unregulated, wildcat state banks. The restrictions on

Table 1.1 Number of chartered banks under the National Bank Act

Year	State	National
1860	1,562	0
1863	1,466	66
1864	1,089	467
1865	349	1,294
1870	325	1,612
1875	586	2,076
1880	650	2,076
1885	1,015	2,689
1890	2,250	3,484
1895	4,369	3,715
1900	5,007	3,731
1905	9,018	5,664
1910	14,348	7,138
1914	17,498	7,518

Source: Adapted from Robertson (1964, p. 306).

note creation were loosened in the Resumption Act of 1875, which promised convertibility, but by this time deposits had almost completely displaced notes as the basic means of payment. It thus became possible to make national bank charters more attractive in country locations by reducing the minimum capital requirements for a national charter from $50,000 to $25,000.[14]

The "incidental powers" of banking in the act had initially been interpreted as including securities transactions, and national banking associations participated in the railway boom, along with state charter banks, underwriting and selling railway bonds that were used to replace their "accommodation" paper, that is, rollover lending to firms for longer-term financing needs. Many national banks also held fixed interest securities as part of their investment portfolios. However, in 1902 the Comptroller ruled that bonds were covered under the Section 29 limitation of 10% of paid-in bank capital for the "total liabilities to any association, of any person, or of any company, corporation or firm for money borrowed, including in the liabilities of a firm the liabilities of the several members thereof" (reprinted in Dunbar, 1897 (1969), p. 183). This section also noted that the "discount of *bona fide* bills of exchange drawn against actually existing values, and the discount of commercial or business paper actually owned by the person or persons, corporation, or firm negotiating the same shall not be considered as money borrowed" and thus exempt from the 10% rule. In 1906 these restrictions were amended to permit lending of 10% of capital plus surplus to a single borrower to a maximum of 30% of capital (cf. Bremer, 1935, p. 96).

As a result of these changes, the activities of national banks had been virtually reduced to discount of exchange bills and commercial and business paper, and a limited portfolio of bond investments, given the Comptroller's challenge to the right of the large New York banks to operate and underwrite securities. The act also forbade real estate investments. In effect, the national banks were limited to issuing notes and deposits against short-term discount lending to business. That is, de facto, they were limited to the restricted definition of commercial banking that would emerge in the 1933 Banking Act. National banks thus remained at an increasing disadvantage relative to state-chartered banks that were able to operate virtually without restriction in the securities business and in real estate lending.

In the Federal Reserve Act, national banks outside the central reserve cities were given limited rights to invest in real estate. All restrictions were to be lifted in the McFadden Act. The basic intention of the act was to continue the "parity" policy by granting equal branching rights and to extend the range of "investment securities" that banks could hold. But even this proved insufficient, and to retain their competitive position, national banks formed independent "security affiliates" that were organized under state charters to place their investments in equities outside the regulation and control of the Comptroller. This facilitated lending against customers' equity and brokers loans, as well as underwriting of securities, including foreign securities. Of particular importance (and examples of speculation and abuse) were the creation of investment trusts that were quoted on the stock market and invested in equity (cf. Reis, 1937, p. 113f). The first such affiliate was organized by First National City Bank of New York, under a state charter, in 1911. This brought a radical change to the operation of national banks.

The result of the policy of "parity" between national and state banks was competition producing lowest common denominator regulation (this was to be rechristened a level playing field when a similar process was applied to savings and loan banks in the 1980s). National banks reduced their "real bills" lending (classified as "all other") by 20 percentage points while increasing their lending against bonds and equity by 9 percentage points, their direct acquisition of such assets by 6.5 percentage points, and their real estate lending by nearly 5 percentage points. These figures do not include the positions of the securities affiliates. The share of "eligible loans" for rediscount at the Fed held by national banks fell by half from 30.2% to 16% between 1923 and 1932.

Table 1.2 Balance sheet composition (%) of national and state charter banks, 1921, 1930

Charter	National Charter		State Charter	
	1921	*1930*	*1921*	*1930*
Investments	25.1	31.6	21.2	24.2
Secured Loans★	16.9	25.9	13.2	11.8
Real Estate	1.7	6.8	13.0	13.3
All Other	56.3	35.7	52.6	50.7 (58.9 in 1928)

★ Secured by bonds and stocks

Source: Bremer (1935, p. 113).

The first quarter of the century was thus dominated by a battle between federal regulators and state regulators that permitted national banks to increase latitude in their securities operations. When this proved insufficient, national banks switched to state charters or sought to circumvent national regulations by carrying out their securities operations under state charter, outside the purview of the Comptroller.

It was the 1907 crisis, triggered by the failure of the Knickerbocker Trust Company in New York, that confirmed that the national banking system, although it might have eliminated the risk of crisis due to the suspension of payment on banknotes, had not eliminated the endemic instability of the American financial system. Most experts laid the blame for this instability on the rigidity of the issue in the National Bank Note system, making lender of last resort activity impossible. This brought additional pressure for change to the national banking system.

To remedy this problem the 1908 Aldrich-Vreeland amendment to the National Bank Act provided for the formation of national currency associations, comprised of national banks and empowered to issue emergency currency notes. Although 286 banks formed a total of 18 associations, this system was inadequate to deal with systemic instability. In 1912 Aldrich proposed legislation to create a National Reserve Association. It was not enacted, although much of the proposal survived in the Federal Reserve Act passed in December 1913. The District Reserve Banks, which replaced the associations, began operation on November 2, 1914.

The motivation behind the act was to eliminate instability by creating a means to "furnish an elastic currency" by "rediscounting commercial paper." To this end the National Bank Note was replaced by a new note to be issued by the new institution. It was not to be another government bank or a central bank on European lines but a "system" of district "reserve" banks, owned by the national banks. The district federal reserve banks were authorized to issue the new currency, the Federal Reserve Note, which was to be legal tender for all debts and which was considered the liability of both the Federal Reserve System and of the US government. The government debt that the national banks had purchased to issue these notes was exchanged for Federal Reserve Notes. The national banks thus lost the right of note issue to the district federal reserve banks.

Just as national banks, the district federal reserve banks had to hold reserves against the notes they issued. The government bonds held under the National Bank System were replaced by a minimum of 40% in gold and the remaining amount backed by commercial paper acquired by discount from the stockholder banks. Government bonds were still eligible as investment assets but were not eligible as backing for Federal Reserve Notes. The new system was thus an expression of the banking principle known as the "real bills" doctrine: the creation of notes backed by self-liquidating, short-term commercial lending.[15] It thus satisfied the requirement of an elastic means of payment, which would expand and contract with the needs of trade and the conditions of the banking system. A member bank that lacked funds to increase lending to legitimate business borrowers could discount commercial bills, representing existing loans to businesspeople in exchange for Federal Reserve Notes at its district reserve bank. On the other hand, if the notes were not needed, they could be used to retire discounted paper. There would thus not be an "excess" note issue to the needs of trade.

It was thus the banking principle, as embodied in the real bills doctrine, that eventually formed the basis for the US Central Bank, in contrast to the British decision in 1844 to adopt the currency principle. Although it is not always recognized, the logical application of the banking principle requires that transactions deposits can be provided only by banks that engage in short-term commercial lending, for only under these conditions will the supply of money automatically adjust to the level of real economic activity. Deposits created to finance long-term investments would contravene this automaticity because they would remain in circulation after the initial expenditures had been taken and remain until the investment was fully amortized. As already mentioned, this reasoning seems to have been implicit in the earlier decisions taken by the Comptroller of the Currency concerning the acceptable range of operations of national banks. But, as seen, during the first quarter of the 20th century, national banks were under heavy pressure from state banks operating in the securities business and were actively seeking ways in which they could also participate in this business despite the rulings of the Comptroller.

Thus, the part of the Federal Reserve Act that was to deal with the problem of the elastic currency and the lender of last resort function was based on a form of banking organization that was under intense pressure for change at the beginning of the century, if indeed it had ever existed. During the boom of the 1920s, banks expanded aggressively into long-term investment finance through the capital markets. As both national "commercial" banks and their "commercial" real bills loans declined as a proportion of the banking system, so did the applicability of the real bills doctrine as the guiding principle for control of the US monetary system. As will be seen, anyone analyzing the future of banking in the US in this period would have concluded that national "commercial" banks were in crisis as the proportion of their lending to business was in continual decline.

As long as the Federal Reserve continued to operate according to the commercial loan principle in conditions in which banks were increasingly making security and bond loans, it would be increasingly ineffectual in terms of elastic control of the currency. Indeed, the Fed soon found that its "qualitative control" over funds through the designation of assets eligible for discounts could not prevent funds flowing into stock market "call" loans and "non-productive" securities lending as the boom progressed. By 1929 the Fed was directly enforcing "qualitative" control by refusing any discounts for banks with any documented lending to support securities purchases.

The Fed had even less control over money creation once the crisis broke, for banks had virtually no commercial paper investments in their portfolios to present for discount, and the major proportion of their portfolios of investments in loans against capital market securities were ineligible for discount. A system that could only support bank reserves by lending against commercial loans and government securities could not provide reserves to support the money supply if banks were predominantly invested in bonds and equity and loans secured by these capital market assets.

This flaw in the operation of the new "elastic currency" was strikingly revealed in September 1931, when Britain left the gold standard. Despite massive gold holdings (expectations of foreign exchange traders have always defied logic), it was widely presumed that the US would quickly follow Britain, and there was a run on the US dollar at the same time as the US domestic banking crisis was breaking. The Federal Reserve found itself virtually helpless between two contrasting currents. To increase the outstanding issue of Federal Reserve Notes, the district banks had to increase their holdings of gold or increase rediscounts of banks' commercial bills. But the banks had only security loans of uncertain value and no business loans. Foreigners, and some Americans, speculated against the dollar by redeeming notes and shipping gold abroad. The Federal Reserve thus found the currency in circulation decreasing at precisely the time when banks needed support. There was no means of reversing the situation; the new currency was not as elastic as had been assumed when it came to providing lender of last resort support to the banking system.[16] The real bills doctrine thus proved to be extremely inelastic when banks were primarily investing in capital market securities or lending to the private sector to finance the purchase of securities.

At the risk of oversimplification, the reform legislation introduced in the New Deal could be interpreted as attempting to restore a banking and financial system similar to that which had been envisaged in the Federal Reserve Act and had been foreshadowed in the earlier rulings of the Comptroller to limit banks' activity to commercial banking. Because the elasticity of Federal Reserve Notes and the operating policy of the Federal Reserve System was based on deposit-taking banks being limited to making short-term business loans, this bank structure was written into the 1933 banking law in what became known as the separation of "commercial" banking from "investment" banking operations. What the Comptroller had failed to achieve in interpreting the National Bank Law, and what had been implicit in the Federal Reserve Act, was now imposed by New Deal legislation in the form of the segmentation of commercial and investment banking.

Decline of banks or the decline of commercial banking?

This is the definition of what is meant by a "bank" in modern discussions of the difficulties being faced by the banking system. It corresponds to neither of the classic forms of bank previously discussed, for it is not a pure "capital" bank, nor is it a pure "deposit" or giro bank. It is a pure issue bank. It is interesting to note that the difficulties faced by this particular form of "commercial" bank had already been noted at the foundation of the Crédit Lyonnais. They were also the subject of discussion at the very time at which the 1933 banking law was making them permanent.

This discussion is most evident in a book by Lauchlin Currie (Currie, 1934), an adviser to the Federal Reserve and the Treasury in the 1930s, who considered commercial banks to "belong to a past era." He supported this position by pointing out that banking statistics for December 31, 1932, indicated that 65% of banks' lending was against security and bonds, and only 8% could be considered as commercial loans.[17] He "sought to explain the decline in bank loans as due to a recognition of the extent to which loans intensify the dangers of a drastic decline in net earnings and of insolvency should gross earnings decline" (ibid., p. 41). He notes that over the period 1922–8 there was a tendency for larger, successful firms to reduce their bank borrowing and that the "great bulk of commercial loans were being made to farmers and relatively small business concerns" as well as to the least successful businesses.

Whether Currie was right in identifying the cause of the decline in business lending, or whether it was simply the fact that firms were encouraged by the banks directing them to their securities affiliates where the stock market boom made it much cheaper to raise funds because the Fed was putting pressure on interest rates, does not change the end result of a decline in the quality and liquidity of "commercial" bank assets. Clearly, a rather different picture would have emerged had the accounts of banks been consolidated with their affiliates.

Currie concludes,

> If economic progress continues to be associated with the increasing importance of larger corporations having access to the stock and bond markets, there is a strong probability that the commercial loan will continue to decline in the future. The decline in the commercial loan, in other words, appears to be intimately related to the changing structure of business which is bringing about a change in the methods of financing of business.
>
> (Currie, 1934, p. 41)

He suggests that banks will be left with savings deposits as a source of funding individual lending, whereas other institutions should be expected to emerge to meet any lending demand beyond the ability of these banks (ibid., p. 152).

Currie, whose investigations deal with the period of the 1920s, was basing his forecast on a linear extrapolation of the history he knew. In the event, the New Deal legislation came in the way of his predictions. Yet, they read as if they had been written in the 1980s, when exactly the same concerns had been raised about the survival of commercial banks. As noted in the introduction, economists are not necessarily interested in banks, and Currie was interested only in commercial banks because he thought the emphasis that was placed on commercial banks in the US stood in the way of an effective reform of the monetary system and an efficient control of the role of banks in the operation of monetary policy.

This marked the watershed noted earlier in the way economists approached the analysis of banks. According to Currie, "Banks derive their peculiar economic significance not from the fact that they are lenders – there are many other lenders – but from the fact that they furnish, in modern countries, almost the entire supply of the community's means of payment." He argued that "[l]oans are not means of payment any more than are houses or wheat," and "[a]part from their connection with demand deposits there is no logical reason to distinguish bank loans and investments from other loans" (Currie, 1934, p. 49). Whether banks lend to firms or against real estate, long term or short, according to Currie, is irrelevant unless they also provide liquid liabilities used as means of payment. Commercial banks are of particular interest not because they lend to business, nor is it important that this source of a commercial bank's business is disappearing; we should only be interested because of the impact this may have on the provision of means of payment. It is only the *Issue* function that is of importance.

Currie's book thus marked a departure from the "banking school-real bills" doctrine that had dominated monetary thinking in the US. Currie calls this the "commercial loan theory" of banking. What bothered Currie was that "[t]he Banking Principle stressed commercial loans as a means to an end – the effective regulation of money. It appears likely that by now the end has become almost forgotten and the means has become an end in itself" (Currie, 1934, p. 37). Although he does not make the point, this is an implicit criticism of the 1933 Banking Act, which returned commercial banks, limited to short-term commercial lending, to the role of sole providers of demand deposits, which had become the major means of payment in the economy.

Currie's conclusion is that structural changes in loan demand (today we would say that the stability of the money demand function had broken down) would vitiate the automatic regulation of the supply of money supposed by the commercial loan principle because of structural changes in demand for loans that need not produce changes in the supply of money appropriate to monetary stability. Indeed, the main point of Currie's book is that there will usually be conflicts between the desirable changes in bank assets and in bank liabilities, which leads him to propose a reform of the system based on a divorce of "the supply of money from the loaning of money" (ibid., p. 152) via the government provision of demand deposits (this was before the Chicago proposals for 100% reserve banking) through what would now be called "narrow" or "core" banks investing in government debt. This is a giro bank, adapted to conditions of suspension of specie payment. Federal Reserve Notes, with partial gold backing, take the place of gold held in the giro bank.

Currie recognized that this would have an impact on commercial banks and their lending to businesses and individuals. He also recognized that there would have to be radical changes made in Fed operating procedure toward more direct control of the money supply. In particular substituting manipulation of reserve requirements applied only to demand deposits in place of discounting to directly change the volume of bank reserves. As Currie notes, "In the older textbooks on banking it was customarily implied that the function of reserves was to afford liquidity. . . . It is now generally held by monetary writers that the function of member bank reserves is to control or limit deposits" (ibid., p. 65).

Currie's analysis was apparently too late for inclusion in the monetary reform plans of the new administration, and the 1933 Banking Act reinstated the commercial bank, restricted to short-term commercial lending, as the linchpin of the new financial system. Little concern seems to have been given to the problems of control of the supply of money expressed in Currie's book. Even the creation of the Open Market Committee had as its goal: operations "with a view of accommodating commerce and business." Other features were clearly directed toward increasing the "qualitative" control over lending, for example, Section 7, which gave the Fed the right to fix the proportion of security loans to bank capital and surplus and, in special cases, to prohibit increases in such lending for up to one year. Paradoxically, the only feature that acts directly on the liability side of the balance sheet, Section 11, which prohibits interest on demand deposits and gives the Fed the power to regulate interest rates on time deposits, is rather a barrier to the introduction of monetary control.[18] There is nothing in the 1933 act to suggest a rejection of the commercial loan approach. Thus, it is the New Deal banking legislation that resolves the crisis in commercial banking that had been identified by Currie by defining commercial banks as the only type of bank legally allowed to operate in the US.

The second decline of "commercial banking": history repeats itself

The post-war period could thus have been expected to be one in which the same scenario of the decline of commercial banks was replayed. It can be seen in the fall of the commercial banks' share of the total assets held by all financial institutions from around half in the 1950s to less than 30% in the 1990s. Yet, this could simply be the effect of the post-war expansion of other types of financial institution, such as savings and loan banks and mutual funds. However, commercial banks also lost part of their traditional lending business to alternative lenders as can be seen from the fact that the share of commercial bank loans in the total indebtedness of non-financial corporations fell from more than 90% in 1950 to less than 60% in the beginning of the 1990s. At the same time, commercial paper grew from a negligible proportion to 12% in the same period, and non-bank financial intermediaries' share grew from 6% to 18%. The remaining decline in the share of commercial bank lending is made up of an increase to about 10% in foreign borrowing. Thus commercial banks were clearly losing their core business lending activity to non-bank competitors over the period. It was not simply the case of an expansion of overall financial intermediation in which new institutions were creating new types of investment assets.

Competition also prevailed on the liability side as banks lost deposits. On the one hand, thrifts and then brokerage houses competed for private household deposits, and other financial assets such as Treasury bills attracted business deposits. This decline in the relative position of commercial banks is similar to that noted by Currie for the 1920s, with the exception that in the post-war period banks were unable to securitize their lending activities or to shift them to affiliate companies because of the New Deal legislation. For this reason the decline was more damaging to the banks, for it was impossible for them to compensate for the decline in lending by offering money market mutual funds, which could intermediate commercial paper, or to compete with commercial paper offerings by packaging loans in investment trusts.

The problem was thus not so much the inability to operate in the sale and trading of long-term securities as the inability to adapt to changes in the form of short-term lending in the market. The decline in the role of commercial banks then did not mean that corporations were being deprived of services offered by commercial banks, simply that these same services were being offered by other financial institutions, usually at a lower cost and with greater efficiency.

It is interesting that the same decline in the share of total assets intermediated by banks took place in France and Britain. Yet, in both countries this trend was reversed because banks had the possibility of adjusting to the new forms of short-term corporate lending. It is for this reason that US banks have been pushed into other areas of business, such as off balance sheet activities, to compensate for the inability to follow changes in their traditional line of business. This is not only activity in derivatives, highly leveraged merger lending, and so forth but also simple activities such as providing lines of credit to back issues of commercial paper by corporations. Indeed, given the low margins on commercial paper issues, banks now often earn more from providing the credit lines guaranteeing commercial paper rollovers than they would had they actually provided the lending.

The post-war decline of commercial banks

The post-war period produced a totally unexpected change in the composition of banks' balance sheets. Although Currie (1934) had noted the rise in private securities lending in bank balance sheets, by the end of the war, the application of the Banking Act had caused such lending to disappear. However, they had been more than fully replaced by purchase of government securities. By 1945, 57% of commercial banks' assets were government security loans (cf. Madden, et al., 1948, p. 88). As noted, this was partially the result of the 1932 Glass-Steagall Act, which made government securities a substitute for commercial loans as collateral for the issue of Federal Reserve Notes. This temporary, emergency measure was made permanent in 1945. The rest was due to the decision to finance the war by means of long-term borrowing at low interest rates rather than by taxation. Most of this government war debt ended up in bank portfolios (the 10% restriction on lending to a single borrower did not apply to the purchase of government bonds!).

This created another situation that had not been foreseen by the commercial loan theory of central banking, which had formed the basis of the creation of the Federal Reserve and its policy actions. The size of banks' holdings of government securities gave them nearly total independence from Fed policy controls over lending in the post-war period. The Fed-Treasury Accord of 1951, which returned control of interest rates to the monetary authority, was important because driving down the price of securities sufficiently to cause capital losses on the banks' portfolio holdings was the only way the Fed could limit banks' sales of securities to finance additional lending. In the immediate post-war period, this was not difficult as most securities had been purchased at interest rates of less than 2%.

However, higher rates on government securities not only made Treasury refunding of the debt more expensive, but it also increased the opportunity cost to large corporations holding bank deposits with zero-interest rates. In addition, smaller depositors where increasingly attracted by savings and loans banks, which were able to offer better rates for their deposits as they were not subject to the ceilings imposed by Regulation Q.[19]

Given the rates that prevailed in the 1930s and during the war, Regulation Q controls were benign: rates on short-term three-month Treasury bills were 3/8%, and long bonds were pegged at 2.5%. The rate advantage on bills certainly did not offset the inconvenience compared to bank deposits, whereas savings and time deposits offered no advantage over long-maturity Treasuries.

When the Fed raised short rates after the war, banks for the first time felt competition as large corporations drew down deposits and shifted into Treasuries to take advantage of short rates, which had risen above 1%. The only possible response available to banks was to try to attract businesses to time deposits in which rates could be raised to remain competitive without exceeding the regulatory limits. But this put them in competition with savings and loan banks, whose shares were not yet subject to Regulation Q limits.

It was the return of inflation in the Korean war boom that convinced the Fed to use monetary policy to counterbalance the excessively expansionary impact of fiscal policy at the expense of supporting an orderly government securities market. It also represented a shift from conditions in which monetary and fiscal policy are coordinated to achieve a common goal to one in which the absence of appropriate fiscal policy required offsetting monetary policy. In these conditions monetary and fiscal policy work at cross purposes and tend to reinforce each other as the natural increase in interest rates, which would be caused by increased economic activity, is reinforced by monetary restraint.

The resulting increase in market rates above the Regulation Q ceiling made it impossible for banks to offset the loss in demand deposits by attempting to shift them to time deposits because their maximum rates were now also below comparable non-bank rates. The use of monetary policy as a substitute for fiscal policy due to international conditions thus had a direct impact on initiating the movements of funds out of the banking system and the use of financial "innovations" by banks to attempt to reverse the decline.[20]

Innovations to protect the corporate deposit base

The drain of funds from bank deposits was reversed during the 1958–60 recession as market rates fell below the Regulation Q maximum. Walter Wriston made his future career at First National City Bank of New York by creating a "treasury bill" for commercial banks, recommending the sale of time deposits to large corporate borrowers in amounts of $1 million[21] that side-stepped the illiquidity of the 180-day maturity by making them tradeable in a secondary market in which other government securities dealers and other banks interested in recovering their large depositors would join as market makers and make money "riding the yield curve" (see Fieldhouse, 1964, p. 46; Mayer, 1974, p. 201). Thus the "negotiable" certificate of deposit (CD) was born on the basis of providing a 50-basis-point premium over short-term Treasury bills and with the same liquidity, provided by the same market makers, as Treasury bills.

The stability of CD deposits for the banks was determined by the permanence of the positive differential between Regulation Q limits and short-term market interest rates. Any rise in market rates that reversed the differential would not only eliminate CD funds, but it would produce capital losses on the banks' securities portfolios, making it more costly to replace the funds. The dependence of the large money center banks on CD funding meant that the use of monetary policy to offset the lack of timely and appropriate fiscal policy could be achieved only by driving banks toward insolvency (fortunately security portfolios, like loans, were not marked to market so that this was not evident from looking at annual reports) and making the banking system more illiquid. It was presumably to prevent this double hit on bank profits caused by monetary restriction that during the first half of the 1960s, the Fed repeatedly adjusted Regulation Q rates upward in step with changes in money market rates.

Because thrifts were not initially subject to Regulation Q, they could compete with commercial banks for small household deposits. The thrifts used this freedom to offer deposits paying rates that in late 1962 were higher than long-term government securities and roughly equivalent to rates on new corporate issues. In 1962 the Fed started to set different Regulation Q limits for savings and time deposits in commercial banks, allowing a time deposit maximum above the savings limit; in 1965 special regulations unified rates on CDs for all maturities over 30 days, but the maximum applied to CDs was 150 basis points above the limit on commercial bank savings deposits. Because savings deposits could be held only by individuals, there was an asymmetry between savings and time deposits that were open to all clients. Franklin National Bank of Long Island took advantage of this anomaly to offer individual savings depositors "time certificates of deposit," based on the higher time rate maximum in $1,000 minimum denominations. This not only caused a shift of funds from savings to time certificates held in commercial banks, but more importantly it caused a massive shift from savings associations to commercial bank time deposits and a concomitant decline in funds available to finance housing.

The introduction of these "consumer" CDs marked the beginning of the savings and loan crisis, for commercial banks had found an effective counter to the competitive advantage of savings and loan banks due to their exemption from Regulation Q. The difficulties, which were caused in the construction industry (particularly in California), led Congress to attempt to shield the thrifts from bank competition. The Interest Rate Control Act of 1966 introduced a special maximum Regulation Q rate for "consumer" time deposits, below the rate on negotiable CDs, and extended these limits to savings and loans banks by making them subject to Regulation Q limits but with a 25-basis-point premium over the rates permitted to banks. This was meant to restore their competitive advantage relative to banks, but it did nothing to shield them from competition from non-bank money market instruments when rates rose above the maximum Regulation Q limits. To complete the attempt to seal off the negotiable CD market from individuals, the Fed introduced a $100,000 minimum size on negotiable CDs at the end of the year.[22]

Any benefit to thrifts of the attempt to restore their competitive advantage over commercial banks was overshadowed by the fact that again in 1966 the Fed decided to offset insufficient fiscal restraint with monetary contraction. However, it decided not to adjust CD limits in line with changes in market rates. This produced the double hit on banks, reducing the value of their Treasury securities and making their CDs uncompetitive. The result was a sharp halt in lending as outstanding CDs were not renewed as they matured and banks were forced to take massive losses on the sale of securities required to raise funds to meet lending commitments to regular borrowers. Although this was called a "credit crunch," it is the equivalent of a policy-induced bank run; it nearly spilled over to produce a capital market break.[23]

At the time this process was described as "disintermediation," with the implication that it would be followed by a process of "re-intermediation" when conditions returned to normal and depositors returned their funds to banks and savings and loans. However, bankers considered the event a "near-death" experience not to be repeated by a return to the *status quo ante*. There was thus a reassessment of bank operations (note that the impact on funding occurred in both commercial banks and savings and loans) that led to the shift from asset to liability management as the banks sought refuge from the possibility of another "double whammy" and the savings and loan banks sought other methods of competing with banks and money market instruments, in particular by means of negotiated orders of withdrawal, which appeared by the end of the decade. The implication was that all efforts had to be directed toward finding sources of funds that fell outside Regulation Q.

These conditions were accompanied by the decision to make the voluntary lending restraints obligatory and the introduction of the interest equalization tax, which resulted from the difficulties of resolving the problem of international adjustment. These two factors reinforced the banks' recourse to offshore non-deposit sources of funding in the Eurodollar markets and the presence of US banks in the London dollar market dates from the 1966 crunch.

Another source of funds was the interbank market for overnight borrowing of reserves, now known as federal funds. Initially classified as "loans," these transactions were eventually reclassified as the sale and repurchase of assets, which exempted them from limitations on the proportion of bank capital that could be committed to a single borrower.[24]

The 1966 episode further aggravated the relations between the banks and their large corporate customers. The inability of the banks to meet their funding needs suggested to corporate clients that they had to find non-bank backup sources of funds, often through issue of corporate paper. Obviously this alternative was only possible for the best credit so that it meant that banks continued to lose their best corporate borrowers as well as remaining subject to competition from money market instruments for their large corporate depositors and savings and loans for their individual depositors.

The Fed again applied monetary restraint in late 1968 and again chose not to raise Regulation Q limits. After 1966 the larger money center banks had come to use the Euromarkets as an auxiliary source of funds whenever rate differentials made it profitable to do so. To offset the $13 billion or so of CDs lost in 1969, they thus fell back on the Eurodollar market.[25] The Fed could have prevented this, and it has been suggested that it did not do so to improve the payments balance and strengthen the dollar,[26] but it is more likely that the Fed wanted to avoid the distressed sales of securities by banks and the risk of insolvency on government debt dealers, which had occurred in 1966. Eurodollar borrowing continued until the economy slowed and domestic rates fell back, making it advantageous to substitute domestic for Eurodollar borrowing. This produced rapid repayments and a rapid deterioration in the settlements balance in 1970 and 1971.[27] The result was increased instability in international capital flows and massive pressure on European central banks, in particular the Bundesbank. Dollar holdings in German banks increased from $2.8 to $12.5 billion between May 1970 and 1971, and the decision was finally taken to float the Deutsche Mark (cf. Bell, 1973, p. 90ff). These movements were interpreted by the Nixon administration as an unsustainable, permanent outflow and the final argument for the August 15 decision to abandon gold convertibility, which effectively ended the Bretton Woods system.

The search for alternative depositors and borrowers

When the oil crisis produced the problem of "recycling" the "petrodollars" earned by the petroleum-producing countries, the large US commercial banks were already established and active in the Euromarkets and eager for the additional source of deposit funds as well as for the developing country "sovereign" credits to replace their eroding base of traditional corporate borrowers. Recycling also provided an easy way for governments to avoid the tricky politics of international institutions accepting risk and responsibility. Much as during the Second World War, when the government would print bonds that the banks could buy through the creation of deposits, the necessary reserves being produced by the repurchase by the Fed of bonds from the banks, now it was the international buyers of petroleum who provided the funds that the petroleum-producing countries deposited with the banks to create the reserves to fund the loans to developing countries.

Instead of the Fed guaranteeing a low, stable "pattern of rates," the Euromarkets used rollover credits to eliminate interest rate risk. However, in 1979 bank balance sheets were hit in virtually the same way as in 1966, when the Fed shifted operating procedure to control monetary aggregates rather than interest rates. With flexible exchange rates, the rise in interest rates caused a sustained appreciation of the dollar. Although the banks were protected from the interest rate and exchange rate risks, this time the double whammy hit their sovereign borrowers, who saw their interest payments increase with every interest rate rollover and the dollar amounts of their interest and principal repayments rise with the appreciation of the dollar. The banks discovered that they were not protected from interest rate and exchange rate risk after all; credit risk had replaced interest rate risk, and defaults brought about the same collapse in the value of their loan portfolios as the rise in interest rates in 1966 had produced on their security portfolios. Once again historical value accounting of loans prevented visible insolvency, but once again the attempt to use monetary policy had operated by reducing the value of bank assets (this time both their syndicated loans and their securities portfolio), producing near insolvency. This time the Fed had to intervene to prevent its own policy-induced bank run when first Poland and then Mexico threatened default and concerns were raised over the solvency of the banking system. And once again, the banks faced the problem of finding alternative sources of funding and lending.

In contrast to the 1966 and 1969 credit contractions, in the early 1980s there was little impact on the volume of lending of the banking system; the banks simply increased the rates they paid for non-deposit reserves, and rollover credits were introduced domestically. It finally required credit controls to bring the expansion in lending to a stop, for increasing market rates no longer appeared to have any impact. Under the Fed's new operating procedures, monetary policy worked only when it made the borrowers, and thus also the banks, insolvent. In the process, interest rates had been pushed to historically high levels in a period of recession.

Monetary control versus prudential control

Not only did the decisions of the banks to increase non-deposit sources of funds after the 1966 credit crunch create increasing difficulty for the Fed in influencing aggregate demand conditions, the extended use of selective controls and high interest rates had led many banks, including large money-center banks, to seek state charters and withdraw from Fed membership. Thus at the beginning of the 1980s the Fed agreed to exchange regulations to insure the stability and integrity of the banking system for regulations to increase its ability to influence economic activity. The Depositary Institutions Deregulation and Monetary Control Act of 1980 responded to the Fed's request for obligatory membership by extending Fed reserve regulations to all deposit-taking institutions, irrespective of charter. The cost, however, was the elimination of Regulation Q controls on time and savings deposits by 1986. It also preempted state usury laws on certain types of lending such as mortgages (removing a major obstacle to domestic adjustable-interest-rate rollover lending) and increased federal deposit insurance protection from $40,000 for deposits up to *and including* $100,000 for all deposit-taking institutions.[28] To reduce expenditures, budgets of the supervisory agencies, in particular the Federal Savings and Loan Insurance Corporation (FSLIC), were cut, sharply reducing the number of examiners.[29]

However, the "more level" playing field introduced by allowing thrifts freedom to offer demand deposits and use interest rates to attract them did not apply to their assets, which remained composed of long-term mortgage loans at low interest rates. Even if they succeeded in defending their deposits through the use of bro-kered deposits, the difference between short-term deposit rates and the earnings on outstanding mortgages meant that most were soon technically insolvent. The asset side of balance sheets was "leveled" in the 1982 Depositary Institutions Act (which brought forward the elimination of Regulation Q by two years) allowed thrifts to engage in certain types of commercial lending and acquire securities that had previously been prohibited. The idea was that access to investment oppor-tunities with higher interest rates would offset the low rates on their outstanding mortgages, giving overall earnings sufficient to cover the increased costs of deposit funds. Investments in commercial real estate and in non-investment grade assets (junk bonds), both prompted by the 1982 act, were the cause of most of the fraud and losses in the thrifts. Thus, although most were already insolvent as a result of the introduction of the "more level" playing field of the early 1980s, savings banks were allowed to continue to operate, raising funds through the use of brokered, government-insured $100,000 deposits and investing in assets with the highest, and thus riskiest, returns available to avoid formal insolvency.

Commercial banks did not need special legislation to permit such activity (the Federal Reserve Act had granted to national banks outside the central reserve cities the right to make real estate loans, and the 1927 Pepper–McFadden Act eliminated these restrictions and in addition provided the ability to deal in investment securities); instead, as they worked their way out of their ill-fated lending to developing countries, they again sought alternative lending opportu-nities. The new freedom to attract funds via rate competition meant that higher yields had to be sought on investments. First, banks lent to oil and gas producers in the early 1980s, just in time for the collapse of the OPEC cartel and of the price of oil; then they moved into commercial real estate, just in time for the tax exemptions on such projects to be withdrawn in the tax reform bill of 1986; and finally they engaged in highly leveraged transactions via bridge lending for mergers and acquisitions, just in time for the collapse of the junk bond market in 1989. All the while the banks' traditional borrowers continued to increase their direct borrowing in the money and capital markets.

It is unnecessary to retell the story of the decline of the US financial system to make the point that the attempt to salvage the savings and loan industry, and the search by commercial banks for a new client base, played a large part in creating output for which there was no real final demand. This prolonged the Reagan boom of 1983 into the second-longest continuous expansion in his-tory. The financial experts had decided that the thrifts would "grow" their way out of insolvency, so they set about making their assets grow. The result was a drugged expansion in which the banks and thrifts provided both the financing and the demand for the production of the oil and gas supply industry, the con-struction industry, the financial services industry, and the real estate developers, architects, lawyers, and so on who were involved in the gas exploration boom, the commercial real estate boom, the merger and acquisition boom, and so forth. It was a case of suppliers creating their own demand because many of the projects, managed by developers who also owned the financial institutions, often had three years' profits front-loaded into them for both the developer and the lending thrift, whether or not the projects were ever completed or sold. One by one these sectors collapsed for lack of final buyers and had to be carried on the books of the financial institutions that had funded them.

Once again it was the Fed that started the attack on the value of bank portfolios when, fearing an outbreak of inflation, which it had been expecting since 1987 (the rate in 1986 was slightly over 1% and jumped in 1987 to 4%, slightly higher than the 1982–5 average), it returned to the tight monetary policy it had initiated in 1987 after the mini-break in the stock market in 1989, reinforcing the fall in asset values. The asset portfolios of banks were thus subject to declines in value due to both the increase in interest rates and to the decline in asset quality. The invasion of Kuwait simply confirmed the recession, which had been held in abeyance for a decade by the smoke and mirrors of the supply-side revolution. The cut in defense spending and the attempts to cut expenditures to reduce the deficit did the rest, while banks contributed by reducing lending and producing the so-called credit crunch.

In the same period, bank regulators moved to counter the difficulties that they believed to have been caused by the widespread use of variable-interest-rate lending. As noted, because rollover lending reduces interest rate risk, it also removes the impact of monetary policy on the value of the bank investments that had been the center of the operation of policy in the 1960s. Higher interest rates no longer necessarily reduce the capital value of assets if both funding and lending rates are automatically adjusted. The risk of rising interest rates is thus transformed into changes in the carrying cost of the borrower's lending and thus in the ability to repay the loan. This is an increase in credit (or default) risk. The increased capital requirement was to have created a larger cushion against these greater credit risks and to increase the cost of making more risky loans by forcing the banks to raise reserves at market interest rates in the capital market rather than at subsidized rates through increased deposits. The more capital a bank borrowed, the higher the risk premium the market would charge, until its funding would be finally cut off.

But, because all of a bank's traditional commercial and industrial lending was given the same 100% risk weighting, this system created the perverse incentive of reducing business lending and of driving banks toward the most risky lending possible within this risk weighting. It thus did nothing to impede the problems faced by the banks in finding replacement lending for the first-class credits that were now borrowing directly through the issue of commercial paper in the money markets. At the same time, it aggravated the conditions of the credit crunch, for as a bank's high risk loans went bad, it either had to go back to the market for more funds or reduce its risk-weighted asset portfolio. This it could do by reducing its 100% weighted commercial and industrial lending, usually through the securitization of the assets and their sale in the capital market and increasing its holdings of government securities carrying a zero risk weighting. Thus, just at the time when conditions faced by borrowers were becoming more difficult, bank lending was contracting as a consequence of the introduction of the new risk-weighted capital requirements. The result has been a rapid accumulation of government securities in bank portfolios and a return to bank balance sheets similar to those of the immediate post-war period.

The French transition from segmented banking to universal banking

The French experience in the post-war period provides an example of a banking system transformed from separation of commercial banks from other financial institutions to one in which all financial institutions were subject to the same regulations. The process was not continuous, but by the beginning of the 1980s, the French system had been transformed from one that resembled the Italian system to one that was similar to the German system. Because part of the concern of French regulators was the loss of competitiveness of the commercial banks, it provides an example of how a segmented system can be converted to allow banks to recover their central position in a unified system.

The background to the banking system during post-war reconstruction

The banking legislation introduced by the Vichy government in June 1941 laid the groundwork for a segmented system by defining different classes of financial institution in terms of specific banking activities (cf. Germain-Martin, 1954, p. 233ff; Burgard, et al., 1995, pp. 18–9, 37–42). Prior to this time banking activity had been regulated as any common commercial transaction under the code of commerce. The new legislation defined banks as firms whose "usual function . . . is to receive from the public, as deposits or otherwise, funds which they employ for their own account, either in discounts or in credit transactions, or in financial operations." Funds "received from the public" are defined as "the funds which a firm or a person receives in every form for the account of a third person, with the understanding that the funds will be returned." Banks, defined as firms that borrow funds from the public that are used to lend short term, were governed by a Bank Control Commission and the Permanent Committee on the Organisation of Banks and Financial Houses. These were primarily self-governing organisms because bankers were in the majority on the former and totally composed the latter, even though membership was by government appointment. Just as under US regulation, any financial institution that did not take retail deposits from the public was not subject to regulation as a bank.

Changes in the post-war period reinforced this segmentation of the system (cf. Germain-Martin, 1954, pp. 234–9). The reason was not, as in the US, to ensure safety to public savings held by banks but rather by the need for more direct government control over the planning and implementation of post-war reconstruction. The most important outcome of this objective was the decision to nationalize the Banque de France as well as the four largest banks: Crédit Lyonnais, Société Générale, Comptoire Nationale d'Éscompte, and the Banque Nationale pour le Commerce et l'Industrie. Legislation, introduced in 1945 and applied from the beginning of 1946, required changes in the control mechanisms of the entire financial system. As a the Ministry of Finance took effective control of the banking system, including the Banque de France. Financial institutions were classified into three broad categories: deposit banks ("banques des depots"), investment banks ("banques des affaires") and medium- and long-term credit banks.

Similar to US commercial banks, deposit banks were eligible to accept public deposits, as defined in the 1941 legislation, for periods up to two years. Their lending to a single borrower could not exceed 75% of bank capital, and their equity participation in an enterprise was limited to 10% of their capital. In fact, echoing the policies outlined for Crédit Lyonnais in the 19th century, their investments in equity were extremely limited. For the deposit banks in aggregate, such investments were less than 1%, whereas their discounts represented 65% and loans and advances 16% of their total assets in 1950. They were thus classic commercial banks, taking short-term deposits and making short-term discounts against self-liquidating bills.

The principal activity of investment banks, on the other hand, was defined as

> undertaking and carrying out equity investment in existing or new enter-
> prises, and granting credit of any length for public or private enterprises,
> which are benefitting, have benefitted or will benefit by such equity invest-
> ment. Only the banks' own funds or funds deposited with them for at least
> two years' duration or to be withdrawn only upon previous notice may be
> used for such investments. The best known of these banks are the Banque
> de Paris et des Pays-Bas and Union Parisienne. These investment banks
> resembled the original German Kreditbanks. Whereas most of the so-called
> Hautes Banques, such as Rothschild, Lazard Frères, Saint Phalle, and Worms,
> primarily manage the investment of the personal fortunes their owners
> and a select group of wealthy clients, they also fall under the definition of
> investment banks.
>
> (cf. Germain-Martin, 1954, pp. 244–51)

A special class of bank, the medium- and long-term credit banks, occupy an intermediate position between the commercial and investment banks. Although they can make loans of maturity up to two years, they cannot accept deposits of less than two years maturity and are subject to the same limits as deposit banks concerning their direct equity investment in enterprises.

The deposit banks were largely excluded from the financing of French post-war reconstruction. Instead the government acted through specialized non-bank financial institutions under its direct or indirect control. The major instruments used by these institutions were lending programs targeted to benefit specific sectors of the economy and granting loans at subsidized interest rates to the borrowers in the selected sectors. The result was the creation of a more or less independent circulation of funds ("le circuit") in which the Ministry of Finance played the role of a surrogate central bank, controlling a system in which funds flowed into post office deposit accounts and other official and semi-official government financial institutions and then were channeled to government institutions coordinating reconstruction lending. The deposit banks entered this independent financial circuit by means of the "plancher d'effets publics," which required them to invest 25% of their funds in government bonds. The requirement was raised to 30% in 1960 (Patat, 1993, p. 303ff).

Thus the French post-war financial system not only separated the deposit banks, which were given a monopoly over deposit taking and limited to short-term investments, but it also provided for the same segmentation of particular flows of credit to targeted users that was present in the US system. Government non-bank financial institutions dedicated to particular types of borrowers, such as Credit Foncier, Credit National, Caisse Central de Cooperation Economique, Caisse National de l'Energie, were created or operated to satisfy the specific requirements of reconstruction planning. This form of organization had the same detrimental effect on the expansion of both deposit banks and private investment banks. However, the negative impact on profitability caused less difficulty because four of the six major deposit takers (only Crédit Commercial de France, operating primarily in Paris and the major commercial centers, and Crédit Industriel et Commercial, a conglomerate of regional banks, remained private) were government owned.

An additional aspect of the reconstruction policy was to encourage bank merger and consolidation to produce large banking groups. The result was the creation of Banque National de Paris (through the merger of Comptoirs Nationaux d'Escompte de Paris and Banque National pour le Commerce et l'Industrie), the merger of Banque de la Union Parisienne with Crédit du Nord, and the creation of the Banque Indo-Suez. These are still the major investment banking groups operating in France.

Dismantling the post-war reconstruction system

Although the structure of the financial system had served the purposes of reconstruction, by the mid-1960s this had been completed, and the French government took steps to reintroduce competitive conditions into the financial sector and to reduce the role of government financial institutions in the financing of the economy (cf. De Boissieu, 1990). One of the first steps in this process was the introduction, in 1963, of sociétés d'investissement à capital variable (SICAVs). From 1966 to 1967 major changes were introduced into the financial system with the aim of increasing the flow of national savings to the banking system and thus diminish the role of the government in intermediating the flow of funds in the economy. Bank lending rates were freed from any controls (except usury limits) to allow the market mechanism to substitute the administered subsidized rates.

Table 1.3 Total bank credit (%)

	1969	1972	1979
Short-term credit	66	54	39
Medium-term credit (mobilizable★)	17	13	11
Medium and long-term	29	34	50

★ Paper with a guarantee from a government non-bank financial institution qualifying for automatic discounting with the Banque de France

Source: Elaboration of Patat (1993, p. 317).

The "cloisson," which had separated deposit banks and investment banks, was removed. To balance this increased freedom to compete in setting interest rates on lending, the government sought to increase the amount and the stability of the funds flowing to the banks by allowing virtually free branching without official authorization and introducing controls on deposit rates, including the prohibition of the payment of interest to eliminate competition for demand deposits.

This marked the initiation of the "bancarization" of the French economy as individuals were encouraged to open bank accounts. By 1980 the proportion of the eligible population holding a bank deposit had risen from 35% to 89%. The figure is currently around 100% (COB, 1995). In addition, attempts were made to shift depositor preferences toward savings and time deposits; special accounts bearing preferential rates or favorable tax treatment were also created to encourage saving for house purchase and investment in small businesses. All special treatment for accounts held in government non-bank financial inter-mediaries was eliminated (although it was not until 1983 that the right to offer some of these special accounts was extended to all private banks). As a result of this legislation, the number of branches tripled, sight deposits doubled, and savings deposits increased by five times between 1967 and 1973. There was thus a substantial shift in the flow of funds from government financial institutions to the banking system.

The other side of the decision to grant greater control to the market in determining the price and direction of finance in the economy was the strengthening of the role of capital market financing. The 1978 Monory Law introduced beneficial tax treatment for stock investments, followed in 1979 by the introduction of the Fonds commun de placement.

A New approach to government control of the financial system leads to a new bank law and full universal banking

In 1982 the Socialist government preserved the shift in emphasis toward more direct financing of industry through the financial sector but also sought to increase the government's ability to direct the broad flows of financing in the economy, in particular toward small and medium enterprises. As an alternative to control via government-owned, non-bank financial intermediation, the government decided to influence the flow of funds as the dominant shareholder in financial institutions operating in a market environment. This was achieved by taking 36 of the largest banks into public ownership and increasing government direct and indirect (through cross shareholdings) control of 124 banks in a total universe of less than 400 domestic French banks.

In 1983 the Delors Act created new, non-equity instruments that banks could issue to raise capital to fund lending to small and medium industries. The desire to change the way government influenced the banking system to ensure compatibility with government economic policy in the face of the 1983 decision to remain within the European Monetary System also led to a decision to revise the legislation governing the financial system. If the government were to act as owners of financial institutions operating within the framework of the market, it was necessary to ensure that government-owned banks did not operate at a disadvantage relative to other banks. Somewhat paradoxically, this led to a series of changes that increased the role of the market in the financial sector as well as a series of financial innovations that were more or less forced into existence by government fiat rather than by the operation of market competition seeking to overcome government constraints.

The decision to nationalize the banks was thus accompanied by a decision to rewrite the prevailing banking legislation to eliminate advantages that were enjoyed by certain "non-bank" banks such as mutual savings institutions and special credit institutions (such as Crédit Mutuel, Crédit Agricole, and the Banques Populaires) and merchant banks over commercial banks. Already in 1979 certain prudential regulations that applied to the banques inscrites were extended to banks accepting deposits with a maturity of more than two years.

The basic idea was that all financial institutions should be subject to the same regulations. It created a single regulatory structure applying to the entire financial system. It still reflects the traditions of the original 1941 legislation but makes clear the elimination of the segmentation with the private banking system, which had continued to characterize the French system even after the 1966–7 reforms.

In contrast to the 1941 legislation, the 1984 law gives the broadest possible definition of banking (cf. Banque de France, 1986, Annexe II, Titre 1er, Chapitre 1, Article Premier) as "Les établissements de crédit sont des personnes morales qui effectuent à titre de profession habituelle des opérations de banque."

> Les opérations de banque comprennent la réception de fonds du public, les opérations de crédit, ainsi que la mise à la disposition de la clientèle ou la gestions des moyens de paiement. (Article 2): Sont considérés comme fonds reçus du public les fonds qu'une personne recueille d'un tiers, notamment sous forme de dépôts . . . (Article 3) Constitue une opération de crédit pour l'application de la présente loi tout acte par lequel une personne agissant a' titre onéreux met ou promet de mettre des fonds à la disposition d'une autre personne . . . Sont assimilés à des opérations de credit le crédit-bail et, de manière générale, toute opération de location assorties d'une

option d'achat. (Article 4) Sont considérés comme moyens de paiement tous les instruments qui, quel que soit le support ou le procédé technique utlisé, permettent à toute personne de transférer des fonds. (Article 5) Les établissements de crédit peuvent aussi effectuer les opérations connexes à leur activité telles que: 1⌐ les opérations de change; 2⌐ les opérations sur or, métaux précieux et pièces; 3⌐ le placement, la souscription, l'achat, la gestion, la garde et la vente de valuers mobilièleres et de tout produit financier; 4⌐ le conseil et l'assistance en matière de gestion de patrimoine; 5⌐ le conseil et l'assistance en matière de gestion financière, l'ingénierie financière, et, d'une manière générale, tous les services destinés à faciliter la création et le développement des entreprises, sous réserve des dispositions léglislatives relatives à l'exercise illégal des certain professions; 6⌐ les opérations de location simple de bien mobiliers ou immobiliers pour les établissements habilités à effectuer des opérations de crédit-bail. (Article 6) Les établissements de crédit peuvent, en outre . . . prendre et détenir des participations dans les entreprises existantes ou en création.

> (Banque de France, 1986, Annexe II, Titre 1er,
> Chapitre 1, Article Premier)

The new legislation thus allows banks to operate in virtually any aspect of finance.

The government appears to have recognized that the decision to reinforce the operation of the market in organizing direct financing of industry would increase the volatility of interest rates and asset prices and that the introduction of universal banking would create the possibility of larger divergences between the maturity of bank liabilities and bank investments. Banks that had formerly operated under government direction with stabilized interest rates would now be subject to risks that had not existed previously. To offset these increased risks would require a more active short-term money market to make the distribution of liquidity more efficient and a capital market that could provide longer-term financing for both banks and firms. In addition, steps were taken to provide additional mechanisms to offset the increased price and interest rate risks that would result from reliance on market-determined prices and the new freedom of banks to enter a wider variety of business. To permit financial institutions to contain the impact of fluctuations in interest rates, the marché à terme d'instruments financiers (MATIF) was opened in 1986; to hedge against fluctuations in the market price of equity or of indices of stock market prices, the marché des options négotiables de Paris (MONEP) was opened in 1987. At the same time encouragement was given to the rapid development of an over-the-counter market in derivatives such as forwards, future rate agreements, and options.

Different from the US, where the financial innovations were largely the fruit of attempts by banks to offset the differential legislation that constrained them to operate in a single segment of the financial markets, in France these innovations were introduced by the government (cf. COB, 1995, p. 122) as part of the support of financial institutions considered as necessary to the successful operation of the banks in the absence of segmentation.

From the point of view of reducing the liquidity risks faced by banks operating in competitive money markets, the decision to extend the financial innovation to introduction of a market for commercial paper in 1985 was not entirely consistent. On the other hand, it was crucial to complete the shift in the allocation of credit to market-determined interest rates. By 1989 the commercial paper market had grown to 15% of banks' short-term lending to business. Whereas bank credit covered nearly 90% of French firms' external financing needs in 1980, this ratio had fallen to 34% in 1986 as a result of the success of commercial paper as a substitute for bank lending.

This process of disintermediation can also be seen in figures provided by the Conseil National du Crédit (in COB, 1995, p. 124ff), which show that the degree of financial intermediation as measured by non-bank borrowing from banks relative to total financing of the economy declined from 58% in 1984 to only 2% in 1993. On the other hand, if bank financing via the acquisition of equity and other forms of bank direct financing to firms is considered the ratios' rise to 66.9% and 22%. Although the direction of the change is the same, it suggests that changes in the way banks provide funding to firms explain part of the decline.

In an attempt to retain their corporate lending business, banks were forced to compete with commercial paper rates. In 1984, 97.3% of French bank lending to corporate credits was at variable rates linked to bank prime rates; by 1992 variable rate lending had fallen to 88.7%, and 44% was linked to money market rates, and only 37% was linked to prime. The trend toward fixed rate lending and linking of variable rates to long-term interest rates has continued, and today the majority of corporate borrowing is linked to long-term market interest rates.

At the same time as demand for bank-intermediated lending was being replaced by issue in the commercial paper market, the source of bank funds was also under pressure. For example, whereas more than 75% of banks' short-term funds in 1980 had been covered by the sale of sight deposits, which by law paid no interest, by 1991 this ratio had fallen to 50%. Total deposit coverage of bank credit fell from 68.2% in 1984 to 59.5% in 1993. The share of sight deposits in total client deposits has remained in the range of 35–40% between 1984 and 1993. In 1985 CDs ("titres de créances négociables") were introduced, but it was not until 1987, when their sales tripled in the course of the year, that they became an important source of bank funding. In that year CDs represented only a fifth of the funds raised by deposit liabilities; by 1993 they were more than double bank demand deposit liabilities. Banks also sought reserves through borrowing in interbank markets. The substitution of market-priced funds for zero-cost demand deposits caused an increase in the costs of funds, moving the pricing of short credits closer to market rates. This process has tended to increase the already high proportion of interbank business carried out, especially by the larger French banks.

A reflection of this change in the structure of financing may be seen in the increasing proportion of firms' long-term financing by means of retained earnings. The self-financing ratio (derived from data presented in COB, 1995,

p. 119) for non-government enterprises rose from 68% in 1984 to 103.1% in 1988 and 105.7% in 1993. Thus, the possibilities for both short- and long-term commercial bank lending to firms that were opened up by the freedom given by the new banking law proved difficult to realize. However, after an initial decline, the share of bank credit ("crédit de trésorerie") in firms' external financing recovered to 50% by 1990, largely as a result of the increased use by firms of financial innovations provided by banks.

The loss of short-term lending to the best corporate clients is the same experience that caused concern for the future viability of US commercial banks and drove them into more risky types of lending and to lend to lower quality credits, such as consumer lending. Thus, the 1966–1967 legislation eliminated the competition of government non-bank financial institutions, and the 1984 bank law eliminated competition from private non-banks by subjecting them to the same regulatory regime; the decision to introduce a greater degree of market determination of interest rates led to increased competition from non-bank forms of direct financing through the market. Indeed, the government appears to have encouraged it.

However, the diverse response of the French banks from those in the US was due to the fact that not only had the regulatory structure been made more uniform, but they were also allowed to operate directly in the newly introduced sectors of the financial services industry. Although the banks were losing their major source of cheap funding and their best clients, they were able to move directly into those areas from which competition was emerging.

Part of the loss in deposits represented a shift in funds into "organismes de placement collectif en valeurs mobilières" (OPCVM), which comprise "sociétés d'investissement à capitale variable" (SICAV) and "fonds communs de placement" (FCP), offering market interest rates. This not only involved household accounts; in 1986, business firms were estimated to own 38% of the funds invested in SICAVs. Thus, just as in the US, French banks were faced by competition for deposits from the equivalent of what in the US were called "money market" mutual funds.

The balance sheets of the OPCVM show their investments as around 60% in short-term assets and 25% in equities. Their short-term investments account for about 85% of the total issue of commercial paper ("billets de trésorerie") and 55% of CDs. Because the new bank law allowed any financial institution to operate an OPCVM, banks were able to recapture some of the their deposit drain by offering their own mutual funds. This produced management fees, custodial charges, and brokerage commissions from the operation of the funds as well as underwriting fees for the issue and sale of the commercial paper by the companies. This allowed them to offset some of the income lost from the narrowing of net interest margins due to competition on lending rates and the rising proportion of funds raised at market rates: their global intermediation margins fell from 2.59% to 1.4% between 1984 and 1993 and net interest margins from 3.0% to 2.2%. Banks had been given complete freedom to set fees and commission charges in 1986.

In this way the commercial lending that had been lost to direct financing by the issue of commercial paper was intermediated through banks' OPCVM, which purchased firms' commercial paper and other liabilities. The banks thus continued to provide lending to firms, only now intermediated by their separately constituted OPCVM, and they continued to earn income, only fees and commissions replaced net interest margins. In terms of the stability of earnings, this shift probably reduced the risks faced by banks, rather than increasing them, for they were no longer carrying the interest rate risk of commercial lending. It also reduced the amount of capital and reserves that the banks had to hold. Thus the kind of money market mutual fund banking that has been prospected for the US has already become common in France and has allowed French banks to preserve their role in financial intermediation and to defend their earnings.

However, the fall in net interest margins due to the increased competition, and the fact that the fee income from the operations of mutual funds was much lower than their prior earnings from intermediated lending, led banks to seek to supplement earnings by offering their clients other types of services, including financial derivatives. However, supplying these services usually also implies investing in these instruments, if only to provide the counterpart to the products offered to clients. This quickly led to the banks' own investments in such instruments. From an imperceptible amount in 1987, banks derivative activities now amount to around three times the size of their balance sheets, reaching a nominal amount of 30,000 billion francs in 1993.

The result was that the banks continued to intermediate lending to firms, and their income has in fact increased. Fee and commission income of French banks is now in the range of 25–40% of their total earnings, which is around international averages. At the same time, the government succeeded in eliminating subsidized interest rates and shifting the allocation of credit to market-determined interest rates. The public now receives market rates on funds held in OPCVM compared to the zero legal rates for sight deposits, and around 75% of bank lending is directly linked to money market rates.

For the three largest banks (Banque National de Paris, Crédit Lyonnais, and Société Générale), commission and trading income represented 48.1% of net output in 1993 compared with 26.9% in 1990.

Table 1.4 Principal contributors to net product of the French banking system in (%)

	1984	1986	1988	1990	1993
Interbank and treasury	−2.3	−9.1	−9.1	−17.7	13.5
Client operations	113.3	90.6	98.2	128.1	110.7
Investment portfolio	−12.4	−4.0	−12.7	−41.6	−48.9
Other operations★	16.2	20.3	22.2	26.3	49.8

★ Includes derivative operations and other non-traditional commercial banking activities

Source: Commission Bancaire (1995, p. 132)

Changes in prudential regulation for the new bank law

In addition to the changes in the financial market that accompanied the new bank act, the government also moved to adjust the regulatory framework, centralizing regulations and introducing a structure more appropriate to the new undifferentiated banking system (cf. COB, and Colmant). This process accompanied the changes in European banking accompanied by the preparation of the Single Market Act and also incorporated those changes. The primary regulator is now the Commission Bancaire, an entity independent of, but operating through, the Banque de France. This is a situation that is similar to that found in Germany between the Bundesbank and the Federal Regulatory agency.

French banks are subject to a number of prudential ratios that constrain the composition of the assets and liabilities on their balance sheets. These include a level of minimum capital and the requirement that their assets exceed liabilities by an amount that is greater or equal to this amount. There is also a risk-asset ratio that sets bank capital to weighted risk items at a minimum of 5%. It covers both on and off balance sheet exposures. The risk distribution ratio limits the exposure to a single credit to 40% of the weighted risk items, again including both on and off balance sheet lending.

A liquidity ratio has been in force for banques inscrites since the 1948 reforms. It requires matching of short-term assets to liquidity-weighted, short-term liabilities. Originally the definition of short term was set at three months, but in response to the new banking law, this was reduced in 1988 to one month. Deposits enter short-term liabilities with a weighting of one-fifth of their total value. This represents the fact that although deposits may be withdrawn instantly, in practice they tend to be highly stable forms of bank funds. The definition of assets is also large, including securities held in repo transactions and the net position of the bank in the interbank market. The ratio now applies to all banks, as defined by the 1984 act, on a consolidated basis. It is currently under review.

A number of additional regulations were introduced as a result of the introduction of universal banking. The first is the ratio of permanent resources, which requires that 60% of French franc domestic long-term assets be funded with long-term liabilities. Long term is defined as positions with a residual maturity of more than five years. French banks are also required to keep a balanced position in their foreign exchange exposures. Total exposure cannot exceed 40% of own capital, with 15% limits on positions in individual currencies. Positions in the European Currency Unit (ECU) or in the European Exchange Rate Mechanism (ERM) currencies carry a 30% weighting.

The balance sheet constraints thus retain the prudential ratios commonly found in segmented systems and add short and long-term maturity matching similar to those of the German system of universal bank regulation. Thus, in an attempt to reduce the potential risks facing banks in the new, market-determined lending environment, the French system limits the degree of mismatching permitted of its unrestricted commercial banks and also provides for the financial innovations that ease the hedging of the risks that they are allowed through the creation of more active and efficient money and capital markets and through options and derivatives markets.

Finally, bank consolidation continued to be actively encouraged. In part this was to provide larger bank capitalization and to increase bank efficiency but also to form banking units better able to compete in European and international markets. At the end of 1994 the five largest banks accounted for more than two-thirds of total deposits and more than 45% of total lending. For the ten largest, the figures are more than 80% and more than 60%, respectively. French banks generated around a quarter of their business from overseas subsidiaries in 1994, up from around 16% in 1984.

All of these transformations, which were initiated to provide an alternative mechanism for government control of the financial system, in fact came to full fruition only after the policy of nationalization of the banks had been reversed. In 1987 the government embarked on a policy of re-privatization of the banking system to allow the banks to increase their private capital to be able to better compete in international markets. From 1987 on the French central bank initiated the practice of using the interbank market to effect its interest rate policy and to influence bank liquidity. The increase in market efficiency and the transformation of financial markets were thus finally used to influence the economy in a rather different way from that which had been envisaged with the change in policy in 1982.

The mixed success of the transformation from segmented to universal banking

There has been dissatisfaction expressed concerning the ability of this type of policy to increase the overall efficiency of the financial system. This would be the case if competition among banks were not that traditionally envisaged as a contestable market. For example, if the supply of funds represented by deposits and the demand as represented by loans are subject to large, non-recoverable fixed costs, for example, in building depositor confidence and building up proprietary information about the conditions of potential borrowers, then banking markets may not be perfectly competitive. In such conditions, pricing at marginal costs could drive down the returns for all banks, but this might not eliminate the least efficient banks because they may retain both clients and depositors. The lack of the transfer of this business to the most efficient banks may thus penalize their actions to increase efficiency by reducing the returns to innovative operating procedures. In this case, increased competition may make the system less efficient.

In summary, the French experience provides an example of the transformation of a segmented banking system in which commercial banks were declining in importance relative to non-commercial bank competitors and direct intermediation. However, the basic factor motivating the introduction of market separation and its subsequent removal was the role that the state was to play in directing economic activity: reconstruction in the 1950s and 1960s and the developing of

French small and medium industry in the 1980s. The reforms in the 1960s were an attempt to move away from subsidized interest rates and directed financing, to increase the efficiency of the financial sector, and to give the banking system a larger role in the financing of industry.[30] The cloisson separating commercial banks was thus lowered to allow banks to replace the role of the government. But, it was also to introduce market pricing of financial flows. It was at this point that lending rates were freed from controls, but deposit rates were set at zero to protect the banks from the increased interest rate risk that they would be facing. However, the liberalization of lending rates also included the introduction of commercial paper, a move that led to reductions in the demand for commercial banks' traditional form of financing. The persistence of subsidized saving deposit rates (in the form of beneficial tax treatment for livret blue, livret A, and CODEVI passbook accounts) for certain types of mutual and cooperative banks then created competition for deposits despite the prohibition of payment of interest on sight deposits. This competition from nonregulated deposit takers thus led to the final elimination of the cloisson by means of the introduction of similar regulations for all types of banks engaged in similar activities. This change of regulation was important for commercial banks, not because it eliminated the competition for deposit funds but because it allowed the banks to engage directly in the new forms of intermediation of commercial lending via the creation of bank money market and investment mutual funds.

Along with the new legislation, new markets and institutions were introduced to allow the banks to deal with the increased risks faced in dealing in a market-based system. However, the banks not only used these possibilities to manage their market risks, but they also used them to augment their declining earnings. The introduction of market pricing had sharply reduced net interest margins, and the banks sought to counter this by seeking to increase earnings by entering into more risky types of investments for their own account. These included real estate investments but also investments in derivative and other instruments that were primarily designed to provide risk hedging for the banks and to generate fee income when offered to clients. Bank profits, which have been falling since 1990, turned negative from 1992.

Thus, on balance, French banks have managed to retain their relative position in intermediating the financing of industry, but this activity is now less remunerative. This has led to attempts to supplement earnings with other activities. Thus, even when banks have managed to retain their position in the intermediation of the funding to business, this has not precluded a shift toward activities that increase in the amount of risk undertaken by the banks.

The lesson that emerges from this experience is that the idea of a commercial bank requires controls and restrictions on the operations of financial institutions that are incompatible with the free market determination of interest rates and the free market determination of the degree of intermediation of financial flows. If the regulations are maintained, while interest rates are allowed to reflect market conditions, segmented commercial banks will experience difficulties. The French government apparently believed that these difficulties would be primarily involved with the increased risks associated with borrowing short-term sight deposits and lending to commercial enterprises at longer terms. It thus moved to constrain these risks and to introduce new institutions to deal with them. However, the real threat that faced the banks was when the introduction of alternative sources of financing for business commercial paper and money market mutual funds, which ensured that market competition could set rates, also reduced the amount of financing that banks could attract at the same time as it reduced the net interest margins on that lending. The freedom to respond to this reduction in earnings, which was given by the new bank law, allowed banks to continue to intermediate by acting to underwrite commercial paper and to operate mutual funds. But, this reduced the risk that the banks carried in providing firm financing and thus the returns that could be earned. In this event the concerns over the increased risks that the banks would face in providing commercial lending in a free market environment were misplaced. However, the new institutions that had been introduced to allow the banks to hedge risk were used to provide more risky forms of investment that would allow them to offset the fall in earnings. Removing the regulations and allowing full-scale universal banking, although it allows commercial banks to offset the loss of their function of intermediating the flows of funds to commercial borrowers, does not prevent the reduction in the profitability of these activities due to the reduction in the regulation of activities.

The attempt to offset the decline in earnings invariably leads to higher-risk investments. This is what has led to the emphasis on risk management, rather than maturity transformation, in most US banks. The French banks appear to have been relatively slow to adopt this change as the returns on their investment portfolios have demonstrated. Whereas US banks have made large investments in new technology related to monitoring the risk-return characteristics of their overall balance sheet activities, in France, the banks have invested primarily in technology to reduce transactions costs to maintain profitability of what is traditionally the most costly of banking activities.

The future of "commercial banks" and the future of banking in the 1990s

In Section 2, two basic types of bank were identified with two aspects of banking, *Income* and *Issue*. These were the "capital" bank and the "giro" bank. The capital bank was primarily involved with generating income from the investment of funds placed at risk for the benefit of its direct owners, the shareholders. The giro bank, on the other hand, was designed as a means to facilitate commercial transactions, that is, to act as a clearinghouse to match debit and credit entries. It was usually a public bank that required no capital and placed no capital at risk.

The historical development of these two types of banking outlined in Section 3 reveals the tendency under pressure to provide convenience for both types of banks to broaden its activities to engage in both investment and provision of transaction services. Investments in capital banks soon came to be used as means of payment, and eventually these banks raised funds for investment by issuing notes and then selling deposits. The giro banks did not usually issue signs or symbols of their deposits and were precluded from investing the funds held on behalf of clients for transfer. But most eventually did issue some type of receipt that functioned as a means of payment and the temptation to use the funds for other, more remunerative purposes usually proved to be too great to resist. The result was that banks developed that combined the two functions in various ways. This produced a decline in *Security*, instability, and default, leading to the imposition of regulations that attempted to restore *Security* by restoring banks to their pure forms of capital or giro. History is replete with prudential regulations designed to require banks to behave as if they were giro banks or capital banks or to strictly limit the extent to which the two activities can be combined.

The best-known regulatory responses are the segmented banking system, introduced in the National Bank Act and New Deal legislation in the US, the application of the Italian Bank Law of 1936, France in the post-war period, and the German prudential legislation regulating the balance sheets of universal banks. The former legislates the separation of deposit-taking banks from investment banks and places restrictions on their activities to make them conform as nearly as possible as giro banks. In Germany, and in France after its bank reform of 1966–7 and 1984–6, banks are free from any legislation restricting their activities, but prudential regulations require separate treatment of their activities linked to the provision of payment services and that relating to investment activities. Maturity matching is required for both short-term and long-term assets and liabilities.

The concept of a "commercial" bank emerged from the development of prudential regulation that produced the legal separation of commercial and investment banks in the US. It stems from the real bills doctrine that limits banks that offer transaction services to the provision of finance for the production and sale of real goods. Thus, the canonical "commercial" bank takes in sight deposits, makes secured loans of less than 90 days to finance work in progress or goods in warehouse waiting to be sold, and holds government securities in its portfolio.

As the description of activities of commercial banks suggests, they can prosper only because of legislation that protects from competition the income earned from their restricted activities. These have included restrictions on interest rates, the provision of deposit insurance, and so forth, which have impeded the operation of the market mechanism in determining the prices of financial assets. As soon as these restrictions are eliminated, usually in an attempt to increase the efficiency of the pricing mechanism in financial markets, earnings fall as net interest margins are reduced and the volume of intermediation falls.

Although commercial banks have been in difficulty repeatedly throughout their history, it was the attempt to give a greater role to the market in determination of prices in financial markets associated with the introduction of monetarist policies in the United States that produced the current crisis of survival. The attempt to counter their declining earnings by moving into higher-risk activities simply aggravated the crisis as the banks were insufficiently capitalized and insufficiently prepared for the new activities. Much the same experience was observed in France, and it is likely to be repeated as Italian banks are granted increased freedom as a result of the new banking legislation.

There was, however, a major difference in France, where the government moved quickly to change the basic bank law to provide for the introduction of universal banking at the same time as it introduced changes in regulations to increase market competition. This did not, however, prevent the former commercial banks in France from experiencing the same types of difficulties as their US counterparts. Indeed, in some cases the difficulties facing the French banks were worse precisely because of the additional freedom they enjoyed to enter new areas of activity. This freedom did, however, allow them to retain their position at the center of the process of providing funds to industry because they were able to form and operate money market mutual funds that attracted the funds of their former short-term deposits to purchase the commercial paper issued by their former corporate borrowers. Thus, they were able to generate fee and commission income to replace the lost net interest margins on intermediation.

The response of the French banking system to this change in organization provides an indication of why the experience has not been more beneficial for the commercial banks. The French government had anticipated that the reduction of controls over financial markets would increase the volatility of interest rates and asset prices. This increased volatility, along with increased involvement in the financing of business by the commercial banks, would increase the risk faced by the banks. A number of steps were thus taken to dampen the volatility and expected risk. Among them was the introduction in 1967 of the zero limit on interest rates payable on short-term deposits to reduce competition for deposits and thus reduce the volatility of deposit funds. The new bank law was designed to prevent unwarranted competition due to special regulatory benefits. Derivatives markets were introduced to provide the banks with additional means of hedging their investments, which were expected to become increasingly volatile. Finally, additional prudential regulations were introduced, requiring rough maturity matching across the short- and long-term sections of bank balance sheets. All of these changes indicate that the government believed that the major risk run by banks would be the increased price and liquidity risks on maturity transformation in the face of more volatile market prices and interest rates.

However, the liberalization of the financial markets to allow greater market determination of prices also meant that the maturity transformation between short-term investments and term lending was not taken over by the commercial banks but was increasingly intermediated through other mechanisms such as money market mutual funds that were able to offer borrowers lower rates and depositors higher rates than the banks. Both the business, and the risk of maturity mismatches that the government had sought to contain, disappeared from bank balance sheets. The expected increase in bank intermediation was instead undertaken by simple middlemen or market makers. To remain in this business, the banks had to organize mutual investment funds themselves, accepting the lower earnings. Thus, the new freedom to operate in a larger range of financial activities given by the bank legislation did not completely resolve their difficulties.

The problem was not the failure to foresee the financial innovation, represented by money market mutual funds, represented potential competition to banks' lending to business. Rather, it was the failure to recognize that commercial bank lending to business was not undertaken primarily to produce maturity transformation and that their income did not result from accepting the risk of maturity mismatches on their balance sheets. Banks operate and profit instead from their ability to eliminate risks. The problem was not the competition from direct intermediation between borrower and lender through the market, which created difficulty for the banks. Instead, the difficulty was represented by the competition from the new financial markets trading, and pricing, financial risks.

What do banks do in the 1990s?

The properly run giro bank did not face risk, and the properly run investment bank ran risks that were recognized and voluntarily borne by its owners given the anticipated returns; neither required risk hedging. On the other hand, the basic problem facing "commercial" banks that tried to combine these two activities was the problem of analyzing risk. This combined form of bank may be viewed as dealing in forward commitments that cannot be fully arbitraged so that there is a risk of non-completion of commitments. Because a successful commercial bank will require a continuous record of meeting its commitments to its creditors, owners, and debtors, non-fraudulent banks will have to take action to hedge the risks caused by the issue of liabilities, which serve as means of payment to provide financing for their investment activities, irrespective of the particular types of assets or liabilities in which they deal. The main objective of such banks is neither income from investment nor from the issue of notes but rather from the management of risk. Thus, a useful way of generalizing the activities of such banks is to assume that these banks will attempt to fully hedge their risk exposures.[31]

The role of banks in the modern financial system

As noted, banks are often presented as providing maturity transformation, borrowing with sight liabilities that satisfy the liquidity needs of household depositors to finance assets composed of fixed-term loans required by business borrowers. This was the basic framework of analysis that motivated the changes in the French system. This activity of maturity transformation is then said to lead to two related types of risk. Funding acquisition of even very short, fixed-term assets with sight liabilities creates "liquidity" risk due to the possibility that the assets cannot be liquidated in time to permit the repayment of liabilities. In addition, there will be "price" risk created by the possibility that assets cannot be liquidated in a timely fashion at a price that permits repayment of liabilities.

Funding assets with liabilities also creates "maturity" or "interest rate" risk determined by the possibility that the cost of liabilities used to fund the assets will change more rapidly than the return on assets, if the liabilities are of shorter term than the assets. If rates are rising, this leads to loss of income and reductions in the capital value of assets, which may also produce price and/or liquidity risk if the value of assets falls below the value of liabilities.

However, with the introduction of adjustable-rate borrowing and lending, maturity mismatching need no longer imply interest rate risk because the interest rate may be reset at fixed intervals during the life of the instrument. If assets and liabilities are "repriced" at each reset interval, a maturity mismatch may be eliminated by fixing appropriate reset intervals. In this case maturity mismatching continues to create liquidity risk, but interest rate or price risk is determined by the matching of the reset intervals, which becomes "repricing" risk. In these cases liquidity and price risks are separated.

Imposed hedging of intermediation risk by regulation

From the point of view of banks as risk hedgers, banks do not carry these risks voluntarily, and they do not earn their profits for bearing this risk themselves. Part of the business of banking is to offset or hedge this risk at a cost that is less than it can charge for intermediation between borrowers and lenders. The other major part of the banking business is to hedge the risk associated with the issue of private liabilities at a cost that is below the bank's net interest margins. This is the risk created by leveraging the liability side of the balance sheet.

Although hedging should be the "natural" result of the action of prudent bankers, in the face of the rash of bank failures and fraudulent behavior in the US in the 1920s and 1930s, the government introduced additional encouragement in the form of minimum required levels of hedging. Thus, in the segmented US system, partial hedging of liquidity risk was imposed through minimum reserve requirements that limited the expansion of bank liabilities, whereas the hedging of market risk was implicit in the restrictions concerning the range of assets in which an institution could operate. Hedging of price and interest rate risk was reinforced by setting maximum limits on the interest rates payable on sight and other short-term liabilities and deposit insurance.

Regulation to provide the same type of minimum hedging is also present in universal bank systems that employ minimum required reserves and have deposit insurance schemes. Balance sheet constraints requiring maturity matching substitute for the restriction on assets suitable for investment in the segmented system. Thus, from the point of view of hedging, the two systems are similar, although the regulations used to impose minimum hedging differ.

Prudential regulations as imposed hedging

This may be better understood by considering the way in which the regulations require banks to hedge their liquidity and/or interest rate risks in both the segmented and the universal bank systems. For example, a 100% reserve requirement against deposits may be interpreted as requiring a bank that has issued a sight deposit to hedge what may be defined as a short forward cash reserve position by holding cash equal to the value of the deposit. Alternatively, a deposit sold by a bank to a customer includes the right to exchange the deposit for cash (central bank reserves) at par on demand at an unspecified future date. The bank may be viewed as having written a put option on the deposit to its customer because the customer has the right to sell the deposit back to the bank for cash at a strike price equal to the value of the original deposit. For the bank this short put option position is formally equivalent to being short reserves. To fully hedge its written put, the bank thus has to take a long position of 100% reserves.

But, a bank that hedges its position at 100% is over hedging because it is covering itself against the simultaneous withdrawal of every deposit, an unlikely occurrence in normal conditions. What it should do is hedge against the most probable level of net withdrawals. This may be done by means of a "delta" hedge. To simplify, the most relevant variable in determining the size of the required long position to hedge the bank's written option is the probability of exercise of the put option, that is, the probability that there will be a reserve drain as the value of customers' cheques paid to other banks and withdrawals of funds exceed collections and deposits. If this probability of withdrawal (equivalent to the probability of exercise of the option) is 10%, then the bank should hold reserves of 10% to hedge its short position. Thus, a system such as the English, in which banks are encouraged to hold particular target proportions of cash and liquid assets, may be interpreted as one in which the monetary authority imposes partial hedging of deposit liabilities on banks.

This analysis has to be modified in the presence of legal fixed minimum reserve requirements, for if they are legally fixed at some minimum, the reserves are not available to meet expected cash drains and thus do not act as a physical hedge. In this case, the legal reserve requirement is rather intended to limit the net creation of bank liabilities to that proportion at which it expects its net drain to be zero over time so that there is no need for physical hedges to meet net reserve drains. In this case the hedge is determined by the official bank regulator when it sets the minimum reserve requirement; because the reserve requirement is fixed, and usually adjusted to achieve monetary policy goals rather than with respect to the liquidity risk faced by individual banks, it is unlikely that the reserve requirement should meet the bank's desired hedge position, leading to the necessity of holding excess reserves or seeking methods to reduce what the bank considers as unnecessary reserves for its desired level of risk reduction.

Under a deposit insurance scheme, an insurance fund effectively guarantees any residual risk to the bank from having written the option, insuring that the forward reserve position is perfectly hedged. Alternatively, the insurance may be viewed as covering the counterparty risk borne by the buyer (the depositor) of the put that the bank cannot meet its option commitment. Thus the bank depositor receives the equivalent of a put option at zero cost through the minimum required reserves and insurance on the deposit. The cost of the option that the bank gives its client (normally it would receive a premium for writing this option) is thus given by the insurance premium paid by the bank plus the foregone interest costs on the minimum required reserves (or on the difference between lending rates and the rates paid on reserves if the central bank remunerates reserve deposits). As long as the lending rate exceeds this figure plus the costs of servicing the account, the bank provides fully hedged maturity transformation without risk and earns positive returns.

It is thus possible to consider prudential regulations imposed on banks as a minimum degree of hedging when there is doubt that banks will naturally undertake sufficient hedging to insure stability of the financial system. Aside from well-known historical exceptions, banks seem to undertake such hedging; indeed in systems without formal regulations, banks operate with self-imposed cash and security reserves, and many have developed private insurance schemes and self-regulatory bodies to impose prudent behavior.

The other point of importance to note is that the formal regulations require hedging to be undertaken in a particular way, usually by the purchase and holding of the opposite position to that being hedged. In the case of reserve requirements, this is the purchase of central bank reserves. However, there are other ways for banks to hedge this risk than changing their holdings of cash or deposits.

The introduction of "market-based" hedging

The hedging of risk can be achieved in two ways. Either by means of holding offsetting positions in the same assets or liabilities, that is, "physical" hedging, or by means of purchasing market-traded instruments that provide compensation of future price movements of assets. The role and influence of the market in the operation of the financial system may be analyzed in terms of the way it provides choice and flexibility for the way banks hedge risk positions.

For example, rather than calling in loans to increase their holdings of reserves, banks can purchase reserves in the overnight federal funds wire markets, or they can use exchange-traded derivative products to change the repricing intervals of term assets. The notional written put, which is sold with a deposit, can be hedged by buying a put or by going long futures or forwards instead of through holding reserves. Looking at hedging as taking place either through positions in reserves, or in terms of market-traded derivatives on reserves, thus allows a different perspective on the way in which the "market" has entered into the operations of financial institutions by providing alternative methods of hedging bank risk.

The first step in this process of increasing the role of the market in the operation of risk hedging was the introduction of "liability management," which involved the use of purchased reserves in the federal funds markets, and was then extended to "bought funds" of all kinds. In this system meeting required reserve requirements was arranged through the day-to-day repurchase operations of the banks in buying and selling reserves in the short-term money market, a series of tomorrow–next contracts. In this system it is no longer necessary to actually "own" reserves to hedge risk because reserves can be borrowed or bought according to need in the market.

The next step was to substitute the hedging of risk by means of taking long positions in the physicals market with hedging provided through the purchase and sale of derivative products, now available primarily through trading in the market. For example, banks could lend term funds at fixed rates, which could be swapped into floating rate lending with reset periods to match that on purchased funds, thus reducing repricing risk. Or fixed rate term lending could be converted into floating interest rate exposure to match a shorter reset interval on deposits through the purchase of a strip of interest rate futures contracts for a series of future maturity dates. When rates rise the futures show a profit, which offsets the rise in the cost of refunding and vice versa.[32]

Credit risk

Liquidity risk and interest rate risk are not the only types of risk faced by a bank when it intermediates funds. A bank will also face credit risk, which is determined by the borrower's ability to repay borrowed funds and interest. A major function of the bank is the proper evaluation of this risk as well as measures to hedge that risk adequately. The approach to bank lending based on "real bills" provides for physical assets as hedge cover or security against credit risk. When risk increases, the decision to place loans on a cash or non-accrual basis and to reserve against them out of current earnings also represents an increase in the physical hedge put in place by the bank to cover its risk. Diversification of the loan portfolio is another method of reducing credit risk. Again, regulations impose a minimum for hedging by banks by limiting the amount that may be lent to a single borrower to a given proportion (traditionally 10% but recently the proportion has been raised in a number of countries) of bank capital.

Credit risk can also be represented in terms of the bank writing a put option to the borrower, which allows him to sell the underlying "security" pledged for the loan at a price equal to the amount borrowed plus any outstanding interest on the loan. A default by the borrower is then simply the exercise of the put option to sell the goods in process or in warehouse to the bank at a price equal to the loan plus outstanding interest.

The bank's possession of collateral as security represents the hedge against this credit risk. The excess value of the security relative to the loan (or the compensating balance held on deposit with the bank), which the bank requires, then has to cover the costs of liquidating the security. The higher the evaluation of credit risk, the greater the required collateral, and the greater the value of the option that the bank writes to the borrower. It is the higher value of the option written to the more risky borrower that is reflected in the decision to charge higher interest rates to less creditworthy borrowers and to require a greater collateral cushion. But, the higher interest rate paid by the borrower in no way provides an offset to the necessity for the bank to hedge the short option, nor does it reduce the cost of hedging. When a bank denies accommodation to a borrower, even if the borrower is willing to pay higher rates associated with the higher option price, it is because the bank cannot hedge the option that it is writing to the borrower at a cost that allows it to cover the costs of funding the loan. It has recently become common to explain this reluctance of banks to use interest rates to ration lending and the use of quantity constraints rather than prices to ration borrowers by the existence of asymmetric information. The approach adopted here is that banks have sufficient information to evaluate risk but simply that the risk cannot be hedged at a profit.

The hedging of credit risk is another area in which markets have come to play an increasing role in bank operations. The increasing use of "asset management" in the form of securitization of bank assets to buy and sell them in capital markets may be viewed as an alternative method of hedging both liquidity and credit risk. This type of hedging also comes into direct conflict with the regulation of hedging produced by segmentation of banking, which limits the type of lending and thus the means of hedging credit risks to the holding of physical assets as collateral or to compensating balances.[33]

Once the operation of a bank is viewed as the joint production of providing funds to finance production and the management of risk, there is no reason to limit the services that banks sell to their customers to the former to the exclusion of the latter. Thus, the shift to an increased role of the market in providing hedging of risk has been accompanied by an increase in the provision of risk intermediation to bank clients. Just as the sale to third parties of their internal mechanisms for transferring funds from one area to another allowed merchants to become merchant bankers, banks now integrate third-party needs for risk intermediation with their own risk management requirements.

Systemic risk

Looking at the role of banks as hedging risk highlights the fact that the evaluations of risk that are required are also changing. In a market-based system bankers are called upon to evaluate not only the risk of the asset but also the risk-reducing characteristic of the hedge instrument. It is a much different operation to estimate the value of a house and then write it down by 50% to reach a collateral value than to estimate the performance of a currency or interest rate swap. In addition, whereas the lending activities of banks under physical hedging tend to be independent events – for example, the failed entrepreneur's house that is taken up for sale by the bank is not likely to be located in a neighborhood in which all entrepreneurs have failed – market-traded hedging instruments are all traded in arbitrage interrelated markets, and thus the ability of various instruments to hedge risk moves together. This suggests that there might be an increase in systemic risk bought about by market-based hedging.

The role of competitive markets in financial systems would then be represented by the type and use of alternative, market-based methods of hedging liquidity, interest rate, and credit risk. For example, instead of matching maturities by selling long-term liabilities to fund the purchase and holding of long-term assets, a system more reliant on the market might be composed of banks that exhibit extensive maturity mismatching of the actual assets held on the balance sheet relative to liabilities but with liquidity, interest rate, and credit risk hedged via the use of market sources of reserves or through the use of market-traded derivative products such as interest rate futures, interest rate swaps, and so forth.

Risk management characteristics of different bank forms

It would thus be possible to characterize the two basic forms of bank in the modern system in terms of their risk management characteristics and techniques. The giro bank, of course, no longer exists but has been replaced by the closest regulatory equivalent, the commercial bank. The income bank still exists in the form of the investment bank.

A "commercial" bank may be defined as having sight liabilities in the form of demand deposits and assets composed of liquid transactions reserves and short-term lending to firms secured by commercial inventory or work-in-process (real bills) payable in 90 days or less. Part of the bank's liquid reserves on any given day are the result of the repayment of loans providing funds that may be relent or repaid to depositors. The shorter the average maturity of the loans, the greater this source of liquidity and the lower the transactions reserves necessary to cover liquidity risk. In the limit, a bank that makes only overnight loans needs no reserves because it has no liquidity or interest rate risk, only credit risk linked to the work in process or the inventory in fact being sold in the goods market at expected prices and in the expected quantities. This would also be the case of a British clearing bank that only invested in one-day to maturity bills from discount houses.

The return on equity invested in such a commercial bank is determined by the difference between the cost of deposits and the earnings on assets or the net interest margin and the ratio of liabilities to equity: the bank's leverage. Again, the limiting case is represented by a zero maximum interest rate paid on deposits with no non-earning liquid reserves aside from overnight loans and minimum capital (maximum leverage) permitted. For lending of longer term than overnight, the net interest margin will be reduced by the cost of hedging liquidity and price risk. This may take the form of the cost of the insurance premia and a reduction in the average return on assets. If the return on assets and equity are to be maintained, interest rates will have to rise or leverage be increased.

For purposes of completeness, note that the bank's liquidity risk could also be reduced by increasing the size of the bank, for if it were the only bank in existence, there could then be no deposit drain. The only liquidity risk would be the possible currency drain arising from a change in public preferences between cash and deposits. Thus, bank size is also a means of hedging liquidity risk by reducing the probability of deposit withdrawal.

The modern equivalent of the "income" bank is the "merchant" or "investment" bank, which employs only its owners' equity capital to invest in real commodities or in the long-term securities of non-bank firms. Because there are no "creditors" other than the owners to be repaid, there is no need for liquid reserves. Return on equity will depend on the income from the assets during the holding period and the ability to resell the bank's investments at expected prices and quantities in excess of cost in the commodity market or the secondary securities market.

Thus, the commercial bank described here is fully hedged for liquidity and interest rate or repricing risk because its assets and liabilities have the same maturity and are repriced at the same interval. Although the investment bank described has no liquidity risk, it is subject to interest rate risk because of the influence on resale price of fixed income assets, not liquidity. For both types of bank, the most important risk is credit risk, and this is presumably more important in the case of the investment bank.

This risk is hedged in the commercial bank by taking collateral and in the investment bank by taking equity interest or writing covenants into long-term, fixed interest contracts. Although neither depends on the use of the market to provide its hedging, each does depend on the operation of external markets for goods and securities as well as the confirmation of expectations of prices and quantities that can be sold in those markets. This would be just as true in a unified system that used physical hedging of risk.

Other configurations will be ranged between these two extremes. Term lending will create liquidity and interest rate risk for the commercial bank, just as deposit taking will create liquidity risk for the investment bank and change the nature of interest rate risk. This will require additional hedging for both. This could be achieved by the commercial bank increasing the maturity of its liabilities appropriately, just as the investment bank could decrease the maturity of its assets. The limit of this convergence is a universal bank with perfect maturity and repricing interval matching. But, this requires a larger concentration of capital, including the appropriate corporate form. Alternatively, new banks might spring up in what are new "niches" of lending, each dealing in a different maturity of matched assets and liabilities. This would be a perfectly segmented system. A system in which independent, distinct commercial banks, savings banks, investment banks, and so forth coexist in the absence of regulations on their area of business, and in which each hedges its liquidity and interest rate risks by matching the maturity of its assets to its liabilities, may be said to be "naturally segmented" because it is the method of hedging used that creates the de facto segmentation. A system of unified banks that also hedged risks would have exactly the same aggregate balance sheet pattern as the financial system with independent commercial and investment banks. The major difference between the two systems then reduces to the size and concentration allowed to the individual banking units.

The question is whether the crucial distinction in a segmented system lies in the independent ownership of different types of bank or in the limitation on the types of assets in which they deal or, rather, in the way in which they choose (or are forced by regulations) to hedge their risk positions – or, to put the point differently, whether the distinction between systems should be based on the definition of the bank's activities or the method by which the bank arranges its hedging.

If there were other methods of hedging risk than direct matching of assets and liabilities, there might be banks that have fixed rate term loans financed with sight deposits with the liquidity and interest rate risk hedged by holding reserves. Alternatively, these banks might hedge the interest rate risk by swapping the fixed rate term lending for floating rate interest payments to match the reset interval of its funding costs. If these alternative methods of hedging are cheaper, then competitive forces will lead financial systems to take on diverse combinations of particular institutions, but there is no reason why this should be a system of purely universal banks. On the other hand, if there are regulations that require particular methods of hedging, which are more costly than those developed by the market, there will be attempts to "deregulate" the system to take advantage of the more profitable methods of hedging.

An example given by the money market mutual funds

A simple illustration of this approach may be provided by inspection of the way credit and liquidity risks are dealt with in a classic collateralized Consumer and Industrial (C&I) loan made by a commercial bank to a commercial borrower. As noted, the classic commercial loan is 90 days maturity against work in progress or goods in warehouse already contracted for sale. They are "self-liquidating" because they are repaid via the completion of the contract of sale of the collateral. The bank effectively does a reverse repurchase agreement in which it "buys" the collateral by granting the company a deposit account, agreeing to resell the collateral to the firm 90 days later at a higher price, which extinguishes the deposit, with the difference between the two prices representing the interest. If the loan is not repaid, the bank retains possession of the collateral.

These loans are thus secured by collateral represented by the goods in warehouse. As noted, this pledging of security could be represented as the sale, by the bank to the commercial borrower, of a put option on the collateral with a strike price equal to the value of the loan. The commercial loan is then the creation of a deposit to the credit of the borrower plus the sale of a put option on the collateral.

The expertise that the loan officer of the bank brings to this transaction is the evaluation of the security and the size of the margin of safety between the expected value of the collateral and the size of the loan. This evaluation is equivalent to determining the fair price of an out-of-the-money put option on the collateral.[34] The determination of the terms and conditions of the standard commercial and industrial loan is then exactly the same exercise as determining the fair price of the option, which is sold to the borrower with the loan. If the option is priced fairly, then the banker has fully hedged the credit risk associated with the loan. In the case of default, the banker "buys" the collateral with the unrepaid loan; the value of the acquired collateral should just equal the amount of the loan plus accrued interest, including any additional collection costs that might be incurred in the sale of the collateral. The bank thus does not bear any credit risk in making the loan; it simply hedges that risk appropriately by setting the terms of the security of the loan.

Liquidity risk represents the deposit liabilities on the other side of the bank balance sheet. Demand deposits represent a commitment by the bank to exchange cash (money base, whether specie or central bank reserves) for the nominal value of the deposit liability at a one-to-one ratio on the "demand" of the depositor. This is equivalent to the bank giving the deposit holder an American put option on the deposit with a strike equal to the current nominal value of the deposit in terms of cash. The value of this option is the liquidity risk faced by the bank. If the bank does not charge for demand deposits, this means that the depositor implicitly receives the value of the put option premium from the bank. This also represents the cost of the deposit to the bank in addition to any costs associated with the operation of the account for making transactions by cheque or transfer.

The option value will be determined by the costs incurred by the bank in hedging its exposure to the put written to the depositor. This hedge is usually in the form of holding the bank's capital as reserves against deposits. The expertise of the banker comes in determining the reserve proportion. This will be roughly the probability of exercise of the option, that is, by the probability of the net deposit withdrawal exceeding the repayment of loans. Legal reserve requirements and deposit insurance are simply methods by which regulators force banks to hedge liquidity risk.

There is no difference in this cost, which is the liquidity premium, whether the deposit is created by a customer depositing cash or by the bank opening a deposit as a commercial loan. From the point of view of the bank, a commercial loan may then be represented as package that contains a spot sale and forward repurchase of a deposit, the sale of a put option on the deposit, and the sale of a put option on the loan collateral. The interest charged on the loan must be sufficient to cover the fair value of the two put options that the bank is writing to the borrower and that represent the costs to the bank of hedging the credit and liquidity risk on the loan. If the bank is to earn any profit on the transaction, its net interest margin must be greater than this.

There are other ways in which this intermediation might be represented. For example, the loan could be represented as a spot-forward swap on the deposit with multiple, embedded repayment options. For present purposes, it is sufficient to note that banks have always been dealing implicitly in options contracts with their commercial clients and that they have always been engaged in the evaluation of the fair value of such contingent commitments. It also shows that if the bank has properly evaluated and covered the risks associated with the loan, it does not "bear" any risk from making the loan and thus does not earn income from risk bearing. Rather, it is a clearinghouse for risks; if it makes a profit, it is from its expertise in evaluating the risk and arranging for the hedging of the loan. This means that bank net interest margins cover the cost of hedging the bank's risk in making loans, and any net profit might better be considered as the equivalent of "fees and commissions" for arranging the risk cover.

If "commercial" banks have been dominant in this form of lending, it must be because they have a cost advantage in doing so, either because of their expertise or because the loan and deposit markets are restricted either for borrowers or for other lenders. For example, the regulations limiting payment of interest benefit banks not only because this limits competition for deposits but also because this keeps down the cost of deposits, which are already a loss-making proposition because of the giveaway put option representing repayment on demand. On the other hand, this cost has to be covered in the interest margin the banks charge to business borrowers. Regulations that are designed to decrease the risk of the transactions accounts of depositors are thus subsidized by borrowers who must bear the cost of hedging of all bank deposits, not only those created through the granting of loans.

It is thus not surprising that banks should have experienced competition for their commercial lending business from commercial paper markets, where borrowing rates do not have to cover the option premium necessary to hedge depositors' liquidity risk. It is also clear that the creation of commercial paper markets should have squeezed bank margins and reduced their business lending.

The response of the commercial banks was to reduce the costs of deposit funds via the introduction of the negotiable CD, one of the first acts of securitization in the financial innovation process. Because the CD was a time deposit, it did not create a liquidity risk similar to a demand deposit. By creating a secondary market for CDs via a system of market makers ready to buy and sell CDs similar to Treasury bill brokers, they could be converted on demand in the secondary market and thus had the same liquidity for the holder as a demand deposit, whereas they paid a positive rate of interest. Banks were thus able to use organized markets to provide deposits with similar liquidity and a higher return than demand deposits. The use of the market allowed the banks to eliminate the hedging costs required to provide liquidity to demand deposits.

Paradoxically, it was this use of the market to create liquidity and reduce hedging costs that led to the creation of money market mutual funds. A CD is little different from a share in a money market mutual investment fund in which the fund operator stands ready to convert at nominal value. Most money market funds notionally fix the market value of their shares at $1, which is exactly what a bank does when it guarantees repayment at par of its deposits to make them resemble bank deposits. However, there is no legal guarantee that this peg will always be met, so the fund has the same risks as a bank and presumably the same hedging costs.[35] In addition, the mutual fund still has to cover credit risks of the commercial paper that it buys. If the fund has larger assets than a bank (which in a unit bank system such as the US is not difficult), then it can reduce these costs through diversification. However, the main savings enjoyed by a money market mutual fund is its lower operating costs, which have only to cover a computer, a mail drop, and a (part-time) investment manager. It thus has none of the overhead that a commercial bank is required to incur to attract deposits.

Money market mutual funds thus do virtually the same things that banks do when they make commercial loans. They collect funds through the sale of shares and make loans to commercial borrowers. They also have to undertake the same risk management as a bank. Their advantage is that they can provide this risk management at lower cost than banks. As seen in the case of France, there is nothing to stop banks from offering these same services by setting up their own mutual funds but with earnings for fees and commissions that are lower than when the banks intermediated lending directly.

Thus, the process that is at work eroding the profitability of commercial banking is not competition for the borrowing-lending intermediation via maturity transformation but in the costs involved in the pricing and evaluation of risk. Because these costs are generally lower in organized markets, their use gives a competitive advantage to their users. Looking at the problem from the viewpoint suggested by the work of Ronald Coase, the line of demarcation between the market and the firm is set by the costs of organization. The costs of covering the risks of commercial lending are lower when organized through markets than when organized directly within banks. This is the competition that commercial banks are facing. It is a competition that they cannot win.

Risk management and the future of banks

Does this mean that banks will eventually die out? That they will be replaced by direct financing through markets or by market traded mutual funds? If by banks one means the canonical definition of a "commercial" bank that issues "short-term" liabilities in the form of demand deposits and transforms them into longer-term assets in the form of business loans, the answer is clearly yes. But this response is based on the mistaken idea that the "commercial" bank is a "natural" form of banking organization. It is not. The discussion in Section 2 should be sufficient to show that there is no "natural" form of bank organization. The response is also based on the idea that banks are simply a conduit providing the intermediation of funds from excess saving units seeking liquid investments to deficit-saving units seeking permanent lending. This is a simplification that is highly misleading, if not mistaken.

As suggested by the previous discussion, the combination of the two main banking forms survives because it is in the business of risk management. When lending involves maturity transformation, the risks are predominantly credit and liquidity risks. Such banks succeed because they manage to eliminate these risks more efficiently than other forms of organization and are able to retain substantial commission and fee income, in excess of their costs of providing risk management, for doing so. The competition that is creating difficulty for these banks is not in the part of their activities involving maturity transformation (except in the cases where this is caused by legislation preventing banks from adopting other forms of lending) but in the management of risk involved in these activities.

If banks are to survive, it will not be by becoming more efficient as maturity transformers but by doing what they have always implicitly done, and that is managing risk more efficiently than other forms of financial organization. To do this they will have to adopt and integrate the more efficient market-organized methods of risk management that have been developed into their own activities. The historical discussion presented here suggests that banks and markets have always developed in a complementary, rather than competitive, fashion. Some of this complementarity can already be seen in the response of banks to the introduction of commercial paper markets. Instead of providing the funding for business loans, they now provide backup lines of credit for firms who issue commercial paper. Thus, a firm that finds it cannot rollover its outstanding issue of paper can prevent default by using the bank loan. This is a form of insurance policy offered by the bank to the firm or a put option that it sells to the firm, which allows the firm to sell the bank its outstanding commercial paper at maturity at a strike equal to par. Banks also provide backup lines to mutual fund operators to ensure that the net asset value of their funds remains at par and the shares can be redeemed as if they are deposits. This can be viewed as a put option sold by the bank to the fund, which allows it to sell shares in the fund at a par strike price. Thus even when the funds are not directly intermediated by a bank, a bank will usually be involved in providing some of the risk management services.

The evaluation of the risks involved in loan contracts by bankers has been traditionally founded on a banking relationship in which a banker possesses complete knowledge of the business activities of the firm. In a competitive financial environment, such intimate relationships no longer exist. Competition to supply financial services to firms would require that each competitor acquire such knowledge, which would mean that each would have such information from every firm, raising difficult problems of proprietary information. Thus, firms are led to introduce in-house expertise in the use of financial markets and the selection of financial services from financial institutions.

Bankers do, however, retain some advantages in dealing with individual clients relative to direct markets. The reduction in the costs of managing risk associated with dealing directly through organized markets depends on the exchange of a large volume of standardized contracts. None of the existing exchange-traded contracts may be appropriate to the particular risks of financing the operations of any single business firm. Banks can continue to provide individual service to clients by offering tailor-made risk management services. By providing individual services to a number of clients, the bank can seek to hedge those risks by internally matching the basic risk characteristics of the services sold to the clients.

This is precisely what giro banks have always done in managing the provision of transactions services to their clients. For example, in their foreign exchange trading, banks will first match clients offsetting purchases and sales, acting as a clearinghouse, and then seek to trade the net position of its clients. This is exactly the same thing that banks can do for the over-the-counter risk management contracts they offer their clients. By matching the long and short positions of the exposures that have been accepted from clients, the bank can eliminate the risk of both parties without taking any risk itself. It can charge fees and commissions for what is essentially a riskless, clearinghouse service. Different from a market, the bank can offer complex structured packages of such contracts, suitable to individual clients, and then break down the types of risk. Any positive net position can then be hedged through an organized markets. Thus, even though organized markets for exchange-traded instruments are cheaper and more efficient, banks will still be more efficient in providing client services because of the greater efficiency of the internal process of netting of risks.

Banks may no longer be primarily involved with lending or maturity transformation. But, they will still provide services such as transformation of interest rate risk by swapping floating rate interest payments for fixed payments, or hedging the future interest costs of future investment expenditures, or hedging foreign exchange rates. And, there is no reason why this should cause any increase in risk for the bank itself.

This is not to say that some banks will not continue to provide traditional banking services or that some will not end up taking more risky positions. For example, banks that persist in concentrating their activity in lending to businesses will find their return to capital falling below the market levels as they lend to more risky borrowers who are unable to tap the commercial paper market. Such banks will be tempted to use the new risk management possibilities to augment their earnings as well as to manage their risks. Derivatives can be used to hedge bank risk, or they can be used as investments to increase bank earnings. For these banks there will be an increase in risk.

It is also clear that banks will have to be of a sufficiently large size to take advantages of these economies of scale and scope in providing risk management services to their clients. One would thus expect to see a greater degree of concentration in the banking sector. For unit banking systems such as the US, this creates particular problems, for the majority of banks are clearly not of sufficiently large size. This suggests that there will be further consolidation or that some sort of arrangement similar to the pre-1914 system of correspondent banking will be developed in which smaller banks serve as a conduit for funds to the largest banks that in their turn provide risk management services to the smaller bank's clients. It is clear from both the French and US data available that only the largest banks are currently active in the use of derivatives in providing client services and their own risk management. Fewer than half of US banks reported derivative holdings in 1996. The top 25 banks accounted for 97% of total derivative activities in the first quarter of 1996 (see OCC, 1996). More than 85% of these positions were in over-the-counter derivatives associated with the provision of client-based services.

It is for this reason it is important for bank supervisors to change their approach to prudential regulations to clearly identify the use of derivatives to augment bank earnings through investment and the use of derivatives to augment bank earnings through a more efficient reduction in the risks associated with providing client services. This suggests that the segmentation of banking systems is not the real issue. The issue is how the risk characteristics of a bank's overall balance sheet are evaluated for prudential purposes. It is not clear that the matching of maturities of bank asset and liability positions, whether within banks or across categories of banks, is the most appropriate way of assessing the stability of bank operations. Indeed, imposing maturity matching by categories of assets may be just as inappropriate in the current banking environment as the segmentation of banks into commercial and investment banks.

The introduction of regulations permitting universal banking might thus be described as a necessary but not a sufficient condition for providing an environment in which banks that formerly operated in protected, segmented markets can adjust to the new, competitive environment in financial markets. First, banks will have to recognize and apply their expertise in supplying risk management services to their business clients. Second, they will have to prove to be more efficient in providing these services than organized markets. Third, they must be regulated in ways that insure that they use the new financial derivative products as part of providing risk management for their balance sheets rather than in providing greater earnings for their investment portfolios. As stated, not all banks will be able to do this, either because of insufficient size or insufficient expertise. The difference between the use of technology in US and French banks is instructive. In France, new technologies have primarily been aimed at reducing the costs of providing transactions services, which means reducing the costs of raising deposit funds. In the US, the major expenditures have been in developing risk measurement and allocation systems, with the most successful banks eschewing retail deposit funds. Because such expenditures will be beyond the resources of most small banks, this again points to a process of concentration or correspondent banking.

Notes

1 This document was originally prepared to serve as a background paper for drafting a general introduction to a research project organized by President Giannino Parravicini to assess the future of banks in Italy. Having undergone several revisions and changes in direction, the plan for a single publication for a coordinated project was abandoned. The present draft thus appears alone. The main conclusions in Section 7 were completed in 1993; the remainder was completed in 1994, except for Section 6 dealing with France, which was completed in the summer of 1996. Further changes in the conditions of the project have meant that what was meant as an introduction to the project is the last to appear.

2 Concerns for the position of banks in the financial system were reinforced by the collapse of the savings and loan banks as well as the solvency of commercial banks so that the question was extended from their survival to their viability. See, for example, Bryan (1991), Pierce (1991), and Litan (1987).

3 Most of the historical references in the discussion of the development of banking are drawn from the discussion in Kregel (1996) and the bibliography cited there.

4 This interpretation follows MacLeod (1892, I, p. 315). Conant (1896, p. 22) notes his reference to "[t]he definition given in an Italian dictionary in 1659 . . . '*Monte*, a standing bank or mount of money, as they have in divers cities of Italy.'" He also quotes Blackstone to the effect that the government of Firenze in 1344, unable to pay a debt of £60,000, "formed the principal into an aggregate sum, called, metaphorically a *Mount* or *Bank*, the shares whereof were transferable, like our stocks." A contemporary observer of the

founding of the Bank of England quoted in Clapham (1945, I, p. 20, italics added) refers to the "seal of [the Bank], being the Britannia sitting on a *bank* of money."

5 Colwell (1859, Chapter XIII) indicates a progressive levy on opulent citizens paying 4% interest, whereas MacLeod (1894, II:1, p. 577) indicates a flat 1% levy paying 5%. Conant (op. cit., p. 21) gives the date of the first forced loan as 1156.

6 The generosity of the Grand Duke was limited – he required indemnification for loss and required the assets of the bank as well as the property of the citizens as guarantee in a contract of "capitolazione," which also applied to all communities of the State of Siena doing business with the bank.

7 Fully titled: "An Act for granting to their Majesties several Rates and Duties upon Tunnages of Ships and Vessels, and upon Beer, Ale, and other Liquors; for securing certaine Recompenses and Advantages, in the said Act mentioned, to Such persons as shall voluntarily advance the Sume of Fifteen hundred thousand Pounds towards carrying on the Warr against France."

8 The Union Bank of Louisiana, chartered in April 1832 was a "property bank" that attracted funds from the northern states and from Europe through the sale of bank bonds. The proceeds were invested in real estate, which served as the security for the bond issue. Banks that found it difficult to raise funds were aided by state governments who issued their own bonds and then turned the funds over to the banks or lent their bonds directly to the banks for resale. Slaves were even permitted to be pledged for up to two-thirds of the collateral for loans.

9 Although, there were limits. For example, the credits the Bank of Amsterdam granted in "bank money," representing official weight coin, against the deposit of circulating coin valued according to its actual weight and against bills falling due, could not be converted into gold on demand. It also issued bullion receipts at a 5% discount to mint price, which could be converted within six months upon payment of a keeping charge of 0.5% for gold and 0.25% for silver (cf. Dunbar, 1909, p. 95ff).

10 Cf. Hammond (1967, p. 332, 355) and Robertson (1955, pp. 142–3). It is interesting to note that the act, sponsored by Martin van Buren, was widely criticized as leading to the over issue of notes for reasons that would now be classified as reflecting the "moral hazard" of generalized insurance. The act is reprinted as Appendix III to Brock (1992, pp. 427–36).

11 Texts of the relevant legislation pertaining to this entire period are reprinted in Dunbar (1897).

12 Barnett (1911, p. 14) notes that because the National Bank Act focused on the regulation of note issue, this led to the idea that regulation was not required for state banks, which could no longer issue notes, leaving deposit banking virtually unregulated. This provided an additional advantage to state banks.

13 This simply shifted the problem to that of differential discounting on cheques issued by different banks and created the problem of non-par clearing of cheques, which the creation of the Federal Reserve was meant to eliminate.

14 Barnett contains an extensive discussion of the factors that made state bank charters increasingly attractive in this period. Among the less well-known is the introduction of deposit insurance in a number of frontier states.

15 The National Bank Act had favored "real bills" lending by exempting it from the 10% limitation, but the size of the note issue was independent of such lending.

16 The solution that was eventually adopted gave the Federal Reserve effective freedom to deal in government securities and opened the way to today's emphasis on the use of government debt as a vehicle for open market policy. The Glass-Steagall Act of 1932 (not to be confused with the Glass Banking Act of 1933, which legislated the separation of the commercial and investment activities of banks) permitted district reserve banks to lend Federal Reserve Notes against government securities for an emergency period of one year. This expansion of eligible discounts is similar to the change in Bank of England discounting policy during the 1825 crisis. It allowed the federal reserve banks to lend

against government securities held by the banks and put downward pressure on interest rates as it increased reserves and the supply of gold available to meet foreign demand (cf. Anderson, 1949, p. 269ff).

Thus the primary role of government securities in open market policy, so well-known today, was the result of the Glass-Steagall Act (1932) and only became institutionalized with the reorganization of the independent Open Market Committee in Marriner Eccles' Banking Act of 1935. The (1932) Glass-Steagall provisions became permanent in 1945, and this, as well as the policy of interest rate stabilization adopted to provide cheap finance for the Second World War, provided the post-war conditions in which government securities became the principle position-making asset for banks when the Fed once again started to use active monetary policy after the 1951 Fed-Treasury "Accord."

17 Figures given by Anderson (1949, p. 264) for reporting member banks show security loans as 44% of total lending in August 1929, rising to 45% in October and 50% in August 1930. Anderson credits this movement to the Fed policy of increasing bank reserves by purchasing government securities, which led to a reduction in discounts of eligible paper at the Fed and an increase in ineligible security lending, which created the necessity of tightening in 1931–1932 (cf. Epstein and Ferguson, 1984).

18 The sudden appearance of this provision in the 1933 banking bill has perplexed commentators, but it seems a natural response to the concerns that had been expressed since the 1920s about the persistence of correspondent relations between member and non-member banks. If non-members could borrow from correspondents who financed the borrowing through the discount window, the "qualitative" control over the use of federal reserves was circumvented; the same thing occurred if members borrowed from non-member correspondents. See the account in Harris (1933), Chapter XIV. Zero rates on demand deposits may thus be seen as a means of eliminating correspondent balances and forcing the concentration of reserve balances in the reserve banks and increasing Fed membership; the regulation of time rates was a means of precluding competition from New York for country bank time deposits for the same purpose. The original bill had included liberal branching privileges to compensate the larger city banks, but these were dropped as a result of opposition from large, as well as country, banks. It is generally reported that the large New York banks were in favor of the restriction of demand deposit rates to decrease their costs, but this has to be weighed against the loss of correspondent relations and the increased control from the Fed over their asset portfolios. It is possible that their experience with the Fed funds market in the 1920s had suggested the cost of correspondent funds would be reduced by more than the loss on services provided. Burgess (1927, p. 120) notes the presence of this "new informal money market which has developed in recent years."

19 The problem was recognized at least within the New York Fed. In a 1960 letter Allan Sproul (1980, pp. 131–2) wrote concerning: "[p]ayment of interest on demand deposits. The passage of time, with its changes in conditions and climate, affects this statutory control also. Of particular significance are the rise in the Treasury bill to the position of the chief liquidity instrument of the economy, the large volume of foreign short-term funds in this market, and the awakening of the treasurers of large corporations and of state and municipal financial officers from their long slumber. As you well know, funds now flow in and out of deposits at banks and into and out of Treasury bill with almost the predictability of tides."

20 Sproul (1980, p. 139) commented on this inappropriate use of Regulation Q as follows: "Originally introduced to try to protect commercial banks from their presumed folly, the authority to fix such ceilings has been stretched to serve as a handmaiden to general monetary policy in bringing pressure to bear on commercial banks to restrict their lending, and as a yo-yo device to shift funds from one type of thrift institution to another in accordance with the ideas of the authorities as to who should get what."

21 The large size of the certificates was not originally intended to exclude small savers but rather imposed by the banks to try to make it difficult for corporate depositors to convert their demand deposits to interest-paying time deposits.

22 This period is chronicled with great insight in Mayer (1974).

23 The crunch started in the spring, when the increase in market interest rates exceeded those of the savings associations just as they were meeting increased competition from the new time deposits offered by commercial banks; in April 1966 outflows of funds exceeded inflows. The crunch at commercial banks did not occur until late August. The run risked producing a securities market crisis through the impact of the forced sales of municipal and government securities by banks on the prices of the inventory holdings of government securities dealers, just when banks were reducing their lending to dealers. Indeed, investment bankers and stock brokers were as concerned about the impending financial crisis as commercial bankers. See the account given by Alfred Hayes (1970).

24 The Fed initially viewed this development as undermining its policy authority but eventually supported the market on the grounds that it would reduce excess un-borrowed reserves and thus make the banks more responsive to changes in reserves. Minsky (1957, p. 173), on the other hand, noted that it also had the effect of making the system as a whole less liquid, and thus more prone to instability, while provoking changes in funding sources that may offset the intention of policy.

25 At this time neither borrowing from subsidiaries (under Regulation M) or from foreign banks operating in the Eurodollar market (under Regulation D) was subject to reserve requirements. Thus, a shift in deposits to an offshore subsidiary not only allowed market rates to be paid to depositors, but it also reduced required reserves. Note that the savings and loans did not have this opportunity but were now subject to interest rate constraints.

26 Cf. Bernstein (1971, p. 194ff) points out how the increased borrowing improved the official settlements balance of payments, although it left the liquidity balance unchanged.

27 The default of Penn Central in 1970 also forced a change in policy, for it placed the entire commercial paper market in difficulty, and weaker corporations found they could no longer rollover their commercial paper commitments and had to return to bank lending to replace the funds. In the face of the rising difficulties at Chrysler, which had substantial commercial paper outstanding, the Fed eliminated Regulation Q limits on time deposits greater than $100,000 to allow banks to fund the required increase in lending to offset the collapse in commercial paper funding. When the commercial paper market returned to normal, this new freedom to compete for funds set the stage for increased rollover lending to Less-Developed Countries (LDCs) and real estate investment trusts (REITs), both of which went bad when the Fed contracted from 1973 to 1974 and rates went to unprecedented levels.

28 This was particularly important because at that time Regulation Q interest rate controls had been abolished for deposits of $100,000 and up so that deposits of precisely this amount were exempt from interest rate controls but qualified for federal guarantee. As a result, a brokered market grew up in which investment banks distributed these deposits to the highest bidder without any reference to the risk conditions of the savings and loans that purchased them.

29 It is important to note a difference between FDIC and FSLIC insurance. The former insured sight deposits, and thus required instant payment up to insurance limits, the latter however insured savings and time deposits or shares in mutual institutions. Repayment was thus only required at the normal term of the deposit, or in the case of a share in a mutual savings bank, the FSLIC guarantee would have been satisfied if the monies were repaid after the final installment of the 30-year mortgage was received by the bank or its liquidator. This was ignored during the crisis.

30 It is interesting to note that the rise in real interest rates that these reforms produced did not produce the widely expected increase in household saving and flows of funds to the financial sector. In fact, there was a sharp reduction in households' financial saving, that is, net of housing and the acquisition of real assets accompanied by a rise in the ratio of self-financing by firms. This was in part due to the suspension of wage indexation at about the same time as the mid-1980 bank reforms, which brought about a shift in the distribution of income. This also reduced firms' demands for external funding. Although

there was a rise in firms' financial investments, such as SICAVs, evidence cited by de Boissieu suggests that these firms also had the highest rates of real capital accumulation.

31 This is not to suggest that this always occurs in the real world. Absence of full hedging occurs in the case of fraudulent activity. Likewise, because full hedging depends on the evaluations of risk, which cannot be made with perfect certainty, there may be conditions that act to change market perceptions and cause "hedging myopia." This is the case of what Minsky has called endogenous financial instability and results from generalized misperception of risks. These problems are outside the scope of this essay.

32 It is in this sense that the US financial system has become more market oriented, not because of increased "direct" financing. The major changes in the banking system have been in banks that have specialized in areas in which the use of such products can reduce hedging costs relative to funding margins and thereby increase revenues. As long as regulations require banks to hedge via physical markets when cheaper, market-traded derivative alternatives exist, there will be pressure for changes in regulations that appear as calls for "deregulation." Because US regulations rely almost exclusively on the use of "physical" hedging, these moves to introduce new market-based methods of risk hedging have been directed toward the elimination of the regulations producing segmentation.

33 On the other hand, other forms of bank lending, such as accommodation and term lending, signature lending, and other forms of non-collateralized lending must be hedged in a different way. For example, banks may diversify their credit risk by swapping loans with other banks whose lending is concentrated in a different sector. Options contracts are also being written against changes in credit quality as expressed in risk premia over safe benchmark rates or in delinquency or default rates on packages of credit. The strike on the option is then expressed as, say, an X% risk premium over the safe benchmark. The owner of an asset whose price will decline with a decline in the credit quality, and thus a rise in the risk-adjusted interest rate on that class of asset, could thus buy a call option at X%, and the rise in the option value as the risk premium rises aboveXx would offset the loss in the capital value of the asset. Alternatively, for exchange-traded assets, such as bonds, buying a put option on the bond price will offset any fall in price due to a rise in the risk-adjusted interest rate (cf. Neal, 1996).

34 The same process is at work in determining the compensating balances that the borrower must hold on a line of credit.

35 Technology played an important role here, for it was only after cheap computational power became available that fund operators could carry out the net asset value calculations that enabled them to introduce unit pricing. See Martin Mayer's discussion in *The Bankers*. In 1995 a number of fund operators, some of whom had expanded their investments to include derivatives, found that the net values of the fund had fallen below $1. Faced with the possibility of having to redeem at less than par, they injected funds to keep the value at par.

References

Anderson, Benjamin McAlester (1949) *Economics and the Public Welfare*, New York: Van Nostrand, Reprinted by Liberty Press, Indianapolis, 1979.

Banque de France (1986) *La Banque de France et la Monnaie*, Paris: Service de l'Information de la Banque de France.

Barnett, George E. (1911) *State Banks and Trust Companies Since the Passage of the National Bank Act*, Washington: Government Printing Office, National Monetary Commission.

Bell, Geoffrey (1973) *The Euro-dollar Market and the International Financial System*, New York: Wiley.

Bernstein, Edward M. (1971) "Les eurodollars: les mouvements de capitaux et la balance américaine des paiements," in Herbert V. Prochnow, ed., *L'Eurodollar*, Paris: Calmann-Lévy.

Born, Karl (1983) *International Banking in the 19th and 20th Centuries*, New York: St. Martin's Press.

Boyd, John H. and Mark Gertler (Summer 1994) "Are Banks Dead? Or Are the Reports Greatly Exaggerated?" *Federal Reserve Bank of Minneapolis Quarterly Review*, Vol. 18, No. 3.

Bremer, Cornelius Daniel (1935) *American Bank Failures*, New York: Columbia University Press.

Brock, Philip L., ed. (1992) *If Texas Were Chile*, San Francisco: ICS Press.

Bryan, Lowell L. (1991) *Bankrupt*, New York: Harper Business.

Burgard, Jean-Jacques, Charles Cornut, and Oliveir Robert de Massey (1995) *La Banque en France*, 4th ed., Paris: Presses del la Fondation Nationale des Sciences Politiques & Dalloz.

Burgess, W. Randolph (1927) *The Reserve Banks and the Money Market*, New York: Harper Business.

Clapham, John H. (1936) *The Economic Development of France and Germany – 1815–1914*, Cambridge: Cambridge University Press.

———— (1945) *The Bank of England*, Vol. I, Cambridge: Cambridge University Press.

COB: Commission Bancaire (1995) "Dix ans d'activité et des résultats des banques françaises," Rapport annuel pour 1994, Paris, pp. 115–54.

Colmant, Hugues (1990) "The Evolution of Institutional Structures and Regulations," in C. De Boissieu, ed., *Banking in France*, London: Routledge.

Colwell, Stephen (1859) *The Ways and Means of Payment*, New York: Augustus M. Kelley, Reprint 1965.

Conant, Charles A. (1896) *History of Modern Banks of Issue*, New York: G. P. Putnam's Sons.

Confalonieri, Antonio (1974–6) *Banca e Industria in Italia, 1894–1904 Three Volumes*, Milano: Banca Commerciale Italiana.

Currie, Lauchlin (1934) *The Supply and Control of Money in the United States*, Cambridge, MA: Harvard University Press.

de Boissieu, Christian (1990) "Recent Developments in the French Financial System," in C. De Boissieu, ed., *Banking in France*, London: Routledge.

Dunbar, Charles F. (1909) *The Theory and History of Banking*, 2nd ed., O.M.W. Sprague, ed., New York: G. P. Putnam's Sons.

———— (1969) *The Laws of the United States Relating to Currency, Finance and Banking From 1789 to 1896*, New York: Augustus M. Kelley, Reprint 1897.

Einaudi, Luigi (1953) "Teoria della Moneta Immaginaria nel Tempo da Carlomagno alla Rivoluzione Francese," in Storia, ed., *Economia, Volume 1, a cura di Bruno Rossi Ragazzi*, Roma: Edizioni di Storia e Letteratura.

Emden, Paul (n.d.) *Money Powers of Europe*, London: Sampson Low, Marston & Co, Ltd.

Epstein, Gerald and Ferguson, Thomas (December 1984) "Monetary Policy, Loan Liquidation, and Industrial Conflict: The Federal Reserve and the Open Market Operations of 1932," *Journal of Economic History*, Vol. 44.

Fieldhouse, Richard D. (December 1964) "Certificates of Deposit," in *Essays in Money and Credit*, New York: Federal Reserve Bank of New York.

Germain-Martin, Henry (1954) "France," in Benjamin Haggott Beckhart, ed., *Banking Systems*, New York: Columbia University Press.

Goldsmith, Raymond (1958) *Financial Intermediaries in the American Economy Since 1900*, Princeton: Princeton University Press.

———— (1969) *Financial Structure and Development*, New Haven: Yale University Press.

Hammond, Bray (1967) *Banks and Politics in America*, Princeton: Princeton University Press.

Harris, Seymour Edwin (1933) *Twenty Years of Federal Reserve Policy*, Cambridge, MA: Harvard University Press.

Hayes, Alfred (1970) "The 1966 Credit Crunch," in David Eastburn, ed., *Men, Money and Policy, Essays in Honor of Karl R. Bopp*, Philadelphia: Federal Reserve Bank of Philadelphia.

Kaufman, George G. and Larry R. Mote (May/June 1994) "Is Banking a Declining Industry? A Historical Perspective," Economic Perspectives, Federal Reserve Bank of Chicago.

Kregel, Jan Allan (1996) *Origini e sviluppo dei mercati finanziari*, Arezzo: Banca Popolare dell'Etruria e del Lazio, Collana Studi e Ricerche.

Litan, Robert (1987) *What Should Banks Do?* Washington, DC: Brookings Institution.

MacLeod, Henry Dunning (1892) *The Theory and Practice of Banking*, London: Longmans, Green, Reader, & Dyer.

———— (1894) *The Theory of Credit*, 2nd ed., London: Longmans, Green.

Madden, John T., Marcus Nadler, and Sipa Heller (1948) *Money Market Primer: A Study of the Institutions and Operations of the New York Money Market*, New York: The Ronald Press.

Madeleine, M.G. (1943) *Monetary and Banking Theories of Jacksonian Democracy*, Philadelphia: The Dolphin Press.

Mayer, Martin (1974) *The Bankers*, New York: Ballantine Books.

Minsky, Hyman (1957) "Central Banking and Money Market Changes," reprinted in *Can 'It' Happen Again?* Armonk: M.E. Sharpe.

Neal, Robert S. (Second Quarter 1996) "Credit Derivatives: New Financial Instruments for Controlling Credit Risk," Economic Review, Federal Reserve Bank of Kansas City.

OCC: Office of Comptroller of the Currency (June 10, 1996) "Derivatives Data – First Quarter 1996 Call Report," Washington, DC.

Orsingher, Rogar (1967) *Banks of the World*, London: Macmillan.

Patat, Jean-Pierre (1993) *Monnaie, institutions financières, et politique monétaire*, Paris: Economica.

Pierce, James L. (1991) *The Future of Banking, A Twentieth Century Fund Report*, New Haven: Yale University Press.

Reis, Bernard J. (1937) *False Security*, New York: Equinox Cooperative Press, reprinted by Ayer Co. Salem, New Hampshire, 1986.

Robertson, Ross M. (1955) *History of the American Economy*, New York: Harcourt Brace.

———— (1964) *History of the American Economy*, 2nd ed., New York: Harcourt Brace.

Schumpeter, Joseph (1934) *Theory of Economic Development*, Cambridge, MA: Harvard University Press.

———— (1954) *History of Economic Analysis*, New York: Oxford University Press.

Sproul, Allan (December 1980) *Selected Papers of Allan Sproul*, edited by Lawrence S. Ritter, New York: Federal Reserve Bank of New York.

Whale, P. Barrett (1930) *Joint Stock Banking in Germany*, London: Macmillan.

2 Financial fragility and the structure of financial markets

Summary

This paper investigates the role of financial structure on the financial fragility of the economy. It argues that whereas structure is independent of the degree of what Minsky calls financial fragility, it will have an impact on the rate of contagion by which financial fragility produces general economic instability. This is independent of the traditional view of instability as being caused by financial intermediation, creating a mismatch of maturities of financial institutions' asset and liabilities but is linked to the quality of the assets against which banks lend when there is a rapid increase in resources intermediated by banks. It concludes by arguing that the present system has become more prone to financial crises because of an increase in the speed of contagion due to a change in the financial structure.

Instability of the economy and fragility of the financial structure[1]

Against the backdrop of the approaching 60th anniversary of the New Deal financial legislation and the inauguration of a new administration facing the task of re-regulation of the financial system, it seems appropriate to reflect on the relationship between financial structure and financial instability. The New Deal regulations were introduced in the aftermath of conditions of extreme financial fragility and one of their express aims was to eliminate the potential for financial institutions to produce instability in the economy. The regulations seem to have been successful, at least until the late 1970s, in preventing another great depression, or to paraphrase, "It" has not (yet) happened again.

Since Minsky developed his now famous "financial instability hypothesis" during the "golden years" of the operation of this New Deal legislation, it must be presumed that he believed that "financial fragility" was not only possible but also present during those years of economic stability. This also implies that in Minsky's view, the New Deal legislation did little to eliminate the potential for financial fragility. As no substantial breakdown occurred in the period, we might conjecture that whereas financial structure is independent of financial fragility, it may play a role in the rate of propagation of fragility or in preventing the transformation of fragility into the "It" of the major instability of the Great Depression.

Minsky's (cf. the introduction to Minsky, 1982) suggestion that the transformation of financial fragility into a more generalized "breakdown" has been prevented by the existence of "Big Government" acting as spender of last (and sometimes first) resort and a "Big Bank" acting as the "lender of last resort" also seems to preclude the importance of the financial structure of the system in the passage from fragility to breakdown; although, it leaves open the possibility of an influence for financial structure on the speed of contagion in the system.

In broaching the question of the impact of financial structure and regulation on the degree of financial instability in Minsky's work, it is important to recognize a basic point of difference from the traditional approach to financial instability. Minsky refers to "instability" as the destabilizing impact of financial conditions on the behavior of the economy as a whole rather than to the "instability" of the financial institutions in the economy. I shall thus propose to define changes in the proportions of "hedge," "speculative," and "Ponzi" financial relations (cf. Minsky, 1986, Appendix A) in the financing of production as producing changes in the "fragility" of the financial system. It is this definition of "fragility" that replaces the traditional conception of financial "instability."

Financial instability and financial fragility

The traditional conception of instability in financial markets stems from the view that financial institutions act as agents that intermediate between savers willing to lend funds and final borrowers seeking to invest funds. This intermediation function not only requires a matching of borrowers and lenders but also more importantly concerns the transformation of the maturity of financial assets from short term to long term, with lenders preferring short-term liquid assets and borrowers long-term more or less permanent fixed interest liabilities. The greater the mismatch between the maturity of the short-term assets issued to savers and the long-term liabilities purchased from investors, the greater the risk that short-term interest rates will rise relative to long-term rates, producing negative net worth and insolvency or a flight of funds called disintermediation as the short-term bid rates lag behind the market. When the volatility of short-term interest rates is modest, the adjustment can be made by cutting back on new lending, reducing net margins and drawing down secondary reserves; this was the method of monetary control in the post-war period. When the movement in short-term rates is substantial, loans must be called, and forced sales of assets may takes place, leading to downward pressure on prices.

Such instability can be reduced in a number of ways. One is to limit maturity mismatching by institutions. This would require a range of different institutions operating in markets for assets of different maturities limited to issuing liabilities of the same maturity, which would imply regulation via the imposition of financial market segmentation. Alternatively, one could have an infinite number of institutions, each operating with an imperceptibly small mismatch, which could be covered by a buffer of liquid reserves. Finally, long-term assets could have interest rates indexed to short-term liabilities; this would eliminate the interest rate risk of maturity mismatching by financial intermediaries but shifts it onto the borrower, who is forced to forego the presumed preference for fixed interest liabilities. Credit risk here replaces maturity or interest rate risk.

In addition to maturity transformation, financial intermediaries are also characterized as producing liquidity through the issue of short-term liabilities against long-term assets. In this process the bank makes an illiquid asset held in the private sector more liquid, while the bank becomes less liquid. The willingness of bankers to create liquidity by lending against a private sector asset (or against the expected income from a private sector asset) depends on the "liquidity preference" of the bank.

Maturity mismatching and liquidity creation are usually linked together. This is the case for banks that lend against real assets by creating demand deposits. On the other hand, in an inter-temporal general equilibrium world, the two aspects are separated, for long-term capital assets are just as liquid as any other financial assets; maturity transformation does not then create additional liquidity. Different financial structures might then be thought to create different relationships between maturity transformation and liquidity creation.

In Minsky's development of the idea, financial fragility represents something more than either the mere possibility, or even the persistence, of financial instability due to maturity mismatching in financial institutions. Rather, fragility is inherent in the successful operation of the capitalistic economic system and results from changes in the liquidity preferences of bankers and businesspeople as represented by changes in the margins of safety required on liquidity creation produced by maturity transformation. Thus, fragility could result even in a perfectly stable financial system as defined under the traditional terminology because of changes in the extent of the creation of liquidity for a given degree of mismatching. In this case, a fall in liquidity preference could take place, and the maturity mismatching would remain constant, as bankers become willing to lend against more risky assets. Then different financial structures may not prevent fragility, but they might have different fragility behaviors, similar, say, to fractal coefficients, concerning the speed with which fragility is transmitted within the system.

Fragility in stable conditions

Minsky's theory takes the US financial system as its reference structure. In particular it is crucially dependent on the negotiations and relationships between bankers and businesspeople and their evaluation of future returns and prospects. It presumes a particular type of banker, the banker of, let's say, the pre-1970 era, before the breakdown of the Bretton Woods system, and still subject to the full force of the Glass-Steagall restrictions on commercial banking. For the businessperson, finance is thus a two-stage affair. Short-term project finance comes from the bank, and long-term takeout finance comes from floating the completed project in the capital market. This is where the rest of the financial system comes in. Investment bankers underwrite the floatation of the project by a primary distribution of securities in the capital market. There is no legal restriction to prevent them from being direct investors, but they usually only act as brokers between firms and investors. There is thus an implicit financial structure in which firms' short-term financial liabilities are held in bank portfolios and firms' long-term liabilities are held in household portfolios, along with banks' short-term demand deposit liabilities.

The ability of the banks to lend to businesses to finance investment depends on there being buyers in the long-term capital market to provide the funds that the firms use to repay the banks' short-term lending to fund investment. The buyers are predominantly households who thus finance the capital stock holdings of the economy. The financial system thus intermediates between firms and households in a two-stage process.

This is rather different from the textbook description that often presents the financial system as the intermediary that makes the requirements of firms for long-term lending to fund fixed capital investment compatible with the desire of households to hold short-term liquid assets. In fact, commercial banks provide sight and other short-term deposits against secured, short-term commercial and industrial lending. Investment banks convert short-term borrowing into long-term borrowing by underwriting long-term primary securities distributions. But because they do not normally take position themselves, there is no "natural" long-term demand for these securities unless it comes from other banks, firms (as is the case in many systems outside the US), or institutions such as insurance companies or pension funds receiving non-discretionary savings, which they invest on behalf of the general public.

To the extent that households provide the demand for the long-term securities, despite their preference for liquid assets, they do so only because the secondary market for equity provides sufficient liquidity to allow them to sell without an impact on market price. It is thus the liquidity provided by the financial institutions operating the secondary market, not the intermediary function of financial institutions, that provides the maturity transformation by which the public's demand for relatively short-term liquid assets is matched to the firms' requirement for permanent sources of finance:

> So long as it is open to the individual to employ his wealth in hoarding or lending *money*, the alternative of purchasing actual capital assets cannot be rendered sufficiently attractive (especially to the man who does not manage the capital assets and knows very little about them), except by organising markets wherein these assets can be easily realised for money.
>
> (Keynes, 1936, pp. 160–1)

Thus the mismatching of maturities does not appear on the balance sheet of any financial institution; the maturity transformations that occur within the financial system, and the associated position risks, are minimized and transferred to the investing public. In this view liquidity is not created via balance sheet transformation but by the creation of sufficient liquidity and depth by brokers matching buy and sell orders in the market with the help of "assigned dealers" (specialists) such as those operating on the New York and American Stock exchanges.

There are thus two different methods of liquidity creation. One is "internal" to a financial institution and results from maturity transformation by banks acting as "dealers" willing to buy and sell loans and deposits at bid-ask differentials. The other is "external" to the financial institutions and occurs in free markets in which brokers seek to match households' requests for liquidity, taking a fee or commission from buyer or seller or both. The extreme case of external liquidity is the mythical Walrasian auction market, which costlessly matches buyers and sellers for all future states and dates.

Financial systems and financial fragility

The US system is often contrasted with European financial systems by noting that the US system is "market based" as opposed to "bank based." This is usually meant to convey the fact that long-term financing takes place through primary distribution of securities in the capital market rather than through banks. The US system is thus said to be becoming more "disintermediated" or more "market based" as the commercial banks' basic clients for commercial and industrial lending in the corporate sector have increased their use of the commercial paper markets to raise short-term finance, thus eliminating the banks from the first stage of the two-stage process of financing investment suggested here.

However, this would be to miss the point of the US system by ignoring the fact that in the US system, it is the liquidity of the secondary securities market that makes maturity transformation via the banking system unnecessary because it allows households to hold long-term securities directly. This reduces the amount of potential maturity mismatching and thus risk on the balance sheets of financial institutions. It seems much more revealing to say that the US system differs from the European system in that in the former, more interest rate and position risks are incurred directly by the investing public, whereas in Europe they are carried directly on the balance sheets of banks. The same is true of European secondary markets, which tend to be dominated by banks or by dealers rather than brokers. Dealers will also tend to carry the interest rate and price risk of their positions on their balance sheets.

This way of characterizing the differences in the system also allows us to pierce what might be called the "veil of market deregulation," which masks the fact that as a result of leveling of the playing field, more and more interest rate, credit, and position risk is being carried on the balance sheets of banks and other financial institutions.

In the US financial system before the 1920s corporate borrowing in the capital market was not extensive. Most corporations were still held by inside groups of owner-managers who implicitly provided the long-term funds for investment through retained earnings or increasing their own equity positions rather than through either bank lending or the market. Chandler (1990, Chapter 3) suggests that it was only in the post-WWI crisis and the 1930s depression, when retained earnings proved to be insufficient, that the large firms depended on either banks or capital markets for anything but working capital and foreign exchange and securities transfer services. Thus, long-term borrowing and long-term lending were directly linked, outside of the financial system and independently of financial markets, but within the class of owners of industry (often with the help of the intermediation of investment banker "brokers" such as J.P. Morgan). This corresponds very closely to Kalecki's idea of the capitalist class financing their own expenditures on consumption and new investment from their own profits, without the need of the financial system to intermediate (cf. Kregel, 1989).

It was the growth of firms to large size that brought change in this structure. On the one hand, firms expanded beyond the abilities of their owners to manage them, but they also outlived their owners. Marshallian heirs, unwilling to continue in their grandfathers' footsteps became politicians and artists and sought to convert their holdings to shorter, more liquid assets by selling their interest to the general public. Antitrust legislation also had an important impact in producing a shareholding public by forcing the breakup of large trusts and causing their shares to be distributed in the hands of many holders. It is difficult to argue that instability in this system was the result of maturity mismatches and position risks due to the fact that banks were unrestricted in the types of assets that they could hold in their investment portfolios.

If instability does not come from maturity mismatching, from banks lending long and borrowing short, where does it come from? In a system such as that which prevailed before WWI, in which capital assets are closely held by the capitalist class, a reduction in the rate of economic expansion and the subsequent fall in prices bring instant ruin to both financial and industrial capitalists as their wealth is decimated. This constraint on their spending brings investment and employment to a halt. Note that in this respect, a wide dispersion of ownership of capital assets in the hands of the general public, with professional managers making decisions on behalf of the industrial firms, means that a fall off in the rate of expansion and a fall in asset prices will be more widely diffused throughout the population and not have as direct an impact on those in charge of the employment and output decisions. But, even in such a system, it is still the case that long-term assets are held directly by the public without the intermediation of the banking system so that maturity mismatching cannot be the basic cause of breakdown.

The linkage between financial fragility and economic instability

The simplest answer that may be given is by reference to the historical record of the 1920s, which suggests that it is the deterioration of the "quality" of the assets held by financial institutions. Part of the problem of quality, especially in the latter part of the 1920s, was linked simply to fraud and misrepresentation. A more important part is linked to excessively rapid expansion of bank resources in the 1920s due to international factors.

Anderson (1979, Chapters 17–19) reports massive gold inflows to the US in the early 1920s to which were added three massive purchases of government securities by the Federal Reserve in 1922, 1924, and finally in 1927 to support the UK return to gold. While bank credit expanded by $11.5 billion between 1922 and mid-1927, commercial and industrial loans were declining after 1924. Between 1921 and 1927 the total of outstanding commercial loans and install-ment credits by member banks declined slightly. The expansion in credit, which was not needed to finance industrial needs, went instead into financing real estate lending, which increased by more than $2 billion in the period, and for loans against securities and direct investments in securities, which increased by about $4 billion over the period. There was also a substantial increase in consumer installment lending. All this sounds very similar to the 1980s, doesn't it?

This shift in the composition of bank assets meant that the amount of com-mercial paper eligible for discount at the Fed declined substantially. Recall that the Fed had been set up for the purpose of making the currency flexible, and this was to be achieved by discounting against business lending. More impor-tantly, it meant that when the loans to real estate and financial market investors got into difficulty, they could not be used for discount at the Federal Reserve; as it was then set up, there was no lender of last resort safety net for this type of lending activity. This is why the most important Glass–Steagall legislation is that of February 27, 1932, which extended the range of assets eligible for discount to include government securities, opening the way to open market policy (cf. Kregel, 1992).

As readers of Frederick Lewis Allen's *Only Yesterday* (Chapter XI) will recall, the 1920s got off to a roaring start with the Florida real estate boom, followed by a crash, which initiated the string of bank failures, which was further exac-erbated by the stock market crash and culminated in the string of bank holidays in February and March of 1933. In a 1931 study of Florida state banks' balance sheets for the period 1922–8, Dolbeare and Barnd (1931) found that the major difference between the balance sheets of failed and successful banks was "the larger and more rapid increase of the resources of the failed banks," which

> created problems of wisely investing the added funds. . . . It was necessary to reach a conclusion as to how long these funds would be left in the bank, and then it had to be decided in what type of assets the funds should be invested. . . . If the return of these funds should be demanded unexpectedly at a later date, and the funds had not been invested properly so they could be recalled at once, the banks would be in serious difficulties. . . . The rapidity of the inflow of new funds . . . made it necessary for the failed banks to decide their policy quickly, and probably led to a hasty analysis of the new loans and securities in which the funds were invested. . . . it is not strange

that mistakes were made, since there is nothing to show that the officers of the failed banks possessed superior wisdom. . . . The large and rapid reduction of their resources in the post-boom periods was the immediate cause of the failed banks closing their doors.

(p. 14)

The study shows that the ratio of loans and discounts to deposits for the failed banks increased from 76% to 81% between 1922 and 1927, while it fell from 71% to 61% for the successful banks. Of the loans and discounts, the failed banks increased their lending on real estate more than threefold during the period, whereas the successful banks increased such lending by less than 50%. As a percentage of resources, real estate lending grew from 14% to 17% for the failed banks, whereas it fell from 16% to 12% for the successful banks.

Even more interesting is the finding that the ratio of equity to liabilities for the failed banks was higher than that for the successful banks in the entire period (except for the year 1925). "In other words the owners of the failed banks were furnishing a larger proportion of the funds for which the banks were liable than were the owners of the successful banks" (p. 34). Investors were clearly attracted to the more speculative, faster-growing banks, although presumably at that time there were no economic consultants to justify their behavior.

The study does not give data on the stock price of the failed banks, but it can be assumed that their rapid growth produced better-than-average increases in prices so that these banks were able to increase their capital by new issues at costs that were lower than the prudent banks. Thus a boom in bank stocks creates cheap funding that is used to finance a boom in real estate. This would be an identical situation what George Soros identifies as the "reflexivity," which existed in the REITs in the 1970s (cf. Soros, 1987, p. 66ff). In such cases neither public scrutiny of bank balance sheets nor capital ratios would have prevented the propagation of the crisis.

As Allen reports, most of the purchases were financed on a 10% down basis against blueprints of development sites, without legal documentation or inspection, and in the expectation of being sold at higher prices before any additional balance was due. As long as prices continued to rise, everyone could continue to meet payments; as soon as prices stabilized, the bottom fell out of the market, leaving the banks that had financed the purchases holding collateral that was often in the form of a pyramid of successive binders without documentation for plots of Florida swamp.

But, this was only a practice run for the stock market boom of 1927, which got underway just as the Florida real estate boom was collapsing. The mechanism was more or less the same, with margin money replacing the down payment and financial assets (also often representing little more than blueprints) replacing plots of land.

In general, it was the rapid increase in bank resources that led to increased laxity in lending criteria as banks competed with each other to find borrowers, producing a decline in asset quality, which emerged as soon as there was a fall in the growth rate of resources. This comes very close to Minsky's definition of financial fragility. It is the fall in the rate of expansion of lending that produces the fall in prices and the ensuing debt deflation. It is the change in liquidity preferences of the banks that eventually leads them to stop liquidity creation rather than the maturity mismatch, which causes fragility.

Eliminating fragility by regulatory reform

From this historical background it would appear that there are two ways in which reform to prevent fragility from producing instability could have been approached. One would have been to try to eliminate the acceleration and deceleration of bank reserves and the creation of liquidity, which means stabilizing the expansion of bank reserves. This is the path that was eventually advocated by monetarist economists who wanted to place the Federal Reserve on a monetary expansion rule. It is also considered impossible by most who recognize the endogenous nature of the money supply and the importance of financial innovations; liquidity cannot be controlled. This is also at the basis of Minsky's belief that fragility is inherent or endogenously produced by the successful operation of the system.

This leaves only the possibility of changing the transmission process by which the excessive growth of liquid resources could produce asset quality deterioration by preventing banks from lending against real estate, financial securities, and other non-commercial assets and by preventing fraud in the creation and trading of investment assets. This is the path that was chosen in the New Deal Banking and Securities legislation. By segmenting commercial from financial or investment banking, the ability of the commercial banks to seek new areas of lending outside the traditional C&I loan was restricted. Lending to real estate was set off in its own protected Home Loan Bank system, and investment underwriting was reserved to non-deposit takers. In this way the system also had imposed on it a type of de facto maturity matching, with institutions segmented by the maturity and risk of the assets in which they dealt.

The securities legislation was meant to prevent fraudulent representation by placing controls on both issuers and purchasers and by regulating the secondary markets in which they were traded. Thus, although legislation could not give bankers "superior wisdom," it could prevent their excessive optimism from finding an outlet in excessively risky, illiquid assets and limit the damage that would be caused. Thus, the structure of the system will not prevent fragility, but it should be able to control the transmission of fragility into instability and crisis. The introduction of New Deal legislation eliminating fraud and the increasing dispersion of share ownership were both factors that damped the propagation of financial distress in the post-war period. The more or less steady expansion that occurred was enough to insure the absence of severe crisis.

It is also true that the New Deal legislation introduced strict market segmentation among financial institutions dealing with different types of asset classes and thus brought about a de facto reduction of potential maturity mismatching in portfolios. In particular it forbad banks from borrowing short and lending against long-term assets. But, this is perhaps the least important part of the stability of the period, for severe mismatching did not exist in the pre-war period.

Is the current financial system more or less "fragile"?

It is both interesting and paradoxical that the modern US system, which is now characterized as one in which "markets" dominate over financial institutions, is one in which a much larger proportion of capital assets are held on the balance sheets of financial institutions. As suggested, one might distinguish this difference in terms of the secondary market for securities dominated by "brokers" and the financial institutions being dominated by "dealers." It is easier to see that markets are increasingly dominated by dealers who do hold assets (and mismatches) on their balance sheets.

This is due, on the one hand, to the rise of large institutional investors. More than half of the outstanding equity of US corporations are held by institutions as fiduciaries rather than by private individuals. Pension funds and insurance companies are particularly important in this respect. However, these are clearly institutions that match long-term demands for assets with the firms' demand for long-term lending. Their growth is largely the result of legislation forcing households to make contractual savings for long-term purposes. Changes in the value of equity thus have a much more diffused impact on the system and do not necessarily have an impact on management decisions as when the inside owners were also the managers. But, the rapid growth of funds to be invested has pushed institutions into investments that bear higher degrees of risk, with both insurance companies and pension funds substantial investors in merger and acquisition and speculative real estate ventures.

However, the other side of this coin is that the size of the institutional "buy-side" has meant that the financial intermediaries on the "sell-side" have had to expand beyond being mere brokers. In addition, banks (both commercial and investment) are increasingly acting as principals investing their own capital to produce earnings that have been lost as commercial lending has moved to the commercial paper market and as fixed commissions on underwriting and broking for secondary trading have eroded brokerage revenues. Thus, an increasing proportion of maturity transformation is for the first time occurring on the balance sheets of financial institutions as banks are freed to compete for an increasingly wide range of assets. The first experiment was with the savings and loans, which were allowed to expand the range of their investments and to compete with other institutions in issuing liabilities, with a rapid increase in maturity mismatching and a rapid decline in asset quality. The financial structure thus has an increasing potential for producing severe maturity mismatches, which increase potential instability. It also has increased potential for increasing competition for assets when there is an expansion in bank reserves or when financial innovation makes reserves more powerful (we used to call this an increase in velocity or in the multiplier). This means more rapid asset quality deterioration in an expansion and a system that propagates fragility more rapidly. The financial structure may then be said to be more fragile and more unstable than in the post-war period, placing more responsibility on the central bank to prevent the expansion of liquidity. It also means that a new administration, eager to promote the expansion of employment by means of an expansionary policy, should act quickly to prevent the possibility of the kinds of "reflexive" processes that increase the risks of rapid fragility propagation should that expansion prove to be successful. Minsky's hypothesis tells us that the fragility will be the natural result of the success of the expansionary policy; rethinking the way banks and financial markets are regulated will be required to ensure that the fragility does not produce another round of excess and then a collapse that allows "It" to happen again.

Note

1 Professor of political economy, University of Bologna, Italy. This paper was presented at the Association for Social Economics Session: "The Current Financial Crisis and Hyman Minsky's Financial Instability Hypothesis" of the Allied Social Science Associations meetings held in Anaheim, California, January 7, 1993, 8:30 am. Financial support from an Italian Ministry for Universities and Scientific Research group (40%) grant: "Non-competitive Market Forms and Economic Dynamics" is gratefully acknowledged.

References

Allen, Frederick Lewis (1931) *Only Yesterday: An Informal History of the 1920's*, New York: Harper Business.

Anderson, Benjamin McAlester (1979) *Economics and the Public Welfare: A Financial and Economic History of the United States, 1914–1946*, 2nd ed., Indianapolis: Liberty Press.

Chandler, A.D. (1990) *Scale and Scope: The Dynamics of Industrial Capitalism*, Cambridge, MA: The Belknap Press of Harvard University Press.

Dolbeare, Harwood B. and Merle O. Barnd (June 1931) *Forewarnings of Bank Failures: A Comparative Study of the Statements of Certain Failed and Successful Florida State Banks, 1922–1928*, Gainesville: University of Florida Business Administration Series, Vol. 1, No. 1.

Keynes, John Maynard (1936) *The General Theory of Employment, Interest and Money*, London: Macmillan.

Kregel, J.A. (1989) "Savings, Investment and Finance in Kalecki's Theory," in M. Sebastiani, ed., *Kalecki's Relevance Today*, London: Macmillan, pp. 193–205.

——— (1992) "Minsky's 'Two Price' Theory of Financial Instability and Monetary Policy: Discounting vs. Open Market Intervention," in S. Fazzari and D. Papadimitriou, eds., *Financial Conditions and Macroeconomic Performance: Essays in Honor of Hyman P. Minsky*, Armonk: M.E. Sharpe, pp. 85–103.

Minsky, H.P. (1982) *Can "IT" Happen Again: Essays on Instability and Finance*, Armonk: M.E. Sharpe.

——— (1986) *Stabilizing an Unstable Economy*, New Haven: Yale University Press.

Soros, George (1987) *The Alchemy of Finance*, New York: Simon and Schuster.

3 Universal banking, US banking reform and financial competition in the EEC[1]

Introduction

The German financial system has become the subject of increasing attention by economists and policy makers in both Europe and the United States. The process of economic and monetary unification initiated with the implementation of the Single Market Act and in prospect of a European Monetary Union is expected to increase competition in EEC financial markets. Since financial institutions will be subject to the principles of mutual recognition and home country regulation, except in the case of prudential controls, competition will also involve national systems of regulation. It is generally assumed that market efficiency is greater the lower the extent of market regulation. On these grounds the German financial system, characterised by "universal" banking with unrestricted entry into all types of financial market, is expected to become the dominant form which will force other countries to introduce similar national regulatory systems or face the prospect of their financial institutions emigrating to Germany to be able to compete on an equal basis with German banks.

In the United States, difficulties in the commercial banking system have quickly followed the crisis of the savings and loans banks. The problems facing the commercial banks are generally believed to be the result of financial market legislation which currently allows non-deposit-taking investment banks to compete in areas such as commercial lending and transactions services which have traditionally been restricted to deposit-taking commercial banks, while preventing the banks from entering those markets, such as underwriting and securities dealing, which have been, and remain, the preserve of investment banks. Since a "universal bank" may engage in both retail deposit-taking and the financing of industry through underwriting, brokerage, and ownership of financial and corporate debt and equity, the unrestricted German system has been suggested[2] as an alternative to the "segmented" US financial system. Support for the unification of banking and finance is also found in some recent studies which suggest that universal bank systems may provide lower capital costs to industry,[3] and thus offer national competitive advantages to those countries who do not impose segmentation.

Critics of "universal" banking have suggested that financial institutions free to operate in all financial markets would present substantial risks of conflicts of interest and fail to provide sufficient investor protection. This might occur, for example, when a bank who is a major short-term lender to a company becomes responsible for advising the company on the issue and pricing of securities which the bank is also responsible for placing with buyers who may also be among its brokerage or trust clients, and which the bank may also buy or sell for its own proprietary trading account. While it is not impossible that the different sections or subsidiaries of a single institution should act in the best interests of its industrial client, its private and trust clients, as well as its own shareholders, the "universal" banking system does nevertheless create a potential conflict of interest between the banks and its various clients which opens a possibility for abuse which is absent by definition in a segmented system.

In addition, active participation in underwriting or proprietary trading may lead banks to take investment risks which are incompatible with their role as deposit-takers and thus as part of a national payments system. In financial systems which operate with implicit government guarantees, explicit deposit insurance, or with central banks charged to provide lender of last resort lending support, this means that some of the increased risk will be borne by the general public. This is the "free rider" problem which emerges (as it has in the US) when government explicitly or implicitly guarantees deposit liabilities of private banks used as public means of payment without exercising detailed prudential control over the level of risk associated with the investments which the bank may undertake with the funds raised by offering guaranteed deposits.

Despite these risks inherent in a unified system, the German financial system appears to have been at least as, if not more, stable than more highly regulated systems, such as in the US, which are based upon strict regulation of market segmentation. The present paper suggests that the success of the German system has less to do with the freedom granted to universal banks,[4] than with the alternative approach to bank regulation and supervision which in certain respects is as restrictive as market segmentation. This has allowed the German system to maintain a pattern of specialisation among financial institutions, as well as a particular distribution of securities ownership between firms, banks and the public.

The legacy of the 1920s Great Crash and the 1930s Great Slump

The US response

Before the crisis of the 1920s the US financial system resembled the then more advanced European financial centres with widespread operation of what are now called universal banks. The response to the "Great Crash" of 1929 and the subsequent series of bank failures, culminating in the "Bank Holiday" of 1933, was embodied in the 1933 Glass Banking Act and the Securities Act of 1933, the Securities and Exchange Act of 1934 and the 1935 Banking Act. This legislation limited financial institutions to operations in segmented markets, defined in terms of the financial "products" traded in them, subject to direct governmental or indirect (via self-regulation) regulation.[5] As a result, the possibility of "universal" banks operating simultaneously in a number of different financial markets was eliminated. It also meant that the US conception of financial market "deregulation" was viewed in terms of freedom of access to different market segments.

The immediate intention of the New Deal legislation, under the pressure of the inauguration day bank holiday,[6] was to restore confidence in the collapsing banking system. This aim was pursued by the creation of a Federal Agency[7] to insure deposits (introduced in the 1933 Banking Act and made permanent in 1935). To prevent the fraudulent activity which had occurred during the boom of the 1920s Federal Reserve Board regulation Q limited bank competition for deposits via price competition,[8] and removed the possibility for banks to use deposits to fund speculative activity by severely limiting the assets against which they could legally lend and forbidding underwriting, ownership and secondary trading and brokerage of corporate securities. In addition, the two Securities Acts strictly regulated the financial viability of underwriters and brokers, as well as regulating the financial viability of the companies issuing liabilities and requiring them to issue full financial information concerning their conditions. It thus excluded potentially weak or fraudulent financial and industrial companies from the capital market, and required those who were admitted to provide full information to potential investors.

The response to the crisis thus provided for recapitalisation of the banks, provision of blanket federal insurance for their deposits up to $5,000, but imposed restrictions on bank competition for funds via price, as well as restricting the destination of those funds to short-term commercial lending or government securities. Restrictions were also placed on both the issue of new securities and the trading of securities in capital markets to prevent fraud. These actions preserved the banking system, but did little to create incentives to increase the flow of long-term lending to firms or the efficiency of the allocation of funds to industrial borrowers. This task was eventually taken on by the Reconstruction Finance Corporation which became the *de facto* source of long-term funding of private industry during the depression, and virtually replaced capital markets.[9]

The German response

The German response to the financial crises of the 1930s is perhaps less well-known and the fact that the universal form of banking, which was born in the 1850s,[10] was preserved rather than abolished, as in the US, has led to the idea that the German system is relatively less regulated and thus more prone to the risks believed to be inherent in permitting banks to finance long-term capital market investments with short-term deposit funds. In difference from the US, the German banking crisis of the 1930s was not primarily the result of fraud or the use of deposit funds for speculation in capital markets. It was the result of hyperinflation in the inter-war period and the extensive reliance on foreign borrowing to finance war reparations. The crisis was set off by an outflow of foreign and domestic funds caused by contagion from the collapse of the Creditanstalt[11] and a run on the Danat Bank[12] after the announcement of the collapse of one of its largest clients led to a bank holiday in July 1931.

In response to the crisis the German government created the Akzept- und Garantiebank to provide the third signatures for bank acceptances which were required in order for them to be discounted by the Reichsbank. As a result of this, and other, rescue operations[13] the German government subsequently came to own 91% of Dresdner Bank, 70% of Commerzbank and 35% of Deutsche Bank. A 1933 government sponsored Banking Enquiry reached the conclusion that there were no structural defects in the banking system and that its organisational form was best left to private initiative, subject only to general overall supervision by the government.

As a result the 1934 German Banking Law (Kreditwesengesetz) created a single supervisory agency with blanket jurisdiction over virtually every aspect of financial activity, aside from insurance. By 1936 the big Berlin "universal" banks had recovered sufficiently to reprivatise themselves and, in difference from the US, the German financial system emerged from the 1930s crisis without any direct government intervention or any major structural changes.

Current German bank regulation

During the post-war reconstruction period, there were proposals to recast the German system along American lines (*e.g.* the Dodge Plan of 1945) in order to reduce the potential for the abuse of power by the large banks and industrial cartels which were thought to have brought the National Socialists to power and provided support for German military pretention. Although the large universal banks were reorganised as independent regional institutions (April 1948), the liberalisation of branch organisation introduced in the Large Banks laws of 1952 and 1956, and finally the elimination of any controls on bank location in 1958, allowed the Big 3 banks (Deutsche, Dresdner and Commerz) to regroup their regional units into national institutions within a decade.

The 1934 Bank Law was replaced in 1962, and amended in 1976, 1985 and 1990. The new law preserved the basic regulation of German banks via a Federal Banking Supervisory Office which was made legally independent of the Bundesbank (reporting to the Minister of Economics), although it mandated close cooperation. It also reconfirmed the position of the 1933 Enquiry that direct control over the structure of financial institutions and their entry into particular financial markets was unnecessary, although it did preserve the power to set maximum interest rates (which was quickly abandoned).

The German Bank Law takes an indirect approach to the problem of bank stability and the protection of depositors by requiring a matched maturity structure of the balance sheets of financial institutions via a set of "Principles Concerning the Capital Resources and Liquidity of Credit Institutions".[14] The most basic of these is the 'liquidity principle' (Principle II), which limits long-term lending to long-term funding, defined as the bank's own equity plus sale of bank bonds, long-term borrowing, 60% of savings deposits and 10% of current accounts and time deposits of non-financial entities. In addition (Principle III) the bank's portfolio of loans, advances, discounted bills, quoted shares and liabilities of other credit institutions cannot exceed 60% of current and time deposits of non-financial entities, 35% of the current and time deposits held by financial entities, 20% of savings deposits, 35% of borrowing with a maturity from one month to four years and 80% of the bank's issue of acceptances, notes, bills drawn on itself and international letters of credit.

The capital adequacy rules (Principle I) require bank capital (including reserves and retained earnings) at a minimum of 1/18th (5.555%) of total lending to firms, individuals and its book credits and non-controlling interests. In 1990 this list was extended to include risk adjusted off balance sheet exposures for financial swaps, forward contracts and option rights. In addition, Principle Ia limits a bank's outstanding acceptances, promissory notes and bills drawn on debtors to a maximum of 1.5 times its own capital, calculated and reported on a daily basis. In 1990 Principle Ia "was amended more substantially to limit all 'price risks' – including in particular those arising from off balance sheet financial instruments – to 60% of a bank's liable capital" (1990, p. 39). Within this 60% limit there are individually binding class limits of 30% for foreign currency and precious metal risks, 20% for interest rate risks from interest rate forward contracts and options, and 10% of other forwards and options on shares and index-linked contracts.

Thus, as a result of the spread of new financial products it has been necessary for Principle I to be "extended to constitute a *general counterparty risk principle* going beyond mere credit risk. Principle Ia . . . provide[s] a general set of rules aimed at containing . . . the *price risks* involved in certain types of transactions which are particularly risk-prone because they require little or no capital input (leverage effect)."[15]

Further, there are regulations on the size of loans: single loans cannot exceed 75% (reduced to 50% in 1985) of the bank's own capital; the five largest loans cannot exceed three times own capital (abolished in 1985) and all large loans cannot exceed eight times loan capital.[16] These large loans, defined as those which exceed 15% of bank capital, have to be reported without delay to the Bundesbank, and all loans above DM 1 million also have to be reported. "The main duty of the recording centre is to ascertain the indebtedness of borrowers who have obtained credits of or exceeding DM 1 million from two or more institutions, and to inform the lending institutions regarding the amount of their borrowers' total credit indebtedness and the number of lenders" (Deutsche Bundesbank, *Annual Report*, 1962, p. 95).

These Principles demonstrate the difference in basic philosophy[17] between the German and US approach to prudential bank regulation and investor protection. The German system does not restrict the field of activity of financial institutions in any way, nor does it attempt to regulate specific financial product markets, rather it imposes prudent banking behaviour on all institutions by requiring a matched maturity structure of balance sheets and imposing minimum capital ratios and maximum risk exposures.[18] Within this structure, financial institutions are free to enter any activity and to act in any market without restriction or other direct government regulation.[19]

It is clear that whatever potential instability which might be caused by a single institution acting as a borrower in the short-term money market and a lender in the long-term capital market is restricted by regulations on maturity matching. Active monitoring of detailed balance sheet restrictions in the German system thus may been seen as a substitute for the market segmentation of the US system.

The importance of post-war reconstruction

In addition to its unique regulatory approach, the German financial system has been conditioned by a series of decisions made during post-war reconstruction. The 1948 currency reform had the effect of wiping financial balance sheets clean, in both the public and private sectors. As a result, until 1974 the German government was a net creditor to the private sector, while families were slowly rebuilding their wealth positions through small savings deposits.[20] In 1950–1 the savings ratio of private households was barely above 2%. Most firms had been able to write down or eliminate their liabilities and to build "hidden reserves" by overvaluing assets (allowing large depreciation allowances against taxable earnings) when they drew up their new balance sheets in Deutsche Mark. New investment was financed primarily from retained earnings and bank financing rather than through the capital markets.[21]

Finally, the undervaluation of the DM with respect to the US dollar stimulated foreign direct investment, as well as exports. Thus, until the mid-1950s there was virtually no activity in capital markets for lack of issues by either the government or firms on the one hand, and from a lack of demand from households, on the other. Although banks had the ability to act as investment banks, they did very little business in this area.

The reconstruction of the economy was intermediated by the banking system as households' increasing savings were held in savings deposits and as firms

Table 3.1 Proportions of households total monetary assets (in percentage)

	Bank Deposits	Building Society	Insurance	Bonds	Share	Other
1950	50.00	2.27	16.82	1.36	25.00	4.09
1960	61.56	7.34	17.70	4.94	7.89	7.18
1970	59.07	8.66	16.69	10.24	4.99	6.37
1980	52.99	6.91	17.03	13.21	2.13	9.33
1989	45.59	4.46	21.84	16.77	2.86	8.29

Source: Tables accompanying the article "The capital finance account of the Federal Republic of Germany for (various years)" published annually in the May number of the *Monthly Report* of the DEUTSCHE BUNDESBANK.

Table 3.2 Firms (in percentage)

	Self Financing Ratio	Share in financial Assets		Share in Liabilities	
		Domestic Deposits	Foreign Deposits	Domestic Borrowing	Foreign Borrowing
1950	71.14	61.88	17.33	48.37	11.16
1960	63.86	50.45	21.68	57.74	7.64
1970	65.79	49.34	25.28	59.74	11.13
1980	67.37	48.71	28.36	60.46	10.18
1989	64.50	40.26	35.85	60.11	9.62
1990	65.00				

Source: Tables accompanying the article "The capital finance account of the Federal Republic of Germany for (various years)" published annually in the May number of the *Monthly Report* of the DEUTSCHE BUNDESBANK.

expansion outpaced the growth of internal funds, they increased their borrowing from the banks. The following tables show the relative stability of bank deposits in household portfolios along with the slow increase in fixed interest assets and the decline in their holdings of equity.

This is matched by the slow decline of the ratio of self-financing to gross investment, offset by the rise in borrowing from domestic banks, along with a slow shift in the composition of deposits from domestic to foreign banks.

The decline of internal funding appears to have stabilised in the 1980s, as corporate earnings improved dramatically. This increase in earnings was also accompanied by a three-fold increase in share prices, and an increase in the issue of corporate equity. Thus, the German market was not immune from the global boom in share prices which occurred in the 1980s and listed companies took advantage of the possibility to increase their equity borrowing. Yet, this did not represent a sharp increase in the role of capital markets in allocating financial resources.[22] At the end of 1990 the number of listed companies was only 42 higher than in 1980, reaching 501, or only one-fifth of the total of public limited companies. There are more than 400,000 private limited companies and 100,000 partnerships in the German economy.[23]

Thus, in the 1980s share financing took on a more important role in providing finance for the small proportion of German firms listed on the stock exchange. At the same time, internal funds also increased and the "own funds ratio" calculated as the ratio of equity capital and reserves to the balance sheet total for public limited companies recovered to 30%, 4 percentage points above the low reached in 1981. New issues were particularly high in 1990 in the boom which preceded the unification. This increase in new issues in the 1980s does not seem to have changed the distribution of share ownership dramatically, although the banks became more active in the process of underwriting the new issues.[24]

The German system might thus be described as one in which households hold deposits in banks which are subject to maturity matching and capital controls

Table 3.3 Pattern of share ownership (percentage of total)

Sector	1960	1970	1980	1990
Households	27	28	19	17
Enterprises	44	41	45	42
Public Authorities	14	11	10	5
Banks	6	7	9	10
Non-Residents	6	8	11	14
Insurance Companies	3	4	6	12

Source: "The significance of shares as financing instruments", *Monthly Report* of the DEUTSCHE BUNDESBANK, Oct. 1991.

Table 3.4 Bank security portfolios (in percentage)

	1985	1986	1987	1988	1989	1990	2/1991
Bonds	92.99	91.48	91.86	91.45	89.63	87.69	88.01
Bank	72.00	71.29	70.28	67.50	66.08	64.60	65.43
< 4yrs	13.03	12.09	11.89	9.49	7.65	14.71	16.60
Public	20.92	20.11	21.51	23.89	23.49	23.03	22.41
Industrial	0.07	0.07	0.06	0.06	0.07	0.06	0.17
Shares	2.53	2.75	2.69	2.40	3.01	3.43	3.27
Industrial	2.33	2.51	2.30	1.93	2.51	2.93	2.75
Investment							
Funds	0.73	0.87	1.13	1.33	1.44	1.97	1.98
Other	0.36	0.66	0.43	0.35	0.49	0.52	0.46
Foreign	3.40	4.25	3.93	4.47	5.43	6.38	6.28
Bonds	3.11	3.54	3.41	3.91	4.75	5.92	5.91
Shares	0.20	0.50	0.45	0.48	0.57	0.36	0.28
	(% of total value outstanding)						
Banks holding of:							
Shares	9.03	10.17	10.72	9.87	11.82	14.42	13.55
Bonds	38.89	38.20	38.77	39.85	37.68	36.49	34.89
Bank	42.75	44.20	46.03	47.86	45.01	43.53	41.94
Industrial	11.26	12.07	11.71	12.52	12.95	14.21	35.70
Public	29.86	25.92	25.71	27.16	25.95	25.18	23.39

Source: *Monthly Report* of the DEUTSCHE BUNDESBANK.

which ensure their stability and thus indirectly assure the safety of household deposits. The production and investment of private firms is financed by short and medium-term bank lending, the proportions of which are determined by the division of wealth between households and financial corporations. The major issuers and purchasers of bonds are the banking system, while enterprises hold over 40% of the shares issued by the small number of quoted companies.

Table 3.5 Firm's liabilities (shares of annual flow – in percentage)

	1980	1985	1986	1987	1988	1989
Bank loans:						
short	29.6	9.00	−3.70	−12.30	−17.90	17.76
long	24.5	37.10	59.40	45.50	36.70	43.33
Institutions	4.5	5.90	−0.60	3.60	1.40	0.1
Bonds	0.9	6.20	11.00	14.30	3.50	−0.0
Shares	6.1	7.70	20.00	11.70	5.60	7.22
Money Market Liabilities	1.0	–	–	−0.60	−0.50	−0.21
Other★	33.4	34.10	13.90	37.80	35.60	30.55

★ Includes households claims under company pension commitments.

Table 3.6 Families' assets (shares of annual flows – in percentage)

	1980	1985	1986	1987	1988	1989
Funds placed in Banks	42.1	40.30	53.20	42.20	51.70	22.97
Currency + Sight Deposits	3.1	4.00	9.70	9.70	10.30	4.51
Time Deposits	31.6	9.30	9.90	6.80	8.20	31.50
Saving Deposits	7.4	27.00	33.60	25.70	33.20	−12.44
Capital Market	20.7	20.50	8.40	22.40	14.00	32.86
Bonds	20.9	17.70	7.30	18.90	11.00	37.00
Shares	−0.7	2.80	1.10	3.50	3.00	−4.13
Insurance	21.2	31.10	30.80	29.60	30.80	29.60
Pensions	11.3	9.00	9.60	8.10	6.80	7.80

Source: Tables accompanying the article "The capital finance account of the Federal Republic of Germany for (various years)" published annually in the May number of the *Monthly Report* of the DEUTSCHE BUNDESBANK.

In such a system there is little role for conflicts of interest within banks, for private retail clients hold only small proportions of capital markets assets in their portfolios and industrial clients seldom require the bank to act as underwriter. Capital market assets are primarily held as investments by the banks and are also a favoured source of bank funds, so that any risk which might occur from the process of borrowing short to finance the holdings of long-term capital assets is limited by the constraints on balance sheet ratios. In a similar way, conflicts of interest between the banks and the borrowing firms are limited by the fact that firms issue little equity or bond debt, and by the fact that the banks are also equity holders in the firms so that good firm performance also means good bank performance.

The structure of the German financial system

In the discussions of the advantages and disadvantages of the German system of universal banking there seems to be a presumption that it is completely dominated by a few, extremely large, universal banks which in addition to being subject to potential conflicts of interest may exercise undue economic and political power because of their size. In the German system this is not the case in any absolute sense; although the universal banks are generally larger than either commercial or investment banks in the US, this is simply because they are not subject to the same constraints on products or geographical location.

Nor is it the case that all banks in the German system operate freely in all markets. As the size distribution of the German financial system indicates, institutions dealing in particular product markets co-exist, and actively compete, with big commercial banks. Just because banks enjoy free entry to all markets does not mean that all banks are active in all markets. Yet, the universal bank form dominates two of the four different types of financial institutions which make up the financial sector: *a)* commercial banks (including the Privatbanken), *b)* public savings and giro banks, *c)* special interest co-operative banks and their giro bank, and *d)* special function financial institutions including public and private mortgage banks, building societies, postal savings banks, consumer credit banks and investment companies.

In general private deposits have been concentrated in the savings banks, although the commercial banks have recently increased their activity in this area.

Table 3.7 Size distribution of financial institutions by volume of business: 1990 (m = million DM, b = billion)

	Number	*Branches*	*<100m*	*100–500m*	*550m-1b*	*1b-5b*	*>5b*
Commercial Banks	341	6552	74	100	43	91	33
Big Banks	6	3234	–	–	–	–	6
Regional	192	2976	28	58	28	54	24
Foreign	60	34	13	19	7	18	3
Private	83	308	33	23	8	19	–
Regional Giro Banks	11	311	–	–	–	–	11
Savings Banks	771	19036	7	275	188	267	34
Co-op Giro Banks	4	33	–	–	–	–	4
Credit cooperatives	3392	17402	1903	1288	134	64	3
Mortgage Banks	36	58	–	4	1	4	27
Private	27	50	–	2	1	4	20
Public	9	8	–	2	–	–	7
Postal Giro System	16	–	–	–	–	–	–
Building and Loans	32	63	1	2	7	13	9
Private	19	63	1	1	4	9	4
Public	13	–	–	1	3	4	5
Special Function	18	34	1	2	2	2	11
Total	4621						

Source: *Monthly Report* of the DEUTSCHE BUNDESBANK.

Table 3.8 Share of deposits by type of bank (in percentage)

	January 1991			January 1985		
	Total Deposits	Sight Deposits	Time Deposits	Total Deposits	Sight Deposits	Time Deposits
Commercial	39.57	51.16	31.77	33.07	45.94	42.61
Big 3	8.41	7.23	8.76	8.39	13.99	7.01
Regional	24.62	37.80	13.59	13.09	17.41	12.05
Private	1.974	1.56	1.59	2.37	2.84	1.74
Regional Giro	18.38	15.33	35.30	15.17	18.65	21.93
Savings	10.27	7.85	6.67	11.26	4.69	4.58
Regional Co-op Giro	10.77	9.95	13.30	14.46	21.37	20.27
Cooperatives	4.75	3.30	1.50	6.49	2.69	1.96

Source: *Monthly Report* of the DEUTSCHE BUNDESBANK.

It is also not the case that there are no geographical limits to the operations of banks. The public savings and giro banks are licensed in each Land, much like State chartered banks in the US, and cannot operate outside their Land. Most of these banks were initially established by local governments to provide financing for public expenditures. Since these banks were operated in the social and economic interest of the areas in which they were located, and since in Europe lower income earners did not generally have access to the commercial banking system until the 1970s, they offered payments services in the form of giro clearing accounts which first linked all the local banks in a single Landesbank Girozentrale, and then through a country-wide clearing via the Deutsche Girozentrale. These banks initially dominated deposit-taking in Germany and still have a position equal to that of the commercial-universal banks. Through their Zentrale organisations the individual savings banks located in single Länder combine to form large multi-branch banks which are able to operate just as the larger universal banks and to compete actively with the large commercial universal banks. Each individual savings bank thus has access to the same national and international markets and can offer the same products and services as any large commercial bank, by participating with other small banks through its regional or national Giro organisation.[25]

It would be inappropriate to push the analogy too far, but the German public savings banks face restriction much like State chartered unit banks in the US system, restricted in terms of branching to a particular region and are much like savings and loans in the restrictions on the types of investments which they may undertake. The difficulties that these restrictions have caused in the US have been alleviated by the operation of the centralised clearing organisations which have allowed the smaller banks to operate as partners in a larger single bank which is not bound by the same regulations.

Banks and corporate control

While the universal bank system does preserve substantial competition and has strong supervisory controls on balance sheets which prevent excessive risk in a single bank which takes both short-term deposits and is free to invest in corporate equity, there is one difference that is of importance. In the German universal-bank dominated financial system, corporate equity appears to be predominantly controlled, if not directly owned, by the universal banks, rather than private individuals (or the representatives of private individuals as in the case of the large US institutional investors such as pension funds, insurance companies, investment and mutual funds). Despite the fact, noted above, that officially reported bank holdings (which understate actual positions) are a relatively small proportion of outstanding corporate equity, this is not a good measure of the influence exercised by universal banks.

First, the Commission of Enquiry on "Basic Banking Questions" set up in 1974 to recommend changes in the commercial banking system reported that in 1974/75 while banks owned only 9% of corporate capital stock, they represented 62% of the votes at stockholders meetings (the "Depotstimmrecht" gives the bank the right to represent beneficial owners of shares which they hold as custodians or in trust accounts) and held 18% of the seats on corporate supervisory boards. In addition, the preponderance of short-term lending in firms' total financing means that banks will be more directly involved on a day to day basis in major financing decisions. Although much has been made of the role of the "Hausbank", most German firms have now outgrown the ability of even the largest bank to provide all their required services, yet the high proportion of short-term lending which must be continuously re-evaluated and rolled over means that contacts between firms and their bankers must be active and continuous. In this way short-term lending takes on a long-term character, and it follows as a by-product of this system that only a small proportion of firms seek public listing to raise equity capital. Until 1990 there were fewer than 500 publicly quoted companies (AG). Indeed, it has been the banks, rather than firms, which have been the most active participants in both the debt and equity markets in recent years.

Conclusions

This review of the German financial system suggests that the most significant aspect is not the lack of regulation permitting universal banking, but rather its diverse approach to regulation which substitutes balance sheet regulations for the controls on liabilities and assets produced in the US by market segmentation and which has thus allowed both universal and specialised banks to co-exist. In this sense the US system was just an indirect method of controlling the maturity structure of bank balance sheets which in Germany is directly applied to all banks.

For the USA

This suggests that those who have considered the introduction of "universal" banking as a possible remedy to the US banking crisis and as a way of providing a "level playing field" for commercial banks with respect to investment bank-broker-underwriters, have not recognised the degree to which this increased freedom could only be countenanced if changes were made to introduce German style banking supervision and balance sheet regulation[26] and would include the following radical steps given the current discussions on banking reform in the US:

1   The introduction of a unified supervisory structure for all financial institutions.
2   Single, national charters for all financial institutions.
3   Detailed balance sheet regulations to match maturities and risks.
4   Free entry of all financial institutions into all areas of business, geographically and by product.
5   No limitation on mergers of financial institutions, either within or across product or geographical area.
6   The elimination of government sponsored deposit insurance.
7   The provision of a public transactions structure for individuals. The Fed already provides a clearing house for large transactions of financial institutions, the Post Office could provide a similar clearing house for small payments for individuals who do not have access to the financial system or who do not wish to bear the risk associated with private transactions structures offered by financial institutions.
8   A full revision of SEC legislation.[27]

Anything short of these provisions would run the risk of recreating possibilities for abuse as great as those which existed in the 1920s and again in the 1980s. It should be clear that the introduction of universal banking is more than just removing barriers between financial product markets to create a level playing field, it requires the construction of an alternative set of uniform barriers in the form of a uniform regulatory structure. It is not clear that either the Congress, or the commercial banks or investment banks recognise the extent of the new regulations which would be required to replicate the supposed advantages of the German system.

Neither is it clear that the potential conflicts of interest, which are absent in the German system due to the peculiar structure of asset holdings which developed in the post-war period, would be absent in the US where equity financing and equity investment form a much larger proportion of firms' funding and households' investments and where proprietary trading forms a large proportion of the earnings of an increasing number of large banks.

For the EEC

As far as the European Community is concerned, most commentators appear to have based their analysis of the dominance of universal banking on the freedom of action allowed to German universal banks, without considering the regulatory restrictions on their balance sheets, or recognising that although this freedom is general to all financial institutions, there is still a great deal of specialisation and substantial size diversity in the German system. Further, since these restrictions are part of the German financial system's "prudential regulation", it is unlikely that Germany would allow foreign based "universal" banks to operate within Germany without similarly strict balance sheet regulations. Nor is it obvious that such detailed regulation would be highly attractive to foreign banks seeking to locate in Germany to benefit from "universal" banking. Indeed, this suggests that the question of competition between different institutional forms within the EEC will be closely linked to the question of the prudential supervision of banks within the EEC. Just as in the US, it seems clear that the major prerequisite for the successful functioning of the universal bank system would be the creation of a single EEC agency with responsibility for bank supervision, independent from the European Central Bank, but which cooperates closely with it. It is interesting to note that the amendments to the Rome Treaty proposed in Maastricht make provision for European Central Bank cooperation with such an independent agency at the Community level, but that as yet no formal provision has been made for its creation. It is unlikely that Germany will relinquish these prudential controls over its own banks, nor will it allow domestic competition from non-German "universal" banks not subject to the same controls, without similar legislation at the Community level. It would appear that a major chapter of banking supervisory law has still to be written by the Community before either full monetary union or the predominance of universal banking in the EEC can be considered a real possibility.

On the other hand, given its regulatory structure, Germany will be better placed to reduce or eliminate the costs imposed by other types of prudential regulation, such as reserve requirements or deposit insurance, which play a relative minor, and technically redundant, role in German prudential regulations and serve only as controls on money creation.

Finally, it is of note that universal banking has not become dominant in Germany, so that there is nothing to suggest that it should become dominant in the Community as a whole, even if this is made possible by the adoption of the Germany supervisory system as the community standard.

Conflicts of interest

While balance sheet requirements can do much to curb the risk of maturity and interest rate mismatches which might occur under universal banking, they can do little to eliminate conflicts of interest. The absence of conflicts of interest within the German system seems to have been the happy result of spontaneous market segmentation resulting from the post-war development of the German economy. If private clients seldom hold capital market assets directly and when banks are themselves the largest issuers and holders of securities, the possibility for the kinds of conflict of interest, or fraud and abuse, such as characterised the 1920s, is greatly reduced, although this has not prevented particular cases within the larger German banks. Since this particular structure of asset holding grew out of the experience of post-war reconstruction under Germany's specific banking law, it cannot be replicated in other countries, nor can it be guaranteed to persist in Germany. The problem of conflicts of interest remains to be tested by universal banks who are active on both the issuing and placing sides of the equity markets.

Bologna
J.A. Kregel

Notes

1 This paper presents a shortened version of the first section of a report entitled "Markets and Institutions in the Financing of Business: Germany, Japan and the USA" prepared for the Jerome Levy Economics Institute Conference "Restructuring the Financial Structure for Economic Growth", November 21–23, 1991.

2 See for example the statements by the President of the Federal Reserve Bank of New York in the summer 1989 and spring 1991 numbers of the FEDERAL RESERVE BANK OF NEW YORK's *Quarterly Review.*

3 See McCAULEY and ZIMMER, and ZIMMER and McCAULEY.

4 It is not intended to give a full representation of the German financial system. Excellent presentations are available in FRANKE and HUDSON and in Italian in BARZAGHI, 1988 and 1991, and NARDOZZI.

5 It also meant that financial institutions could not follow synergies in their activity because they were restricted by regulations defined in terms of financial products while markets were increasingly forming around the purchase and sale of "risk"; thus regulations tended to cut across the economic boundaries of the new markets which were developing.

6 Franklin Roosevelt's first act as president after his inauguration in March 1933 was the declaration of a "bank holiday" closing all banks in the banking system. Bank failures for the post-Crash period were:
    1930: 1,350; 1931: 2,293; 1932: 1,453; 1933; 4,000; 1934: 57.

7 Most accounts point to the fall in bank failures to 57 in 1934 as evidence of the success of the deposit insurance program. But the Glass Act was not passed until June and its deposit insurance provisions did not come into operation until the beginning of 1934, leaving unexplained how the banks survived from March to December–the answer is a piece of Hoover legislation, the Reconstruction Finance Corporation which had been supporting banks from February 1932 (Bank of America) and provided the capital necessary to reorganise the balance sheets of the banks which emerged from the bank holiday by direct purchase of, or lending against, preferred stock or capital notes of commercial bank and trust companies, authorised by an emergency bill passed on March 9. See JONES, pp. 17–87. The RFC thus became the owner of substantial interests in class C banks, the weakest banks which were allowed to reopen. As Jones points out, "This program of putting capital into banks prevented the failure of our whole credit system. It was carried out without loss to the government or the taxpayer" (JONES, p. 26).

8 It has also been suggested that the preclusion of payment of interest on deposits was to offset the cost of insurance premiums which were one-half of one percent of the banks' deposit liabilities. The magnitudes do not seem comparable.

9 For those convinced by Kindleberger's representation of the Reconstruction Finance Corporation as the US equivalent of the Italian IRI, one should recall that IRI was a holding company created to receive the equity of (usually failed) corporations removed from

failing banks' balance sheets, while the RFC was operated as if it were a commercial bank, generally limiting lending to good collateral; IRI could not make Jesse Jones's statement that it had not lost the government or the taxpayer any money!

10 As Barrett Whale points out, these Kreditbanks did not initially accept public deposits, but were similar to investment partnerships which only put its partners' capital at risk. They generally lent money to small or newly formed initiatives in the hopes of recouping the investment with a profit when they floated their equity in the companies on the capital market. Deutsche was the exception to this general practice. Only after the crisis of 1873 did these banks actively seek deposit funds, partially through absorption of failed banks.

11 Which had recently merged with the insolvent Boden-Creditanstalt, heavily exposed to industrial borrowers. The French government considered the announcement of the Austro-German Zollverein a *de facto* "Anschluss" of Austria by Germany and a violation of the Treaty of Versailles; this led to rumours, but apparently no more than that, of the withdrawal of funds by French banks from the already weak Creditanstalt and a generalised run on the bank. *Cf.* C.P. KINDLEBERGER, 1987, chapter 7.

12 The Darmstädter und Nationalbank. The Darmstädter was founded in 1853 as the Bank für Handel und Industrie was the prototype of the "new model" of German banks or Kreditbanken which eventually evolved into the universal bank. *Cf.* P. BARRETT WHALE, p. 9.

13 Part of which were the famous large public works programs which were initiated in 1932 as pump-priming for private sector investments. When the latter failed to appear military spending provided a ready substitute. The financing of these expenditures was undertaken by some 31 public "central credit institutes" which may be classified as providing financing for: public works and utilities, personal credit, agricultural credit, manufacturing credit, rural settlement and cultivation of the soil, and urban credit and building, *cf.* POOLE. They very much resemble a decentralised RFC and is a much closer equivalent than IRI.

14 DEUTSCHE BUNDESBANK,*Annual Report,* 1962, pp. 97ff. These Principles simply made formal the "Guiding Ratios for Credits" which had been applied previously by the Bank Deutscher Länder and then the Bundesbank.

15 The detailed procedures for the calculation of the risk adjustments and the computation of the exposure limits is given in DEUTSCHE BUNDESBANK, *Monthly Report,* August, 1990. The weights are generally in line with those in the EEC Solvency Ratio Directive based on the Cooke committee proposals for the BIS international capital adequacy requirements.

16 In addition, in the 1985 amendment to the Banking Law these regulations were redefined to apply to the consolidated balance sheets of banking groups, *i.e.* to include any company in which the parent bank has 40% capital interest or "direct or indirect controlling influence".

17 The approach suggests the German "Ordnungs-" or "Order-" approach to theory and policy based in the work of Walter Eucken which gives priority to the design of the rules and institutions making up the economic framework or "Order".

18 Since the 1974 Herstatt crisis (which was the result of fraudulent foreign exchange trading) there have been additional regulations limiting open foreign exchange positions to 30% of capital plus reserves and retained earnings and the creation of two institutions to insure depositors' funds: In 1974 the Bundesbank set up the Liquidity-syndicate bank which accepts bills drawn by banks facing liquidity shortages which can be discounted at the Bundesbank, and in 1976 the banks themselves created a private "deposit insurance fund" which reimburses individual depositors for up to 30% of the bank's most recently published net worth statement. Bank membership in both institutions is voluntary.

19 It is for this reason that legal reserve requirements to insure that "prudential" levels of reserves are maintained by financial institutions are redundant in the German system, although they do provide an important additional tool of monetary control.

20 This helps to explain why open market operations have never played a very important part in monetary policy–the Bundesbank had to be given powers to force the government to create financial assets which it could trade in the markets.

21 In addition, the tax credits used to encourage investment provided an interesting impact on financial markets. Tax rebates were given on the entire value of interest free loans made by individuals or corporations for the financing of housing, shipbuilding and reconstruction investment by third parties. The loans were taxable when called. See WAL-LICH, pp. 160ff. Wallich estimates that up to 20% of investment in the housing sector was financed in this way. Accelerated depreciation allowed the firms to keep most of their profits, as assets were overvalued in the preparation of the new DM balance sheets.

22 This increase, however, is not directly visible in company accounts. The average issue prices for new shares in the 1980s was four times par value. The increase in equity is given in terms of par value, while the excess of issue over par is entered as reserves in company accounts.

23 In 1987 a secondary market (the "geregelter Markt") was instituted with less stringent listing requirements for smaller firms. At the end of 1990 there were more than 150 enterprises listed. Also in 1987 "Risk Capital Investment Companies", limited liability public companies which raised capital in the stock market to lend to small and medium sized companies unable to meet listing requirements, were introduced. At present there are fewer than twenty such companies.

24 *Cf.* "The significance of shares as financing instruments", see *Monthly Report* of the DEUTSCHE BUNDESBANK, Oct. 1991.

25 This is similar to the correspondent system which existed in the US before the Pepper-McFadden Act of 1927 and the 1933 Glass-Steagall Act. In the absence of this legislation a natural evolution of this system would have been for the larger money center banks to take participations in their regional correspondents to form large national clearing structures which channeled funds to the larger main banks of a form very similar to that in Germany.

26 It is interesting to note that in precisely the period in which capital adequacy requirements were being introduced on an international basis, a comparative study of the financial structure of the G-10 countries (CUMMING and SWEET) did not even consider balance sheet restrictions imposed by the national supervisory authority.

27 Since the SEC is the result of the segmentation between deposit banking and investment introduced by the 1930s legislation many of its activities would be redundant in a universal system under a single supervisory authority, in particular most of the consumer protection provisions concerning information disclosure by firms and securities institutions. Its basic activity would remain oversight of organised financial markets.

References

Barzaghi, Alessandra, "Repubblica Federale Tedesca" in *Manuale per il 1993 e oltre – le strutture creditizie*, G. Vaciago, ed., Milano: Edibank, 1991.

Barzaghi, Alessandra, "Repubblica Federale Tedesca" in *Sistemi creditizi a confronto*, Servizio studi della Camera dei deputati della Repubblica Italiana, Roma, 1988.

Cumming, Christine and Lawrence M. Sweet, "Financial Structure of the G-10 Countries: How does the United States Compare?" *Federal Reserve Bank of New York Quarterly Review*, Winter, 1987–8.

Deutsche Bundesbank, "The New Banking Law and the Deutsche Bundesbank's Cooperation in Bank Supervision", *Annual Report*, 1962, pp. 94–110.

Deutsche Bundesbank, "Business Finance in the United Kingdom and Germany", *Monthly Report*, November, 1984, pp. 33–42.

Deutsche Bundesbank, "Amendment of the Banking Act", *Monthly Report*, March, 1985, pp. 35–41.

Deutsche Bundesbank, "The New Principles I and Ia Concerning the Capital of Banks", *Monthly Report*, August, 1990.

Deutsche Bundesbank, "The Significance of Shares as Financing Instruments", *Monthly Report*, October, 1991, pp. 21–8.

Francke, Hans-Hermann and Michael Hudson, *Banking and Finance in West Germany*, New York: St. Martins Press, 1984.

Jones, Jesse (with Edward Angly), *Fifty Billion Dollars: My Thirteen Years with the RFC*, New York: Macmillan, 1951.

Kindleberger, Charles P., *The World in Depression: 1929–1939*, Penguin, 1987.

McCauley, R.N. and S.A. Zimmer, "Explaining international differences in the cost of capital", *Federal Reserve Bank of New York Quarterly Review*, Summer, 1989.

McCauley, R.N. and S.A. Zimmer, "Bank cost of capital and international competitiveness", *Federal Reserve Bank of New York Quarterly Review*, Winter, 1991.

Nardozzi, Giangiacomo, *Tre sistemi creditizi*, Bologna: Il Mulino, 1983.

Poole, Kenyon E., *German Financial Policies 1932–39*, New York: Russell & Russell, 1969.

Whale, P. Barrett, *Joint Stock Banking in Germany*, London: Macmillan, 1930.

Wallich, Henry C., *Mainsprings of the German Revival*, New Haven: Yale University Press, 1955.

Zimmer, Steven A. and Robert N. McCauley, "Bank Cost of Capital and International Competition" *Federal Reserve Bank of New York Quarterly Review*, Winter, 1991.

4 Market forms and financial performance

Introduction[1]

The government regulation of financial markets introduced in most developed countries during the 1930s represented an attempt to impose a particular form on financial markets that would make them less prone to the instability experienced during the inter-war period. These regulations must be judged a success as major financial crises were avoided for a quarter of a century after the end of the war. However, in the mid-1960s signs of strain were visible. During the 1965 "credit crunch," the US came close to a major securities market crisis. Paradoxically, rather than providing impetus to tighten the regulatory structure, the reappearance of financial instability in the US initiated changes that have eliminated many of the 1930s regulations. This is because the regulations themselves were considered the cause of instability. On the other hand, when instability has reappeared in other countries, such as the failure of the Herstatt bank in Germany, the response has been a continued extension and refinement of regulation to meet changing market conditions.

There thus appear to be two clear, divergent regulatory trends represented by the US and German systems. The form of financial institutions and the structure of financial markets also differ markedly in the two countries. In Germany banks are free to operate in any area of money and capital markets, whereas in the US banks are restricted to a circumscribed set of financial operations such as deposit taking and short-term lending to commercial enterprises, and most capital market operations are forbidden to them. For this reason German banks are often identified as "mixed" or "universal" banks, whereas in the US "commercial" banks are "separated" or segmented from non-deposit-taking "investment" banks that are allowed to operate in capital markets. It is also common to contrast the German "unified" banking system with the "compartmentalized" US system.

This difference has also been characterized as that of "market-based" versus "bank-based" systems. Because a US "commercial" bank is precluded from both direct investments in the equity capital of non-financial businesses and the underwriting, distribution, and market-making of their securities, such financing will take place via direct sale of securities to the public by investment banks acting as underwriters. In a system based on restrictions on commercial bank assets, the allocation of capital is "market intermediated." In contrast, when banks are free to engage as principals in long-term financing or direct ownership of business, as they are in Germany, it is presumed that banks substitute for the operation of capital markets in allocating capital. Such systems are considered to be "bank intermediated." The relation between market form and financial stability is thus often approached in terms of a comparison of "bank-based" versus "market-based" financial systems.

Such simple distinctions may not be adequate to express the most important aspects of the diversity of financial systems. For example, generally stable conditions characterized compartmentalized post-war US financial markets, but conditions in countries such as Germany, Holland, Belgium, and Austria, where unified banking prevails, were no different. Further complicating the issue, Great Britain, whose banks have freedoms similar to universal banks, is usually classified along with the US as a "market-based" system, whereas countries such as Italy, France, and Japan, which until recently had compartmentalized systems imposing "separation" of commercial banks from other forms of banking, are usually considered to be "bank-based" systems.

Finally, it seems obvious that there is nothing to prevent investment banks operating in "compartmentalized" systems from internalizing intermediation, investing on a long-term or ownership basis. It is not so much the existence of compartmentalization as the size of their equity capital and constraints on their ability to raise non-deposit funds that prevents such activity. Nor is there any reason why universal banks should not choose to specialize to operate exclusively as either short-term commercial lenders or as underwriters of long-term industrial finance if this offers the highest return on equity. The difficulties involved in defining the "bank-versus-market" distinction unambiguously, with reference to the difference between compartmentalized and unified banking systems, suggest that these may not be the most appropriate categories for dealing with the relation between market form and financial instability.

Forms of bank organization

The New Deal banking legislation in the US was in large part based on the belief that the collapse of the US banking system was due to the capital market activities of banks' securities affiliates. The legislation thus attempted to increase the stability of the financial system separating banking institutions from those dealing in investment finance. It expressed the widely held belief that "universal" banking systems, which allow banks freedom to enter virtually any area of activity, are inherently more risky than "compartmentalized" systems. This proposition may be illustrated by means of a highly simplified definition of a "bank" as a firm that funds the acquisition of income-earning assets by issuing liabilities. This notional "bank" earns profits from the difference between the costs of its liabilities and the income of the assets acquired. Figuratively, this could be expressed as earning income by "riding the yield curve" for different types of assets. This highlights the fact that bank net interest income results from taking spread positions on interest rates. Income is thus directly influenced by interest rate movements that may be figuratively represented by shifts in the position and shape of the yield curve. It also highlights the fact that bank income will be influenced by the ability to anticipate changes in the yield curve.

The *ideal type* "commercial" bank in a compartmentalized system may then be represented as restricted to operating on a small stretch of the yield curve for a particular type or risk class of asset, say, 90-day loans secured by goods in warehouse or in process funded with zero-interest sight deposits. Universal banks, on the other hand, are free to play wherever they like on (or across) the full range of curves for any risk class of asset they choose.

On this characterization it seems obvious that universal banks will be subject to greater interest rate and liquidity risks because they are less certain to be able to sell assets at prices that will allow them to repay their short liabilities on demand. They will also have greater risk of becoming insolvent because the value of longer maturity assets will generally be more sensitive to shifts or inversions in the yield curve as well as being traded in less liquid markets, whereas the returns on their assets will remain fixed (or may fall if asset prices or dividends fall) when short-term funds have to be replaced at higher costs. Universal banks would thus incur additional liquidity risk and interest rate risk and have more volatile earnings and thus a higher risk of illiquidity and insolvency.

The perception of greater instability of the mixed bank is thus explained by the fact of the greater freedom that it has to incur risks by playing on a wider range of the yield curve as well as across a wider range of asset risks. The universal bank should thus be considered as more unstable than the commercial bank when faced with rapid changes in financial market conditions and asset and liability prices.

History seems to support this view, for it is now generally accepted that the fragility of the mixed bank form was an important contributing factor to financial instability experienced in Germany, Italy, Austria, and the United States in the 1920s and 1930s. Indeed, it was precisely this experience that led to changes in US and Italian bank regulations to place limits on the field of operations of banks.

How to make mixed banks more stable

In terms of the simplified definition of a bank adopted here, the most obvious remedy for the financial instability, which was perceived to have been caused by mixed banking, was to limit their activities to the short end of the yield curves for particular, low-risk assets. This leaves the rest of the curve (and all the curves representing the other types of assets in the economy) to investment banks that are free to accept the additional risk but only with their own capital, not the funds of risk-averse depositors. Such a decision would simply reflect a long-standing banking tradition, first enunciated in the "real bills" doctrine. This is the solution that the 1933 Glass Banking Act attempted to introduce in the

US. In a sense it reflected an attempt to return to the structure of the pre-1920s US system in which the bulk of private individuals' savings had been held in mutual savings banks, in credit unions, and as savings deposits in commercial banks on a long-term basis to finance long-term assets like residential housing. State and national charter commercial banks offered commercial services to companies such as deposits, discounting, and foreign exchange, whereas private, non-chartered and largely unregulated bankers offered underwriting and merger and acquisition advice. Most state-chartered banks and national banks were forbidden from offering such "non-banking" services.

This traditional structure is also reflected in the original design of the Federal Reserve System in the early (Simons) and later (Friedman) proposals for 100% reserve requirements as well as the currently popular proposals in the US for "core" and "narrow" banks limited to investing depositor funds in "risk-free" government securities. All of these proposals are based on the idea that financial stability can be insured by limiting commercial banks to providing transactions accounts to the public on a fee-for-service basis, leaving investment banks to carry on the high-risk investment financing functions of "mixed" banks.

There are a number of difficulties with such a "solution" to the problem of financial instability. The first is that such separation places limits on commercial bank earnings and growth. The income generated from fees and the net interest spread may not provide market remuneration to bank capital. This will limit growth potential. Both of these factors may provide incentives for commercial banks to seek other areas of activity or extend investments to those bearing higher risks.

Another difficulty with such proposals to resolve instability is that "investment" banks (e.g., the non-commercial banks in the US and the Istituti di Credito Speciale in Italy) have shown no revealed preference for engaging in higher-risk activities and do not generally play the rest of the yield curve that had been the province of "mixed" banks. In general, the investment banks created by the introduction of compartmentalized banking systems in the 1930s have not taken over the investment financing role that had been typical of mixed banks in the 1920s. Rather, investment banks in the US have tended to use their funds for underwriting the issue of new capital securities and short-term trading of existing securities as dealers or market makers in the longer segment of the yield curve forbidden to commercial banks.

Provision of liquidity versus provision of long-term finance

This behavior of investment banks in compartmentalized systems has produced an alternative method for providing long-term finance. By making capital markets more liquid, the market-making activity of the investment banks may increase the attractiveness to the general public of holding long-term assets. By taking only very short-term trading positions in long-term assets, investment banks are able to reduce much of the price and interest rate risk associated with investment in such assets.[2] Investment banks in a compartmentalized system have in fact tended to be traders rather than risk-taking, long-term investors in the capital assets of non-financial business. The role played by investment banks has not been to provide the long-term finance for the capital development of the economy, which has been the province of universal banks, but rather to make capital markets more liquid.

Despite formal compartmentalization of the US system, commercial banks also participate in this process of providing liquidity to capital markets, if only indirectly. Although investment banks do commit their own capital, the majority of their position taking is financed by short-term borrowing, usually from commercial banks. Despite Glass-Steagall legislation, US commercial banks have always been free to lend short-term against capital securities as collateral. Of particular importance in the US is the overnight "call money" market, which finances the inventories of the major market makers in both private and public securities. More recently this has been extended to the provision of bridge loans to finance merger and acquisition deals arranged by investment banks.

The "separation" is thus not between risk-limited commercial banks making short-term business loans and risk-loving investment banks committing their own capital long-term but between banks (both commercial banks as lenders to the investment banks and the investment banks as dealers) that reduce one class of risk, liquidity risk, by acting as market makers, whereas households bear the market price risks of holding long-term investments. The more efficient the banks are in reducing liquidity risk, the more willing households will be to accept price risks, the greater the amount of direct capital market intermediation will be through the financial markets, and the lower the price risk will be borne by financial institutions.

From the point of view of the economic system as a whole, this type of organization may reduce overall risk because it spreads price risk over a larger base because there are more households than investment banks. As households generally borrow less to finance their asset holdings (margin requirements are higher than capital and reserve requirements placed on institutions), they are less likely to experience insolvency as a result of price risk.

This type of organization is what might be classified as a "market-based" system. But, its characteristic feature is the distribution of risks across different types of banks and households rather than financial intermediation taking place via banks or through the market. A financial system operating in this way may be subject to less risk, and may be considered more stable, than one in which mixed banks are free to play the yield curve as they please.

But, this leaves an important question unanswered: why banks in a unified system manage their capital investment activities differently from investment banks in a compartmentalized system and appear to be willing to undertake the additional price risks of direct investment in long-term assets. The "facile" answer is that it's not their money but the depositor's that is at risk in a mixed bank. The "easy" answer is that they earn higher returns on such investments, and this offsets any additional risk.

The first response is facile because it implies that households are indifferent to risk. In any case, history suggests that such indifference can quickly turn into pressure to impose regulations on bank operations. The second answer is too easy, for although some argue that direct and durable relationships between banks and companies improve the information available to banks so that selection and monitoring of borrowers are improved, these same advantages are presumably available to investment banks in compartmentalized systems that nonetheless choose not to take advantage of the higher risk despite the potential for higher returns.

Both answers imply that the additional risks identified in mixed systems should produce a tendency for bank form to converge to the lower risk system of separation of commercial banking and industrial finance, either through direct governmental regulation or the operation of the law of natural selection. Yet, universal bank systems have persisted over long periods and, in the case of Germany, have survived the deep financial crisis of the 1930s. This suggests that either the perception of additional risk incurred by such banks is mistaken or that they have evolved protection systems and alternative methods of reducing risks. The question that has to be answered is how mixed banks have managed to avoid the price risks associated with financing their investments in long-term capital assets.

The German example of mixed banking

Some historical background

The evolution of the German financial system provides insight into this question. The German Effektenbanken or Kreditbanks, following the example of Crédit Mobilier and Société Générale, introduced the British idea of joint-stock banking. They played an active role in financing German industrialization in the second half of the 19th century. These were not the only financial institutions in the German system that included note-issuing "noten" banks, joint-stock mortgage banks that issued Pfandbriefe against mortgages on real property, Landesbanken, operated by the provincial governments, which provided local authority financing and provided giro services, Sparkassen, created by municipal authorities to encourage savings, and cooperative credit societies grouped together by the Zentralgenossenschafteskasse, which acted as their central bank. Both the notenbanken and the Hypotheken (mortgage) banks were more closely regulated than the Kreditbanks because they issued special credit instruments, which the latter theoretically did not.

The German banking system experienced difficulties during the 1857 crisis. The difficult financial conditions during the Franco-Prussian war meant that the Kreditbanks often had to support the prices of the shares of the companies they held in their investment portfolios and to carry larger holdings of company stocks than desired. French reparations, starting in 1871, and a liberalization of company law that allowed virtually free formation of companies without government approval set the stage for the creation of additional banks, including two of today's best known "universal banks," Deutsche (1870) and Dresdner (1872).

At this time the formation of a new company was achieved by means of a "simultan (or Ubernahme) Gründig" in which the investment bank invested its own capital and took an active interest in company affairs until shares could be sold to the public at a profit in the stock market. The original model for a Kreditbank was a joint-stock venture that invested its shareholders' capital in forming new companies; they acted as venture capitalists. The first Kreditbanks, which are the ancestors of today's grossbanken, did not borrow short-term from the public by taking deposits. The vagaries of the economic cycle led to periods of frenetic issue activity interspersed with crisis; the result was great variability in bank earnings. This led to a good deal of consolidation and rapid growth of successful survivors.

The Kreditbanks also organized and participated in underwriting syndicates, or Konsortien, for government loans to reduce risk. Thus, all new securities that came to the capital markets did so through the banks acting as underwriters for new firms, existing firms, or the government. The banks also served as official sponsors for the admission of share issues to trading on the official exchanges. The banks were thus the dominant players on the stock exchanges (much like US investment banks).

To smooth earnings the banks set up wholly owned joint-stock subsidiaries to create branches throughout the region. Some sought to expand business abroad and to finance trade, which eventually led to raising short-term funds via deposit taking directly via special offices, "depositkassen," to compete with the "sparkassen" (savings banks). Deutsche Bank was the first to do this (in Berlin) in 1871, largely for its trade financing operations. The move into deposit taking and giro business continued as the Kreditbanks absorbed failed deposit banks. In the crisis of 1873 Deutsche absorbed seven other banks. In fact, Deutsche was not active in industrial underwriting until the late 1880s.

Thus the German Kreditbanks were similar to a private Wall Street bank before 1930 – the fundamental difference being that they were better capitalized than their US counterparts because they were founded as joint-stock banks to invest their equity in industrial ventures and had large subsidiary branch networks. Because they looked upon company investments as short or medium term, and because they offered combined deposit-underwriting facilities to the firms they had launched on a long-term relationship basis, they were more actively involved in the operation of the stock market than British merchant bankers or US investment bankers.

German response to the banking crisis of the 1930s

This structure was to emerge virtually untouched from the financial turmoil of the 1930s, which so changed the face of the US financial industry. The German banking crisis of the 1930s was different from the US. It was not the result of a speculative frenzy in stocks, nor was there a run on the banks by domestic depositors. It was the lagged result of hyperinflation in the inter-war period that decimated the large joint-stock banks' equity capital and led to extensive reliance on foreign borrowing. The banks thus encountered difficulties only when the flows of foreign funds into Germany were reversed by the attraction of the late 1920s US stock market boom and rising US interest rates. Conditions worsened with the defeat of the government coalition in September 1930, which brought the National Socialists to prominence. The condition of the banks became critical with the collapse of Austrian Creditanstalt and a run on the Danat bank after the collapse of one of its largest clients. The savings banks and their central giro institutions were also in difficulty as a result of their lending to local and state governments, of which they were formally a part, and their dependence on foreign borrowing. After a "bankers" rescue attempt failed because of Deutsche Bank's refusal to participate, the Danat folded on July 13, 1931. This produced a domestic run on the large banks.

The German government declared two bank holidays in rapid succession in July 1931, and payments were not resumed until August 1931. The government was well placed to respond to the crisis, for its direct presence in the financial sector included the Reichskreditgesellschaft and a large number of special purpose banks that had been created in the 1920s. The government also formed the Akzept und Garantiebank to provide the third-party signatures required for bank acceptances to be discounted by the Reichsbank. This provided temporary liquidity; a more durable solution was provided by the reorganization of the private banks by the Golddiskontobank, which took equity ownership and extended emergency credit in a way that foreshadowed the actions of Jesse Jones of the US Reconstruction Finance Corporation after the US Bank Holiday in 1933. The German government came to own, directly or indirectly through the Golddiskontobank, 91% of Dresdner Bank, 70% of Commerzbank, and 35% of Deutsche Bank.

A government-sponsored banking enquiry, proposed on the expectation that it would recommend abolishing mixed banking, was eventually carried out under the National Socialist government. It reported in 1933 that there were no structural defects in the banking system and that its precise organizational form was best left to private initiative, subject only to general overall supervision by the government. It should be recalled the government already had extended ownership and virtual control over the financial system.

The German Banking Law (Kreditwesengesetz) of 1934 embodied this view of the structure of the system and was limited to the creation of a single supervisory agency with jurisdiction over every type of financial institution (except insurance companies). It set the basis for the current bank legislation and included the creation of the Bank Supervisory Board, which was to license banks, required monthly reporting, and made provisions for maturity matching and reporting of large loans. The big Berlin "universal" banks were reprivatized by 1936. Thus, despite similar practical reactions to the crisis to those in the US, the German financial system emerged from the 1930s without any major changes in financial structure similar to the separation of commercial and investment banking.

Stability of German mixed banking in the post-war period

The performance of the German system in the inter-war period conforms to the presumption of the inherent instability associated with mixed banking. It does not, however, support the belief that such banks provide a substitute for the capital market. The operation of German universal banks was closely linked to the existence of an active stock market. The basic difference is that although mixed banking was retained, the instability normally associated with it was nonetheless eliminated in the post-war period.

The explanation of this seeming paradox can be found in the German bank law of 1934, which still serves as the basis for bank regulation. In general, it does not restrict banks to the types of business they can engage in (although there are some restricted areas). Instead it places constraints on the composition of bank balance sheets. These take the form of "Principles Concerning the Capital Resources and Liquidity of Credit Institutions."[3]

The most basic of these is the "liquidity principle" (Principle II). It broadly limits long-term lending to long-term funding, which is defined as the bank's own equity plus the sum of the outstanding bank bonds, long-term borrowing, 60% of savings deposits, and 10% of current accounts and time deposits of non-financial entities. In addition, Principle III limits the bank's portfolio of loans, advances, discounted bills, quoted shares, and liabilities of other credit institutions to a maximum of 60% of current and time deposits of non-financial entities; 35% of the current and time deposits held by financial entities; 20% of savings deposits; 35% of borrowing with a maturity from one month to four years; and 80% of the bank's issue of acceptances, notes, and bills drawn on itself; and international letters of credit.

Finally, the capital adequacy rules of Principle I require bank capital (including reserves and retained earnings) to be at least 1/18 (5.555%) of total lending to firms, individuals, and its book credits and non-controlling interests. In 1990 this list was extended to include risk-adjusted off balance sheet exposures for financial swaps, forward contracts, and option rights. Principle Ia limits a bank's outstanding acceptances, promissory notes, and bills drawn on debtors to a maximum of 1.5 times its own capital, calculated and reported on a daily basis. In 1990 this was amended more substantially to limit all "price risks," including in particular those arising from off balance sheet financial instruments – "to 60% of a bank's liable capital" (1990, p. 39). Within this 60% limit there are individually binding class limits of 30% for foreign currency and precious metal risks, 20% for interest rate risks from interest rate forward contracts and options, and 10% of other forwards and options on shares and index-linked contracts.

As a result of the introduction of new financial products, Principle I has been

> extended to constitute a *general counterparty risk principle* going beyond mere credit risk. Principle Ia . . . provide(s) a general set of rules aimed at containing . . . the *price risks* involved in certain types of transactions which

are particularly risk-prone because they require little or no capital input (leverage effect).

There are also regulations on the size of loans: a single loan cannot exceed 75% (reduced to 50% in 1985) of the bank's own capital; the five largest loans cannot exceed three times own capital (abolished in 1985); and all large loans cannot exceed eight times loan capital.[4] Large loans, defined as those that exceed 15% of bank capital, have to be reported without delay to the Bundesbank, and all loans above DM 1 million also have to be reported.

> The main duty of the recording center is to ascertain the indebtedness of borrowers who have obtained credits of or exceeding DM 1 million from two or more institutions, and to inform the lending institutions regarding the amount of their borrowers' total credit indebtedness and the number of lenders.
>
> (Bundesbank Annual Report, 1962, p. 95)

In simple terms the regulations imposed in Germany as a result of the 1930s crisis produced the practical equivalent of the separation of commercial and investment banks by imposing asset separation within the balance sheet of a single "mixed" bank. A German bank is required to maintain a generalized matching of assets and liabilities within particular segments of the yield curve and risk classes. Reduction in liquidity risk for banks holding long-term capital assets is achieved by imposing a rough matching of maturities of assets and liabilities in the long and short segments.

However, such regulation does not necessarily eliminate price risk. Price risk would only be eliminated if banks matched the particular payment and return characteristics of assets and liabilities, using fixed interest borrowing to fund fixed interest lending of the same terms, and the sale of bank equity to investors to match bank investment in the equity of non-financial firms.

In this respect it is interesting to note that the joint-stock form of German mixed banks in the pre-war period matched equity liabilities with equity assets, much like closed-end venture investment funds. It is even more interesting to note the absence of financing by the sale of new equity in public securities markets and the dominance of fixed interest lending in post-war German capital markets. Despite the absence of regulatory changes, there has clearly been a structural change in the system after the war that has produced a shift from reliance on the equity market to reliance on bond market financing as the central element in the long-term funding of bank investments.

First, just as firms eventually outgrew the ability of their "hausbanks" to finance them, it is clear that it would have been difficult for banks to expand their own equity sufficiently rapidly for banks to provide "external" financing via equity capital for the expanding industrial sector. If the use of pure equity finance had remained dominant, then the German banks would also have become predominantly market makers in securities rather than long-term lenders.

Second, the 1948 currency reform wiped out accumulated asset positions and eliminated the secondary capital market. The financing of firms' investment in the post-war reconstruction period took place primarily through retained earnings and short-term bank borrowing. This implied a radical change in the method of operation of the large banks. First, they could not finance and under-write the issue of shares in the formation of new firms because there was no capital market in which to sell them once the companies were launched. It also meant that the mechanism by which the banks lent short term to finance fixed investment by companies until additional shares could be floated in the securities markets to extinguish the short-term indebtedness could no longer be completed.

As the post-war recovery strengthened, the banks accumulated demand and time deposits and made short-term loans to firms, which could be rolled over only into medium and long-term loans (the ratio of short to medium-long lend-ing was split about evenly in 1954), because they could not be "securitized." The banks were thus faced with an ever-increasing maturity mismatch. Financ-ing reconstruction, in the absence of capital markets, thus recreated instability because deposits could be withdrawn at any time, creating a liquidity crisis, and any change in yield differentials, such as might be caused by inflation, might cause insolvency if short rates had to be increased rapidly to retain deposits while long-term lending rates remained fixed. The former was a threat for the smaller banks, but for the larger banks with extensive branches, the threat of a deposit drain was small. The inflation threat applied to all banks. There was an additional threat due to a loss in deposits from a drain of deposits abroad, but this possibility was eliminated by the existence of controls on both trade and financial flows. This may also explain the concern to maintain balance of payments surpluses, which were achieved very rapidly and have been defended tenaciously in the face of international criticism long after the reconstruction period. There were a number of policy initiatives to attempt to revive the equity market, none of which had any substantial impact.

The shift from the stock market to the bond market

To meet the balance sheet regulations imposed by the banking law, banks started to issue bonds, which were initially held within the financial sector, and then started to be sold to the public. In this way long-term fixed interest liabilities matched term lending, and reliance on bond finance became a substitute for the pre-war use of the equity market. In effect, the banks substituted long-term lending for their portfolio investments in equity and bank bonds for issues of their own equity. The German system is thus no less dependent on capital mar-kets to reduce risk than the US system; both require well-functioning securities markets to provide a reduction in price risks. There is a difference in the type of asset used to provide the maturity matching, with bonds replacing equity in the post-war period. More important, however, is the increased degree of inter-mediation, which has remained characteristic of the post-war system.

It should be noted that despite the freedom accorded financial institutions under German banking law, not all operate in all markets, as universal banks do.

Financial institutions dealing in particular product markets coexist, and actively compete, with the big descendants of the Kreditbanks. Further, government regulation does limit entry to some markets such as insurance and mortgage lending. The four different basic types of financial institutions that make up the financial sector include the following:

a) commercial banks (including the "privat" banks),
b) public savings and giro banks,
c) special interest cooperative banks (and their giro bank), and
d) special function financial institutions including public and private mortgage banks, building societies, postal savings banks, consumer credit banks, and investment companies.

Whereas the large "universal" banks represent a majority of first category, the majority of private household deposits are concentrated in the savings banks. Neither is it the case that there are no geographical limits to the operations of banks. The public savings banks and giro banks are licensed by the regional governments, much like state-chartered banks in the US, and are limited to operations within their land. Most of these banks were initially established by local government to provide finance for public expenditures. Because these banks were operated in the social and economic interest of the areas in which they were located, and because lower income earners did not generally have access to the commercial banking system until the 1970s, these banks also offered transactions services in the form of giro clearing accounts, which first linked all the local banks in a single Landesbank-girozentrale and then through a country-wide clearing via the Deutsche Girozentrale. These banks initially dominated deposit taking in Germany and retain a position equal to that of the commercial-universal banks through their Zentrale organizations. The individual savings banks located in single länder combine to form large, multi-branch banks that are able to operate just as the larger universal banks and to compete actively with the large commercial-universal banks. Each individual savings bank thus has access to the same national and international markets and can offer the same products and services as any large commercial bank by participating with other small banks through its regional or national giro organization.

It would be inappropriate to push the analogy too far, but the German regional public savings banks face restriction much like state-chartered banks in the US system, restricted in terms of branching to a particular region, and are much like savings and loans in the restrictions in the types of investments that they may undertake. The difficulties that these restrictions have caused in the US have been alleviated by the operation of the centralized clearing organizations that have allowed the smaller banks to operate as partners in a larger single bank that is not bound by the same regional controls. Although the large universal banks play an important role within the German system, a great deal of specialization and competition remain.

Thus the overall financial structure, which has been produced by German prudential regulations and the peculiar experience of post-war reconstruction, is a basic factor in explaining the stability of the German system and its ability to hedge price risks. Large changes in asset prices have little impact on households because fixed price, short-term bank liabilities predominate their financial asset holdings. Neither do they have a large impact on firms because their funding comes primarily from retained earnings and long-term bank borrowing. Price risks are thus concentrated on bank and insurance company balance sheets. Given that banks are required by the prudential regulations to hold these assets, they are not considered as trading assets and will usually not be sold. Banks' profits and their ability to lend is thus little influenced by volatility of asset prices and interest rates. Price risks are thus effectively contained.

Bank liquidity risks are contained by the large proportion of savings deposits in household deposits as well as the concentrated structure of the banking system. In the German system, a shift to liquidity by the public is simply a question of clearing among the larger bank giro institutions or the creation of central bank money. A short-term, system-wide demand for liquidity can easily be absorbed without any impact on asset prices or the solvency of the banks.

Consideration of the German example suggests that instead of referring generically to "mixed" or universal banking systems, it would be more informative to refer to balance sheet-constrained mixed banks, such as banks operating under the German type of supervisory regulations. If a mixed bank handles its investment portfolio according to the German prudential principles, it should be no more prone to instability than any other form of bank. In terms of the simple definition of a bank given here, German banks operate under regulations that "separate" or "segment" the yield curves on which they operate into long- and short-term regions. Banks are free to spread only within each region of the curves. The only difference between a system composed of separate commercial and investment banks and a German system of combined or unified banks is that broad maturity matching is imposed by limits on the types of business that a commercial bank may engage in, whereas for a universal bank, it is imposed by limitations on the asset and liability structure of its balance sheet. The fact that neither investment banks, nor mixed banks, are willing or able to raise sufficient equity capital to provide full equity financing for the industrial sector leads to long-term financing via public equity markets in the former and reliance on bond market finance in the latter. In the US this was caused by the dominance of private partnerships and the total absence of joint-stock investment banks, whereas in Germany it is primarily due to the impact of the post-WW II currency reform.

Differences between the modern German and US systems

Despite the general presumption of lower risks for segregated banks, the experience in the US has been far different. There are a number of reasons for this, but three stand out. First, the deregulation that took place sharply eroded the degree to which banks matched the maturities of their assets and liabilities. Commercial banks were not in fact restricted to 90-day commercial loans financed by sight deposits of the simplification used earlier. They had already started making term loans during the Second World War and expanded the practice in peace time. They also operated over an increasing range of types of assets.

In addition, the removal of restrictions on interest rates payable and on the liquidity of different type of deposits created instant maturity mismatches, for example, in the thrifts that made them subject to both liquidity and price risks that they could not hedge and remain profitable. The tightening of spreads caused pressure on earnings and growth, which made increasingly risky activity attractive and caused capital ratios to fall dramatically.

The second is the absence of free geographical expansion through branching and the predominance of the unit bank structure until the 1980s. The risks implicit in this structure were largely absorbed by deposit insurance. It is often argued that in the modern banking system, there is no such thing as a run because gold convertibility no longer exists. The public has to deposit its money somewhere, so that the banking system as a whole cannot lose reserves, and if the public chooses to hold banknotes, these can be created on demand by the Federal Reserve. However, there is a basic difference between this proposition as applied in Germany, where most of the redepositing is in other branches, or can be handled between the clearing centers without recourse to the central bank, and the US system, where banks in difficulty, because they are covered by federal deposit insurance, can raise deposit rates and thus attract brokered deposits from the large investment banks. The German system provides for the offsetting of reserve losses without deposit insurance.

The third difference between the US and German systems is the changing structure of asset holding in the US and the role of investment banks in their role of providing liquidity for holders of capital securities.[5] Table 4.1 gives both a comparison of the US and German systems and the changes in the structure of asset holdings. The small, and falling, share of individual ownership of equity in Germany is notable. In the US, on the other hand, the shift from individual ownership to institutional ownership is clear. Recall that part of the stability of the segmented system was identified in the wide distribution of equity among the general population, which created a wider dispersion of market risk of holding long-term capital securities.

This is disappearing in the US as large institutions become the dominant proximate holders.

This is important because of the role that was attributed to investment banks as providing liquidity to capital markets, which make equity investments attractive to private households. Clearly, it is no longer the private household that is the major direct purchaser of equities.[6] Now, liquidity has to be provided to large institutions engaging in active portfolio management. This has brought about two basic changes in the structure of financial markets. The first is that to provide liquidity to the markets, investment banks have shifted from brokering and trading to dealing as their predominant activity. Acting as a broker matching orders of household investors who generally adopted a buy-and-hold strategy

Table 4.1 Common stock ownership – US and Germany – 1979 and 1988 – % of total outstanding common shares

1979	USA	Germany
Financial institutions	15.8	12
Commercial banks	0	8
Insurance companies	2.9	
Pension funds	8.2	4
Other financial	4.7	
Non-financial business	9.1	35
Individuals	72.2	29
Foreigners	2.9	15
Other	0	10
1988		
Financial institutions	30.4	15
Commercial banks	0	9
Insurance companies	4.6	
Pension funds	20.1	6
Other financial	5.7	
Non-financial business	14.1	40
Individuals	50.2	16
Foreigners	5.4	21
Other	0	8

Source: Prowse, in Sametz (1991, p. 50)

requires little capital, and trading can be tailored to capital available and borrowing. Markets dominated by large institutions will be moving larger volumes
of securities more frequently, often requiring market makers to take significant
positions. The increased necessity for dealing by market makers requires a
larger amount of capital. Most US investment banks in the 1970s finally moved
to joint-stock form, raising capital via the markets. Commercial banks have
become more involved in lending to "position-taking" dealers and in providing
bridge lending to finance mergers and acquisitions.

The result has been a shift in the US from a system of provision of liquidity
based on low-capital, broker markets to highly capitalized, dealer markets in
which the dealers making the markets are much more exposed to changes in
asset prices than brokers. The risk reduction, which was achieved by investment
bankers acting as a short-term traders of capital assets, has been sharply reduced.
As Keynes emphasized, there is no such thing as liquidity for the system as a
whole. The shift to a large-institution, dealer-dominated securities market has
meant that system liquidity comes much closer to the liquidity available to any
individual dealer. A system-wide demand for liquidity cannot be averted without threatening bank insolvencies because commercial banks are major lenders
to investment banks against their security portfolios. This means that price risks

are no longer borne only by household portfolios but also by the financial system. The US financial system, thus, has become increasingly vulnerable to price risks, which explains the attention that is now placed on risk management. Most of the stabilizing features of a "compartmentalized" system have thus been lost and are in the hands of risk managers. But, the instruments used to provide risk management are also traded in markets by dealers and are subject to the same system constraints on liquidity. It is thus not surprising that the US system has recently experienced more financial market instability than the German system despite the fact that unified systems are generally perceived to be more unstable than segregated systems. But, this is because the German system is not now a traditional "unified" system, and the US no longer has a traditional "compartmentalized" system.

This suggests that the most important distinction in analyzing the relation between market form and financial instability is in the way maturity matching is imposed on financial institutions. In the US since the New Deal, it has been imposed by dictating a particular financial structure, whereas in Germany it has been imposed by dictating a particular balance sheet structure. In retrospect, it seems that the US approach would have required more frequent revision of the legislation defining the permissible activities of commercial and other banks to take account of changes in competition and technology, whereas the German approach required frequent revision of the balance sheet controls and supervisory responsibilities. It seems to have been easier to make the latter changes than the former. Indeed, the US has simply acted to soften the legislative constraints on permissible banking activity without introducing any alternative regulation in the form of balance sheet controls used in the German system to enhance stability. This is primarily because the legislation, rather than the method of imposing maturity matching, is seen as the cause of instability. The comparison between mixed and compartmentalized systems suggests that this assumption has no basis.

Notes

1 I am grateful to Andrew Cornford and Hyman Minsky for constructive criticisms received in drafting this paper. It draws on work for an Ente Einaudi research project on the future of banking. A detailed account of the implication of universal banking for reform proposals in the US and the EU may be found in Kregel (1992).

2 Capital requirements applied by the SEC to investment banks and broker firms also provide incentives to act as dealers because highly liquid dealer inventories absorb less capital than investment assets as they have a lower "haircut" applied to them. Capital requirements are thus lower the more liquid the assets held. This factor is especially important given the partnership form of such banks, and their low capitalization, until the move to incorporation in the 1970s.

3 The regulations given here are those that applied after the war, and with additions and modifications, up to the beginning of 1993, when significant adjustments were required to make German law compatible with the EU Banking Directives.

4 As a result of the Herstatt collapse, a 1985 amendment to the banking law extended these regulations to consolidated balance sheets, that is, to include any company in which the parent bank has 40% capital interest or "direct or indirect controlling influence."

5 These issues are dealt with in more detail in Kregel (1993).
6 By 1994 households and financial institutions held roughly equal proportions of total out-standing corporate equity – around 47%. See *New York Stock Exchange Fact Book 94*, New York, April, 1995, p. 83.

References

Deutsche Bundesbank (1962) "Annual Report," The New Banking Law and the Deutsche Bundesbank's Cooperation in Bank Supervision, pp. 94–110.

——— (March 1985) "Amendment of the Banking Act," pp. 35–41.

——— (August 1990) "The New Principles I and Ia Concerning the Capital of Banks".

Kregel, Jan Allan (September 1992) "Universal Banking, US Banking Reform and Financial Competition in the EEC," *Banca Nazionale del Lavoro Quarterly Review*, No. 182.

——— (February 1993) "Instability of the Economy and Fragility of the Financial Structure," University of Bologna, Working Paper #158.

New York Stock Exchange (1995) *Fact Book 94*, New York: New York Stock Exchange.

Prowse, Stephen D. (1991) "Comments on the Changing Role of Institutional Investors in the Financial and Governance Markets," in Arnold W. Sametz (in collaboration with James L. Bicksler), ed., *Institutional Investing: The Challenges and Responsibilities of the 21st Century*, New York: Business One Irwin.

Sametz, Arnold W. (in collaboration with James L. Bicksler), ed. (1991) *Institutional Investing: The Challenges and Responsibilities of the 21st Century*, New York: Business One Irwin.

5 Some considerations on the causes of structural change in financial markets[1]

Economic theory has never had a great deal to say about markets, much less about financial markets, and even less to say about changes in institutional structures. It is thus something of a paradox that economic theory, and in particular general equilibrium theory, has attempted to generalize a particular form of financial market organization to the analysis of the operation of markets in general. Because of the insistence that general equilibrium theory is independent of any particular institutional structure of the economy, some critics have concentrated on the unrealistic nature of the ideal market form implicitly assumed in the theory, rather than on the real problem, which is the presumption that this ideal form is universal.

Walras's description cannot be faulted for lack of realism. It can be faulted because it only applies to some financial markets. The London gold pool fixes prices just as Walras described, and Keynes is witness that Walras based his idealized version of the process of price determination on the Paris Bourse [Hicks 1982, 296].

The difficulty is not that the description of the manner in which prices are determined is unrealistic, but that a particular price determination process used for some commodities (gold) or financial assets cannot be extended indifferently to every type of commodity and service, irrespective of their characteristics. Since Smith and Ricardo, it has been common to distinguish between the factors that determine the prices of reproducible and non-reproducible goods. The corollary—that markets for goods with different characteristics will have different structural organizations—had to wait for Book 5 of the *Principles* by that famous neo-Ricardian, Alfred Marshall. Unlike Walras, Marshall was almost exclusively concerned with the study of markets and the factors that distinguish their diverse structure and organization. Thus, the basic criticism of Walras is his excessive generalization (or perhaps misplaced concreteness): the prices of manufactured goods are not determined by the same type of market organization as common stocks at Palais Brongniart.

Thus, despite its claims to the contrary, general equilibrium theory is based on a very particular form of market organization, and its results cannot be considered as independent of institutional organization. The basic contribution of general equilibrium theory may then be reevaluated as having shown unequivocally that a modern capitalist economy could not function on the basis of a daily auction market such as the nineteenth century Paris Bourse. This revelation is perhaps not earthshaking, but its recognition is sufficient to make the point that traditional economic theory has been excessively influenced by institutions claimed to be orthogonal to the "deep" theory, when, in fact, they condition the entire theory.

That economists have always been implicitly aware of this can be seen in the fact that the example usually given of a perfectly competitive Walrasian market is the stock market. Better informed (American) economists usually recognize that the existence of market makers in the form of "specialists" on the major U.S. exchanges render even this justification of the assumption of perfectly competitive Walrasian market problematical. Yet, up to the beginning of the 1980s, most of the world's stock markets, aside from England and the United States, were still patterned after Walras's Paris Bourse. Indeed, it appears that all financial markets (with the possible exception of London) started out as ideal-type Walrasian tâtonnement markets. There are now hardly any left.

If the relevance of Walrasian general equilibrium theory is crucially linked to this particular market form, then its disappearance suggests that the theory will either have to be abandoned or reconstructed on the basis of an alternative form of market organization. The latter alternative may be seen in the attempts to formulate a neo-Walrasian theory that is independent of the "auctioneer" and based on some form of "fixed" or administered prices. But, this attempt is subject to the same criticisms of failing to recognize that it is implicitly invoking a particular form of market organization that is not generally applicable to market exchange in a capitalist economy.

The simultaneous existence of a wide range of market organizations in the economy suggests that they are in a process of constant evolution, which will have an impact on economic theory. General equilibrium theory can survive unscathed by structural and institutional change only by ignoring this process of internal evolution. The most common approach to the problems of how to incorporate variable and evolving markets into analysis has been via "transactions costs" of organized markets.[2]

A cost of capital approach to market organization

Is there an alternative to the transactions costs approach? I think there is, but transactions costs have become so encompassing that it is difficult to differentiate. The obvious place to start is by noting that a market is an institution and as such, an organization, and like any other organization, it requires maintenance. This maintenance has an economic cost. Now, those who reason in terms of transactions costs will argue that this is precisely what is covered by the term. The important question is not the existence of these costs, irrespective of how they are defined, but rather who bears the costs of maintaining the market institution.

Let us look at the idealized Walrasian market and remember that the first financial markets were in streets, alleyways, and public coffee houses; the overheads represented by the Palais Brongniart were thereby avoided. The major cost was labor. The man who stood by the chalk board with the list of stocks, called out the prices, balanced the bids and offers, and wrote up the price–the infamous "auctioneer"–had to be fed.[3]

In the type of market Walras described, brokers met once a day at the same time in the same place to trade stocks. This trading was organized by calling out stocks one by one and fixing the price for each sequentially. When the stock is called, an employee acting on behalf of the brokers proposes a price and tries to match all the buy and sell orders[4] announced at that price; if he cannot match all of them, he tries another price until he succeeds. The final price becomes the official market price, or the fix. All orders to buy or sell at this price are executed, as are orders to buy at a higher price or to sell at a lower price. There is thus a single price, which is the same for both buyers and sellers. This is a market in which there is perfect information because all orders, which exist at any price, are presumed to be in the possession of the agents and are publicly exhibited when the associated prices are announced. In Walras's day, the *agents* themselves, being officials of the crown with monopoly access to the market, could not place orders on their own account, so there could be no abuse of this information. This is what I have called, following Braudel,[5] a "public market" since all information is exposed simultaneously to all participants [Kregal 1990a]. The process of price determination is sufficiently short so that information can be considered as given. Once the price of the last stock is fixed, the market "day" is over and no trading takes place until the following day. It is thus a "discrete" market, which trades only at discrete intervals, with periodic fixed trading "suspensions" during which new orders are collected on the basis of the new information that reaches clients. The basic difference between a "call" market and the Walrasian mechanism is that prices are fixed sequentially–once a price is fixed, there is no going back to make a different bargain for a stock higher on the list on the basis of the fixed price for a stock lower on the list. The primary costs of this type of market are limited to the chalk and the wages of the auctioneers, with secondary costs including the building and fixtures.

Wages are the primary indirect cost associated with brokers acting as agents on behalf of clients. The broker commits no own funds, nor does the auctioneer, who is usually a salaried employee of the group of brokers trading in the exchange; however, neither requires capital in order to function. The market thus provides an order-matching process that produces liquidity by waiting between trading sessions to allow sufficient market and limit orders to accumulate. In addition, when a stock is called, if there is a large imbalance in buy and sell orders so that price will move by more than a fixed percentage from the previous "fix," the stock is suspended for the day to allow more orders to accumulate.

Liquidity in a "public" market is a function of both the flow of orders to the market and the time between "calls," not the agents' nor the auctioneer's capital; since it is "public" liquidity, it carries no direct cost. The liquidity of the market is an externality associated with the size and the organization of the market. Call markets thus have low capital requirements, and rates of return will be relatively unimportant in determining its costs of operation. Furthermore, since it operates without *agents* or the auctioneer taking own position, their solvency will be independent of changes in market prices. Costs of operation will thus also be independent of the evolution of the prices that are set in the market.

The dealer market

Now, let us consider the opposite of the Walrasian call market, a continuous-trading dealer market in which official or registered dealers are obliged to quote bid-ask prices at which they are willing to trade at minimum size. Market liquidity is provided by an individual dealer's willingness to take the other side of any trade. This could be called a "private market," because all trades are negotiated bilaterally and sequentially between the customer (or his broker) and the dealer. Since the dealers are required to trade at their quotes, a bargain can be executed at any time but only at the price the dealer sets. The dealer feeds himself by setting a spread between the prices at which he is willing to buy and the prices at which he is willing to sell. This bid and ask spread is supposed to allow the dealer to sell at higher prices than he buys. But, this is only the case if the market is stable or rising. Whenever a dealer accepts a trade, he is changing his investment position. If his bid is accepted, he must buy stock. In a stable market, if he can subsequently sell the stock at the higher ask price, his profit is given by the difference. If he does a lot of business, he does well–presumably just as well or better than the auctioneer.

But, if the market is not stable and a dealer's bid is hit again and again, he will be accumulating stock without selling. To do this, he has to have capital available (either his own or borrowed) to finance his increasing position; the more stock he buys, the lower his free capital becomes, and the lower is liquidity in the market. As the market moves continuously in one direction, the dealer will try to retain his liquidity by adjusting his quoted bid price downward; if he still wants to sell at a higher price than he bid for the stock he now owns, the bid-ask spread will have to widen, and transactions costs or the "cost of providing market-making services" will rise as liquidity falls, further eroding market liquidity.

But now there is a second element in the cost of making prices in a dealer market–the capital used by the dealer to make his position will have to be remunerated at the market rate of return, and overall trading activity will have to be such that capital remains intact. The bid-ask spread has to cover not only daily maintenance, but also the interest paid to the bank (or what could have been made by using own capital in alternative employments) and any losses incurred when the market moves consistently in one direction or another. In a dealer market, the movement of both prices and interest rates will have an impact on liquidity and on "transactions" costs. This impact, in turn, will effect the flow of orders to the market and the earnings of the dealers, leading to higher spreads and influencing the level of prices that are set in the market. The reason for this difference from the "call" market is that liquidity in a dealer market is "private" liquidity–it belongs exclusively to the dealer or has to be borrowed by him.

Dealer markets might then be called "capital intensive" forms of making market prices. They are supposed to be more liquid than call markets because they provide for continuous rather than discrete trading, but this is only true in stable or rising markets; in falling markets, the widening of the bid–ask spread will very soon reach a level that brings trading to a standstill. Private dealer markets are not necessarily either cheaper or more liquid than call markets. High interest rates, for example, should not only dampen expectations and reduce stock prices, but also should have a larger impact on dealer markets than on call market costs of trading, causing order flow to be reduced in the former relative to the latter.

The recent experience of the International Stock Exchange in London illustrates why dealer markets are "private" markets. In order to protect their capital and to try to earn returns on capital advanced, it is now the case that there are no firm dealer quotes for any but the smallest sized bargains, and instantaneous transactions reporting has been suspended: market participants may not know either the prices or the quantities at which trades are being made until a day later! Market transactions take place in private between consenting adults—so much for the stock exchange as our example of the perfectly competitive market.[6]

There are thus at least two alternative "ideal types" of financial market organization. The "fix" price market popularized by neo-Walrasian theory should not be considered as a more realistic description of markets because it eliminates the "auctioneer," but rather as a market in which prices are produced by dealers who substitute for the auctioneer, and which has a different capital and cost structure and may therefore have different responses to economic events.

If we now turn to the question of how such diverse market organizations can coexist, or how organization might change from one into another, the answer should be found in the differences in costs and returns to capital. It is also linked to Adam Smith's dictum that the division of labor is determined by the extent of the market. What Smith seems to have intended by division of labor, we now call technology, which means that costs and returns will determine the evolution of trading technology. The evolution of the New York Stock Exchange provides us with an example.

The breakdown of a call market

Until about 1870, the New York Stock Exchange used a call system similar to the Paris Bourse. In the middle of the century, around 25 listed stocks were listed on the Exchange, which had started (as had most organized exchanges) by trading government securities, not industrial shares. When the railway boom hit the United States, there was a large increase in issues. The monopoly position of NYSE traders was also being threatened by curb traders and a continuous market in the "big room" (similar to the trading in the "coulisses," the hallways of the Paris Bourse). The response was to incorporate the big room traders into the exchange. Thus, the extent of the market expanded very rapidly, in terms of both the number of shares and the number of brokers trying to trade them.

This situation created diseconomies for the prevailing labor-intensive technology of the call market.[7]

First, the list of official and unofficial stocks became so long that it frequently could not be finished before the next scheduled call. Thus, although the delay between calls got shorter, the delay between trading in any individual stock tended to increase. Second, the process of taking the balance of buy and sell orders as prices are called out is easy when there are a few brokers, but when the number of brokers participating in a call becomes large, it becomes virtually impossible to process the information rapidly. In short, the labor-intensive technology of the call markets broke down when it became large. Something had to be found. What was found was a new division of labor, a new trading "technology," in which the list was split into a number of shorter lists, and the trading floor was reconfigured to contain a number of trading "posts," each calling the stocks on one of the lists. This reconfiguration meant that an original list could be completed in a shorter time since each mini-list was called simultaneously.

But, this attempt to preserve the call system proved to be its undoing. Under the call, each broker was present to contribute his orders to the fix of the price of every stock on the list. Physics teaches us that a mass—even a broker—cannot be present in two places at the same time. With simultaneous mini-calls taking place, a broker could not be present at all of them. Hiring clerks to represent the broker at the other posts would have only made the overcrowding problem worse. The only solution was to abandon the call and to introduce continuous trading at each post. A broker could thus make his bargain at one post at 10:00 and move on to the next post to make a deal at 10:10. Thus, continuous trading was born to get around the laws of physics. It seems that for a short period, both the call and continuous trading coexisted.

But, if continuous trading solved the problems created by space, it introduced a second problem: time. In a continuous market, spatial or geographical sequencing replaces temporal sequencing, but it also makes temporal sequencing random. It was now possible for a broker to miss a bargain since there was nothing to guarantee that all brokers with orders for a particular stock would arrive at the post at the same time. This "random order arrival" may produce order imbalance, even when the overall supply and demand present in the market is perfectly matched.

Imagine two brokers, one with an order to sell Radio at 49 or above and the other to buy at 51 or below. There is no guarantee that they will meet and complete their bargain at 50, since they may not reach the post at the same time and, indeed, may ignore the existence of each others' order. Clearly, prices may behave very differently in discrete call markets than they do in continuous trading markets. In general, because of the spatial and temporal fragmentation of trading, continuous markets will be less liquid and more volatile and have more frequent order imbalance than a discrete call market.

The volatility caused by random order arrival produced a market response in the form of "floor traders," who dealt for their own account rather than taking orders from customers. These traders were willing to step in and take the opposite side of trades they felt certain they could unwind during the day. They thus provided continuity in order arrival. Now, let's return to the brokers trying to trade Radio.

If the broker trying to sell arrives at the post in the morning and finds no counterparty to his trade, a floor trader would step in and offer to be the counterparty, buying at 49. When the second broker arrived in the afternoon to buy, the floor trader could again act as counterparty, selling to him at 51 and taking a two dollar profit for his effort. The floor trader thus became the intertemporal intermediary, earning his living off the spread between his buying and selling prices: Here we find the origin of bid-ask spreads. This activity required little or no capital because the floor trader expected to close out his positions within the course of the trading day, but it did require a good deal of information about prices and orders in particular stocks.

Thus, because brokers knew they were missing bargains because of random arrival, they started to leave orders with floor brokers who began to specialize in certain types of shares. Out of the combination of the floor trader and the floor broker, the figure of the "specialist" emerged as a response to the volatility that was created by the introduction of a new trading technology for the outmoded call system.[8]

It should be clear that the specialist was never meant to "support" stock prices or keep them constant, only to offset the volatility caused by random order arrival. He seeks a stable and orderly market, not "fixed" prices. Thus, from the auctioneer of the call system who was not a market participant emerges the specialist who is a floor broker and a dealer (which is what the floor trader becomes). The specialist is a dealer who, like the original floor broker, is not presumed to take position on his own account outside the trading day in any but exceptional circumstances.

Note that like the original call system, the new system does not require appreciable capital. The floor trader usually unwound his positions before going home—he made his money by buying cheap and selling dear at a spread that eventually became the bid-ask spread. The leaving of orders with other brokers required instructions and eventually became the limit orders on the specialist's book. These are offers to buy and sell that are backed by customer capital, not the specialist broker, so again it is public liquidity. The system thus retains its labor intensity and keeps its capital costs low.[9] Had Walras written the *Elements* in 1920 in New York, we would have had the "specialist" instead of the "auctioneer" organizing the market; it would have been a theory of temporal and spatial arbitrage and speculation in a continuous trading market instead of recontracting in a discrete call market. It would have been criticized as being just as irrealistic when extended to all markets generally.

Currently, the specialist system is also experiencing diseconomies due to changes in the extent of the market, which is primarily due to the size of the average trade that occurs on the market. As large institutions such as pension funds, mutual funds, and insurance companies have larger and larger amounts of money to invest, portfolios have become larger, and portfolio adjustment thus requires trades of large blocks of stocks or of combinations of large blocks called program, or basket trades. The larger the size of a given buy or sell order, the smaller the probability of finding a counterparty willing to take the entire bargain without a large change in price. Thus, liquidity is reduced, and volatility is increased, raising the risk that is run by the specialist in acting as the counterparty. Specialists thus run the risk of having to carry larger inventories of stock over time, which requires an increased capital base. The capital requirements of the market also increase. At the same time, large traders dislike having their trades move prices against them, because price erosion represents a transaction cost just as a bid–ask spread or a commission does. They have increasingly attempted to avoid these costs by trying to prearrange or match orders off the market through the block trading desks of large brokerage houses or investment banks, which reduces the flow of business to the market and thus decreases the "public" liquidity available. The result is a market that is less liquid and requires more private capital to retain liquidity. But, private capital requires a market rate of return, so that transactions costs increase, driving more orders off the market. It is in this context that the dealer system, a purely private market with private capital, was proposed as the natural evolution of the stock market trading organization. Yet, this is not necessarily the case.

From call to broker–dealer to dealer markets or back to the call?

At the beginning of the twentieth century, the specialist system was the natural response to the difficulties created by rapid expansion in the extent of the market. But, had the computer and telecommunications revolution occurred in 1900 when the call market was experiencing diseconomies, rather than now when the broker-dealer system is experiencing difficulties due to large size, the natural response would have been the same as that which can be seen in most of the world's parliaments faced with an increase in the number of elected representatives: electronic voting and tabulation systems have replaced the counting of hands for and against.

If each broker has a computer linked by modem to the central market-making computer, it makes no difference how many brokers participate in the call; they do not get in each others' way. Neither is there any difficulty in tabulating their bids and offers at particular prices. Furthermore, there can be as many stocks to trade as one likes, for the computer can handle the determination of the equilibrium market price of virtually any number of stocks trading simultaneously. Additionally, there is technological progress since the system is no longer limited to sequential determination of stock prices on the list. New technology makes the call market correspond even more closely to the Walrasian ideal type. Yet, it cannot resolve the problem created by time-space continuity. Everything cannot happen in the same time in the same place. Computers may be able to calculate prices of different stock simultaneously, but brokers cannot yet enter them in that fashion.

It is interesting to note that such a system already exists[10]–the near perfect Walrasian call market–but as yet very few traders use it. And it is not clear that it will eventually dominate existing markets for several reasons. The first reason, as already indicated, is the fact that it has become possible in 1980 rather than 1880 when the call first experienced difficulty. At that time, it would only have put the auctioneer on the unemployment roll. Today, it would replace a substantially larger number of brokers and specialists, since orders could be made directly to the system by principals. Furthermore, it would make physical exchanges redundant because trades can be entered from brokers' offices or customers' houses. Thus, there are substantial vested interests in preserving the existing system.

The reason for the success in preserving the existing system is that the degree of perfection of a financial market depends on its organization, but it also depends on its being a perfect monopoly. Competition cannot be allowed in the production of prices. Until the perfect market reaches this minimum size, the costs associated with a lack of order flow will outweigh its technological and liquidity advantages, so that the process of simultaneous competition between diverse forms of market organization really cannot operate.

Real and financial dealer markets and call markets

Thus, there are two possible paths open for the future development of stock market organization: a return to the public market-public liquidity single price call system based on new technology or the private market-private liquidity continuous trading bid-ask price system based on dealers. The further extension of the latter would appear to confirm the idea that financial markets are coming to resemble commodity markets more and more, because the product market is usually characterized by a dual organization in retail and wholesale markets. The bid-ask spread charged by the dealer in the financial market is replaced by the wholesale-retail margin charged by wholesalers and retailers. Since these markets are in general not auction markets, but the prices are fixed by retailers, they are what Hicks had in mind when he talked about "fix price" or administered price markets. They are basically the same as bid-ask dealer markets, which are also "fix price" or administered price markets. But, they are two different types of fix price markets. The difference is found in the distinction between reproducible and nonreproducible goods. In product markets, the flow of production relative to stocks is high, because producers have the ability to control supply by changing the level of output, so that they can keep ex-factory prices fixed and allow first inventories and then production to adjust to keep price stability. (The Japanese have eliminated the inventory adjustment and have pushed all of it onto secondary suppliers.) On the other hand, in financial markets, stocks are large relative to the flow of new assets; financial market makers can only influence supply by building inventory, which means taking position. Position requires committing own capital, which will also be small relative to outstanding stocks and will have a cost that is related to current interest rates. Such action would never be taken to stabilize prices, except when the expectation that the rise in price would exceed the interest carrying costs. Financial market dealers have no interest or ability to keep prices stable.

All this comes very close to Coase's idea that markets can be analyzed by traditional economic methods if we only bother to do so. But, what Coase pointed out was that this analysis could not be done within neoclassical theory, because markets were incompatible with the premises of perfect competition assumed in the theory. On the other hand, if we go back to classical theory—and with a little help from Marshall—markets can be analyzed by normal economic theory. What does this tell us about economic theory in the context of institutional change? Quite simply that a theory that is a description of a particular form of market organization cannot be used to analyze the evolution of market organization. On the other hand, as experience has shown us, it can be impervious to changes in the overall structure of the economy, for it can always introduce special ad hoc assumptions to explain anomalies among its basic assumptions and the evolution of the actual economy.

Notes

1 The author is Professor of Political Economy, University of Bologna. This paper, which represents a summary of work carried out within the research group "Non-competitive Market Forms and Economic Dynamics" sponsored by a Ministry of University, Scientific and Technological Research (MURST 40 percent) research grant, was presented at the annual meeting of AFEE in New Orleans, Louisiana, January 1992 as a result of a travel grant from the Italian National Research Council (CNR).

2 This approach builds on Hicks's [1935] original insight that money could only be introduced into general equilibrium theory via explicit introduction of "transactions costs" associated with organized financial markets. Hicks was soon followed by Ronald Coase [1937], who did not use the same term, but referred to the uncertainty associated with the use of markets. In modern times, the transactions costs approach has been associated with Douglas North by Hicks himself in his *A Theory of Economic History* and *A Market Theory of Money* and by Oliver Williamson. This approach has been more concerned with explaining the substitution of "market" for "nonmarket" relations, while paying little attention to the organizational structure of markets and their evolution over time and across different goods and economies.

3 In addition, all the *agents de change* had their *charges* with clerks and supplies to be supported, as well as mistresses and so forth. The fixed commission on trading is to cover all these labor costs of the agency function of traders and is independent of the maintenance cost of the "market" itself.

4 Orders may be given for a particular price, now called a limit order, or for the average price or for the fix, i.e. the equilibrium price. These latter orders give some flexibility in determining the price that will balance the largest number of orders.

5 The term "public market" came from Fernand Braudel, *Civilisation Materielle, economie, capitalisme,* vol. 2, xve-xviie, giede, Paris: Arurand Colin, 1979.

6 Some of the other problems that have been encountered in London are discussed in Kregel [1990b].

7 I have dealt with some of these questions in "Financial Innovation and the Organization of Stock Market Trading," *Banca Nazionale del Lavoro, Quarterly Review,* December, 1988, pp. 367–86.

8 The exchange folklore is that the first specialist was a broker who broke his leg and was thus immobilized at the Western Union post and offered to execute limit orders for other brokers.

9 And, according to critics, the system keeps the specialists' earnings excessively high, as well as creating a potential conflict of interest when a single individual trades as an agent and for his own account.

10 It is called SPAworks, for Single Price Auction, operated by Wunsch Auction Systems until 1991 when it became the trading system for the Arizona Stock Exchange. It currently trades stocks by means of a computer operated call auction system.

References

Coase, Ronald. "The Nature of the Firm." *Economica*, New Series, vol. 4 (1937): 386–405.

Hicks, John Richard. *Collected Essays*, vol. 2. Oxford: Blackwell, 1982a.

———. "A Suggestion for Simplifying the Theory of Money." Reprinted in *Collected Essays*, vol. 2. Oxford: Blackwell, 1982b.

———. *A Theory of Economic History*. Oxford: Clarendon Press, 1969.

———. *A Market Theory of Money*. Oxford: Clarendon Press, 1989.

Kregel, J. A. "Financial Innovation and the Organisation of Stock Market Trading." *Banca Nazionale del Lavoro, Quarterly Review* (December 1988): 367–86.

———. "Market Design and Competition as Constraint to Self-Interested Behaviour." In *Economic Policy of the Marekt Process: Austrian and Mainstream Economics*, edited by K. Groenveld, J. A. H. Maks, and J. Muysken, 45–57. Amsterdam: North Holland, 1990a.

———. "Mutamenti nella Struttura delle Negoziazioni e 'Block Trading' nei Principali Mercati Azionari." In *IRS-Rapporto sul Mercato Azionario 1990*. Milan: Il Sole 24 Ore, 1990b.

Part II

Minsky–Fisher, financial instability

6 Margins of safety and weight of the argument in generating financial fragility[1]

No one who has heard Hy Minsky describe the negotiations between a bank loan officer and a potential business borrower will ever forget it. The dissection of the *pro forma* statement of prospective cash receipts and commitments for the proposed investment project is the focal point of the process that determines the acceptable margins of safety for both the borrower and the lender. And the idea of financial fragility is built around changes in these margins of safety.[2] It is the slow and imperceptible erosion of these margins of safety that produces financial fragility. When margins have been reduced to the minimum, even the smallest departure of realizations from expectations creates conditions in which firms have to deviate from their planned actions in order to meet fixed cash flow commitments. This can mean delayed payment or distress borrowing. If this is unsuccessful, investment plans may be delayed, and distress sales of inventory or of productive assets may be necessary. The result is a Fisherian debt–deflation process, which produces falling prices, rising real debt burdens, and the reversal of the normal laws of supply and demand. Lower prices increase supply and reduce demand.

Minsky's main contribution to the description of these events was to point out that they were inevitable. He formulated them as an endogenous process in which sustained economic stability produced financial fragility. It has become common to describe this process of endogenous creation of financial fragility as one of mutual contagion in which the entrepreneur's optimism, reinforced by his past record of success, eventually overcomes the natural scepticism embodied in the banker's query "How are you going to repay the loan?" Thus, as tranquil conditions turn to upswing, bankers are induced to sanction lending based on *pro formas* with lower margins of security. Projects in which receipts always covered outflow commitments by a large margin are followed by projects in which expected earnings in some particular periods may fall short but over the life of the project cover gross cash commitments by a large margin. The result is a shift from hedge to speculative financing units. In this account, bankers are willing to sanction this decline in margins because their appetite for risk has risen along with that of their clients. In the final step, bankers throw caution to the wind and lend against projects that do not cover their commitments in any period. The only margin of safety is the expectation of being able to borrow to meet the shortfall. Fragility turns to instability since there is no solution except a debt deflation or a structured workout in which the banks absorb the losses over time while the firms restore their balance sheets.

The problem with this story is that it requires that bankers are disingenuous or that borrowers are dishonest. The former has an explanation in speculative bubbles, the latter in asymmetric information. But Minsky always maintained that bankers were inherently skeptical and insisted on margins of safety because they doubted the borrowers' estimates of future cash flows. One of the reasons was that the banker was usually better informed about the overall market environment and potential competitors than the borrower. In short, bankers are neither gullible nor irrational.

Thus, for such an endogenous, evolutionary process of the reduction of margins of safety to take place, it would seem that it should be based on something more than the susceptibility of the banker to the siren song of the borrower and his/her inflated *pro forma*. Even though bankers may have a better general knowledge of local competitive conditions or the future plans of competitors, they will have no better knowledge of future conditions than anyone else. As a result, the basic determination of the decision to lend will be based on the J. P. Morgan rule[3] of the creditworthiness of the borrower. A "good credit" can be identified only by looking backward at past repayment performance, not by making hazardous future predictions.

Further, since a bank is an ongoing enterprise, the banker wants to know how he/she will get the money back from a borrower, but he/she is more interested in the answer to the question, "Can I lend to this client again?" And this will be decided primarily by past repayment performance, by "credit history" as much as by the figures on the *pro forma*. There are thus a number of factors that will cause the banker to give more importance to evaluation of the "credit risk" of the borrower than to the evaluation of the risks inherent in the use of the funds for a particular investment project. This, of course, implies looking backward rather than forward and assuming that the future will repeat the past.

Now, it is a characteristic of a period of stable expansion that the population of borrowers with good repayment histories is increasing. Errors that would have emerged in more difficult times are converted into success by the growth of the market and income. In such conditions, it is not necessary to assume that the banker becomes less skeptical or diligent in making his/her credit assessments or that he/she becomes more enthusiastic and optimistic in evaluating future earnings for margins of safety to be reduced. It is just that the universe of borrowing experiences becomes increasingly positive. It is the expansion that validates more risky projects, rather than any change in evaluation on the part of the lender.

The problem of declining margins of safety would then be the result of a slightly different cause: the method the banker uses to evaluate the risk of a loan. On the Morgan principle, this will in general be to evaluate the credit risk of the borrower and to use the credit history of the borrower to predict the future. It should be clear that this is not irrational, for as Keynes reminds us, in conditions in which the future cannot be known with certainty, the assumption that the future will repeat the past is as good as any other. The banker may be considered to reason as follows: Let the primary proposition, p, be: "the borrower is a good credit risk (will pay interest and principal on time)." A secondary proposition, p|h, will indicate the banker's degree of rational belief in p. Included in the information set, h, will be the credit history of the borrower. As a period of expansion goes on, the amount of positive information in h increases and in doing do increases the weight of the argument in favor of accepting p as a correct assessment of a borrower's creditworthiness. The borrower will thus be preferred to other potential clients. But, as the expansion goes on, there are more and more "good credits" who represent acceptable margins of safety.

The second factor that the banker will consider is the riskiness of the project itself. This primary proposition about project risk would be that "this investment will meet its *pro forma* return." But the information content of h for this proposition is close to zero since "our knowledge of the factors which govern the yield of an investment some years hence is usually very slight and often negligible" [Keynes 1936, 149–50] so that p|h offers little guidance. The decision to lend would in this case be based primarily on convention or average opinion (cf. Keynes's [1972, 156] belief that bankers prefer to fail in a "conventional . . . way"), which means by reference to the types of projects other banks are financing. Again, neither of these depends on excessive enthusiasm or misrepresentation.

Thus over time, bankers will be lending to borrowers they previously would have refused (or would have lent only at higher margins of safety), and they will be concentrating lending to projects in particular areas simply because everyone else is doing so. As in any evolutionary process, the participants need not realize what is actually taking place: the banker does not realize that he/she is reducing his/her margins of safety. Indeed, as far as the banker is concerned, the ability of his/her clients to meet the payment of interest, based on their past performance, is if anything improving. Therefore, the margin of safety is not declining since the weight the banker attaches to the borrower's accumulating positive repayment history increases with continued timely repayment. The banker thus becomes even more convinced in proposition p relating to credit risk, which comes to dominate the proposition relating to project risk since the weight of the evidence is stronger. We might say that there is a tradeoff between the margin of safety and the weight of the argument. The combination of the margin of safety and the weight of the argument remains stable over the expansion, and the banker does not perceive any increase in credit risk exposure. The problem is that the weight of the argument cannot be used to meet the loss of income from loans placed on an accrual basis.

From the point of view of the borrower, a similar process takes place. But, the borrower starts from the second primary proposition of the banker. The primary proposition is that the project will generate sufficient earnings to provide timely repayment of interest and principal and produce the highest possible rate of return of those projects considered. The decision to request financing from the banker will be based on rational belief in a secondary proposition in which h is virtually empty. However, as time goes on, the accumulating experience of actual results meeting or exceeding expectations leads to a more or less automatic reinforcement of the belief that project returns can be forecast correctly. The weight of the argument thus increases, or to put it another way, the borrower becomes more sanguine about believing the estimates of future receipts despite the fact that there is no factual basis for them.

Anticipated future earnings growth thus becomes an increasingly more certain substitute for current liquidity as a margin of safety against fluctuations in earnings due to errors in earnings forecasts. A 2 percent forecasting error can be offset much more rapidly if the economy is expanding at 5 percent per annum than if it is expanding at a half-percent. Indeed, it seems to be a statistical property of expansions that they are less volatile than contractions. Thus, as the cycle proceeds, the expected forecasting errors tend to be reduced as expectations become increasingly confident.

Thus, both the borrower and the banker become more confident, without any necessity for euphoria or excessive optimism. Increasingly "optimistic" *pro formas* in a cyclical expansion thus represent a rational reaction to the evaluation of past events as expressed in higher probabilities of success. But, as Keynes points out, success is due to no particular expertise on the part of the entrepreneur, but simply to the fact of investing in an expansionary environment. The problem is not that the banker starts to finance speculative rather than hedge projects, or ponzi rather than hedge projects. Indeed, the *pro formas* in all probability do not reveal these changes as the borrowers revise earnings estimates upward in the light of past experience, and they will be confidently accepted by the banker. But there need be no misrepresentation, since the banker will be primarily concerned with past credit history as a measure of the reliability of the *pro forma*. If there are any doubts based on the plausibility of the *pro forma*, the decision will be circumscribed by the actions of other banks, since refusing a loan simply means loss of market share. This not only means that the plausibility of the *pro forma* will be of secondary importance, it also leads to the banker failing to fully exploit proprietary knowledge of overall market and competitive conditions. The results are overinvestment and concentration of risk.

It is tempting to say that bankers are using inappropriate methods in evaluating their margins of safety. Instead of looking at credit histories and the behavior of other banks, they should be looking at the impact of unforeseen events, such as changes in monetary policy on the ability of clients to repay. From the point of view of the fragility of the *pro forma* estimates, the margin that they should be looking at is the reaction of prospective cash flows to conditions in which interest rates will have risen to choke off the expansion, so that both interest costs are rising and cash receipts are falling short of expectation, putting pressure on the acceptable margins of safety-or what are now called "stress tests" of bank balance sheets.

The tripartite classification of borrowers would thus be made by reference to the impact on margins of safety of a change in interest rates. A firm for which the margin of safety is positive for any probable (say two standard deviations) increase in interest rates may be classified as having fully hedged its future cash commitments. One in which the margin of safety is insufficient for some peri-ods is speculating that the rise in interest rates will not be such as to increase the number of those negative earnings events to the point that it reverses its positive net present value (or turns its "wind up" value to the banker negative). Finally, the firm that as a result of a probable rise in interest rates has to go back to the banker and capitalize its interest payments in a renegotiation in order to prevent bankruptcy is practicing "ponzi" finance. Hedge, speculative, and ponzi financing positions at current interest rates may all have the same flows of cash commitments, but they will have different margins of safety to protect them from probable changes in future interest rates and increasing future payment commitments.

Here we have added an additional set of forecasts to those in the *pro forma*, the forecasts of the likely change in interest rates and the duration of the change. A 25 basis point change has a much different impact on margins of safety than a 75 basis point change or an expectation of a string of 25 basis point rises spread out over a year. However, this does not solve the problem, for all the models that evaluate balance sheet risk in this way base the probability of a change in interest rates on the past performance of interest rates. In an expansion, these measures will be declining in the same way as the weight of the argument about borrow-ers' credit history is increasing. Bankers, like most others, seem to be very bad at formulating interest rate expectations. Indeed, the majority of bank failures (before the 1980s avalanche) were the result of the impact on bank investment portfolios of mistaken bets on interest rates [cf. Sprague 1986]. At the end of 1993, surprisingly few bank economists were predicting the rise in interest rates that took place in 1994.

Thus, the process of increasing financial fragility need not be accompanied by misinformation, asymmetric information, excess optimism, or irrationality. The more things change, the more things appear to remain the same as far as margins of safety are concerned. Financial fragility need not necessarily be visible in terms of changes in the composition of the quality or composition of the assets on balance sheets. Nonetheless, margins of safety are being eroded, and risk is increasing. We are thus left with what is the major strength of Minsky's idea of financial fragility. You cannot prevent it if you try. Indeed, trying is not rational. It is the natural result of the rational operation of a capitalist system.

Notes

1 The author is Professor of Political Economy, University of Bologna, Italy. This paper was presented at the annual meeting of the Association for Evolutionary Economics, New Orleans, Louisiana, January 4–6, 1997.
2 I have always presumed that Minsky took both the idea and the terminology from Graham and Dodd's *Security Analysis,* which identifies the earnings coverage of total interest com-mitments as the most comprehensive measure of the margin of safety. The margin of safety offers protection against the untoward events that confirm the fact that past performance is not a conclusive predictor of the future.
3 "[A] man I do not trust could not get money from me on all the bonds in Christendom" [J. P. Morgan, cited in Chernow 1990, 154].

References

Chernow, Ron. *The House of Morgan*. New York: Simon and Schuster, 1990.

Graham, Benjamin, and David L. Dodd. *Security Analysis*. New York: Whittlesey House, McGraw-Hill Book Company, 1934.

Keynes, John Maynard. *The General Theory of Employment, Interest and Money*. London: Macmillan, 1936.

———. *Essays in Persuasion*, vol. 9 *The Collected Writings of John Maynard Keynes*. London: Macmillan for the Royal Economic Society, 1971.

Sprague, Irwin. *Bailout: An Insider's Account of Bank Failures and Rescues*. New York: Basic Books, 1986.

7 Managing the impact of volatility in international capital markets in an uncertain world

International capital flows and financial instability

International financial flows are the propagation mechanism for transmitting financial instability across borders. They are also the source of unsustainable external debt. Managing volatility thus requires institutions that:

* promote domestic financial stability;
* ensure that domestic instability is not transmitted internationally; and
* ensure that international institutions and rules of the game are not themselves a cause of volatility.

International institutions as a cause of volatility

These three aspects were well understood by the architects of the postwar international trade and financial system. It was their basic belief that it was the unsustainable interallied debt and German reparations that brought about the instability in international capital flows that contributed to the 1929 stock market crash and the collapse of the multilateral trading system, all contributing to the Great Depression and laying the groundwork for the Second World War. A sustainable peace, as well as economic prosperity, thus required policies to manage domestic credit systems as well as the international flows of borrowing and lending. Resolving these questions required increased government control, as well as regulation and surveillance of private and international capital markets.

In the United States, the stock market break brought the introduction of New Deal banking legislation that determined the activities permitted to financial institutions with directed prices and quantity constraints on markets. At the international level, the proposed solution was to remove international financial flows from the private sector, placing international financial intermediation under government supervision.[1] In the words of U.S. Treasury Secretary Morgenthau, the purpose of the postwar reform of the international monetary and financial system was "to drive the private money lenders from the temple of international finance."[2]

Keynes's proposal for an international clearing union went a step further, according to Paul Einzig (1944), and would have completely eliminated private-market currency trading. Thus both exchange rates and capital flows were to have been subject to coordinated intergovernmental decisions. The basic objective was to limit the size of external financing for external deficits and thus to limit the size of any country's external debt.[3] Countries would be shielded from instability created by the monetary and fiscal policies of other nations and transmitted through capital flows or exchange rate fluctuations.

While the main objective of the United States was to insure that financial instability did not interfere with the restoration of a free, multilateral trading system, Keynes's main objective was to gain the autonomy from the gold standard necessary to implement domestic policies of full employment. Under both approaches this meant a "managed" currency to replace the gold standard.

However, the international financial system that was eventually adopted reinstated the gold standard, with the dollar replacing gold,[4] and preserved the role of private financial institutions in foreign exchange transactions and in intermediating international financial flows, but with one important difference emphasized by Robert Triffin—the dollar was a national currency whose supply depended on the country's external balance, while gold was the currency of no nation and had relatively inelastic supply. Nonetheless, the objective to minimize the role of private financial institutions in the intermediation of capital flows and exchange rates remained. However, placing the dollar at the center of the system while the United States had a large and seemingly indestructible current account surplus made U.S. financial institutions the center of international intermediation and supplies of international liquidity. Although international capital flows came to play an increasingly important role in the international system, in the end the demise of the system was as much due to speculation generated by the Triffin paradox as it was to the transmission of domestic instability via international flows. This was clearly a case of instability generated by the system itself, rather than being transmitted by the system.

However, by the end of the 1970s there was clear evidence of the role of domestic financial instability in creating international stability transmitted by international capital flows. As noted above, the object of both the United States and UK proposals was to limit the increase in foreign indebtedness by limiting the ability of countries to run sustained external surpluses. The commitment to a fixed dollar parity was the first constraint, for when reserves were no longer sufficient to finance a current account imbalance, a country was obliged to draw against its credit at the International Monetary Fund (IMF). Soon after its inception, such drawing ceased to be automatic and included conditions on domestic policy, directed to reversing the imbalance. Failing correction, an exchange rate adjustment was added. The main point was that after reserves were depleted, imbalances could only be financed by borrowing from the IMF and this was accompanied by policies that made further financing unnecessary.

However, this all changed in the 1970s when private lending became a major source of balance of payments financing. This was due to the response of U.S. banks to the 1966 credit crunch as banks shifted from "asset management" to liability management practices, including funding through foreign branches operating in the nascent eurodollar market in London. Thus the beginning of the dismantling of the New Deal regulations on the U.S. domestic banking system provided the impetus for the return of private international capital flows and became the primary vehicle for the recycling of petrodollars in the mid-1970s that was accompanied by a lapse in risk assessment on private loans and deficient national supervision that emerged in a full-scale regional financial crisis in Latin America, starting with the Mexican default in 1982.

This raises the question of what might limit capital flows or limit their volatility. This will depend on the potential that a country has to raise the resources required to meet external claims. This can come from four possible sources. During Bretton Woods they were limited to:

- a positive net balance on goods and nonfactor services trade;
- foreign exchange reserves generated by past current account surpluses; and
- multilateral or bilateral public development assistance or debt relief,

but, in the 1970s, after the return of international capital flows, they were supplanted for long period by:

- net private capital inflows.

As already noted, the problems of increasing volatility in international capital markets arises because the latter option allowed countries to escape the Bretton Woods limitation on capital flows to short-term trade credits.

From the point of view of Hyman Minsky's analysis of financial fragility, under Bretton Woods countries were encouraged to have hedge financial profiles, with balanced external payments positions and reserves sufficient to act as a margin of safety against fluctuations in net export earnings. When the cushion of official reserves was not sufficient to meet payments and keep exchange rates from speculative attack, reserves could be supplemented by official lending by multilateral institutions such as the IMF. The majority of such lending was to industrialized countries with balance of payments difficulties caused by internal or external shocks that turned what could be classified as a "hedge" financing profile into a "speculative" profile in which they could not meet payment for current goods and services at the existing fixed exchange rate. In exchange for temporary bridge financing from the IMF, the country agreed to adopt tight monetary and fiscal policies designed to reduce income sufficiently to bring about a fall in imports relative to exports (that were supposed to rise but usually also fell, but by less) in order to produce a reverse flow of resources in the form of a current account surplus that could be used to repay the official lending and replenish reserves. It is clear that such a system carried a deflationary bias since all countries could not have hedge financing profiles unless there was an external source of liquid reserves via a lender of last resort.

The basic philosophy behind this approach was that a commitment to a fixed exchange rate was identical to the commitment to pay in a timely fashion included in any financial contract so that devaluation was equivalent to a partial default on debt service to nonresident holders of domestic assets. The system was organized on the presumption that on average, over time, countries applying appropriate monetary and fiscal policies to preserve price stability would have a balanced external position and would always be able to meet their financial commitments in terms of foreign currency at their declared par rate with the dollar. Bretton Woods was a system organized for a world dominated by trade amongst more or less similar countries with individual countries occasionally falling into speculative mode due to an unforeseen internal (excessive wage increases relative to productivity) or external shock (loss of a protected export market), which could be countered or offset by changes in internal (domestic absorption) policies. While the adjustments were implemented the payment shortfalls were met by official lending. It was only in the extreme case of fundamental disequilibrium that exchange adjustments (expenditure switching) were contemplated as a complement to internal adjustment policies. Thus the accumulated stocks of external sovereign debt of most countries remained very low and the majority of international capital flows involved direct investments, for example, by American companies setting up operations in Europe before the creation of the European Economic Community (EEC) and in Latin American countries, primarily in the areas of natural resource extraction.

After the collapse of the Bretton Woods System, default on domestic–currency denominated external commitments became acceptable in the form of flexible exchange rates. Thus this exchange rate partial default risk on foreign claims that had been borne by the multilateral financial system and by national governments in the form of the cost of reserve balances was shifted to the individual lender. One way in which lenders could hedge against this risk was to denominate foreign loans in their domestic currency.

At the same time, international capital flows became increasingly important; first in providing adjustment finance, but more importantly in making it possible to allocate capital internationally on the basis of highest returns. Financial flows were no longer controlled in the interests of market stability, but were now directed to achieve efficient international allocation of capital. This provided the justification for the recycling of the dollar balances of the petroleum exporting countries to Latin America in the 1970s. It had long been presumed (despite the objections of economists such as Nurkse and Singer) that developing countries provided higher returns because of their low capital stock, while capital-intensive developed countries faced diminishing returns to investment. Whether or not the presumption that risk–adjusted returns in developing countries are superior to developed countries is correct, the rise in lending to developing countries in Latin America as petrodollars were recycled, followed by the sharp reversal of U.S. interest rates and the appreciation of the dollar, quickly converted what had been hedge/speculative financial profiles of these countries into Ponzi financing schemes with negative net present values.

After the traditional Bretton Woods adjustment solution of current account surpluses to meet the debt service brought such substantial declines in income as to produce what came to be called the "lost decade" of growth in Latin America and the risk of political instability, a solution was eventually found in the Brady Plan. Given that no debt relief or official assistance was forthcoming, and with outright default considered as jeopardizing the stability of the global financial system, there was only one remaining solution from the list given above—to borrow more to meet outstanding financial commitments. This is the traditional solution to a Ponzi financing scheme—the problem was to find a willing lender.

Debtors sought to attract funds by opening their internal markets and deregulating their capital accounts by introducing what has come to be known as the Washington Consensus policies. In addition, funds were raised directly through the issue of a securitized structured financing issue of Brady bonds. This involved the creation of a special purpose entity that held U.S. Treasury discount bonds as assets. Against these assets they issued Brady bonds equal to the (higher) maturity value of the Treasury securities, using the difference to buy in the country's outstanding debts in the secondary markets. In addition, two or three interest-only U.S. Treasury strips were purchased to meet the initial interest payments on the Brady bond issue; the rest of the interest payments would be produced by the recovered debt. These Brady bonds were sold to institutional investors because they were given investment-grade ratings on the basis of the fact that they held U.S. Treasury collateral and U.S. Treasury interest payments. This was one of the first steps on the road that led to AAA collateralized mortgage obligations (CMOs) of subprime mortgages that used a similar procedure to create a market though ratings leverage.

Policy to stabilize external financial flows[5]

Building on Minsky's approach, stability can be increased by measures that ensure that firms maintain hedge financing profiles defined as financial management that insures that exogenous changes in cash commitments are matched by changes in cash inflows to meet them. At the international level, hedge financing means ensuring that net export earnings are more than sufficient to cover debt servicing needs in every future period. Since net export earnings for developing countries are generally highly volatile due to reliance on a small number of export commodities with highly variable demand and prices, this might involve calculation of the volatility of net exports over a period of time and then limiting borrowing to the amount that generates debt service equal to average net export earnings less a cushion of safety represented by, say, two standard deviations. Reserves could be held to cover all or part of the two standard deviation cushion of safety over debt service. However, reserves and private credit lines that also have been used are generally very costly, since the former usually have a negative carry and the latter include international risk premia on private lending. One method of reducing these costs of reserves would be intraregional reserve pooling across countries with different export baskets. This comes close to the idea behind Keynes's clearing union proposal, which represented the pooling of reserves across surplus and deficit countries. Alternatively, countries limiting their debt service to average net export earnings could be given unconditional automatic drawing rights on their reserve tranche, as originally proposed for the IMF, or special drawing rights (SDR) balances of an amount equal to the required cushion of safety.

An alternative means of supplementing the reserve cushion would be for central banks to purchase far "out of the money" put options on their currencies (i.e., to sell their domestic currency against the dollar) as a technique for defending the exchange rate in the presence of large speculative outflows. Since out of the money options have a minimal premium, the strategy would have low costs; as the currency weakens from capital outflows, the options would increase in value and could be exercised to provide additional reserves to stabilize the currency. The positive influence on reserves will exist even if the central bank uses the foreign exchange to sterilize the funds used to exercise the put contract (buy the foreign exchange).[6]

There are other strategy options for official intervention in the foreign exchange markets. For example, the sale of covered calls on foreign currency (a commitment to sell the foreign currency held in central bank reserves against the domestic currency) could also be used to defend an upper limit (maximum depreciation) for the exchange rate. Likewise, in order to prevent an undesired currency appreciation, the central bank could write (sell) put options on a foreign currency (a commitment to buy the foreign currency with domestic currency).[7]

Preventing a speculative profile from becoming a ponzi profile— matching cash inflows and outflows

The second aspect of Minsky's approach is to ensure that countries that are hit by external shocks that transform their financing profiles from "hedge" to "speculative" should be able to return quickly to hedge financing rather than being transformed into Ponzi financing. Here the provision of temporary liquidity is important, as is the necessity to ensure that external shocks do not have an asymmetric impact on cash flows and debt payment commitments. This would involve the specification of financial liabilities that are linked through a derivative contract to cash inflows, i.e., to either the sales or prices of exports.

Whether or not open financial markets and free financial flows provide net additional resources to a country, they should provide a more efficient means of changing the profile of future cash flows and bearing the risks over the occurrence of such flows. Thus, just as a bank attempts to manage its interest rate and liquidity risks or a firm attempts to manage its interest rate or translation exposure on foreign earnings, a country should attempt to manage its own financial fragility by managing its balance sheet so as to match its earnings more closely to its commitments.

This is a different objective than attempting to borrow enough reserves to build up an arsenal or a *blindaje* that wards off speculators in the short term. Such a policy may, however, create even greater financing difficulties in the medium to long term because it raises debt service (the borrowing costs are higher than the returns from investing the reserves).

Examples of matching cash receipts and cash commitments by means of natural hedges already exist, although they have not been fully exploited due to the traditional IMF approach of providing adjustment loans. Par and discount bonds issued by Mexico, Venezuela, Nigeria, and Uruguay in exchange for their defaulted commercial bank loans in their Brady restructurings carried "Value Recovery Rights," an instrument similar to a warrant entitling the holders to payments in addition to the fixed interest coupon when the issuer sells more petroleum than some benchmark (e.g., the amount for a specified base year or average of years or some excess above the average price for that year). Thus, as petroleum sales increase (either from an increase in sales or an increase in price), cash outflows due on the bonds increase, increasing the effective rate of return on the outstanding bonds. Ideally such instruments should be designed to have a symmetrical impact on cash inflows and outflows, so that when financing ability declines the cash commitments decline in step. Basically, the idea is to make fixed interest obligations behave more like variable return equity and have the lender take on part of the volatility risk of the debtor's earnings in exchange for a reduced risk of default.

Another approach[8] proposes that the government whose foreign exchange earnings are heavily exposed to a specific industry (such as oil) agrees to exchange (swap) the returns from the beneficial ownership in the government company's foreign exchange reserves for the returns on an asset (a developed country asset or a global equity index portfolio) whose return would be less volatile than oil prices. This should lower the spread on government bonds since the volatility of the income stream now servicing the bonds will be that of the lower volatility equity index. However, while such a proposal should reduce volatility, it would not produce full hedging since developed country stock prices are likely to be highly correlated to commodity prices and, in particular, to petroleum prices.

An alternative method to match inflows to outflows relies on participation of the private sector in providing liquidity to a country that is unable to meet its current commitments (Lerrick 2001). Instead of providing emergency bailout funding, the IMF would purchase American-style put options (to be exercised at any time) from creditworthy private sector financial institutions that give the Fund the right (but no obligation) to sell to the sellers of the options floating rate notes issued by the major emerging-market governments with international indebtedness if they are in difficulty in meeting their cash commitments because of a reversal of flows or an external shock. The notes would be issued with a short maturity, carry a high, variable interest rate, and would be publicly traded. This provides an automatic inflow of funds from the private sector when the country is facing difficulty and would provide bridge funds that permit the crisis-stricken borrower to restructure its outstanding debt, if necessary, and to obtain long-term financing (both from the capital markets and from the development banks for structural adjustment programs). The condition on the exercise of the options would be an agreement by the issuing government to an IMF-sanctioned adjustment program or fulfillment of the preconditions of an IMF Reserve Augmentation Line (RAL), with no presumption of IMF or bilateral official financing.

A slightly different approach to the same problem would have the multilateral financial institutions create an investment fund that would intervene in the sovereign debt market of a country having difficulty meeting its commitments, offering to buy all its outstanding debt stock at a large discount from the expected value in the event of restructuring. This is equivalent to having the multilateral financial institutions writing put options at far out of the money strike prices on a developing country's outstanding debt, setting a floor to the market price since the buyer of the option would always be certain to be able to sell the debt at the strike price. If this occurs and the country eventually recovers and the price of its debt rises, the profits would accrue to the investment fund (Lerrick and Meltzer 2001). Developing countries with sovereign wealth funds could also undertake the creation of such a stabilization fund.

Emerging-market borrowers have already introduced a number of different types of innovative financial instruments to smooth the time profile of their stream of future payments commitments, such as issuing bonds with a (European) put option that allows the investor to redeem the bond at a predetermined date before the maturity date. If the government believes that its credit rating will improve and the price of its bonds increase over time as spreads decline, investors will have no interest in early redemption and the option will not be exercised. This would allow the government to issue longer maturity debt and spread its payments commitments more closely to its expected cash inflows. However, this strategy is based on the presumption of improvement in future conditions; if this is not the case they will increase the cost of debt service if the option is exercised and contribute to precipitating a crisis.

The use of these sorts of hedging instruments has a cost, but so does the use of contingent credit lines or preemptive borrowing to hold additional reserves. But the costs involved in such hedge strategies increase when times are good, rather than increasing when times are bad, and thus provide stability to the financing profile. In effect, this balance sheet approach to financial stability attempts to blend the variable cash flow aspects normally associated with equity instruments with the fixed cash flow aspects of bonds.[9]

However, there are two important deficiencies in all these proposals to provide stability in the international financial system by ensuring hedge financing profiles or providing liquidity to temporary speculative profiles. First, they suffer from the same fallacy of composition that Keynes attempted to eliminate through his proposal for automatic liquidity through the clearing union—it is not possible for every country to attain hedge, or even speculative, profiles. Second, imposing hedge or speculative profiles on developing countries implicitly prevents the global increase in welfare that is presumed to result from free mobility of international capital and the use of net resource transfers from developing to developed countries in simultaneous support of both global growth and development. This is because a hedge profile implies that the country's cash inflows are more than sufficient to match cash outflows, which means an external surplus and reverse resource transfers.

External flows as a sustainable source of domestic finance

There is however, a basic difficulty with the maintenance of a hedge profile for a country that is integrated into the international trade and financial system. The first problem is that not all countries can maintain a current account surplus at the same time. At least one country has to have Ponzi financing position if others are to have hedge or speculative positions. In the current international environment there is no method to compensate or insure that country from instability. This should have been the role of the clearing union (but it was not created) or the IMF (but it has not chosen to play that role). This point is nothing different from the accounting identity that says if one domestic sector desires to net save, then the other sectors in aggregate must dissave.

There is, however, another demonstration of the difficulty of maintaining a hedge financing position through an external surplus. This is because an external surplus must be initially based on a commercial surplus, which, in the absence of any other capital services or capital account transactions, will cause an accumulation of foreign claims that will generate foreign interest earnings that are credited to the capital services account of the balance of payments. These credits on current account will reinforce the positive credit balance of the current account and, unless the country is willing to allow an increasing amount of real consumption to be replaced by notional income, eventually produce a capital services account that will "crowd out" real exports of goods and services, with a negative impact on employment and consumption. This calls into question the sustainability of the current account balance over time, but, at the same time, calls into question the ability to run a hedge financing scheme to ensure domestic stability.

Evsey Domar provided the answer to the question of whether such a hedge financial scheme could be sustainable by adapting a prior argument concerning the sustainability of debt-financed public investment. As long as capital outflows increased at a rate that was equal to the rate of interest received from the outstanding loans to the rest of the world, the inflows created on the factor service account by the interest and profit payments would just be offset so there would be no net impact on the trade balance. On the other hand, if interest rates were higher than the rate of increase in foreign lending, the policy would become self-defeating and the trade balance would eventually become negative to offset the rising net capital service inflows. Eventually the continually rising factor service flows would turn the trade balance negative.

With respect to the stability of the financial system, it is interesting to note that the Domar conditions for a successful long-term hedge financing strategy are the precise equivalent of the conditions required for a successful Ponzi financing scheme from the point of view of the rest of the world (or the required deficit country). As long as the rate of increase in inflows from new investors in a pyramid or Ponzi scheme is equal or greater than the rate of interest paid to existing investors in the scheme there is no difficulty in maintaining the scheme. However, no such scheme in history has ever been successful—they are bound to fail eventually by the increasing size of the net debt stock of the operator of the scheme. Paradoxically, in the present global context, it is not the hedge financing countries, but the United States—the required deficit country—that is operating a similar type of Ponzi scheme. Thus the only hedging scheme is one that keeps imbalances from becoming too large. In the absence of IMF control or a clearing union, capital controls present the only possibility to keep the financial imbalance within reasonable bounds.

Internal instability as a source of external instability

A much more important source of volatility comes from instability in domestic financial markets being transmitted internationally by international capital flows and the operation of international banks across borders. This can take two forms, an excessive increase in national liquidity due to domestic policies producing excessive inflows or outflows, or the collapse of a financial boom leading to an excessive demand for liquidity that produces a global liquidity crisis. These have been the predominant sources of crises in the last quarter century. Examples are the shift in U.S. monetary policy in the late 1970s, producing the return flow of capital to the United States from Latin America; the global liquidity crisis that followed the Russian exchange rate crisis of 1998 and the collapse of Long Term Capital Management (LTCM) in the summer of that year; and the current crisis in international markets. These last two examples have the common characteristic of being liquidity crises. This is largely due to changes that have taken place in developed country financial markets over the last twenty years.

The characteristic feature of the new financial architecture that was built up in the United States in the 1990s paralleled the Washington Consensus in restoring the market as the basis of pricing and allocation of finance. This represented a reversal of the New Deal legislation that had given the government the central role in regulating financial markets. At the same time, greater reliance was placed on market discipline to regulate financial institutions. In this progressive dismantling of government oversight, broker dealers saw the elimination of fixed commissions on equity trades, commercial banks and thrifts saw the elimination of fixed deposit rates, and investment banks used the introduction of self-registration to shift from relationship-based to transactions-based underwriting of capital financing. This increased role for market competition amongst financial institutions led to a rapid increase in financial intermediation, or financial layering, that caused a decrease in market transparency and the information that is essential to the effective operation of the market mechanism.

One aspect of market information that is required for the operation of the market is a commodity that is sufficiently homogenous to allow competitive pricing in exchange. As far back as William Petty, economists have recognized the importance of homogeneous commodities as a prerequisite for the operation of competitive markets and the role of prices in providing market information.[10]

Aside from corporate equity, that are homogenous by legislation, other financial assets are usually considered to be too idiosyncratic and particular to be priced and traded in competitive markets. Thus they have traditionally been dealt with through bilateral negotiation through financial institutions acting as intermediaries such as brokers and dealers.

One of the major changes introduced by the new financial architecture based on the market mechanism was the creation of new, uniform financial products that could be traded and priced more efficiently. However, they were often created in ways that reduced the transparency and information required by the market. An example of the creation of new instruments may be seen in the unbundling, or financial engineering, of financial instruments. Stripping the interest coupons from fixed income instruments allowed the creation of a series of short-term instruments that could be compared to other trade short-term instruments. It created the possibility of transforming fixed income instruments into floating rate instruments, and instruments that were negatively related to interest rates could become positively related to interest rates. A whole series of new products were created, but without the creation of organized markets to trade and price them; rather, providing better definition of products tended to blur the differences between different kinds of products. They also shifted the role of the market from valuation to arbitrage. The role of the market mechanism was less to provide price discovery than to identify mispricing through arbitrage across the different components of the instrument. The actual price was less important than the equalization of the whole to the sum of its parts.

The emphasis on the operation of the market led to the search for uniform assets that could be traded in areas that had previously been presumed to be untradeable because of their inherent incomparability and heterogeneity. Starting with automobile and credit card loans, the process was extended to banks' commercial and industrial loans, and even to residential and commercial mortgages. Here the homogeneity requirement was produced through the help of the law of large numbers and ergodicity. But, not only was the definition of the product opaque, once again the markets in which they were to be traded were not organized markets, but arms-length transactions over the counter.

All of these newly created products had one characteristic in common; they represented the title to specified, distinct expected future income flows—interest and principle on a bond, a loan, or a mortgage in which the counterparty in the transaction is the final borrower and completion depends on the flow of income earned by the borrower validating the instrument.

A slightly different example is to be found in the reintroduction of financial futures and options that was initiated by the return to floating exchange rates after the collapse of Bretton Woods. These derivative instruments were traded in organized and, initially, highly regulated markets. However, regulations were progressively relaxed and trading moved increasingly "over-the-counter." The Enron "loophole" that allowed exemptions for proprietary electronic over-the-counter trading was exemplary of this trend. Thus new products such as gas and electricity futures were created, but the market conditions were such that there could be no market discipline and their prices were easily manipulated.

These products are different from traditional financial instruments in that their valuation is not dependent on the performance of future income of the borrower, but on the future movement in a specified price on which the return on the contract is derived. Thus the ability of the seller to complete the transaction is independent of the performance of the underlying investment and validation is usually sought through the provision of margin collateral that is deposited with the exchange clearing house acting as guarantor. Neither the buyer nor the seller need have any direct interest in the performance of the underlying commodity. But, the absence of an organized market is even more damaging to market discipline since it shifts the risk of completion for both buyer and seller from the exchange clearing house to the counterparty.

Much has been said about the increase in leverage that was produced by the spread of derivatives. But it is important to recognize that bank lending is also levered lending, with bank capital playing the same role as margin requirements in standard derivative contracts. A more important difference is the handling of counterparty risk and the risk on the source of the ability to meet the repayment conditions.

Structured loan vehicles combine both aspects and create a different combination of repayment risk. For example, in a below-libor loan that combines a standard loan with the sale of an option on a financial or real variable, the size of the loan becomes variable and the ability of the borrower no longer depends on the income that is being financed, but on the movement of the specified price. As more and more lending is done through structured product, the ability to repay becomes increasingly dominated by price risks that are independent of the ability and operation of the borrower's real productive activities.

Thus financial markets became more dependent on pricing the probability of future events rather than on the valuation of future income flows from financed activity or on the credit of the borrower. Both these assessments require the anticipation of future events and both are built on assumptions about the past behavior, but the former refers to the assessment of credit risk and the business plan of the borrower and is thus based on specific information, while the latter is an attempt to forecast an essentially unknown future universe.

While it was normal for investment banks and broker dealers to assess the price of their positions daily since they were funded by short-term (often overnight) money, this had not been the case with commercial banks and savings and loans. The justification was that since the investment bank portfolio might have to be liquidated in the case of a funding shortfall, it was required to mark its assets to liquidation value to determine solvency. But the commercial banks' short-term deposits were assumed to be sufficiently stable and loans sufficiently collateralized that they did not have to be formally revalued since they would normally not have to be liquidated. Similarly thrifts were expected to hold mortgages to maturity so the only relevant value was the maturity value of the principal. However, the creation of bundled securities of uniform characteristics brought an extension of the application of mark-to-market rules to all financial institutions, further delinking the determination of asset values from the assessment of underlying income flows, even when they were present.

However, the most important innovations that were introduced into the new financial architecture related to a little-noticed activity—the leveraging of credit ratings. The plain vanilla interest rate swap is often presented as simply the exchange of the commitment to pay a variable interest rate for a fixed interest rate on a given loan principal. However, such instruments are usually constructed on the basis of the difference between the credit rating from the fixed borrower and the floating rate borrower, providing both the possibility of borrowing at rates below that they would pay with a direct issue. Again, the transaction obscures market information since the fixed rate lender may have no idea that the fixed rate issuer is not servicing the bond. Indeed, in many deals the fixed rate borrower with the higher credit rating was encouraged to issue. The transparency of information on these contracts could be further exacerbated when leverage was added, to either the fixed or floating leg.

A more recent example of this credit leveraging is AIG's use of the AAA credit rating of its insurance subsidiaries to create AIG Financial Products (AIGFP), which functioned as a virtual stand-alone investment bank. In particular, it provided principal protection or other guarantees to structured fund products built from index, equity, bond, mutual fund, and hedge fund portfolios, as well as loans and loan facilities involving limited recourse to fund vehicles. It could compete in these markets, not because of the capitalization of the trading unit, but because of the credit rating given to the parent holding.

In particular, it allowed AIGFP to sell credit default swaps with margins determined on the basis of that rating even though it was the strength of the insurance subsidiaries that supported the credit rating, but whose assets could not act as cushions against loss on the derivative operations. When these contracts lost value and AIG had to provide collateral, it was the holding that was responsible and its inability to provide margining for the positions brought down the entire company.

All of these structures followed the Brady bond pattern of leveraging credit ratings from one set of assets to another that had no similar credit characteristics. The applications to the securitizations in the mortgage market and then the subprime market are obvious. Structured finance entities may then be seen as representing a method of manufacturing a credit rating through the structure of the assets and by leveraging credit ratings through the process of credit enhancement provided by monoline insurer guarantees or first loss entities.

What is less obvious is the fact that financial markets no longer evaluate the credit of the issuers of financial assets or the processes that generate the discounted present values of income flows. Instead they trade credit risk and invest in credit risk directly. The limit of the unbundling process of financial engineering is to reduce every financial instrument into its individual risk components and then to trade them separately or recombined in packages to exhibit designed risk characteristics that meet investment objectives. Thus the homogeneous commodity required for the efficient operation of the market mechanism that has been produced by financial engineers is risk. Indeed, the current dominance of the credit default simply reflects the fact that it is risk that is being traded, not cash flows.

This has two important consequences. The first is that by reducing everything to a single, similar characteristic, it reduces the very diversity upon which stability of the financial system depends. Thus, while individual risks may be diverse, changes in risk levels will tend to be highly correlated, reducing the effectiveness of any strategy to provide risk reduction.

Secondly, in difference from a cash flow on a bond or a stock, risk has no unambiguous definition since it depends on the ability of the future to repeat the past. The use of standard statistical techniques that are at the basis of most risk analysis have been criticized in a number of ways. First, economists such as George Shackle consider most economic events as unique and thus not subject to measurement by statistical probability. Paul Davidson[11] has pointed out that standard risk analysis depends on financial variables being represented by a stationary ergodic series. Nasim Taleb has noted that for most financial variables the marked leptokurtosis representing their deviation from normal distributions is usually represented by one single event. Normal sampling techniques will seldom cover a sufficiently long time period to provide a true representation of the distribution and thus of the variance as a measure of risk. An event that occurs on average every ten years would require a series that covers at least thirty years and might still not cover the event, which, when it occurs, would be unforeseen. The more unique the event the, less likely that it will be included in any data series (which is simply a way of saying that there is no correct definition of the population size required to calculate measures of volatility).

Benoit Mandelbrot (1997) has shown that financial variables are better represented by a power function, but with no certainty of the value of the exponent. He notes the importance of long-run serial dependence in financial data, measured by the Hurst coefficient, as well as the Noah and Joseph effects (catastrophic interruption to serial dependence and ordering of events), and suggests alternative measures of risk based on fractal, rather than normal, distributions.

As Keynes stressed, diversity of opinion is important to stability, which raises the question of how information in the market is transmitted. Common opinion or convergence of opinion leads to instability. Network analysis provides an approach to answering this question. Are more degrees of separation better for dissemination of information and diversity? Baran's analysis of centralized, decentralized, and distributed networks suggests that distributed networks are less vulnerable to attack (this is how information is transmitted on the internet). Centralized networks, on the other hand, are subject to higher risk of attack and thus to an abrupt change in opinion. Richard Kahn (1954), in a famous article, suggested the balance of the objectives of agents in the market. A market dominated by widows and orphans who hold assets for income will behave differently from a market populated by bond traders who profit from changes in capital values.

In addition, as noted above, whatever measure of risk is used, the presence of risk arbitrage can reduce transparency and increase volatility.

Finally, in modern financial markets, risk analysis itself has become a commodity and is outsourced to private, profit-making institutions—credit rating agencies that were not originally designed to provide this information for financial assets, but have been called upon to serve this function. However, there is no pricing mechanism to evaluate the effectiveness or efficiency of their products.

It is important to recall that the trading of risk is to optimize the relation between risk and return. There is only one way to completely eliminate risk, and that is to swap a long and a short position in the same asset, which achieves a perfect negative correlation with no basis risk. However, this condition is rarely satisfied in financial markets. This means that traditional measures of risk tend to predominate decision making by financial institutions.

Taleb (2008) has performed an analysis of the power coefficient on high frequency financial data for a broad range of instruments. He concludes that the value is between two and three, with a mean absolute error greater than one. He notes that this mean error has massive consequences on predicted results. The expected value of loss in excess of a certain amount multiplied by more than ten times is the result of a change in the coefficient that is less than its mean error—and "[t]hese are the losses banks were talking about with confident precision!"

If there is no coherent way to measure risk, then the domestic financial system will always be a source of potential international disturbance unless there are international measures to dampen the transmission mechanism or measures are taken to return financial systems to credit assessment rather than risk arbitrage. This is less a question of international capital flows than a question of the cross-border operation of transnational banks. As long as banks' business models are directed toward risk arbitrage and risk leveraging, and as long as they operate internationally, they will be a source of international financial instability.

Notes

1 A post-Bretton Woods United Nations expert panel that included Nicholas Kaldor proposed that all international development lending be done by national governments issuing domestic bonds, the proceeds of which would be administered through the World Bank. See United Nations (1949).
2 Quoted in Gardner (1956).
3 The "Keynes Plan" envisaged an international clearing union that would create an international means of payment called "bancor." Each country's central bank would accept payments in bancor without limit from other central banks. Debtor countries could obtain bancor by using automatic overdraft facilities with the clearing union. The limits to these overdrafts would be generous and would grow automatically with each member country's total of imports and exports. Charges of one or two percent a year would be levied on both creditor and debtor positions in excess of specified limits. This discouragement to unbalanced positions did not rule out the possibility of large imbalances. Part of the credits might eventually turn out to be gifts because of the provision for canceling creditor-country claims not used in international trade within a specified time period.

4 Reports of the negotiations suggest that Keynes never approved the use of either gold or the dollar: " . . . in September 1943, Keynes told White that the United Kingdom did not contemplate going on to a gold or a dollar standard, but might be prepared to accept a unitas standard. Whenever the matter was brought up, he categorically rejected the idea that the dollar should be given a special status, and he continued to take the same line at Atlantic City when the subject briefly cropped up there. [. . .] The change from 'gold' to 'gold and U.S. dollars' was lost in the ninety-six page document the chairmen of the delegations would sign a few days later. Whether or not any of them noticed it, or understood its implications, it seems that none of them expressed any reservations about it. Keynes would not find out until later, when he studied the Final Act" (Van Dormael 1978).
5 Much of the material in this section comes from J. Kregel (2004).
6 See Taylor (1995).
7 Many of these strategies are discussed in the *Hannoun Report* (BIS 1994).
8 See also Favero and Giavazzi (2003).
9 Michael Pettis (2001) has noted the importance of the fact that the price behavior of emerging-market distressed fixed-interest sovereign debt more resembles equity than bonds for the design of hedging strategies to reduce financial fragility.
10 See Roncaglia (1985).
11 See for example, Davidson (2002).

References

Bank for International Settlements (BIS). 1994. *Macroeconomic and Monetary Policy Issues Raised by the Growth of Derivatives Markets (Hannoun Report)*, November. Basle: BIS.

Davidson, Paul. 2002. *Financial Markets, Money and the Real World*. Cheltenham, UK: Edward Elgar.

Einzig, Paul. 1944. *Currency After the War—The British and American Plans*. London: Nicholson and Watson.

Favero, Carlo A., and Francesco Giavazzi. 2002. "Why are Brazil's Interest Rates so High?" IGIER, Universita Bocconi, Milano, mimeo, July 14.

Gardner, Richard. 1956. *Sterling-dollar Diplomacy*. New York: Oxford University Press.

Kahn, R.F. "Some Notes on Liquidity Preference." Manchester School, September, 1954.

Kregel, Jan. 2004. "External Financing for Development and International Financial Instability." Discussion Paper Series, No. 32. Washington and Geneva: Intergovernmental Group of Twenty-four.

Lerrick, Adam. 2001. "Financial Crises: The Role of the Private Sector." Statement presented to the Joint Economic Committee of the Congress of the United States, March 8.

Lerrick, A., and A. Meltzer. 2001. "Beyond IMF Bailouts: Default without Disruption." *Quarterly International Economics Report* (May). Pittsburgh, PA: Carnegie Mellon Gailliot Center for Public Policy.

Mandelbrot, Benoit. 1997. *The Misbehavior of Markets: A Fractal View of Risk, Ruin & Reward*. New York: Basic Books.

Neftci, S.N., and A.O. Santos. 2003. "Puttable and Extendible Bonds: Developing Interest Rate Derivatives for Emerging Markets." Working Paper WP/03/201. Washington, DC: The International Monetary Fund.

Pettis, Michael. 2001. *The Volatility Machine*. New York: Oxford University Press.

Roncaglia, A. 1985. *Petty: The Origins of Political Economy*. Armonk: M.E. Sharp.

Taleb, Nassim Nicholas. 2008. "The Fourth Quadrant: A Map of the Limits of Statistics." Edge [9.15.08]. Available at: http://www.edge.org/3rd_culture/taleb08/taleb08_index.html.

Taylor, C.R. 1995. *Options and Currency Intervention.* London: Centre for the Study of Financial Innovation.

United Nations. 1949. *National and International Measures for Full Employment.* Lake Success, NY: United Nations.

Van Dormael, Armand. 1978. "Gold and the U.S. Dollar." Available at: http://www.imfsite. org/origins/confer3.html.

8　The natural instability of financial markets[1]

What is financial instability?

It is usually believed that economics is the study of market exchange – this is the "catalactic" view associated with Mill. This is the approach behind supply and demand, the two sides of an economic transaction. Economists explain how individuals reach their decisions concerning supply and demand by reference to a behavioral ideal – the rational economic man. This has led to the "efficient markets" hypothesis, which implies that any and all information that is required for rational economic decisions is contained in prices determined in competitive markets. However, this approach has one important drawback. As Ronald Coase (1991) has pointed out, it provides no explanation of markets themselves. This is confirmed by the fact that financial institutions that comprise the markets exist because they reject the efficient market hypothesis. Every offering memorandum for an investment fund contains the affirmation that the fund will achieve above-market returns because of its ability to exploit market imperfections.

There is an alternative approach that views economic exchange as time transactions – what, in finance terminology, are called "spot-forward swaps." This approach argues that there is no such thing as an instantaneous, simultaneous exchange that exerts no influence after it occurs. Time transactions involve a commitment to do something today against the promise of a commitment in the future. This is true of both real and financial transactions. When you buy a consumption good, you pay today on the expectation of a certain kind and quality of services that can be received from the good after purchase (and into an extended future for durable goods).[2] An entrepreneur who engages in production buys inputs of labor, materials, and capital today on the expectation that he or she will receive sufficient sale proceeds in the future to meet the costs and achieve a target expected profitability. All financial transactions are an exchange of money today based on the expectation of the receipt of money at future dates. All these transactions are similar because they involve decisions made today on the basis of expectations of the conditions that will prevail in the future. Only if expectations of forecasts of future conditions are correct will the future transactions be realized. This is the assumption of rational expectations.

However, in real markets it is only natural that expectations should be disappointed and future commitments should not be honored. This approach has its roots in the works of Knight, Fisher, Schumpeter, and most importantly, Keynes. It is the essence of Keynesian economics that it is the expectation of uncertain future events that determine present decisions to enter into economic activity. From this point of view, the most important question is not whether prices contain all available information but how to prevent the natural transaction failures caused by unforeseen future events from creating chronic instability.

Traditionally there are two approaches that have been proposed. The first is what Lionel Robbins called the "Classical Theory of Economic Policy" – referring to the Classical economists such as Smith and Ricardo. He argued that they believed that the government should provide the appropriate regulatory framework to ensure that market economic transactions produced acceptable results. According to Robbins (1952), "[T]he pursuit of self-interest unrestrained by suitable institutions, carries no guarantee of anything except chaos" (p. 56). To prevent the chaos that could prevail in a self-interested response to disappointment required regulatory buffers – suitable institutions – that curbed undesirable behaviors and limited undesirable results.

The second is an extension of the efficient markets paradigm that notes the necessity of complete markets for all future dates and events to allow hedging the uncertainty surrounding future commitments through forward transactions. This is the position that appears to have been behind the decisions of the Federal Reserve to refrain from extending regulations to increasingly sophisticated financial product engineering in financial markets. Here an increase in the breadth, depth, and completeness of financial markets should allow the risks of non-completion of transactions to be spread to those in the system most able to bear them and prevent the transformation of disappointment into instability.

However, there is a third approach to the question of financial instability – that given by Hyman Minsky's (1982, 1986) financial instability hypothesis. Minsky followed Keynes in arguing that the results of financial transactions in a sophisticated capitalist economy are inherently uncertain. However, he went further and argued that there was an endogenous process, much like increasing entropy in nature, in which periods of successful completion of financial commitments led to an increasing uncertainty of completion. It was the nature of economic stability to create the seeds of its own destruction by leading individuals to engage in financial transactions increasingly less likely of completion. This can be called an increase in "financial fragility." Thus, even if the financial system were stable, it would produce increasing fragility in which it was ever more susceptible to a major economic disruption. From this point of view neither regulation nor complete and perfect markets could ensure financial stability – indeed, they could be a cause of instability.[3]

The fact that Minsky developed this financial instability hypothesis during the "golden years" of the operation of New Deal banking regulation suggests that he believed that "financial fragility" was not only possible but also present during those years of economic stability. This also implies that in Minsky's view,

the New Deal legislation did little to eliminate the potential for financial fragility. As no substantial breakdown occurred in the period, we might conjecture
that whereas financial fragility is independent of financial regulation, regulation
may play a role in the rate of propagation of fragility or in preventing the transformation of fragility into major instability such as occurred during the Great
Depression.

Minsky's (cf. the introduction to Minsky, 1982) suggestion that the transformation of financial fragility into a more generalized "breakdown" into financial
instability has been prevented by the existence of a "Big Government" that acts
as "spender of last resort" to support business and household balance sheets and
a "Big Bank" that acts as "lender of last resort" to support financial institutions'
balance sheets. Because there is little current possibility of creating a global
government to provide anticylical fiscal policy or a global central bank to act as
lender of last resort, it seems clear that this method of damping instability is not
available at the global level.

The recent evolution of the financial system: more or less "fragile"?

Starting in the mid-1980s, there has been a gradual erosion of the limits of the
regulatory segmentation imposed on the financial system under the 1933 Glass-
Steagall legislation. This process has been called "deregulation." It was primarily
the result of a decline in bank income that many thought would threaten the
existence of commercial banks.[4] US commercial banks' share of the financial
assets held by all financial institutions had fallen dramatically from around 50%
in the 1950s to around 25% in the 1990s as banks suffered competition for both
their deposit business (from thrifts and nonregulated money market accounts)
and their commercial and industrial loan business (from commercial paper).

Because existing regulations gave little possibility of entering new lines of
business, flexibility had to be sought within existing regulations. Section 20 of
the Glass-Steagall Act had restricted commercial banks from potentially profitable capital market activities such as the sale and management of trust and investment funds. Although they were permitted transactions in certain securities,
such as Treasuries, they were prohibited from affiliating with firms "engaged
principally" in underwriting and dealing in securities, like corporate bonds and
equity. The intention was to prevent banks from recreating the securities affiliates that had been one of the engines of the 1920s stock market boom and were
subject to widespread fraud and manipulation. However, in a series of rulings
in the 1980s, the phrase "engaged principally" was reinterpreted to allow banks
to form affiliates to engage in these activities if the earnings they generated did
not surpass specified limits. Thus, it was deemed acceptable for a bank holding
company to form a subsidiary that conducted permissible activities that were
sufficiently large to be considered its principal activity, leaving it free to engage
in some lesser proportion of otherwise prohibited activities in which it was
considered not to be "principally" engaged. The Federal Reserve first authorized

such a subsidiary in 1987 under what was called the "Section 20 exemption" that allowed these subsidiaries to generate up to 5% of net earnings (eventually increased to 10% and in 1997 to 25%). Commercial banks eventually came to operate 51 securities subsidiaries, including some well-known securities firms such as Citigroup's acquisition of Solomon Smith Barney, a merged investment bank and brokerage house. The first securitized investment vehicle (SIV, of which more to follow) was created (it is reputed by employees at Citibank London) in 1988 under this regulation.

This deterioration in segmentation has also worked in the opposite direction with securities firms and insurance companies linking up with certain types of depository institutions known as "non-bank banks," such as international Edge banks, industrial loan banks, credit card banks, and with deposit units through the acquisition of a single thrift, known as a "unitary thrift." For example, American Express acquired an industrial loan bank with about $12 billion in assets. As banks sought new avenues of revenue aside from the disappearing business of borrowing retail deposits and lending to commercial firms, they thus moved more into securities. This led to an emphasis on proprietary trading (embarked upon by Bankers Trust) and into increasing their fee and commission incomes. In particular, as the savings and loan industry was imploding in the 1980s, banks increasingly expanded their construction lending, producing the collapse in real estate of the end of the 1980s and the Greenspan strategy of leading against the wind, which basically means keeping short rates sufficiently low so that banks could rebuild their capital by riding the yield curve between short rates and medium-term rates on government securities.

Thus, the banking system that emerged from the 1980s real estate crisis was one that no longer serviced business lending (per the real bills doctrine) and was no longer primarily dependent on net interest margins for its income but on the ability of their proprietary trading desks to generate profits and Section 20 affiliates to produce fee and commission income. There was less to distinguish a commercial bank from an investment bank other than that the former continued to offer government-insured deposit, whereas the latter offered uninsured money market mutual fund accounts.

Largely as a result of this gradual erosion of the segmentation between the activities undertaken by commercial deposit and loan banks and investment banks operating in capital markets, in 1999 Congress approved the Gramm-Leach-Bliley Bank Reform Act, which allowed commercial banks to expand the range of their capital market activities and investment banks to expand their "commercial" banking activities. The new legislation repealed key provisions of the Glass-Steagall Act to permit a modified form of German universal banking, amending the Bank Holding Company Act of 1956 to permit the holding company owners of commercial banks to engage in any type of financial activity. At the same time it allowed banks to own subsidiaries engaged in a broad range of financial activities not permitted to banks themselves. As a result, banks of all sizes gained the ability to engage in a much wider range of financial activities and to provide a full range of products and services without regulatory restraint.

However, this change in legislation and change in the structure of the financial system did little to halt the decline in the share of assets intermediated by banks proper. It simply allowed them to operate these activities in other affiliated units of the bank holding companies or to the subsidiaries of banks. Ben Bernanke, the chairman of the Board of Governors of the Federal Reserve, has indicated in a recent speech on the impact of banks on economic activity that

> non-bank lenders have become increasingly important in many credit markets, and relatively few borrowers are restricted to banks as sources of credit. Of course, non-bank lenders do not have access to insured deposits. However, they can fund loans by borrowing on capital markets or by selling loans to securitizers.

He notes, however, that "banks do continue to play a central role in credit markets; in particular, because of the burgeoning market for loan sales, banks originate considerably more loans than they keep on their books" (Bernanke, 2007).

This shift from a "segmented" commercial banking system to a universal banking system has done little to halt the share of financial assets that are held on the balance sheets of the banking system. However, banks have succeeded in improving their incomes by shifting from reliance on net interest margins to proprietary trading income, fees, and commissions. In short, banks no longer are the direct source of financing for business or households. Instead they have become "arrangers" or "originators." They create financial assets that they then sell to a subsidiary that in turn, sells them in the capital market to non-bank financial institutions, such as pension funds, insurance companies, or to the general public. And, as in the 1920s, hardly any of these assets represent financing for business – the majority is consumption (credit cards or automobile lending) or real estate (mortgage or home equity).

This shift has been supported by two factors in addition to the changed regulatory structure – improved computational power and the formal introduction of minimum ratios of capital to risk-weighted assets. The impact of computational power can be seen in the creation of money market mutual funds whose net asset and, thus, redemption value are set at $1.00 to make them the formal equivalent of a liquid bank demand deposit. Without computers this could not be accomplished because it requires complicated balancing of portfolios to ensure that redemption of shares always produces a $1 net asset value. The role of computation in the pricing of derivatives such as options is also important, as is the ability to perform sophisticated statistical testing to create statistical arbitrage and relative value trading strategies. Accompanied by the introduction of scoring models to assess credit quality, this meant that the role of the loan officer was no longer the direct assessment of the risk of the project, the credit risk of a borrower, or the value of loan collateral but rather entering standard borrower characteristics into a computer, often without ever meeting the client.

As noted, as the Basle Accord was being completed in the late 1980s, US banks were already increasing their use of off balance sheet financial affiliates. The initial impetus was to extend into capital market activities and increase fees and incomes associated with traditional lending. An offshore or domestic off balance sheet-affiliated entity would not only produce operating fees and commissions from its administration by the bank, but it would also provide management fees and additional capital for the bank's proprietary traders. The introduction of the Basle Accord simply reinforced this income-driven change in bank lending activities off balance sheet. The business of banking changed from being one of holding assets to generate income from interest rate spreads to one of moving assets – the traditional activity of brokers and investment banks. But, in the process, the role of banks as specialized evaluators of credit and providers of liquidity to the system has been lost. And herein lies much of the explanation for the current round of instability.

As the dot-com boom of the 1990s collapsed amid the revelation of off balance sheet-structured entities at many of the large communications and trading companies, banks looked for other sources of assets to be traded and managed as the collapse of the high-technology stock boom led households to seek alternatives to equity investments. Real estate provided an answer for investors; mortgages and consumer credit provided the answer for the banks. Thus, as banks sought to maximize the throughput of loans that would create fee, commission, and management income, households increased their indebtedness, financing an expansion in household expenditures that pulled the US rapidly out of recession and provided the engine for global expansion (as well as the historic rise in the US trade deficit).

The major tool that has been employed in moving assets off balance sheet is asset securitization. This is a technique that has been in use at least since the introduction of Brady bonds and played a large part in the provision of mortgage finance after the collapse of the savings and loan industry in the late 1980s. It involves the creation of an independent special purpose entity – like an investment trust – that issues liabilities, usually fixed interest, whose proceeds are used to acquire fixed income assets. The interest received from the assets creates the income from the trust that is paid or passed through to the investors in the liabilities. The creation and management of the trust by the banks generate setup, servicing, and management fees. The assets acquired by the trust are those that the bank has originated, again for fees, that it does not want to keep on balance sheet. The liabilities issued by the trust are thus debt obligations collateralized by the assets purchased from the bank. The collateral may be grouped together in combinations to generate particular desired characteristics in their income stream – activity that also creates servicing and management fees. The returns from the assets are also structured, with the "senior" tranche receiving more than its fair share of the income. It will thus be able to meet its commitments to pay a particular rate of return, even if some of the assets held in the trust are impaired. Because of the extent of its "overcollateralization," the senior tranche is given an investment-grade rating by a nationally recognized statistical rating organization, insuring a demand from pension funds, insurance companies, and trusts. The remaining assets produce income that is paid to one or more "residual" tranches and will receive income only if there is no default and expectations are realized. These will not receive investment grades and would be sold to investors, such as hedge funds, seeking higher returns from riskier assets. In this way, a pool of noninvestment-grade assets can provide the basis for the issue of investment-grade securities by the trust.

As the success of these structured assets began to produce more high-risk residual tranches, it became difficult to find buyers. This problem was solved by creating another set of collateralized debt obligations whose assets were the residual tranches from existing structures. Again, a "senior" tranche was created through overcollateralization, given an investment-grade rating, and residual trances could reemerge as investment-grade paper. In some, to ensure sufficient overcollateralization, the structure would be complemented with an implicit loan guarantee by the originating bank or a credit default swap written by the organizing bank, by an insurance company, or through insurance from a "mono-line" insurer that guaranteed the returns to the "senior" tranche. Here the assessment of credit risk of the collateralized obligation was not initially on the credit risks of the assets in the structure but of the structure itself bearing sufficient overcollateralization to compensate for the credit risk of the underlying assets.

Now, there are two aspects of this process that produced fragility when applied to mortgages. The granting of credit risk as investment grade by a credit rating agency was initially meant to represent the degree of liquidity of an asset,[5] not its probability of default or the size of loss in the case of default. Mortgages in general, and collateralized mortgage obligations in particular, were by nature less liquid than corporate securities that had been the major category of asset rated by the agencies. Nonetheless, credit rating agencies generally applied the same principles that they had used in evaluating corporate fixed-income securities – an area in which there is a sufficiently long run of data to have reasonable statistical evidence of performance. For the liabilities of the special purpose entities dealing with mortgages or collateralized obligations comprising mortgages, this was not the case. Thus, as the market continued to expand throughout the beginning of the new millennium, a period of stability in the Minskyian sense prevailed, and the ability of these collateralized structures to meet their expected commitments to senior and residual tranche investors led to increased confidence and a reduction in the implicit cushions of safety against non-completion in the form of falling levels of overcollateralization. And not only did the degree of overcollateralization fall, as the demand for traditional mortgages started to decline, banks and independent loan originators sought new clients by offering more attractive terms and reducing qualification standards for "nonconforming" mortgages, that is, mortgages that did not conform to the conditions for placement with the government-sponsored mortgage guarantee enterprises such as Fannie and Ginnie Mae, Freddy Mac, and so forth.

For these "subprime" and Alt-A mortgages, the statistical record upon which to base overcollateralization ratios to ensure investment-grade rating status was even sparser and often nonexistent. Nonetheless, obligations composed of subprime mortgages with no payment history as collateral were created with senior tranches that were rated as investment grade, representing an additional reduction in the cushions of safety behind the structures.

Finally, most of these collateralized obligations were themselves purchased by special purpose investment entities that issued structured assets or by pension funds and insurance companies so that there was very little market trading in the securities to create a basis for market valuation. Thus, their value was usually created by means of a statistical model that either had no historical basis for its parameters or on the basis of existing structures that did not have similar performance characteristics. Thus, the undervaluation of risk and the declining cushions of safety were joined by an overvaluation of potential returns and valuations.

Nonetheless, the intended result – a large and growing source of income for banks (and for the rating agencies) – also produced a largely ignored and unnoticed increase in financial fragility. But, as long as house prices continued to rise, and new households were found to continue to demand new or refinanced mortgages, the increasingly fragile and uncertain payments commitments continued to be met. As long as new mortgages continued to fuel the demand for houses, the higher prices for houses continued to validate the overvaluation of the senior tranche assets and produce excess returns for the residual tranches. Thus, the success in the completion of payments commitments came more to resemble a Ponzi scheme that required increasing mortgage originations to produce the payments on the existing structures, with the addition of increasingly risky mortgage terms and quality and continually declining cushions of safety.

As noted, the credit rating agencies were crucial in the credit arbitrage that was at the basis of the success of structured securitization. The agencies also experienced a Minsky-style decline in credit standards that reinforced the declining cushion of overcapitalization. Because the rating agencies were usually directly consulted in the design of the securitization, they were primarily responsible for determining the appropriate overcapitalization or equity cushion that was considered to be investment grade. An issuer of a structured product would always contact a number of rating agencies to find the agency that would grant investment grade with the lowest and least costly credit enhancement. Thus, a more conservative assessment of the risks by a rating agency would never become effective because it would not be chosen. And, as time went on without difficulties in the market, the more conservative risk assessments would be revised to conform to the less conservative assessments that were being used by successful originators, in part to insure business, and in part because the history of stability at these assessment levels seemed to confirm the less conservative risk estimates as correct. This, along with the lack of statistical history on which to model the default characteristics of the assets, also contributed to the decline of the equity cushion required of the structures (Adelson, 2007, p. 11).

There were other players that joined this parade – independent mortgage originators who only wrote mortgages that they then sold on a wholesale basis to banks, which placed them in pools for collateralization. Others set up finance companies that used loans from banks to fund nonconforming mortgages that they originated, repaying the bank loans with the proceeds from the securitization of the mortgages. All of these institutions depended on being able to sell on short-term financed mortgages through collateralized structures to banks or directly to capital markets.

Finally, as mentioned already, in the late 1980s banks had created structured investment vehicles to move assets off their balance sheets and increase their non-interest income. In these structures, the special entity purchases structured assets or mortgages and finances them through the issue of short-term (asset-backed) commercial paper and longer-term equity notes. This is a rather different structure than the collateralized obligations that generate income through the creation of investment-grade assets out of noninvestment-grade assets, primarily through credit ratings arbitrage. Here, the income comes from the interest spread between the short-term paper issued to fund the acquisition of the long-term structured assets or the old net interest margin of pre-deregulation banking. This spread income was then increased by leverage created from overselling the commercial paper. At the peak, SIVs had issued around $400 billion of the total asset-backed commercial paper outstanding of $1.2 trillion.

The SIV is based on the same principle as a bank that funds loans with short-term liabilities, levered up by a deposit multiplier, and thus has the traditional form of maturity mismatch. But, there are important differences from the point of view of financial fragility. Banks create deposits that are the formal equivalent of US government debt by making loans – an SIV cannot automatically place commercial paper by investing in structured assets. Thus, the combination of maturity mismatching and liquidity creation common to banks is absent.

Second, banks hold reserves with the central bank and in the form of secondary reserve assets to meet a potential deposit drain – the SIV has no formal support structure in the case of a commercial paper "drain." Finally, a bank can always go to the central bank as lender of last resort to discount its loans, whereas an SIV can only sell its assets in the case of distress. The liquidity and stability of the SIVs thus depended on bank liquidity – that is, the sale or substitution of the commercial paper with bank loans. Although banks have argued that they are formally not committed to back up the commercial paper issued by the SIVs that they have created, manage, and administer, they nonetheless have a de facto responsibility to do just that if they are to avoid insolvency. Because there were no formal credit lines and were to off balance sheet entities called "variable interest entities," they were not formally reported on consolidated financial statements, nor was capital required against them under the Basle Accords.[6] Thus, an SIV resembles a small bank – but without bank regulation or supervision. In addition, despite statements to the contrary, the bank creating the SIV retains its exposure to the assets in the SIV that serve as collateral to the commercial paper. When the commercial paper is not renewed, the banks must step in and either buy the new issue of commercial paper or make loans of an equivalent amount. These will count against the bank's capital ratio, and the bank may find it impossible to meet its commitment. It is important to note that whereas the majority of assets in SIVs are mortgage assets, they also include other structured products as well as credit card receivables, auto loans, student loans, and so forth, all of which are subject to the same increasing fragility as the mortgage-backed assets.

It is interesting to note that this model of funding long-term mortgage assets with short-term commercial paper was not restricted to the US. Similar examples caused the insolvency of two banks in Germany as well as a real bank run for Northern Rock in the UK. Indeed, estimates of global bank risk exposure in asset-backed commercial paper is as high as $900 billion. The impact of the uncertainty over the value of the assets behind the paper and the uncertainty over the size of the implicit bank funding commitment led to a dramatic decline in outstanding commercial paper and a sharp upward spike in short-term interest rates in both the US and Europe, producing an acute liquidity crisis.

Thus, by 2006 the US system was one that could be described in Minskyian terms as highly fragile, with low cushions of safety and one that had impaired liquidity provision due to the increased use of security affiliates. It could only avoid a breakdown into instability as long as house prices continued to rise, as long as the flow of new mortgage applications continued, as long as interest rates continued to fall, and as long as none of the structured assets were actually sold in a market to give their mark-to-market value.

It is not clear what set off the collapse. As in most financial crises, in all probability it was in some area of the financial system that had nothing to do with mortgages. On the other hand, some of the subprime mortgages had been sold on an adjustable rate basis, and as reset dates approached in an environment of rising interest rates, many borrowers were unable to meet their mortgage service. Already in 2006 the rise in house prices appeared to have reached a peak. As default rates rose – beyond the untested assumptions of the models that had been used to create the collateralized debt obligations – foreclosures increased, and house prices started to decline. In addition, as already mentioned, the SIVs were interest-spread vehicles with profitability determined by the positive difference between long and short rates. However, in this period the rise in US interest rates was accompanied by an inversion of the yield curve in which short rates rose without a comparable adjustment in long rates, thus squeezing the interest spread and profitability of the SIVs. As their profitability declined, the value of their assets was also falling due to the increasing rate of default and falling house prices due to foreclosures. This led to a decision by investors not to rollover the commercial paper financing of the SIVs, creating the need for banks to step in to provide loans to avoid full liquidation of portfolios.

Thus, the stage is set for a typical Minsky debt deflation in which position has to be sold to make position – that is, the underlying assets have to be sold to repay investors. This will take place in illiquid markets, which means that price declines, and thus, the negative impact on present value will be even more rapid. In this environment, declining short-term interest rates can have little impact, and it is understandable that the secretary of the Treasury – a former head of Goldman Sachs who was present at the creation of many of these structures – has proposed a Super Special Purpose Entity to hold these assets, thus avoiding the need for them to be sold to make position. Unfortunately, the government has not proposed financing the entity but has asked banks to do so. Given their current capital ratios, they will be unable to do so without reducing these ratios to levels that impair their credit ratings.

Finally, the new entity would solve only the problem of the banks and their holdings of "senior" tranches (which, as noted, says nothing about their creditworthiness), it does nothing to solve the problem of the hedge funds holding the residual or toxic tranches that may now be without value. When these losses are reported to investors in sharply lower net asset values, they are certain to lead to massive redemptions by their institutional and pension fund clients. Because hedge funds are normally highly leveraged, this will put pressure on their lenders and their prime brokers – exactly the same banks that currently have to increase their lending in support of their SIVs and their holdings of senior tranches of collateralized obligations. They could choose to make margin calls on the declining value of the hedge fund assets pledged as collateral, but this would simply aggravate their existing problems.

As already noted, the damage from a debt deflation will be widespread – borrowers who lose their homes, hedge funds that fail, pensions that are reduced – so the net overall impact will be across a number of different sectors. However, in difference to what Alan Greenspan argued in defense of financial engineering to produce more complete markets – that it provided for a better distribution of risk across those who are willing to bear it – the risk appears to be highly concentrated in core money center banks that, at present, are increasingly unable to bear it. The Feds survey of lending conditions currently suggests that banks are curtailing lending and tightening credit conditions. This suggest that lending to households, whose spending in the current recovery has been financed by structured finance, is likely to decline dramatically. If the availability of household finance collapses, it is also likely that the long predicted, but never realized, retrenchment of consumer spending may become a reality, buttressed by the continued decline in the dollar, producing rising import prices. That, along with rising petroleum prices, will further reduce real incomes and make meeting mortgage debt service that much more difficult. The system thus seems poised for a Minsky–Fisher style debt deflation that further interest rate reductions will be powerless to stop.

The Fed has already stated that it will accept asset-backed commercial paper as collateral for discount window lending and granted Section 23A exemptions to two large US banks, allowing them to increase their lending to affiliates over existing limits. These measures, along with the Super Fund proposal, are all meant to avoid a "market" solution to the problem in the form of debt deflation. Given that the crisis appears to be similar to that which led to the breakdown of the financial system through debt deflation in the 1930s, a similar remedy in the form of a Reconstruction Finance Corporation and re-regulation of the system would seem to be the most efficient means to prevent, in Hy Minsky's words, "IT" from happening again.

Notes

1 Senior scholar, The Levy Economics Institute of Bard College; distinguished research professor, Center for Full Employment and Price Stability, University of Missouri – Kansas City; and professor of finance and development, Tallinn University of Technology. The author is indebted to Mario Tonveronachi for his insightful comments on an initial draft.
2 And environmental economists would also note that they also produce waste and pollution that also must be considered.
3 It is important to note that Minsky's approach was not one of either "rational" bubbles or of speculative mania. Instead he argued that it was the nature of periods of realized expectations to induce individuals to adjust their own defenses against the possibility of non-completion of time transactions. See Kregel (1997, pp. 543–8).
4 See, for example, George G. Kaufman and Larry R. Mote (1994) or the even more extreme book by Lowell Bryan (1991).
5 "It is notable that in coming up with the NRSRO system, the SEC held that it was appropriate to apply lower haircuts to securities 'that were rated investment grade by a credit rating agency of national repute, because those securities typically were more liquid and less volatile in price than securities that were not so highly rated.'" See Whitehead and Mathis (2007, p. 3).
6 And, if my reading of Basle II paragraph 580 is correct, the same will be true under the new approach.

References

Adelson, Mark (2007) "The Role of Credit Rating Agencies in the Structured Finance Market," Testimony Before the Subcommittee on Capital Markets, Insurance, and Government-Sponsored Enterprises of the House Committee on Financial Services Regarding the Role of Credit Rating Agencies in the Structured Finance Market, Washington, DC, September 27.

Bernanke, Ben (2007) "Remarks," Federal Reserve Bank of Atlanta's 2007 Financial Markets Conference, Sea Island, Georgia, May 15.

Bryan, Lowell L. (1991) *Bankrupt*, New York: Harper Business.

Chandler, Alfred (1990) *Scale and Scope*, Cambridge, MA: Harvard University Press.

Coase, Ronald H. (1991) "The Nature of the Firm," in O. Williamson and S. Winter, eds., *The Nature of the Firm: Origins, Evolution, and Development*, Oxford: Oxford University Press.

Kaufman, George G. and Larry R. Mote (May 1994) "Is Banking a Declining Industry? A Historical Perspective," *Federal Reserve Bank of Chicago Economic Perspectives*, Vol. 18, No. May, pp. 2–21.

—— (1997) "Margins of Safety and Weight of the Argument in Generating Financial Fragility," *Journal of Economic Issues*, Vol. 31, No. 2, pp. 543–8.

Minsky, Hyman Philip (1982) *Can "IT" Happen Again: Essays on Instability and Finance*, Armonk: M.E. Sharpe.

—— (1986) *Stabilizing an Unstable Economy*, New Haven: Yale University Press.

Robbins, Lionel (1952) *The Theory of Economic Policy in English Classical Economics*, London: Allen and Unwin.

Whitehead, Julia M. and H. Sean Mathis (2007) "Finding a Way Out of the Rating Agency Morass," Prepared Statement to the Subcommittee on Capital Markets, Insurance, and Government-Sponsored Enterprises of the House Committee on Financial Services Regarding the Role of Credit Rating Agencies in the Structured Finance Market, Washington, DC, September 27.

Part III

Minsky's theory in an international context

Financial globalization and emerging markets

9 Currency stabilization through full employment

Can EMU combine price stability with employment and income growth?

Summary introduction

The introduction of the Euro in 1999 will see the completion of a process initiated by Roy Jenkins's decision to breathe new life into the Treaty of Rome by reviving the project for a common currency. The path that has led from the Exchange Rate Mechanism, to the Single Market Act, to the revision of the original Treaty in Maastricht has meant a transformation of the original objectives from a free trade zone to a zone of price stability. This has meant that other economic policy objectives have been subordinated to price stability, and many countries have had to sacrifice growth and employment to attain the prerequisites for what the Germans call a "culture of stability." Although these other policy objectives could be ignored for a short period, once the Euro was introduced, they would have to be faced. The original project for price stability overlooked these problems because it was presumed that price stability was a necessary and sufficient condition for the resumption of the kind of growth and employment experience that Europe had experienced before the Vietnam war and the oil crisis. However, this has not been the case.

The process of globalization of trade and production has created additional difficulties for the European unification project. In particular, it has raised the question of competition from developing countries using cheap labor. This has created competitive pressure on firms as well as on the least skilled in the labor force. It has also brought to the forefront the importance of relative labor costs and the focused attention on the role of the behavior of wages and the labor market in attaining price stability. Most European countries now practice some sort of wage policy as the basis of maintaining price stability. Similar to the idea that price stability will produce growth, these seem to be based on the idea that wage stability will improve employment levels. Again, this has not been the case. Indeed, the stability of wages and prices appears to have been the result of creating excess supplies of both labor and productive capacity, both in Europe and abroad.

It thus appears to many that the objectives of wage and price stability will be incompatible with the objectives of high growth and employment, with the Growth and Stability Pact introduced to ensure that priority is given to the former. Yet, it seems clear that this potential conflict will have to be resolved if the European project is to succeed. If this were only an internal European dilemma, the risks might be on the side of a repetition of the past experience of stagflation. However in an increasingly global environment, the risks seem to be tilted in the opposite direction of excessive unemployment, deflation, or even depression. It is clear that the past methods for dealing with the social implications of this conflict will not be sufficient to the task. First budget deficit limits written in the Growth and Stability Pact will increasingly impinge on social safety nets so that attempting to ameliorate unemployment though income supplements and other benefits will eventually come into direct conflict with the objective of price stability. These same limits will apply to the use of fiscal expenditure policies to support aggregate demand.

A common currency represents a radical change in the monetary organization of Europe, designed to ensure that EMU produces a "stability culture." It will require a radical alternative approach to resolve the dilemma of combining price stability with full employment and achieving potential growth. Such an alternative has recently been advanced in the employer of last resort (ELR) proposal (cf. Mosler, 1997–8; Wray, 1998). It suggests the application to the labor market of a simple principle already employed to provide price stability in most financial markets – the use of a market maker. The specialist in the New York stock market plays such a role when he or she buys or sells for his or her own account to dampen price fluctuations. He does not "fix" prices, in the sense of keeping them invariant, but rather counters random movements in an attempt to prevent them from becoming cumulative. Prices are thus stable when their variance is lower.

As Nobel prize winner John Hicks has pointed out, virtually every successfully functioning market in a capitalist economy has the equivalent of a specialist who administered prices by providing residual supply or demand. The basis of the radical alternative behind ELR is to turn the labor market into a full-fledged capitalist market with a market maker who would act as residual buyer and seller of labor, offering to employ any worker unable to find a job at a fixed wage or releasing any worker who chooses to leave for a better alternative. Just as the market price automatically eliminates excess supplies of product, such a proposal would eliminate the formal concept of involuntary unemployment – there would always be a supply of jobs to meet demand for them. By providing an administered residual wage, it would also reduce the variability of wages and thus provide stability to wage levels. The ELR proposal has been put forward as a means of providing full employment. But it can also be viewed as a means for introducing stability of wages, which would make it easier to achieve the culture of stability in the absence of employment.

The next two sections of this paper deal with the reasons why a new approach to the unemployment problem is required. The third considered the ELR proposal as a means of combining price stability with high employment. The final section provides considerations on its introduction into the economic policy apparatus of the European Union (EU).

Why Europe needs to try a new approach to price stability

Throughout the 1980s European economic policy, largely under the direction of Margaret Thatcher, played a single tune called TINA. This is an acronym for the slogan "There Is No Alternative" to the policy of stable prices to achieve stable growth rates with high employment levels.[1] As a result, fiscal and monetary policy were increasingly directed toward reducing inflation rates to the exclusion of all other policy objectives because this was a precondition for all other policy objectives. Because inflation was considered to be caused by an excess supply of money financing an excess demand for goods, monetary growth was restricted, interest rates were raised, and budgets were slashed to keep demand in line with available supplies.

In this context, the completion of the European Single Market, first broached in the Milan Summit in 1985 and initiated in 1993, was viewed as a measure that would promote economic growth without raising money supply growth or increasing fiscal deficits. But, it soon became clear that the benefits of increased intra-EEC demand from the creation of a single market could be fairly shared among the member countries only if relative price changes were determined by changes in productivity rather than the increasingly variable and unpredictable exchange rates that resulted from the behavior of the United States dollar and differences in the evolution of member country policies. As a result, the single market policy to create non-inflationary demand was transformed into a project to establish a full EMU[2] to reinforce the price stability that was considered a prelude to expanding output and employment. For almost all countries, meeting the convergence criteria involved reducing government spending and tightening monetary policy. Somewhat paradoxically, the policy which was meant to support demand by creating inflation was thus transformed into a policy to reduce demand and ensure nominal convergence of economic variables.

This policy has been successful beyond any expectation. The average rate of inflation for the EU in the period 1975–84 was over 10 percent. For the period from 1984 to 1993, when the single market was due to take effect, it had fallen by more than half to 4.5 percent. The rate of price increase for the EU is now below 2 percent, with Greece showing the highest rate of 3–4 percent. Taking the traditional measure of price stability as the 2 percent level that the Bundesbank reported to the German Constitutional Court as satisfying its responsibility under the Bundesbank Law to stabilize the value of money, the EU countries that are likely to enter the EMU have experienced conditions of price stability for around three years. However, the real rates of output growth, which averaged 3.2% during the dismal inflation decade of the 1970s, fell to an average of 2.25% for the decade of the 1980s and in the first seven years of the current decade have collapsed to 1.7%. With stable prices Europe has grown only about half as fast as during the period of higher inflation.

The average unemployment rate for the period 1970–9 was barely over 4%; for 1980–9 it was just under 9%; while for the current decade to 1996, it has gone over 10%. The figures for 1997 and 1998 will average well over 11%. Employment, which had grown by only an annual average of 0.4% in the period 1979–89, has fallen to only 0.15% per year in the present decade to 1996. This is not really surprising, given the fall in the average rate of GDP growth in the face of high rates of productivity growth. But, even the rate of productivity growth has been declining, from an annual average rate of 5.8% in the period 1979–88 to 4.2% in 1990–6.

That the present approach to price stability has not been able to produce high, stable growth may be seen in the simultaneous decline in output gaps (i.e., the difference between potential output and actual output) and average GDP growth rates, which indicate that potential output is converging downward toward the declining rate of actual real output growth. The simplest explanation for this performance is the decline in investment, which has accompanied the decline in inflation. For the first time in the post-war period, the share of investment in GDP is now higher in the US than it is in Germany. Indeed, if one compares the experience of the US and the EU in the 1990s both experienced falling inflation rates, in the US investment and consumption have been rising along with the growth rate. In the US the budget deficit and the inflation rate have been reduced by high growth rather than being considered a prerequisite for high growth. Inflation rates in the US have been continually falling and are currently near the 2% level. This suggests that there are alternative paths to the creation of stable growth and employment that are also compatible with price stability.

If Europe continues these trends, and potential growth falls toward a declining actual growth rate, with productivity expanding at rates that are roughly double GDP growth, the result can only be rising unemployment or lower labor force participation rates.[3] Clearly, the single market and a "culture of stability" are not sufficient to allow Europe to exploit its potential income growth. Is there perhaps another way?

Is export-led growth a viable alternative for Europe?

It has been suggested, also a favorite British position, that external demand could provide a source of non-inflationary growth because it does not require fiscal deficits, faster money supply growth, or increased household expenditures.[4] Export-led growth usually involves exchange rate adjustment, but with Europe about to embark on an experience of irrevocably fixed exchange rates, the same result can be produced by a fall in the domestic rate of inflation caused by nominal wages rising at less than the rate of productivity growth providing a real depreciation of the currency and an increase in external demand to offset the decline in domestic demand. The problem with this approach is that it is virtually identical to the old-fashioned concept of the beggar-thy-neighbor devaluations that plagued Europe in the 1920s. The current version, using wage reductions and real exchange rate changes rather than nominal exchange rate adjustments, is often defended as preferable to the earlier version because it produces the benefit of internal price stability and nominal exchange rate stability.

Nonetheless, it remains a policy that can only be practiced successfully by a single country relative to the rest of the world. It is wholly inappropriate for a country that is part of an integrated economic area that has a high proportion of its trade within the group and is about to introduce a single currency so that exchange rates will become irrevocably fixed. Export-led growth in the context of EMU can only mean relative to the rest of the world outside the EU. It is not a policy alternative that can be operated by any single member country. Yet this seems to be precisely the policy that some countries are employing to solve their unemployment problems. And it can only reduce the possibility of solving the problem for the union as a whole.

As an example, consider current German wage policy.[5] It is widely believed in Germany that its current difficulties of slow growth and rising unemployment are due to excessively high absolute wage levels. This is despite a persistent and rising trade surplus, a current account that has returned to surplus, a GDP deflator less than 1% and a Consumer Price Index (CPI) inflation rate below 2%. Nonetheless, it is argued that recovery of employment levels will require lower wages. The results of a policy that has set the target for wage growth at the inflation target over the last two years has been a reduction in unit labor costs of around 3.5% over the period, a real depreciation of the DM by more than 10 percent, a continued fall in the inflation rate (abstracting from the impact of "fiscal" inflation caused by a change in indirect taxation), and growth in exports at double-digit figures.

This radical adjustment has occurred in the presence of stagnating consumption demand growth of less than 1% per annum, investment in manufacturing that has only recently started to respond in export sectors, and unemployment that has reached unprecedented levels and continues to rise. Rising net exports have not offset the negative impact on domestic demand of the decline in real wage growth, rising unemployment, and the reduction in government expenditures.[6] Despite real depreciation, increased international competitiveness, and price stability, growth in output and employment remain at historically low levels.

But, this policy is not only failing to operate successfully in Germany. As noted, this policy cannot be employed by a single country within a group of countries linked by a single currency without negative effects on the others because all will eventually be forced to adopt the same policies. If the rest of Europe does not follow Germany in keeping wage increases down to the target inflation rate (which is lower than the rate of productivity growth), the result will be exactly the same as if their nominal inflation rates were excessive relative to the inflation rate in Germany, and they will be losing intra-EU competitiveness. The culture of nominal price stability would simply reproduce differentials in real terms. While previously these differences would have appeared as real appreciations of exchange rates relative to Germany, and have been eliminated by nominal appreciation of the DM before the EMU, the differences will now appear in terms of differential real returns to capital and labor in Germany relative to the rest of the EMU. Although there will no longer be any national balances of payments to finance or exchange rates to defend, there will still be flows of funds among countries, and the same instability will result. In simple terms, Germany will be draining domestic demand from the rest of the EU.

Note that greater independence of any individual EU country in managing its own fiscal policy would change this picture very little. If France or Italy decided to expand domestic demand, it would be quickly drained out of the country – it would no longer show up in the German balance of payments surplus and an Italian deficit, as before the EMU, but now appear as increased expenditure flows from Italy to Germany, with the Italian fiscal deficit deteriorating and credit risks on Italian securities increasing. While both labor and capital costs will be rising in Italy relative to Germany, this will only exacerbate the divergences and make a policy of downward wage convergence more pressing. The single currency will bring the positive benefit of releasing European economies from having to contract their domestic expenditure policies to defend their exchange rates relative to the DM, but it brings with it the cost of requiring that they contract their nominal wages to defend the competitiveness of their domestic production against cheapening German imported goods.

Alternatively, Germany might be said to be exporting its unemployment to the rest of the EU member countries. The other members of the EMU can only allow their nominal wage levels to evolve independently of Germany to the extent they can rely on productivity growth in excess of that in Germany. If productivity growth is roughly constant across countries, they will have to reduce their growth of wages below current inflation and productivity growth levels in their tradable sectors to defend their employment levels. The result will be that beggar-thy-neighbor nominal exchange rate depreciations are replaced by beggar-thy-neighbor reductions in wage costs and prices. Competition for foreign demand by wage reductions in a single country will produce competition within the single currency area fought through price deflation, and this will be the case irrespective of the fact that there is currently no question of excessive national rates of growth of wages or prices in Europe. As mentioned, the inflation convergence for the potential members of the EMU has for some three years been within the 2% threshold, considered as price stability by the Bundesbank. Restoring German external competitiveness will only produce internal deflation and increased competition for a falling aggregate total of EU demand, leading to further downward pressure on prices of manufactured goods and larger differences between manufactured and service prices.

The question then is whether the increase in demand from outside the EU resulting from real depreciation of the Euro will be sufficient to offset the decline in internal demand. Whereas external trade was a very large proportion of each member country's GDP before unification, it will become a very small proportion after unification. The order of magnitude is not likely to be sufficient to offset the reduction in EU demand. Further, because the Euro will float against the dollar and the yen, and given the German obsession with a "strong" Euro as evidenced in recent Bundesbank policy, if the Euro were to appreciate relative to these currencies, this would eliminate any benefits that might have accrued from the reduction in unit labor costs. If the Euro behaves as the

German mark has done over the last 20 years, this means that in the medium-term, it will appreciate to maintain a roughly constant real effective exchange rate, with nominal appreciations offsetting any changes in relative unit labor costs. Export-led growth as a medium-term policy thus cannot produce any increase in EU demand and can only aggravate the conflict between growth and price stability by placing price stability in jeopardy of deflation.[7]

From the point of view of maintaining fiscal balance, deflation is just as damaging as inflation, for declining nominal GDP will reduce government receipts, whereas the rising levels of unemployment will increase social transfer payments. Given the commitments in the Growth and Stability Pact, this will create even greater pressure for reform of the existing social welfare programs. Larger numbers of individuals will be provided with sharply reduced support programs.

If the EMU is to be successful, it will require policies that prevent a weak Euro and excessive inflation, but it is even more likely to require policies that prevent excessive strength of the Euro and the risk of price deflation. Thus, the current policy of export-led growth based on increasing international competitiveness appears even less promising in reaching accommodation between price stability and growth and argues for a new approach to the issue.

Supply-side policies for the labor market

This discussion suggests that the key to price stability and to the problem of unemployment both lie in the evolution of wages. Increased wage flexibility is unlikely to provide a solution to rising unemployment, and the increased competitiveness that downward flexibility is likely to produce is unlikely to generate sufficient external demand to offset the negative impacts on consumption growth and investment. Nonetheless, the current global environment of rapidly changing technological conditions and global competitiveness do suggest that there is a need for increased labor flexibility. In economic terms, this means that labor must return to being a variable factor whose use changes with the needs of current production plans. In crude terms, this means greater flexibility in laying off workers, in hiring and firing, and in temporary or part-time work contracts. Resisting these changes in the face of competition from emerging economies with diverse social and cultural support systems creates the risk of higher levels of permanent unemployment.

The changes required to increase flexibility are often considered as supply-side changes – making labor supply more flexible. But they cannot be separated from demand-side changes because greater workplace flexibility makes labor incomes more variable and thus makes consumption expenditures more volatile and less predictable, which dampens the willingness of entrepreneurs to invest. To put the problem from a slightly different point of view, the worker and the employer are looking at the same market in two different ways. The employer is interested in an input that has a variable cost, whereas the worker is interested in a steady flow of income from employment. The employer is looking at the market for a variable resource input, labor, whereas the worker is looking at a market for a fixed income-earning asset, a job. From the point of view of the worker, there is an insufficiently flexible supply of jobs, whereas from the point of view of the employer, there is an insufficiently flexible supply of workers. Introducing flexibility in the labor market makes incomes and prices more variable; introducing flexibility in the job market makes incomes and consumption more stable. There would seem to be an area of unexploited mutual advantage between labor and employers in making both sides of the market more flexible. The free market mechanism does not seem to be capable of providing the solution, yet financial markets solve similar problems on a regular basis. Market makers exist to ensure flexible supplies at the same time as they dampen the price fluctuations from random variations in supplies and demands coming onto the market. The "specialist" on the New York Stock Exchange is an example. Most of these institutional arrangements rely on holding inventories, or what may be described as "buffer stocks," to provide a compromise between the competing needs of flexibility by buyers and sellers to be able to trade on a continuous basis in conditions of price stability.

Because labor is not a storable commodity, and thus cannot be held in a buffer stock, the produce of labor is storable, substituting a variation in labor time for variations in inventories or investment in increased labor skills that allow the transfer of present output into more valuable future output. Indeed, attempts have been made in this direction, in terms of "labor hoarding" by individual firms, but without much success. This is because the produce of labor is held in the specific form of the output of the individual firm. Because it is difficult for a firm to differentiate a random cyclical downturn from a decline in the demand for its own product, such schemes can be successful only if demand patterns remain stable such that it is the general level of demand that adjusts rather than a shift in tastes away from the product. In current conditions of high technological change, and Japanese just-in-time inventory management, labor hoarding in this way does not seem plausible.

Instead, the produce of labor would have to be for a "general" output, that is, something that is in general demand and will be required independently of both cyclical change and changes in demand patterns. In general, such goods are defined as "public" rather than "private" goods (note that this distinction refers to the characteristics of the demand for these goods, not to whether they are produced or supplied publicly or privately). Whereas the idea of a buffer stock of goods may not be successful on a private basis, it may be more plausible if instituted on a public basis, with the public sector playing the role of intermediary, providing the residual supply of jobs to offset the desired flexibility of the private sector. This would mean that although workers could not necessarily count on holding the same job through time, they could be certain that a job would always be available. Flexibility in labor supply, in the sense of being willing to shift more readily between employers would then be compatible with a more steady stream of wage incomes and a return to more stable patterns of consumption. Such a scheme has been suggested by Mosler (1997–8) and further elaborated by Wray (1998) as the "Employer of Last Resort" (ELR) proposal, with the government acting as the market maker to stabilize prices and to ensure flexibility of the supply of jobs as ELR.

If such an ELR program of flexible residual government employment were to replace current unemployment and social support schemes, this would just be a return to the original intentions of employment insurance schemes, which were meant to provide short-term income maintenance for periodic loss of a job due to the short-term cyclical fluctuations of the economy. The unemployment benefit was never conceived to be a long-term support for the unemployed or to provide welfare to the needy. This is not to say that these schemes should not exist, only that they should be separate from the policy to ensure full employment.

An ELR program would resolve the problem of unemployment by definition because the supply of private and public sector jobs would always be equal to the demand. Anyone who chose not to work would have made a voluntary decision to exit the active labor force, whereas anyone unable to work would be eligible for public welfare support.

But, the role of an intermediary is not only to absorb excesses and deficiencies of supply and demand relative to equilibrium but also to smooth price differences around that equilibrium. If the public sector is to play this role and act to stabilize wages, there must be some conception of the equilibrium wage. Obviously, there is no single "equilibrium" wage in the economy but a range of wage differentials for different labor skills that spreads out from some base wage. Just as the central bank sets the policy interest rate, and offers to buy or sell overnight money at that rate, leaving the private sector intermediaries to determine the rates on every other type of financial asset, the public sector could set the "policy" wage rate and leave the determination of wage differentials to the private labor market. Many governments already do this implicitly when they set a minimum wage for private sector employment. But there is no need for the government to legislate the minimum wages that should be paid in the private sector. If the public sector becomes the residual job supplier, it only needs to set the rate at which it will buy labor. The private sector is free to set any rate it wishes for contracts undertaken in competitive markets on a free and voluntary basis. In more or less the same way that money market interest rates are today below the Fed funds rate, the private sector may set wages below the public sector rate, and if workers prefer these wages and conditions, they are free to accept them. All that is required is the alternative of a public sector job at the policy rate.[8]

Setting a "policy" wage for ELR workers would then provide a fixed point around which the overall wage level would be determined. If the demand for labor is falling, workers will be moving increasingly into public employment at the policy wage, which will limit the downward movement in labor income as government deficits expand and provide automatic stabilization in domestic demand. The opposite will occur in periods of expansion. It is to be expected that the differentials would contract or spread out with the changes in private sector demand but would be protected from absolute declines. This means that workers avoid "depreciation" in the value of labor on the downside and depreciation in the value of their wages on the upside of the cycle.

In another sense, the government has an advantage over individual private firms in acting as the market maker. Just as for any intermediary, there will be occasions in which wages will have to be adjusted to preserve a minimum buffer stock. But, instead of raising wages in cases of depletion of the pool of public sector employment, it would be possible to use fiscal restraint to dampen demand as the ELR wage is reduced, thus reducing the upward pressure on wages as lower-skilled workers are drawn into the labor force. Thus, private sector entry wages would not rise, with the beneficial effect of offsetting the fall in productivity that occurs due to "hiring path diminishing returns" as lower-skilled, relatively untrained, labor enters the private sector labor force. Thus, fiscal policy remains necessary as a tool of restraint in an expansion, whereas the automatic stabilizers are free to operate in a decline. In a sense, the policy could be considered as one of using a Non-Accelerating Inflation Rate of Unemployment (NAIRU) but with the NAIRU set at zero unemployment.

There is one last advantage of such a proposal over traditional "Keynesian" fiscal policy measures. The use of government expenditure policy to offset cyclical fluctuations in demand has suffered from two nearly irremediable defects. The first is the time that is required to adopt the required legislation to change expenditure levels. The second is that expenditure levels have come to be determined primarily by political considerations rather than by the needs of the cyclical stability of the economy. The ELR scheme would eliminate both of these difficulties. First, the public employment programs would be prepared and legislated in advance – paradoxically this is very similar to the way the Hoover administration conceived of government intervention in the economy. Thus, there would be no delay in approving programs that would be implemented on a priority basis depending on the availability of ELR labor.

The second advantage is that the programs could not become self-perpetuating or politically motivated. Government expenditures would automatically contract as the economy expanded as the result of lack of labor to carry them out. If political considerations argued in favor of maintaining projects, they would have to be justified and funded on the basis of private market costs and returns, which was the original intention of Keynes's stabilization policy through public works. This would be facilitated through the creation and evaluation of government expenditures on the basis of a capital and current account budget – the current account budget being roughly balanced within the limits of the 3% maximum given by the Growth and Stability Pact and the capital account budget determined by the cyclical movement of the economy, where by definition deficits equal gross investment expenditures.

Application of the ELR proposal in the European Union

The discussion of current policy in the EU suggests that there is a more important issue that an ELR scheme would resolve. As argued, differential wage policy in different countries may create a risk of deflation with the EU. The problem involves setting of the "policy" wage rates in different countries at the appropriate level with respect to differential national rates of productivity growth. Under a single currency one should expect convergence, not only of interest rates but also of prices. The tendency toward deflation highlighted here is aggravated by German nominal wage growth being set at the target inflation rate of 2% when the rate of growth of productivity is substantially higher than this, with the result that German unit labor costs fall faster than in the rest of the EU and have created a real depreciation of German-produced goods.

From the point of view of the EU, there are two questions that have to be resolved. The first is the level at which the policy wage should be set in different countries. The second is the adjustment of the policy wage through time. The level should be set with respect to unemployment benefits, or to minimum wages, or other criteria such as national wage scales. However the level is set, it should be adjusted over time on the basis of the national average growth of productivity to prevent beggar-thy-neighbor reductions in national wage scales. This should be done to ensure that the stability of nominal wages with respect to prices does not produce deflation.

A stabilization scheme patterned on the ELR proposal would have two clear benefits for the EU. The first would be to reduce volatility in incomes while providing flexibility in labor supply. This should make consumption expenditures more stable and be beneficial to investment expenditures, reinforcing the stability of domestic demand, the major requirement for European recovery. At the same time, the increased flexibility should provide higher productivity, and this should also support investment. Together these two factors should allow potential capacity to grow and increase the private sector demand for labor, decreasing the number of residual jobs that have to be supplied by the public sector.

Second, it provides a mechanism for stabilizing wages and thus prices at the same time as it provides a defense against the inbuilt tendency toward deflation in the EU. By providing support for both investment and productivity, it also means that standards of living should be rising as prices remain stable in the medium-term.

One advantage of such a program is that it increases the supply of public goods at virtually no cost, for it transfers idle workers receiving unemployment benefits to productive employment, providing public infrastructure and training. One of the most undesirable impacts of the TINA policies has been an almost total absence of maintenance of public infrastructure. This proposal allows that problem to be met at minimal costs.

There is, of course, one remaining question. The program has potential costs to national government budgets, and there is the question of the permissibility of such expenditures under EU regulations. There is a static and a dynamic aspect to the first question. First, there will be cost savings due to the reduction in unemployment benefit (which will vary from country to country depending on its existing system) for those who are truly involuntarily unemployed (those who are disabled or are receiving income support for other reasons, such as single parents, etc., should not be affected). Then there will be a dynamic effect due to the positive impact on tax receipts as a result of higher incomes, consumption, and investment, leading to higher productivity and higher potential growth rates. Against this must be set the static costs of paying for the labor employed and the organizational structure. The balance of these impacts, at least in the short-term, are likely to create an increase in the government deficit, which would be attenuated by the increased potential capacity and income growth over time.

However, attention must also be given to the accounting of the expenditures for ELR employment. When assessing a county's budget position with respect to the reference values for admission to phase three of the EMU, both the Maastricht Treaty and the Growth and Stability Pact instruct the commission to take into account the relation between the government deficit and gross investment expenditures. The presumption is that a country would be permitted a deficit that is higher than 3% if this was committed to necessary public infrastructure investment expenditures. It is probable that most of the increased expenditures would be classified as investment or maintenance in physical or human capital. Indeed, it would be highly desirable that much of the residual supply of jobs would involve increasing the skill levels of workers through education and on-the-job training in areas of labor market tightness.

Finally, although there is nothing to stop an individual country within the EU from introducing such an ELR stabilization policy, the advantages for price stability clearly depend on it being introduced on an EU-wide basis. Such a policy would render unnecessary any additional oversight of the European Central Bank or the creation of the Euro-X committee to promote social policy.

Notes

1 This is a modern version of the idea advanced in the 1930s that recovery could occur only if profits were increased by reducing wages. A variant was that investment could occur only if saving were increased by reducing consumption expenditures – because wage earners were the primary source of consumption and profit earners the primary source of saving, it came to the same thing. Kalecki argued against the former, and Keynes argued against the latter. At about the same time, Jerome Levy made the same discovery by answering the question of what determined profits.

2 Note that this is the correct specification of EMU rather than the often used, but erroneous, EMU.

3 In a Ricardian world this would not be a problem because none of the EU countries currently has a fertility rate that is even near the 2.1 replacement level, so the decline in population would eventually solve the unemployment problem if immigration can be limited. Only from this point of view does reducing foreign residents aid in solving the unemployment problem.

4 Note that this is little different from the justification for the Single Market Act as a means to increase economic integration and thus intra-EU exports.

5 It has been given official sanction during the presentation of the German Government's Annual Economic Report by Economics Minister Rexrodt, who announced: "More jobs would be created only if wage increases lagged the growth of productivity for the foreseeable future" (Norman, 1998).

6 Nonetheless, despite monetary growth rates near the center of the announced target range and inflation within the 2% target, the Bundesbank has recently raised the short-term repo rate from 3.0% to 3.3%, a clear signal that it is concerned about the compatibility of either government fiscal policy or union wage policy with the objective of price stability. This

seems to confirm the link between nominal wage growth and inflation, producing falling unit wage costs determined by productivity growth. The official explanation is to insure that the new common currency starts its life without any incipient inflationary pressures. An alternative explanation is that it has reduced its inflation target for the beginning of EMU to zero.

7 It is also necessary to consider the global context. German exports to Asia expanded by more than 10% in 1997, up from 6% in 1996, and exports to Eastern Europe rose by a quarter in 1997, largely due to growth in developing countries rather than any change in German competitiveness. Then 1998 brought falling demand, along with falling prices of imported goods from developing countries and primary commodities, adding to the risk of deflation in the EU. Thus, from the global point of view, the current policy may be self-defeating and thus unsustainable. Given that nearly every country in the EU has a positive external balance, the risk is not only for internal deflationary instability but for global instability.

8 This simply reflects what in fact occurred under the gold standard, where individual governments fixed only the rate of conversion between gold billion and the standard units of domestic coinage. It was left to the free market to determine international rates of exchange and to keep them stable. Under the gold standard no government gave a guarantee as to the value of its own currency in terms of foreign currency. Yet, the private gold market produced stability of exchange rates via international arbitrage.

References

Mosler, Warren (Winter 1997–8) "Full Employment and Price Stability," *Journal of Post Keynesian Economics*, Vol. 20, No. 2, pp. 167–82.

Norman, Peter (Thursday, March 12, 1998) "Rexrodt Hails Change in Jobless Trend," *Financial Times*, p. 3.

Wray, Larry Randall (1998) *Understanding Modern Money: The Key to Full Employment and Price Stability*, Upleadon: E. Elgar.

10 Yes, "it" did happen again—a Minsky crisis happened in Asia[1]

The St. Louis Cardinals and the Asian crisis

The Asian financial crisis is doubly unfortunate, first of all because it has set income and wealth levels in these countries back some ten years. But, it is also unfortunate because had Hy Minsky been alive to point out to policy makers that they were dealing with a debt deflation the worst excesses might have been prevented. Those of you who knew Hy might instantly object that Hy knew virtually nothing about Asia. But, that has not stopped hundreds of our colleagues from mistaking what went wrong in Asia. And in Hy's case it probably would not have made much difference. Hy only claimed to be an expert in one thing — the St. Louis Cardinals. But, I think we can make a good guess at what he would have said about the crisis, for it was a clear case of the Minsky instability hypothesis.

As you may remember, Hy spent a good deal of time explaining why "It", that is, the Great Depression, Can't Happen Again. But, in the case of Asia it did. And this is also a lesson for why it might happen again, outside the Far East. First, Hy insisted on the beneficial impact of Big Government in providing a floor under aggregate demand. Free falls in asset prices could not happen if there was a guaranteed floor under incomes. The Bigger the Government, the firmer that foundation and the more stable the economy. Not that this didn't cause other problems, but it meant that you could only go down so far. If we take a look at the vital statistics of the Asian economies, we see in general that they have small governments. And those governments tend to run persistent surpluses. There are no firm foundations here. This is not to say that government played no role. We have heard a lot about "crony capitalism" in Asia. But, this sort of income support does not provide the kind of aggregate demand support that Hy thought was beneficial to avoiding instability.

Hy also thought that a Big Bank, an active central bank willing to intervene actively by lending at the discount window in support of asset prices, and thus of bank solvency, was of crucial importance. Hy did not believe in tying one's hands or currency boards or other forms of shooting financial markets in the foot. It is true that central banks are common in Asia, and in some countries they are active on the policy front. But, in the current crisis a major portion of the lending to firms and financial institutions was in foreign currency, Yen and US dollars, which meant that the local central bank was constrained in its ability to act as lender of last resort by the size of its dollar reserves. They could not follow the Bagehot principle of lending without limit. Of course, they had the (non)-choice of adopting floating exchange rates, but this would have made their ability to act that much weaker.

Thus, the two basic elements that preclude financial instability and have prevented "It" from happening in the post-war period, were both absent in the Asia economies. Detailed knowledge of the region would not really have been necessary to have allowed Hy to reach the conclusion that these economies were subject to financial instability.

But, Hy would have been curious to discover the sources of the financial fragility that produced the financial breakdown in the Asian region. I think he also would have been particularly critical of the analysis that was used as the basis for the policy conditions that were attached to international support measures in the aftermath of the crisis. The rest of the paper seeks to outline these two points.

Financial fragility and development

We all know the aphorism that says bankers should only lend to people who don't need the money. This seems to reflect the experience of most developing countries. When they need to borrow, they find it difficult to do so; but when they are receiving foreign investment funds it is difficult to stop them coming in. What the aphorism presumably intends to convey is that bankers should only lend against good collateral, so that their loans are secured and credit risk is reduced to a minimum. But, as George Soros (1987, p. 81) has pointed out, in financial markets based on expectations of future values, the very act of lending may change expectations and thus the "fair" value of the collateral used to secure the loan. This suggests a positive relation between the value of collateral and the value of the loan it secures — lending may strengthen the firm and thus the bank. On the other hand, a firm that fails to secure lending may have to enter into distress sales or reduce activity, reducing the value of its assets that it had promised as collateral, as well as the value of collateral pledged against outstanding loans.

It is interesting that while this positive relation seems to apply to individual firms, it does not reflect the experiences of developing countries. Here the general rule has tended to be that the more that is lent, the lower the value of the country's assets. Why has lending created this difficulty? Before, Soros had become a household name, Hy (e.g. 1975) had set out an analysis of the risks involved in financial leverage that may help to explain why Soros's proposition tends not to work in many developing countries. Minsky's analysis is based on the sustainability of cash flows generated by the composition of assets and liabilities on company balance sheets. Borrowing the concept of a "margin of safety" from Benjamin Graham, Minsky defined the financing of a firm's operations as "hedge" finance the asset side of the balance sheet produces expected cash inflows from operating projects that always exceed the financing costs and operating expenses, including dividends for shareholders on the liability side of the balance sheet, by a sufficient "margin of safety" or cushion capable of absorbing any unforeseen changes in cash inflows and outflows.

If the cushion covered say 2.33 standard deviations of the historical data on past gross operating returns, then the firm would be unable to meet its cash flow commitments on average only one time in one hundred. A company that is expected to meet its payments with 99% probability is close to what the banker's aphorism means when it says it does not need the money.

As the cushion of safety declines and the probability of being unable to meet cash flow commitments rises, there will be a point at which it is 99% probable that there will be some future periods in which the cushion will not be sufficient so that the firm will not be able to meet its payment commitments. Nonetheless, the cumulative cushion over the life of the loan may be sufficient to cover them, so that the project has a positive net present value. The firm may need an extension on occasion, but by the end of the loan it will have met all interest and principal payments. This is what Minsky calls a "speculative" financing position, for both the banker and the borrower are speculating that by the end of the project there will be enough money to repay the loan, even though there may be shortfalls along the way. This is really what we have in mind when we say that bankers should make good credit assessments.

Finally, when the cushion of safety is non-existent and there is a high probability of shortfalls in nearly every period, the firm may have to borrow additional funds just to be able to meet current commitments. This Minsky calls "Ponzi" financing, making reference to a well-known pyramid investment scheme. These are companies that need to increase their borrowing just to stay in business, but to which, according to the aphorism and good credit assessment, bankers should not lend under any circumstances.

Minsky notes that in a capitalist economy in which the future cannot be predicted and is subject to unforeseen change, the value of the financing positions put in place by bankers will change with variations in macroeconomic variables. For example, a change in domestic monetary policy that causes interest rates to rise has two effects on leveraged financial projects. First, it reduces the present values of the cash flows expected to be earned from operating the projects. Second, it increases the cash flow commitments for financing charges when lending is primarily short-term or set on an adjustable or rollover basis. For a firm with a high proportion of imported inputs, or export sales, or foreign borrowing, a depreciation in the exchange rate will have the same effect on cash flow commitments as an increase in interest rates. In addition, it may also reduce estimated cash flows if import costs rise by the full amount of the devaluation, while export prices in foreign currency are reduced in an attempt to increase market share or stimulate rapid sales. For countries operating in an open trading system these two exogenous changes usually occur together and reinforce each other since higher interest are often used to defend a weak currency and to stabilise a currency after devaluation. Cushions of safety would thus have to be larger for firms operating in countries with open capital markets.

For some borrowers the cushions of safety will not be sufficiently large to cover exogenous changes in both interest rates and exchange rates and may be sufficient to transform them directly from hedge units into Ponzi financing units. The result is an overall increase in the lender's credit risk on outstanding bank loans, since the borrower's cushion of safety is now smaller. There is also an increase in borrower's risk for the firms as they find it more difficult to realise their initially expected cash flows. The *fragility* of the domestic financial system thus increases with either a rise in interest rates, or a depreciation of the currency.

Obviously, this same reasoning can be applied to domestic banks that are allowed to borrow and/or lend in international capital markets. They will require higher cushions of safety to cover the possibility of changes in international interest rates or the exchange rate. But, a bank is in an even more exposed position. A rise in interest rates and a depreciation of the exchange rate not only reduces the present value of its domestic cash flows (represented by the interest payments received from its outstanding domestic loans) and increases the interest costs of its foreign funding, it also reduces the credit quality of its loans and reduces its own credit rating. It will thus have to pay higher credit spreads on its international funding which it will be unable to recover through higher interest rates charged to its domestic clients. If the change in rates is sufficiently large banks may also find themselves suddenly in the condition of a Ponzi unit in which cash inflows no longer cover cash outflows, and the value of assets no longer provides cover for its liabilities for any future date. The net present value of the bank falls below zero and it becomes technically insolvent.

The natural response of a banker would be to cut down on funding costs by reducing lending to firms classified as hedge and speculative units and by calling in lending to ponzi financing units. As noted, the speculative and ponzi firms need increased finance just to stay in business. But, the bankers may have no choice but to cut off support if the banks themselves have become Ponzi units; they may be forced to reduce their lending because their own funding sources refuse to roll over or extend credits. Obviously, domestic banks will also be unwilling to lend to each other, so the domestic interbank market will also contract, leading to a generalised difficulty in completing payment of current cash commitments. As both firms and banks attempt to reduce their foreign currency exposure, market imbalances may occur, leading to a breakdown in the foreign exchange market as well. As a result a financially fragile system may be transformed into a financially *unstable* system.

In such conditions, ponzi financing firms have no choice but to reduce their own cash outflows, delaying current payments to suppliers, cutting back on expenditures, and by attempting to raise cash by selling out inventories, and what output they can continue to produce with current inventories of inputs, at distress prices. If this is insufficient to cover cash flow needs, they will be forced to sell any other assets they may have, or to generate liquidity by suspending current investment projects or even selling capital equipment.

They will also layoff or fire workers who represent a cash drain. The result, in contradiction to Say's Law of Markets, is a generalised condition of excess supply in all markets, placing downward pressure on prices of both output and assets. Such conditions appear peculiar because generalised excess supply will also be accompanied by declining overall demand (which is usually thought to rise when prices fall) as a result of the suspension of investment expenditures by ponzi firms, the general decline in investment due to the tightening of monetary policy, and the fall in consumption caused by the fall in household incomes and increased unemployment. This will place additional pressure on short-term money markets, and may even push short rates upwards as credit conditions deteriorate, current payments are delayed and more financing units seek temporary financing to keep operating.

Endogenous financial fragility

There is an alternative means of generating the same results. Rather then being produced by exogenous changes in economic variables that render cushions of safety insufficient to insure stable expansion, an endogenous process may lead to an underestimation of the risks associated with certain investment plans and thus to the provision of cushions of safety that are too thin. This may occur in periods of economic stability in which the weight of past positive experience increases the expectation of future success, and the memories of past crises fade from the collective memories of bankers and managers. This reduction in the estimates of probable loss will lead to a reduction in the cushion of safety thought to be prudent. Usually both of these process work together, a "stable environment" is usually characterised as a period without major external shocks. Thus cushions of safety are reduced with the lowered expectations of negative shocks. Usually these shocks are identified in terms of changes in sales or financing conditions. But, as noted above, changes in exchange rates have a similar impact to changes in interest rates. Thus, a period of prolonged exchange rate stability may lead to over optimistic assessments of the stability of the domestic currency values of foreign commitments and similar reduction in margins of safety relating to foreign cash commitments or inflows. This endogenous change in margins makes the passage from a fragile to an unstable system that much more rapid in the event of an exogenous shock.

This combination of events in which rising supplies and falling prices leads to falling demand (rather than demand increasing with falling price as in the traditional analysis) is what Irving Fisher called a "debt deflation" process. Minsky's extension of the process emphasises the fact that the rising credit risks that result are reflected on bank balance sheets in the form of increased charge-offs and a general decline in asset quality which will eventually place some banks in difficulty as their capital cushion is overwhelmed by loan losses, and a full fledged financial panic is set off. This spread of fragility from the productive to the banking sector characterises the passage from financial fragility to financial instability and crisis.

The Minsky crisis in Asia

Minsky's original analysis of the passage from financial fragility to financial instability is based on a change in domestic monetary policy or the persistence of stable domestic conditions. But, as seen above, the analysis is easily extended to an exogenous shock in exchange rates for companies operating in open trading systems and to banks borrowing and lending in international markets. With increasingly interdependent capital markets and increased capital flows, the impact of a change in monetary policy would then have to be extended to a change in the monetary policy of the largest international lenders. Changes in interest rates of the major international lenders, especially the US and Japan, have been especially important in creating financial instability in developing countries during the debt crises of the 1970s and 1980s, and are a major factor in the current Asian crisis. However, the current crisis has been exacerbated by an additional element: the conditionality on the lending of the multilateral agencies.

Why is this crisis different from other developing country debt crises?

As noted above, the normal scenario for a developing country financial crisis would involve domestic firms borrowing in foreign currency from foreign banks at interest rates which are reset at a short rollover period. Note that it makes little difference if the loans have a short or long maturity, the point is the change in interest costs on cash flows produced by the short reset interval for interest rates. Short reset periods mean that a rise in foreign interest rates is quickly transformed into an increased cash flow commitment for the borrower, instantly reducing margins of safety. If the change in international interest rate differentials leads to a depreciation of the domestic currency relative to the borrowed foreign currency, then the cushion of safety is further eroded by the increase in the domestic currency value of the cash commitments and the principal to be repaid at maturity. Finally, if the government responds to the weakness of the domestic currency in international markets by increasing domestic interest rates in order to stem currency speculation or to attempt to attract foreign demand for the currency, domestic demand may be adversely affected and domestic cash flows will be reduced and domestic financing costs will be increased. Firms may thus pass rapidly from hedge financing to Ponzi finance units as the result of a rise in foreign interest rates. Whether this increase in financial fragility turns to instability and crisis will depend on the willingness of foreign banks to extend additional foreign currency lending to cover the payment shortfalls on current commitments. If they follow the bankers' aphorism, they may be unwilling to do this. As a result, firms may be forced to attempt to improve their foreign earnings by increasing foreign sales. But, this usually leads to falling prices in international markets which compounds the losses from depreciation of the exchange rate, and any cutback in domestic operations simply makes domestic demand conditions worse. The knock-on effect thus hits both the domestic financial system and the foreign banks, who now have increasingly dubious loans on their books. If both foreign and domestic banks' capital cushion is insufficient to absorb the losses, then fragility turns to global systemic instability. In any case, the initial shock, as well as the recommended policies, combine to increase fragility and thus make instability possible in any exchange rate crisis.

The Asian crisis was slightly different, since most Asian countries sit uneasily between two international capital markets: Japan and the US. Japan is a major creditor to the area.[2] After a period of high interest rates introduced at the beginning of the decade to collapse its speculative bubble, Japanese domestic interest rates have recently been at historical lows. Likewise, the value of the Yen against the dollar has move from a high of around 80 Yen/$ to the current lows of Yen 135. Since most of the Asian countries have adopted policies of stabilising their currencies (this does not necessarily mean rigidly fixed rates) against the dollar (or against a currency basket in which the dollar is a major component), an appreciation of the Yen against the dollar is also an appreciation relative to Asia and represents an increase in Asian domestic currency cash flow commitments on borrowing from Japan. But this does not normally create a financing problem, since the rise in the value of the debt and current payments commitments is more than offset by Japanese producers increasing the outsourcing of their production into Asia in response to their loss of competitiveness. This is the famous "hollowing out" of Japanese manufacturing industry, and is visible in the large foreign direct investment flows into Asia earlier in the decade.

However, the reversal of the trend appreciation of the Yen relative to the dollar, along with historically low interest rates, has meant that Japanese investors placing short-term funds in Asia have benefitted from both a substantial interest rate differential and a possible exchange rate gain as the Yen depreciated. This has created incentives for substantial short-term flows from the Japanese financial markets as banks and other international investors borrow short-term funds in Japan and lend them to Asian banks or firms. Since the Yen had reached an historic peak against the dollar, there was also the distinct possibility of profit from any appreciation of the dollar. These flows were further supported by the creation in a number of countries, Thailand is an example, of special "offshore" financial centres to increase the role of domestic Asian banks in the intermediation of international capital flows in the region.[3] These made it easier for funds to be borrowed in low-interest rate markets, such as the US, and invested at higher Asian rates. However, these facilities did not retain a sharp division from domestic money markets and soon became a conduit for foreign lending to domestic banks and caused sharp expansions in domestic lending. Under pressure to liberalise their financial markets, many countries had lifted restrictions on lending, and with manufacturing industry showing declining profitability, most of these funds went into the more "remunerative" areas of property development and financial speculation.

This increase in short-term flows tended to further reinforce the strength of the Asian currencies and to further decrease their competitiveness relative to Japan, making them even more dependent on sales to US dollar markets. Thus the shift from Yen strength and high Japanese interest rates to Yen weakness and low interest rates has helped to bring about a shift from long to short-term flows. This created a situation in which the exchange rates were being supported by temporary capital flows, while domestic production was losing competitivity to Japan and other non-dollar markets. At the same time, Asian producers were being challenged by Chinese entry into many of their labour-intensive markets and their higher technology markets were rapidly becoming commoditized as prices were dropping rapidly. Thus, the strength of exchange rates did not really reflect the underlying strength of competitivity of the manufacturing sector. This was exhibited by the deterioration of foreign balance for most of the Asian countries throughout the 1990s.

The market's attention was attracted to the diverse behaviour of the real and financial sectors when the Bank of Thailand decided not to intervene to rescue the country's largest finance company, Finance One, in the Spring of 1997. The failure took on special importance because it occurred against the background of increased uncertainty in international capital markets concerning the evolution of international interest rate differentials. In the beginning of May 1997, the view that the Japanese economy was engaged in a full-fledged recovery gained increasing support (although there was virtually no hard evidence to support this belief[4]) and there was a sharp appreciation of the yen and a sudden rise in Japanese short-term interest rates on expectations that the Bank of Japan would move quickly to raise its discount rate.[5] Politicians who had long been pressing the Bank of Japan to raise interest rates (to increase the interest income on their retired constituents' savings) suddenly appeared likely to succeed and market opinion quickly shifted toward confident expectations of higher Japanese rates. As a result, funds that had been borrowed at low interest rates in Japan and Hong Kong, and invested at substantially higher rates in Asia, were quickly withdrawn and returned to Japan, supporting the appreciation of the yen and putting increasing pressure on Asian reserves and exchange rates.

These two factors together brought a sharp reversal of the short-term funds flowing into Asia, putting pressure on exchange rates. Domestic banks in the area facing a sudden decline in foreign funds responded by calling in their loans to domestic companies, primarily in the area of real estate and financial speculation. Of course, all this was a false alarm, the Japanese economy was in fact in a free fall decline, not a rapid recovery, the Bank of Japan had no intention of increasing rates and the Yen quickly reversed direction and moved back toward 130 Yen to the dollar.

It thus seems quite clear that the financial crisis in Asia is to a large extent the combined operation of the endogenous and exogenous factors cited above. The fact that exchange rates had remained generally stable relative to the dollar for so long clearly led to a reduction in margins of safety for both borrowers and lenders, domestic and international. And it is clear that this stability was self-reinforcing: the longer exchange rates remained stable, the higher the market considered the probability that they would remain so; the more funds international investors were willing to commit at lower margins of safety the higher were foreign exchange reserves which appeared to increase margins of safety. The capital inflows that kept the currencies stable thus implicitly increased fragility. They also decreased the ability to finance the commitments on those flows by reducing the competitiveness of manufacturing exports.

External shocks were represented by the volatility of the Yen-dollar exchange rate and the associated changes in relative interest rate spreads and the flow of arbitrage funds into and out of the region, which put increased pressure on the already thin and declining margins of safety. Further, some international regulatory factors played a role. When Korea joined the OECD, Korean government debt took on a special zero-weight status and led to improved rating for all Korean debt, which encouraged foreign inflows since Korean rates were substantially higher than other OECD country rates.[6]

Once the reversal of capital flows had exposed the fragility of the existing margins of safety, this brought attention to a series of other factors which had been present in the market for some time, including a series of prior bank failures (in Indonesia and Thailand) and corporate bankruptcies (in Indonesia and Korea), warnings from the Bank for International Settlements and rating agencies, rising real exchange rates, and current account deficits that had been higher than those which had brought grief to Mexico (Thailand had a current account deficit over 8% of GDP in 1995 as the Tequila crisis spread through Latin America). International funds started to be withdrawn from Thailand and there were a series of contained speculative attacks against the currency that were countered by the Bank of Thailand operating aggressively and successfully in the forward foreign exchange market. Unfortunately, it had to halt this policy when its forward commitments exceeded its reserves.

The central banks of the region first reacted with a concerted policy to defend exchange rates, but after the Thai baht was devalued, a number of countries, recognising the risk to competitiveness of remaining linked to an ever stronger dollar and fearing contagion of the speculative currency attacks, engaged in a series of rapid preemptive devaluations to delink from the dollar. In the space of less than three weeks, Thailand, Philippines, Malaysia, Singapore and Indonesia gave up exchanges rates that had been stable against the dollar for extended periods. The aim was to discourage speculators and thereby avoid the increase in interest rates that would have been required to protect the currency. But in the space of three weeks the movement in exchange rates wiped out the already insufficient margins of safety for domestic banks and corporate borrowers. Thus a policy which seemed sensible from the point of view of international currency markets, did not prove to be successful domestically. First, it placed both firms and banks in difficulty for the reasons already described above. Firms and banks were instantly transformed from speculative to ponzi enterprises. Second, as in the case of Mexico, the delinking from the dollar did not discourage, but rather encouraged, speculators and when countries did not initially respond with tighter monetary policies and actions to cut domestic demand the markets interpreted this as unwillingness to take strong measures in defence of their currencies.

However, from the point of view of most of these countries, and with the support of IMF Article IV consultations, they considered themselves to be dealing from positions of strong economic fundamentals or of having already taken the measures required to return their economies to sustainable positions. Indeed, most had government budgets in rough balance or in surplus, their current accounts were improving (this was the case of Malaysia, Thailand and Korea) from their worst levels as the result of tighter domestic policies, inflation rates were contained and stable, growth was strong and most were taking actions to bolster their banking and financial systems with the help and express approval of the IMF.

Nonetheless, as currencies failed to stabilise interest rates were raised to punitive levels, reinforcing the negative impact of the exchange rate depreciation on the balance sheets of both firms and banks. At this point the elimination of margins of safety rebounded negatively on the foreign exchange rate as both banks and firms sought to limit the damage from the rising dollar and rising interest rates by repaying as rapidly as possible the outstanding foreign currency debt. Domestic banks and corporations thus joined the speculators in selling the domestic currency against dollars. But, in difference from Latin American crises, this was not so much a case of capital flight as simple covering of open foreign exchange positions. The result was a free fall in both the exchange rate and asset prices in many countries as financing units sought "to make position by selling position", selling anything possible to raise funds and reduce cash payment commitments and foreign exposure. A Minsky debt-deflation crisis, or a Soros-type reflexive process, thus got underway. Unfortunately it was not recognised as such, and the policies that were implemented actually accentuated the crisis.

What is to be done — what has been done?

What would have been required to avoid a full scale debt crisis is a debt moratorium, and then a debt "workout" in which cash flows are rescheduled on a sustainable basis. But, such a "workout" is only possible if the deterioration in the cushion of safety is from hedge to speculative finance. If all positions have become ponzi positions, the firms will all have strictly negative net present values, and there is no rescheduling possible which can resolve the problem. To prevent cases of extended insolvency, policy must act to try to stem the downward spiral while firms are still in the stage of speculative financing. The obvious and direct way to do this is to underpin cash flows to firms by supporting domestic demand and by reducing their financing costs, either through debt standstills or reductions in interest rates. This leaves productive capacity in place that can increase export earnings to repay foreign debt, and prevents the gridlock of the banking system caused by generalised nonpayment, default and credit downgrades. Hy has argued in favoured of such "workout" on an international scale for some time.

However, when the IMF was called in to provide support for the Asian economies it appears to have judged the crises to have been caused by imprudent banking practices and excessive lending, leading to excessive balance of payments deficits. IMF support conditions were centred on the improving the balance of payments and patterned on the previous experience in the Mexican-Tequila crisis. In order to prevent erosion of the devaluation due to the price inflation that was expected to arise from the increased import prices and the increased demand from the bailouts of the banks, and to keep imports down, domestic demand was constrained through a reduction in government expenditures and tight monetary targets. To further cut domestic demand and stabilise the devaluation, interest rates were raised. Finally, financial institutions that did not meet international capital standards were ordered closed immediately or operations suspended pending plans for recapitalisation. The objective of the policy was to restore international confidence and bring about a return of short-term capital flows that would make the actual use of the IMF and other conditional funding from the multilateral agencies or governments unnecessary at the same time as it laid the basis for an increase in exports and a reduction in imports which would eventually make capital inflows unnecessary.

However, as noted above, the collapse of exchange rates had not been due to banks financing excess demand for imported consumption goods, but rather, financing imports of capital goods by firms. It was the firms' and banks' balance sheets that had to be supported. The IMF conditions only made their positions worse. First, the flight of foreign capital meant that they had to replace their short-term financing, but at sharply higher rates from domestic banks. Second, with falling global demand, firms became increasingly dependent on domestic demand, but fiscal policy was ensuring that demand would be falling. The original estimates were for small reduction in growth. All three IMF-assisted countries now will be in full blown recession for 1998 and most probably through 1999. Thus, firms had rising short-term financing costs and collapsing income flows to meet them. Third, firms that had borrowed abroad had to repay foreign lenders. Given the long period of relatively stable exchange rates, much of this borrowing had not been hedged, and thus had to be repaid in foreign currency. But, export receipts were falling and the value in domestic currency was rising daily. It was originally thought that the sharp devaluations would cause an export boom similar to that in Mexico. However, firms could no longer obtain finance to purchase imports or meet payrolls, they thus sold position to make position and started to sell from inventories. Just as Minsky's debt deflation theory predicted, the result was a rapid fall in the export prices, while import prices rose in step with the devaluation of the currency. Thus, although trade balances did improve, but only because there were no longer any imports and exports were dumped in distress so that the price effect more than offset any quantity impact, leading to further reductions in the terms of trade. For example, in Korea, the index of export prices fell from an average of 72.4 in the third quarter to 60 in January, the lowest level since 1988.

In addition, tight monetary policies caused an increase in trade financing costs. Commission for letters of credit on domestic transactions in Korea increased from 0.065% to 0.1% and for foreign currency transfers increased from 0.5–0.1% to

0.3%. Credit lines have been reduced and payment penalties increased. Thus, the export capacity of most firms was constrained by the inability of get finance to continue current operations. Mexico had not experienced these problems, first because the majority of its debt was consumer and mortgage debt, and second because the majority of exports took place through the maquilladoras that did not depend directly on the domestic financial system.

Of course, these policies are exactly the opposite of what was required from the point of view of stopping a Minsky debt-deflation crisis. The conditions imposed by the IMF considered the crisis as a flow problem — imports were greater than exports, and tried to slow the first flow and accelerate the second on the expectation that a current account surplus along with capital inflows attracted by high interest rates would stabilise the exchange rate. But, the problem was a stock problem, as firms and banks tried to liquidate their stocks of goods and assets to liquidate their stocks of foreign exchange debts.[7] In Keynesian terms it was a problem of a shift in liquidity preference, not a problem of a shift in spending propensities that had to be achieved.

Thus, international investors reacted rationally, noting that a slowdown in domestic demand could only worsen the cash flows of firms, while the increase in interest rates could only worsen their financing costs. Since import prices would rise and export prices would in all likelihood fall it would become more difficult to earn foreign currency to repay foreign debt. The default on domestic debt would make it more difficult for the banks to finance current production to be sold for export and make it more difficult to repay foreign borrowing. Further, the decision to close banks meant freezing all existing financial arrangements. Solvent banks would be unable to recover any of the funds (partial payment is always better than no repayment at all) lent to suspended banks, and thus would be in even greater difficulty. The IMF conditions thus aggravated the financial fragility and initiated a debt deflation process that meant the crisis would be prolonged and have substantially greater costs in terms of bankruptcy and unemployment.

The market's implicit recognition that this was a "debt deflation" crisis and not just a "debt" crisis may be seen in the pressure on the Hong Kong currency and asset markets. According to any definition of economic "fundamentals", there was little reason to expect difficulty in Hong Kong, either in the asset market or in the foreign exchange market. Hong Kong has already had its experience with fraudulent trading and overexposed banks in the 1987 stock market break. Its banking system is regulated on standards that are at least equivalent to British standards. The currency is backed by a currency board holding US dollars in an amount that covers not only the circulating HK dollar notes, but all sight deposits, by a substantial multiple. Thus every HK dollar, and deposit created by banks lending HK dollars for speculation, could be redeemed in US dollars and there would still be something left over. Beyond that, China holds US dollar assets that are approximately three times as large as the Hong Kong Monetary Authority's holdings. Thus, the Hong Kong banks were not at risk, nor was the HK dollar. The cushions of safety of the banks were substantially higher than the minimum that was suggested by the International Risk-based Capital Standards. Nonetheless, both the Hong Kong stock market and the HK dollar came under heavy selling pressure that precipitated the October 27 sell off in other developed markets. Market Irrationality? Seen in the context of a Minsky crisis, not at all. The key again is the movement of rates. If there is full conversion of HK dollar liabilities into US dollars, there should be no impact on the exchange rate. However, if the HKMA is forced to convert substantial amounts of HK dollars, this puts direct pressure on domestic money market interest rate. Higher domestic rates will raise financing costs, and thus put pressure on construction companies and property developers, as well as the banks that finance them. These are the companies that make up the majority of shares in the Hong Kong stock market. Further, higher interest rates increase the carrying cost for borrowed stock. Thus, any pressure on the currency, even if successfully resisted, would instantly place pressure on stock prices as investors sold out position and property companies sought to raise liquidity by marking down prices. After the decision of the Taiwanese government to devalue the Taiwanese dollar international investors quite naturally looked for signs of weakness or hesitancy in defense of the Hong Kong dollar. It thus became impossible for Hong Kong (until then the only country untouched by the crisis) not to make a pre-emptive response by increasing interest rates. For a foreign investor, there was thus a near certainty that eventually either the Hong Kong dollar would come under pressure if interest rates were not raised, or the HK MA would be forced to increase interest rates preemptively. If this prevented the anticipated depreciation of the currency it would be at the cost of a sharp fall in the stock market. Thus, even if an investor could be sure of exchange rate stability, he could also be virtually certain of stock price instability and falling domestic property prices. There was thus no way to avoid a loss on holdings in Hong Kong, and after the losses sustained in other Asian markets, investors sold out of the one market with perfect fundamentals on a perfectly rational understanding of the difference between stock imbalances and flow imbalances.

Is the crisis over?

If the analysis of the crisis as a Minsky debt deflation rather than a simple balance of payments crisis is correct then the response is no, the crisis is not over and the success of IMF policies in restoring external short-term flows of funds will not be sufficient to resolve the crisis. This is because, at currently prevailing exchange rates, as mentioned above, most firms are still insolvent. The short-term paper, issued by the firms and held by the banks has simply been rolled over. If the restructuring of the banking system proceeds these credits will become non-performing and the firms will be in default. Thus, even in the case of Korea, where an international debt rollover has been arranged to resolve the dollar shortage for the current year, the problem of the outstanding corporate commercial paper held by the commercial banks remains. Further, the debt resolution has simply been pushed to the future. The Korean Institute of Finance predicts that starting in 2001 these debts will start coming due and will represent annual interest charges of around $10 billion. Further the reported commercial paper holdings of the best capitalised banks represents about 2% of equity. For other banks it will be substantially higher. Most of this paper was rolled over as the crisis broke at the beginning of December and has again been rolled over in March. Since most is expected to be in default, any real restructuring of the banks will have to write these loans off as total loss. Further, a large percentage of the loans are held by Japanese banks, and these may have to be recalled if Japan continues to encounter the clear symptoms of incipient debt deflation. In Indonesia, there has been little need for a roll over in order to provide dollar balances as Indonesian dollar reserves appear more than sufficient. The problem is that firms cannot afford to purchase the dollars that they need to repay their debts and remain solvent. Unless the exchange rate returns to more normal levels, they will eventually have to cease operations. It is interesting to note that the rates that were being quoted when the creation of a currency board was under discussion of 5,500–6,000 Rupiah are rates at which most major corporate borrowers are considered solvent.

Thus, there is a second stage of the crisis still to be played out involving the recognition of the ponzi nature of most of productive enterprise and the associated downward adjustment of their valuations. The same will be true of the banks holding the firms' short-term debts. Although the external financing crisis has been stemmed, the internal financing crisis still remains to be resolved. As an order of magnitude, at the end of 1996 the won/$ exchange rate was 844, short-term interest rates were 12.2%, and three-year corporate bonds bearing a bank guarantee paid 12.6%. After touching 2000, the exchange rate at the end of January was around 1800 and overnight interest rates are 25% and three year rates 21.2%. At the beginning of April the exchange rate is around 1400, overnight interest rates are around 22% and three-year around 19%. Thus despite the claims that the situation has stabilised, firms are facing both exchange rates and interest rates have increased by 75 to 90% respectively, after having roughly doubled from November to end December. This means that financing costs have roughly doubled in won terms, while the domestic value of foreign indebtedness is about three quarters higher, for about a three-fold increase in the interest charge on cash flows and on outstanding foreign indebtedness. This is far beyond any plausible margins of safety.

The first step in the third phase of the crisis will then be to restore stability to asset markets, which means having both buyers and sellers, borrowers and lenders. This will allow producers to increase exports and the process of adjustment to begin. However, much of the productive capacity will in fact be closed by bankruptcy. And the fall in prices will be less than the change in exchange rates due to the fact that most Asian exports are import-intensive, so that import costs will be rising in dollar terms, and domestic costs will also be rising as the impact of depreciation on the domestic price level works through to domestic costs. It is also likely that capital flows will also return, through foreign purchases of domestic productive capacity (to operate or to close, as occurred in East Germany). It is for this reason that it is difficult to determine appropriate exchange rates. At current exchange rates, this process should be extremely rapid, and will certainly bring calls from developed countries, swamped with imports, for protection measures.[8] This would preclude adjustment via the expansion of net exports and leave only the restoration of capital flows of the original IMF design. But, this implies increasing reliance on high interest rates and/or the sale of domestic assets at cut rate prices. Neither of which are capable of curing the current debt deflation.

Notes

1 Visiting Senior Scholar, The Jerome Levy Economics Institute; Professor of Economics, University of Bologna and The Johns Hopkins University
2 The share of Indonesia's long-term debt denominated in Yen is 38%, for Malaysia it is 40%, for Thailand 53%, and for the Philippines 38%.
3 Japan was not the only source of arbitrage funding. It was also profitable to borrow funds in the US to lend in Asia, as well as within Asia. For example, the crisis in Indonesia is reputed to have been aggravated by Korean investment banks' refusal to roll over lending to Indonesian corporates that they were funding with borrowing in Hong Kong. Korean investment banks also held substantial positions in Brazilian "Brady" bonds and Russian government bonds, all financed with funds borrowed in international markets. This is one of the reasons why the crisis had such widespread repercussions, as far away as Latin American and Eastern Europe. This should be seen as anything out of the ordinary — when Poland defaulted on its debt in 1982, leading to the 1980s debt crisis, Brazil was one of the creditors.
4 The IMF World Economic Outlook for May 1997 gives a forecast for real GDP growth of 2.2%, down from 3.6% the previous year and suggests that "recovery is likely to continue at a moderate pace" (p. 15).
5 The move was all the more important because it "was of a magnitude that market participants considered quite unlikely, even as late as 5 May. As the yen appreciated rapidly between 5 May and 9 May (the market) began to reflect a significant probability of large further appreciations" (IMF, November 1997: 19).
6 From the discussion above of the reinforcing effect of interest rate and exchange rate changes, it should be clear that banks operating in open developing countries should have margins of safety that are higher than those operating in less open developed economies. Yet, the application of international capital requirements, which were being introduced (and were being met) by most banking systems in the region, apply a uniform minimum capital ratio.
7 Korean conglomerate carry debt ratios of from 400% to 700%, a large portion of which had become short-term and foreign funded, either directly or indirectly, over the last five years.
8 Up to the present, US semiconductor manufacturers, such as Micron, European shipbuilders, such as Fincantieri, and numerous Japanese and Latin American producers have threatened antidumping measures in WTO or to unilaterally impose tariffs on goods from Asia.

References

Graham, Benjamin and David L. Dodd. *Security Analysis*. New York: Whittlesey House, McGraw-Hill Book Company, 1934.
IMF, *World Economic Outlook*, Washington D.C., May, 1997.

————, *International Capital Markets*, Washington D.C., November, 1997.

Korea Herald, "Banks' Tight Policies Hurting Exports," February 26, 1998.

————, "EU to Consider Punitive Tariffs on Korean Goods, Fenruary 27, 1998.

Korea Times, "Export Prices Lowest Since 1988," February 26, 1998.

————, "Exports Face Mounting Resistance," March 2, 1998.

————, "Prolonged Economic Recession Is Feared Due to Surging External Debt Burdens,"
  April 16, 1998

Minsky, H. P., *Can 'It' Happen Again*, Armonk, New York: M.E. Sharpe, 1982.

Minsky, H.P., *John Maynard Keynes*, New York: Columbia University Press, 1975.

Soros, George, *The Alchemy of Finance*, New York: Simon and Schuster, 1987.

11 The Brazilian crisis

From inertial inflation to fiscal fragility

Introduction

In a previous paper[1] I argued that the financial crisis in Asia was radically different from those that have plagued Latin American since 1982. In simple terms, the Asian crisis was not caused by excessively large fiscal and trade imbalances leading to inflation, speculative pressure on overvalued pegged exchange rates and financial sector collapse characteristic of crises in Latin America. Instead, the crises in Asia were closer to a classic Minsky-Fisher debt-deflation process built on the endogenous reductions over time of risk premia on investments in Asia that lead to a buildup of short-term commercial bank lending reinforced by interest rate differentials. The reversal of these flows, initiated by a change in the market perception of international interest rate movements led to pressure on exchange rate bands that caused the majority of both corporate and financial borrowers to experience a net present value reversals and a massive "sale of position to make position" and a downward spiral in asset prices and exchange rates. In short, a capital account reversal rather than a current account imbalance, was the source of the Asian problems. The persistence of the downward pressure on prices was caused by the conversion of virtually every financing unit into a "ponzi" operation, in difference from a traditional current account crisis in which it is only the relative prices of traded and non-traded goods that are affected. The rapid upward reassessment of risk premia then led to a classic Minskyian scenario in which financial institutions cut back sharply on lending as they struggled to strengthen balance sheets and virtually cut off credit to the economy.

Despite these differences, there was one aspect of the crisis in Asia that was reminiscent of the experiences in Latin America in the 1980s and 1990s. That is the rapidity with which the Thai devaluation spread to other economies in the region that had exhibited what appeared to strong macroeconomic fundamentals. Indeed, just as economists were insisting on the fundamental strength of the Indonesian economy at the end of 1997, those with a long memory will remember that similar statements were made about the strength of the Brazilian economy relative to Mexico at the end of 1982. Just as political leaders and economic policy makers in Asia were slow to accept the possibility of contagion from the Thai crisis because they believed (perhaps justifiably on the basis of IMF evaluations of their economic fundamentals) that their economies were fundamentally strong, the same reluctance was present in Brazil's reaction to the 1980s crisis. Indeed, it is interesting to note that just as Indonesia contributed to the IMF led international rescue package offered to Thailand in July of 1997, Brazil was one of the creditors represented in the London Club when Poland declared it was unable to meet its debt service commitments in the Spring of 1982.[2,3]

It was an external interest rate shock that detonated the Minskyian instability in both Mexico (both in 1982 and 1994) and Thailand. The unraveling of the highly integrated levered balance sheets of financial institutions and corporate borrowers in Thailand led to the outbreak of the Minsky crisis in which private agents were forced to liquidate position to make position. A large proportion of this reaction was simply the scramble for foreign exchange cover by domestic producers. The process was contagious because of the interlinkages of financial sector balance sheets and production processes across the region, and indeed across the entire globe.

But, just as the Indonesian crisis was different from the Thai crisis, the Brazilian crisis differs from the standard Latin American crisis. In the next section we look at the recent history of the fight to tame Brazilian inertial inflation to identify those factors that produced a particular strong balance sheet structure in the private sector in Brazil, but caused financial fragility in the public sector capable of generating a classic debt deflation process.

Fighting inertial inflation

Brazil's reaction to the 1980s debt crisis created substantial differences in its economic and financial structure relative to other Latin American countries. Brazil had little problem with its foreign balance. After the 1980s crisis the trade balance remained in surplus from 1983 until after the introduction of the Real Plan in 1994. This was primarily due to the use of a flexible exchange rate policy designed to preserve export competitiveness. Although Brazil had a large public sector debt of around 50% of GDP in 1986, it had not been created by a buildup of a large stock of private foreign assets (that in many countries was due to capital flight), but rather was used in large part for the funding of the 2nd National Development Plan which started in the 1970s to strengthen the internal productive structure of the economy and provide increased export capacity. Like most other heavily indebted Latin American countries in the 1980s, the size of the public debt was increased by the government assuming responsibility after 1982 for virtually all foreign currency debt contracted by the private sector during the syndicated lending boom of the 1970s. The evolution of Brazilian internal debt was strongly influenced by the persistence of hyperinflation. Falling fiscal revenues due to lags between assessment and payment were in part offset by the use of a financial transactions tax, while the lags between budget allocations and expenditures ensured endogenous reductions in real spending. The result was a falling ratio of net public sector debt to GDP to around 30% by the time of the Real Plan.

With inflation causing a rapidly decline in the real value of government debt, it is difficult to convince the private sector to hold it, and the solution was found in the eventual introduction of full inflation indexing of government bills with high liquidity. The logical consequence was that as long as the government had a fiscal imbalance that had to be financed, there could be no money supply policy independent of this objective. Indeed, given the full indexing of financial assets, there was a preference for government debt over currency, and much as occurred in Italy in the same period, the former might be said to have formed the effective money supply. As a result of the rapid inflation fiscal policy was not a viable policy tool, nor was money supply control, leaving the interest rate as the only policy tool. This had a number of consequences that are not in the annals of conventional economics, but are well known to economists from countries that have experienced high and persistent or inertial inflation. First, the interest costs of the outstanding government debt becomes a major component of government expenditure and thus of the government deficit. This means the interest rates becomes both a direct and an indirect source of inflation. Further in Latin America in the 1980s the level of interest rates relative to the rest of the world had virtually no impact on capital inflows, since capital markets were characterised by what is euphemistically called reverse net resource transfers — i.e. net capital flows were negative so that Brazil was providing resources to the rest of the world and in particular to the US, irrespective of interest rate differentials. There was also no impact of high interest rates on the exchange rate, given the size of the inflation differential and the policy of active intervention to preserve competitiveness through devaluation.

The important point of difference from other Latin American economies was thus that Brazil was not building up an excessively large imbalance on foreign account, nor was the exchange rate becoming overvalued, net public debt as a share of gdp was declining, and while low from historical perspective, its growth rate was on average above other economies in the region. However, to achieve this result in conditions of hyperinflation and full indexing meant abandoning active fiscal policy and the impossibility of controlling monetary aggregates. The only policy tool available to try to stem the hyper inflation was high real interest rates. However, this interest rates policy reinforced the hyperinflation by causing:

- a direct increase in the costs of capital since there was no long-term capital market,
- an increase the government deficit, since the outstanding debt was directly linked to short-term rates.
- an increase in the rate of inflation through the impact on capital costs and on the fiscal imbalance.

High interest rates to control inflation reinforced the inflation that spiraled into indexed inertial hyperinflation, and impeded the full development of private long-term capital markets. Thus when policies of market liberalisation were introduced to replace the system of government directed development financing, there was no private sector market structure available to take its place. The financial system had lived the life of a rentier on the float created by the adjustment lags in the indexing system of financial contracts. Indeed, there was hardly any long-term business financing to be done. Only the State continued to invest in any appreciable magnitude and this peculiarly Brazilian characteristic of efficient State financing of investment was under increasing attack from the rapid deterioration of government finances and the push toward increased liberalisation from the multilateral financial institutions and the Collor government.

The key to breaking out of what was becoming hyperstagflation was thus to find a substitute for high interest rate policies and reduce the level of interest rates. Two factors initiated this process. One was the liberalisation of foreign trade introduced by the Collor regime in 1990, the other was the return of international investment inflows to Latin America at about the same time. Led by Mexico's new economic policy introduced by the Salinas government in 1988, capital flows returned to Latin America after the introduction of the Brady solution to indebtedness. The Brady plan implicitly accepted that Latin America would never be able to repay its debts to commercial banks in the short term by increasing net exports, so that it would have to borrow in private international capital markets to do so. That the return of foreign capital to Brazil was independent of any changes in domestic conditions can be seen in the fact that foreign exchange reserves more than doubled between 1991 and 1992 despite the failure of the Collor plan to reduce hyperinflation to even two-digit levels. These inflows formed the counterpart to the deterioration in the trade account that was produced by the increased in imports and reduced exports as foreign competition displaced local producers as the process of tariff reduction and liberalisation of foreign trade was accelerated.[4] Paradoxically, it was this process of trade liberalisation and the return of capital flows that provided the background that allowed for the success of the Real Plan.

The Real Plan was in many respects similar to the earlier reform plans, including the elimination of indexing of wages and prices as a major component, with the nominal exchange rate the anchor for price stability. Nonetheless, interest rates continued to be the major instrument of economic policy. What had changed with respect to the previous plans, was that the Real Plan benefitted from the new post-Brady world of restored capital flows and the developed country portfolio managers' obsession with portfolio diversification and the exploitation of excess returns in emerging markets. In this new context of increasingly free global capital flows, interest rates now had an impact on both capital inflows and on the exchange rate. Indeed, the early period of the Real Plan saw an appreciation by as much as 15% in the Real–US dollar exchange rate, which was originally intended to have been maintained at dollar parity. This real Real appreciation also contributed to the rapidity of the decline in the inflation rate. The introduction and early success of the Real Plan also reinforced the return of net capital inflows by providing evidence of economic improvements, and reinforced the reversal of the exchange rate policy of the previous period from maintaining competitiveness through devaluation to maintaining competitiveness by creating pressure on domestic producers from foreign imports. Since it was difficult for domestic producers to adjust their costs rapidly; the real appreciation of the Real simply produced a growing payments imbalance in the new context of liberalised foreign trade.

The foreign capital flows that matched the growing trade imbalance also had an impact on fiscal conditions, since the Central Bank adopted a policy of sterilisation of inflows in order to protect its inflation fighting monetary policy. This sterilisation, involving selling domestic currency bonds at high interest rates to acquire foreign exchange that was invested at low foreign interest rates, produced "negative carry" that fed directly into the current budget deficit. This reinforced the deterioration in the fiscal positions created by the rapid decline in the inflation rate. Just as banks had been able to make politically influenced loans in the knowledge that hyperinflation would quickly shrink them from the balance sheet, government had been able to make expenditure commitments that were rapidly reduced in real terms. The absence of inflation meant that the rate of growth of fiscal revenues fell while the already approved indexed expenditures were slower to adjust, producing an increase in real expenditures, some of which was visible in increased household incomes, producing a fall in the saving rate and financing a consumption boom.

The rapid fall in inflation created rising real incomes as prices slowed more rapidly than other asset prices and the prices of more liberalised imports fell with exchange rate appreciation. This led to a rapid increase in consumption, in particular on imports. Finally banks were forced to find real lending business to replace the inflation–float, and started to lend aggressively to consumers in the absence of any quick pick up in business borrowing, adding further fuel to the consumption boom driving imports.

Thus, while the Real Plan was immensely successful in eliminating inflation, the continued reliance on high interest rates reinforced the imbalances on foreign and domestic account and reversed the economy from one of inertial inflation to tendential deflation. It was this tendency to deflation that led to the exchange rate crisis under the Real plan. The best way to understand it is by referring to Minsky's favourite analytical technique: analyse the impact of a change in interest rates on balance sheets. But, in the present case it is the government balance sheet and the structure of its debt that will be of crucial importance. And, what will be required is an analysis of the impact of changes in interest rates on the net present value of the Brazil and Co.

A public sector debt deflation process

First, it is important to note that the success of the Real Plan was on capital inflows buttressing the nominal exchange rate anchor in the face of rising current account imbalances. The success of the Plan thus made necessary domestic interest rates that were sufficiently high to produce a sufficiently large international interest rate differential to sustain capital inflows. Any attempt to reduce rates unilaterally ran the risk of reducing the capital inflows and increasing vulnerability to foreign shocks. Given the size and structure of government debt and expenditures, high interest rates also meant permanent fiscal imbalance through the impact of interest service on the government deficit. The high interest rates that were required to ensure the capital inflows that kept the exchange rate stable, along with trade liberalisation, produced a rising import imbalance. The capital inflows in excess of what was required to finance the current account imbalance was countered by sterilisation of the inflows at negative carry that also increased the government deficit and thus outstanding debt. Any attempt to offset this vicious circle which did not involve interest rate reduction would require lower government expenditures, which along with the high interest rates produced depressed internal demand and lower growth — as well as lower tax yields. The Real Plan could not restore Brazilian growth with price stability because it contributed a distorted internal public debt structure and could not have adopted an expansionary monetary policy, even if the government had desired one.

In addition, the Real Plan was introduced in the same year as the Mexican Tequila crisis broke out in Latin America. This placed the entire strategy in jeopardy and required a policy response of extremely high interest rates to protect Brazil from contagion and preserve capital inflows. The result was to place further pressure on the fiscal deficit as the foreign balance continued to deteriorate as the exchange rate continued to appreciate in real terms. The decision to introduce a controlled nominal depreciation of the currency was finally taken in 1995, but the continued decline in the rate of inflation was sufficiently rapid that the new exchange rate regime gave little relief to exporters and the real appreciation appears to have continued, although with a declining nominal rate.

Although the return of capital flows to Brazil in the 1990s started as short-term speculative flows, the stabilisation of the economy soon brought the return of foreign direct investors. This reinforced the negative impact of liberalisation on the trade balance. Brazil had been a relatively closed economy, and as such most Brazilian firms produced primarily for the domestic market. Thus, even the liberalisation of the import of capital goods by domestic firms did little to provide an offsetting increase in exports, while the operations of transnational corporations involving the final assembly of semi-finished goods all tended to increase the import content of exports and raise the trade deficit that would be associated with a given growth rate. Or, to put the point differently, the reduction in growth necessary to restore foreign balance was continually increasing over the period after the introduction of the Real Plan. This is a response similar to that of Mexico, but without the benefit of the linkage to the expanding US economy. Indeed, Brazil was enjoying an internal consumption boom.

But there is another, often unnoticed impact of international financial market integration and the use of high domestic interest rates to attract foreign investments. Since increasing global capital flows meant an increasing proportion of Brazilian public debt came to be owned directly or indirectly foreigners. Thus the rate of interest effectively paid to foreign holders became the domestic Brazilian rate. Further, increasing proportions of the debt were dollar indexed, but paid domestic interest rates. The net result was that an increasing proportion of the domestic Brazilian debt was indexed to the overnight domestic interest rate, and thus an increasing proportion of the externally owned debt was also linked to the domestic overnight rate. Just as profits on foreign direct investments, these interest earnings appear as a debit item on the services, or liquid balance of payments. They represent the same threat of instability as the unremitted profits of foreign direct investors.[5] Changes in domestic interest rates thus have an increasing impact on the current account deficit as well as on the fiscal deficit and they may be expected to move in tandem. This is a vicious circle that is similar to that caused by high interest rates under the period of hyperinflation. To attract the capital inflows required to keep the exchange on its target path and balance the fiscal and foreign deficits has required increases in interest rates that simply increase the size of the foreign and fiscal deficits. Fighting inflation through exchange rate stability via increased interest rates has brought price stability, but at the cost of the foreign balance which eventually undermines exchange rate stability. Indeed, this policy has not only immobilised the interest rate as a policy tool, but it has also blunted fiscal policy as a result of the impact of debt service on the deficit. Brazil is widely believed to have a fiscal crisis, but its ratio of fiscal pressure (tax take to GDP) is not far different from that of most developed countries and like Italy it has had a primary government budget surplus (although this has been due in some cases to the accounting of revenues from privatisation) — the deficit is entirely composed of debt service. Thus, continuous reduction in fiscal expenditure is required to offset the impact of interest service on the debt, while increasing exports are required to offset the effect of higher interest rates on the services payments of the current account balance.

While the success of the stabilisation policy in reducing inflation depended on large capital inflows, the interest rates that this required produced a deterioration in both the fiscal and foreign balances that eventually created doubts about the long-term success of the policy and a reversal of capital flows. In difference from Asia, virtually all market participants recognised that the policy was not tenable as a long-term development strategy, and the capital outflow occurred slowly, between July and January, rather than all at once. The result, however, was exactly the same. A full scale exchange rate crisis.

Private sector stability after the real plan

Thus, the crisis in Brazil was due to the impact of rising interest rates on the public sector balance sheet. The natural question to ask is why the Minsky crisis did not occur in the private sector as it did in the Asian crisis and why the crisis was so much less severe. While the locus of crisis in Asia was private corporate and bank balance sheets, this was not the case in Brazil, where there were only isolated banking insolvencies[6] and no major corporate failures. As a result of the country's previous history of hyperinflation, the market for long-term capital was not well developed, and firms held little fixed interest debt. Banks, on the other hand, had survived the inflationary period by earning income from inflation arbitrage and treasury operations,[7] and had advanced little in term lending to the private sector. Thus the corporate sector was not highly indebted to the banking system (although many banks held corporate equity as an inflation hedge). In 1997 the average debt of the corporate sector was only 30 per cent of owners' equity. A survey of around 100 quoted Brazilian companies showed internal funds averaged just under 60 percent, and equity around 20 percent of total funding, for the first three years of the Real Plan.[8] Firms thus relied on internal funding or had direct access to rapidly developing equity markets. In addition they did not have large foreign-currency exposures.

Loans represent less than half of bank assets in Brazil, and an increasing proportion of lending was to households to finance consumption expenditures, much of which was in foreign currency and created a threat of bankruptcy among households not seen in either East Asia or the Russian Federation. However, private banks in June 1997 are estimated to have had only 15 billion real in foreign-exchange denominated lending (only 21 per cent of total loans). Only 19 per cent of their liabilities was foreign-currency denominated, although the figure may have been as high as 50 per cent for foreign-owned banks. Thus, banks do not have the kind of currency mismatches that characterized other recent crises.[9]

Furthermore, Brazil had just emerged from a major restructuring of the banking sector following the banking crisis that started in 1994–5.[10] From July 1994 to December 1997 the central bank intervened in 43 banks, 32 of which were private, and liquidated all but one of the latter.[11] Strict supervisory and regulatory provisions were also introduced, with capital adequacy requirements stricter than those in the Basle Capital Accord.[12] As much as 20% of the Government's outstanding debt was created as part of this process of Bank restructuring. Thus, unlike in East Asia, it was the Government and the central bank which were most exposed in foreign currencies through the issue of dollar-linked debt to both foreigners and residents, in particular to banks which used it to hedge their exposure when providing forward cover to commercial clients.

While an increasing proportion of capital inflows into Brazil were for direct investment, even when the inflows financed Brazilian imports of capital goods,[13] they were used to increase capacity to serve the large internal market and thus generated little in the way of increased export earnings for the service of external debt. One of the features of rapid development in East Asia had been the ability to insure that the inflows were invested in export capacity that provided foreign exchange for debt service. This reflects the higher share of investment in Asia compared to Brazil. Indeed, the difficulties started in many Asian countries when returns on such investments fell and the continuing capital inflows were invested in financial engineering and real estate.

The Brazilian crisis had other special features. Although it had widely expected been to produce a collapse in the entire region, or even a major global market break, thus far it has produced neither. In difference from Asia, Brazil is a relatively closed economy, its imports accounted for only around 1% of global imports in 1997. Further, regional integration is much more recent than in Asia;

while 22% of Brazilian imports are from Latin America, 65 per cent come from developed countries; and about 16 per cent from Mercosur partners.

Whereas the East Asian crisis had been characterized as a private rather than sovereign debt crisis, the greatest foreign exposure in Brazil was that of the public sector. In East Asia the process of economic collapse was one of debt deflation, as the private sector sold domestic currency to repay foreign loans, and sold domestic stocks and even equipment to repay debt because of the extremely high internal interest rates. Brazil, on the other hand, while it also sold assets in an attempt to forestall the crisis, the sales took the form of the privatization of large portions of the public sector which covered a substantial proportion of the current account financing needs and had, if anything, a positive impact on the balance sheets of the entities involved.

In Brazil the major damage to the private productive sector was due to the impact on demand and capital costs of the attempt to avoid crisis by defending the exchange rate. Industry suffered from penal interest rates from the autumn of that year, that peaked at monthly rates of 4.5 per cent on working capital loans at the end of 1997 and never fell below 3.3 per cent during 1998 even though inflation had virtually fallen to zero. On the other hand, the principal focus of government policy was on improving the fiscal balance, through, inter alia, a reduction of expenditure by 3 per cent of GDP. The depreciation of the currency improved competitiveness without producing large losses on the balance sheets of private enterprise, but since the outbreak of the crisis Brazil (like East Asia before it) has been plagued by the disappearance of trade credits, and the improvements that have taken place in the foreign account have been primarily due to import cuts. Moreover, although the stabilization of the currency has allowed the Central Bank to reduce interest rates, to around 22 per cent by the beginning of the summer, these reductions have not yet fed through to private-sector lending rates.[14]

On the other hand, the crisis had also a number of positive aspects for the private sector. Banks had been large holders of dollar-linked government debt in their portfolios, and a number of investment banks reported record profits as the result of futures positions taken in anticipation of the depreciation of the currency. This is another reason for the relatively benign character of the crisis. Since Brazil was one of the first countries to have been hit by contagion from other regions, there was clear advance warning of possible difficulties. Further, it was widely accepted that the currency was overvalued. Thus foreign and domestic investors were given adequate time to make an orderly withdrawal of capital and arrange for necessary hedging, as well as to unravel complicated derivative strategies, well before the country ran out of reserves. Indeed, the devaluation had been so widely anticipated that several investment banks incorporated the impact of a possible devaluation in their growth forecasts for 1999 as early as the last quarter of 1998. Many private banks returned to the international capital markets at the end of the first quarter before the Government launched a Brady swap issue in April.

After the East Asian crisis it became widely recognized that target levels of fiscal surpluses agreed with IMF had contributed to the depth of the recession.

Thus they were revised to allow Governments the possibility of running fiscal deficits. However, in Brazil this has not been the case, and even larger primary surpluses to offset the increased costs of debt service caused by the depreciation of the currency have been part of the conditions for the provision of multilateral lending. One reason for this may have been fear that the devaluation would rekindle hyperinflation. But after a one-off rise in prices the inflation rate has come down to levels similar to that before the crisis. Nevertheless, even though the entire fiscal deficit is due to interest payments and the effects of higher obligations on foreign-currency debt brought about by the collapse of the currency, Brazil is aiming for a primary surplus of 3.2 per cent of GDP in 1999.

While the crisis in Brazil has had a relatively limited contagion effect, its domestic implications are rather similar to those for the Russian economy. In the run up to the devaluation, forecasts of the impact on the real economy of the high interest rates and government austerity necessary to defend the exchange rate were for a contraction of 4–6 per cent in 1999. The implication was that the key to reducing the government deficit and debt was unlikely to lie in raising the primary surplus, since reduced spending or increased taxes needed for such a fiscal adjustment would squeeze the private sector and prove counterproductive. Rather, interest rates would need to be reduced below the growth rate of the economy, failing which there would be a risk of prolonged economic stagnation as restrictive policies were increasingly applied to reduce the debt but simply creased the deficit and outstanding debt. The floating of the currency reduced the need for these restrictive measures to manage the currency and thus growth forecasts were quickly revised upwards. Thus, Brazilian policy faces a dilemma which cannot be resolved by measures that restrict output growth below its potential.

Is this a crisis? Delfim Netto estimates that the current rate of growth of the Brazilian labour force is around 2.7% per annum and that productivity growth is around 3.5%, which means that Brazil requires a growth rate in excess of 6% to keep the level of unemployment from rising. There seems to be no plausible way the economy will be able to generate that rate of growth without drastically reducing interest rates. Just as Italy and the UK in 1992 were judged to have exchange rate targets (and thus interest rate policies) that were incompatible with politically acceptable rate of unemployment, Brazil was also so judged by international markets by the end of 1998. Given the interest rates that prevailed in Brazil before the outbreak of the crisis, the policy was already untenable, since export growth was not sufficient to cover the increasing deficit on the services balance. The Asian crisis forced the issue by pushing up interest rates to levels which produced visible changes in both the foreign and fiscal balance and forced the introduction of fiscal austerity policies which made the impact on employment growth clear and visible. The slow drain of reserves and the slow flight of foreign investors[15] meant that a meltdown of the Asian style was avoided, but no amount of additional reserves in could change the basic fact that the interest rate on most of the outstanding debt obligations was higher than either the rate of growth of the economy or the rate of growth of exports, and thus neither the fiscal nor the foreign balance could improve without a drastic fall in interest rates. The exchange rate thus had to be left to the market.

There are some who suggest that this will be achieved as Brazil produces a large export surplus as a result of the devaluation. But, much like the initial Asian response, and given the Brazilian structure of trade after liberalisation, the trade surplus is being produced through a fall in imports that is more rapid than the fall in exports, as the sharp decline in incomes cuts consumption and imports. This suggests that any decline in interest rates that leads to a resumption in growth high enough to reduce unemployment is likely to recreate the foreign imbalance, requiring a return to high interest rates and more fiscal austerity leading to another reduction in growth.

Policy alternative

The real question facing Brazil in identifying an alternative strategy is what the aim of policy is to be. Is it to borrow more from abroad by restoring confidence in the currency and attracting foreign lenders or is it to earn more by attracting foreign buyers for Brazilian output? Is the aim of fiscal policy to reduce the deficit by cutting expenditures or by increasing the rate of growth of gdp. If it is to be the latter, then the recent return to capital markets is not a sign of health, but of weakness. The failure of exports to expand is not a sign of health, but of weakness, as is the recovery of the exchange rate. If improvement is an increase in capital inflows, an appreciation of the currency, but interest rates above 20%, then the Brazilian crisis, following the path of Mexico, will not be the last.

In domestic capital markets, lenders are supposed to exercise diligence and governance in order to insure that no borrower becomes excessively leveraged so as to present a threat to the stability of the financing system. The example of LCTM in the US suggests that even in the most advanced form of governance, supervision and control, the market is not capable of imposing discipline in time to limit exposures to safe levels. This has now been admitted even by those who champion the minimum amount of regulation and maximum amount of freedom in capital markets (cf President's Working Group on Financial Markets, 1999, p. viii). Global market mechanisms are even less well developed, which suggests that the responsibility for limiting leverage to that which is compatible with domestic economic stability must lie with national governments. This implies some for of rationing of capital inflows when they exceed that which an economy can safely absorb in the context of its domestic stability policies. Given the strong qualifications required for the validity of the Modigliani–Miller theorem (which says that capital structure has no impact on a firm's performance) finance economists have investigated the optimal degree of leverage for an individual firm. Perhaps it would be more appropriate if instead of discussing the control of capital flows the question were posed in terms of the optimal degree of leverage for a developing country.

Notes

1 "Yes, 'It' Did Happen Again — A Minsky Crisis Happened in Asia," Jerome Levy Economics Institute Working Paper # 234.

2 It is also germane to the argument made below that Korean banks were large, leveraged holders of Brazilian bonds at the outbreak of the Asian crisis

3 Thus, although I argued that the Asian crisis was different from Latin American crisis, I would also like to argue that the crises in countries like Indonesia and Brazil were different from those which hit the countries (Thailand and Mexico) that originally sparked their respective regional crises.

4 Delfim Netto, 1998, notes that Brazil went from being a net exporter to being a net importer of cotton, with Argentina being the main beneficiary.

5 I have discussed the impact on financial instability of these flows in "Some Risks and Implications of Financial Globalisation for National Policy Autonomy," *UNCTAD Review 1996,* March 1997.

6 The Central Bank provided emergency dollar credits at below-market rates to Banco Fonte Cidam (which was subsequently sold to Banque Nationale de Paris) and to Banco Marka, both of which had taken derivative positions based on maintenance of the exchange-rate regime. Banco Boavista was sold to France's Crédit Agricole, and Grupo Espirito Santo of Portugal made large capital injections into its Brazilian investment banking operations.

7 Inflationary transfers of income are estimated at some 4 per cent of national income and provided some 40 per cent of bank earnings.

8 Although the share of debt was rising and equity finance falling over the period. That this might be an overstatement of firm indebtedness is suggested by a independent analysis of the total volume of private sector loans to industry which shows a peak in 1993 and falls by over 50 per cent in the year of the introduction of the Real Plan; by 1996 volume had only reached about two-thirds of the 1993 level. See Tables 3 and 5 of Claudia Nessi Zonenschain, "Estrutura de Capital das Empresas no Brasil," *Revista do BNDES* Vol. 5, No 10 dezembro, 1998.

9 Cf. IMF, Brazil: Recent Economic Developments. IMF Staff Country Report, No. 98/24, Washington, DC, April 1998.

10 As part of the liberalization of trade and finance in the late 1980s Brazil liberalized the licensing of new banks by domestic (but not foreign) entities. Many of the entities founded since the late 1980s came to grief with the rise in interest rates that took place at the time of the Mexican crisis and during the attempt to calm the boom generated by the introduction of the *Plan Real.* 80 per cent of all interventions took place after the introduction of the Plan.

11 If the period is extended to December 1998 the number of banks liquidated or absorbed by other banks rises to 76 out of a total of 271 with the cost of the restructuring reaching 11% of 1998 GDP.

12 Further information on the restructuring of the Brazilian banking system can be found in IMF, Brazil: Recent Economic Developments, op. cit.

13 Roughly 25 per cent of Brazil's imports are capital goods, while about 55 per cent are raw materials and fuels.

14 From October 1998 to May 1999 consumer credit rates increased by 21 per cent, while the Central Bank's base rate fell by 46 per cent. Rates on commercial lending fell by only 4 per cent. The spread between bank rate and the consumer lending rate was over 12 times and 5.5 times in May; see Study by the National Association of Financial Executives, reported in *O Globo,* 16 May 1999, p. 38.

15 US banks cut their exposure to $18.6 billion by the end of September, a reduction of 25% between June and end September.

References

Delfim Netto, Antonio, "O desemprego é a âncora do Real," in *Visões da Crise*, Rio: Contrapunto, 1998.

Kregel, J.A., "The viability of economic policy and the priorities of economic policy," *Journal of Post Keynesian Economics*, Winter, 17:2, 1994–1995, pp. 261–77.

———, 1997, "Some Risks and Implications of Financial Globalisation for National Policy Autonomy," *UNCTAD Review 1996*, March.

———, 1998, "East Asia is Not Mexico: The Difference Between Balance of Payments Crises and Debt Deflation." In *Tigers in Trouble*, Jomo K.S., ed., London: Zed Books.

———, 1998, "Yes, 'It' Did Happen Again–A Minsky Crisis Happened in Asia," Working Paper #234, Annandale-on-Hudson, N.Y.: The Jerome Levy Economics Institute.

Ohno, Kenichi, n.d., "Exchange Rate Management in Developing Asia: Reassessment of the Pre-crisis Soft Dollar Zone," mimeo, Asian Development Bank Institute.

President's Working Group on Financial Markets–United States. 1999, "Hedge Funds, Leverage and the Lessons of Long-Term Capital Management: Report of the President's Working Group on Financial Markets," Washington, D.C. April 29.

Summers, Lawrence, 1998, "Deputy Secretary Summers Remarks Before The International Monetary Fund," U.S. Government Press Release, 2286, March 9.

UNCTAD, *Trade Development Report* 1995, Geneva: United Nations.

12 Financial liberalization and domestic policy space

Theory and practice with reference to Latin America

Introduction

Although they were not included in the original policy proposals of the Washington Consensus, opening domestic capital markets to foreign capital inflows and deregulation of domestic capital markets have been crucial elements of structural adjustment policies practiced by Latin American developing countries and as part of the conditionality attached to IMF and World Bank lending programs starting in the 1970s. Support for these measures comes from a straightforward application of the neoclassical approach to efficient distribution of economic resources on a global level. It notes that this position still dominates the thinking of multilateral institutions, despite the fact that it is based on a faulty theoretical justification, as demonstrated by the 1960s Cambridge controversies in the theory of capital.

Even before the theoretical debates in capital theory, Keynes had criticized similar policies in the 1930s. He reached the conclusion that such policies would eliminate what is now called a country's domestic "policy space," that is, its ability to pursue domestic economic policies directed at maximizing output and employment.

This chapter will present and assess the traditional explanation and justification of opening domestic capital markets to improve domestic growth conditions and outline the criticism based on the Cambridge capital debates. It will also present Keynes's analysis of similar proposals in the 1930s, presenting his argument that such policies eliminate domestic "policy space." It will then present an alternative justification of the benefits of open international capital markets put forward to solve the conflict between full employment policy and price stability presented in the 1960s, noting that this approach may be considered as providing the initial justification of the application of these policies in Latin American countries in the 1970s, leading to the lost decade of growth and employment in the 1980s. This assertion is supported by reference to the experience of the major Latin American countries – Brazil, Mexico, and Argentina – in adopting policies of structural adjustment based on continued opening of domestic markets in the period of the 1980s and the subsequent financial crises that reduced or eliminated their ability to operate independent domestic policies. It concludes by presenting Keynes's recommendation on how to retain policy autonomy and assessing the ability of developing countries, particularly in Latin America, to operate autonomous domestic policies in support of full employment in conditions of open international capital markets and potential policy alternatives.

Theoretical support for global financial liberalization

The theoretical support for global financial liberalization is to be found in the basic neoclassical theory of market efficiency. One of the first to support the continued existence of free international capital flows in the post-war period, in contrast to those who believed that international capital flows should be mediated by governments through the new Bretton Woods multilateral financial institutions, was Jacob Viner. In Viner's words,

> The basic argument for international investment of capital is that under normal conditions it results in the movement of capital from countries in which its marginal value productivity is low to countries in which its marginal value productivity is high and that it thus tends toward an equalization of marginal value productivity of capital throughout the world and consequently toward a maximum contribution of the world's capital resources to world production and income.
>
> (Viner, 1947, p. 98)

The veracity of this position that follows from the assumption of the efficient distribution of resources by international capital markets has never really been questioned. But there is an implicit assumption that lies behind this reasoning as it applies to the flows of capital between developed and developing countries. That implicit assumption is that the return on investment is higher in developing countries than it is in developed countries. The reason for this is usually supported by reference to the longer experience of capital accumulation and thus the greater accumulation of capital and higher capital intensity of production believed to prevail in developed countries. Higher per-capita incomes in developed countries are thought to provide higher savings ratios than in lower pre-capital income developing countries. Finally developed countries are thought to be experiencing declining labor forces and aging populations, relative to young, larger populations in developing countries. Thus, transferring financial resources from high-saving, capital-rich, aging developed countries provides them with a means of increasing returns, assuring their income in retirement, while it increases income growth and employment by providing the financing for investment in higher-return endeavors in developing countries.

However, this approach, based on the maximization of the return to capital resulting from free international capital flows relies on the number of subsidiary assumptions such as the following:

1) A negative relation exists between capital intensity and rate of return.
2) It is possible to identify differences in capital intensity between developed and developing countries.
3) Foreign capital inflows from developed countries are in fact used to increase productive domestic investment.

4) If foreign capital inflows do not satisfy Point 3, and are primarily invested in financial assets, then there is a high elasticity of substitution between financial and real assets.

5) Fixed exchange rates or insurable exchange rate risk.

However, as a result of the Cambridge controversies in capital theory, few of these implicit assumptions part generally valid. We now know the following:

1) The theorems on capital reversal and double switching shows that it is possible for increasing capital intensity to be associated with higher, rather than lower, rates of return to capital and that the same rate of return may be associated with the same degree of capital intensity. As a result it is impossible to establish a general relation between capital intensity and rate of return. This means that the returns to capital in developing countries may be lower in developing countries even if capital intensity there is lower. Simply, there is no univocal relation between capital intensity and value productivity of capital.

2) Because capital is a produced good, its value depends on the prices of the capital and labor inputs necessary to produce it. Because it is a durable good, its value depends on the rate of return used to calculate present values. It is thus impossible to measure capital intensity unambiguously.[1]

In addition to the capital theory debates, history has suggested several reasons to be skeptical about the traditional view.

3) Foreign capital inflows tend to have little impact on rates of domestic investment. Most studies suggest that the impact is marginal. On the other hand, there is evidence that increased foreign capital inflows are associated with increasing domestic consumption.

4) Finally, the impact of capital flows tends to be concentrated in investment in financial assets, and the impact on domestic financial conditions does not produce a change in the relative prices of financial and real assets that leads to a substitution of the former for the latter. The majority of foreign inflows are attracted by high domestic policy rates on financial assets, and because these are policy rates, their impact on domestic monetary conditions is offset by the monetary authorities.

A modern version of the Viner postulate

There is however a more modern justification for financial liberalization that deals not with capital flows themselves but with the liberalization of the movement of financial institutions. In the words of Lawrence Summers, former deputy Secretary of United States Treasury:

> The case for capital account liberalization is a case for capital seeking the highest productivity investments. We have seen in recent months in Asia – as at many points in the past in other countries – the danger of opening up

the capital account when incentives are distorted and domestic regulation and supervision is inadequate. Inflows in search of fairly valued economic opportunities are one thing. Inflows in search of government guarantees or undertaken in the belief that they are immune from the standard risks are quite another. The right response to these experiences is much less to slow the pace of capital account liberalization than to accelerate the pace of creating an environment in which capital will flow to its highest return use. And one of the best ways to accelerate the process of developing such a system is to open up to foreign financial service providers, and all the competition, capital and expertise which they bring with them. The recently concluded global financial services agreement demonstrates that countries recognize these beneficial effects of external liberalization.

(Summers, 1998)

Here the argument is that the success of financial liberalization requires domestic institutions and monitoring that can best be provided by the free entry of foreign financial service providers. Although this argument does not provide a response to the criticisms just noted of the implicit assumption that lies behind the theoretical support of financial liberalization, its empirical support is equally suspect. We know from the report of the Argentine parliament that foreign banks operating in Argentina were the first to exit in 2001 and that not only did they transfer their capital out of the country, but they also provided the means for their clients to exit after the imposition of the "corralito."[2] They clearly did not contribute to creating a stable domestic environment (Tonveronachi, 2006).

In addition, there is substantial evidence that foreign banks operating in Brazil are less efficient than domestic banks[3] and that when foreign banks are allowed to take over or merge with domestic banks in Latin America, they tend to do so with the best-performing banks rather than improving the operation of badly performing domestic banks (Williams and Williams, 2007).

Keynes's position on financial liberalization

In an extension of a view that had already taken shape in the 1920s, Keynes's *Treatise on Money* Volume II subtitled the "Applied Theory of Money" undertakes a detailed analysis of the impact of an international system with global financial flows under an international standard such as the Gold Standard. Keynes's criticism here is more mundane – dealing with asymmetric adjustment in different aspects of the economic system.

In discussion of a return to the degree of financial liberalization implicit in the operation of the pre-war gold standard he raises

a doubt whether it is wise to have a currency system with a much wider ambit than our Banking System, our Tariff System and our Wage System. Can we afford to allow a disproportionate degree of mobility to a single element in an economic system which we leave extremely rigid in several other respects? If there was the same mobility internationally in all other respects as there is nationally, it might be a different matter. But to introduce a mobile element, highly sensitive to outside influences, as a connected part of the machine which the other parts of which the other parts are much more rigid, may invite breakages. It is, therefore, a serious question whether it is right to adopt an international standard, which will allow an extreme mobility and sensitiveness of foreign lending, while the remaining elements of the economic complex remain exceedingly rigid. If it were as easy to put wages up and down as it is to put bank rate up and down, well and good. But this is not the actual situation. A change in international financial conditions or in the wind and weather of speculative sentiment may alter the volume of foreign lending, if nothing is done to counteract it, by tens of millions in a few weeks.

(Keynes, 1930, Chapter 36)

The major difficulty with financial globalization was that it implied uniform rates of interest in all countries and thus the loss of national policy autonomy. The quotation given comes from Chapter 36 of the *Treatise on Money* and bears the title "National Policy Autonomy." There he gives a clear assessment of the impact of international capital flows on domestic economic conditions. He notes the conflict between policy to support international investment flows and policy to offset the impact on the economy of the cyclical behavior of domestic investment decisions. In the discussions of development theory, we would today talk of "national policy space" for developing countries. Keynes is arguing that financial liberalization precludes a country from using monetary policy to offset fluctuations in domestic investment rather than requiring the use of interest rates to influence international capital inflows. The loss of policy autonomy was thus caused by a policy conflict – low interest rates, required to offset a decline in domestic investment would cause a decline in foreign investment.

Policy paradoxes in the US in the 1960s

These types of conflict restricting policy autonomy are not new. In the US, after the dollar shortage had been replaced by a dollar glut, there was also policy conflict between internal and external equilibrium. This conflict concerned both monetary and fiscal policy. If external account in equilibrium at less than full employment, expanding demand by active fiscal policy produces an external deficit, but if the external account is in deficit at full employment, restrictive fiscal policy reduces domestic demand and raises unemployment.

This conflict was resolved by the Fleming-Mundell[4] creation of policy space through external capital inflows. This approached proposed that monetary policy be used to attract capital inflows to finance the current account deficit that would occur at full employment produced by the use of expansionary fiscal policy. External capital flows in open capital markets thus provided policy space if the "assignment problem" was suitably resolved to use the fiscal instrument to target domestic equilibrium and the interest rate to target external equilibrium.

Solving policy paradoxes after the Latin American debt crisis of the 1980s

The same sort of justification was used in 1980s to provide policy space for Latin American countries facing unsustainable debt burdens built up during the large increase in international financial liberalization in the 1970s. After the failure of the attempts by these countries to generate sufficiently large current account surpluses to meet their debt service obligations because of the reduction in growth rates that this required, the Baker Plan was replaced by the Brady Plan, which proposed the use of domestic policies and financial derivative structures to allow countries to eliminate inflation and support growth by allowing them to return to international capital markets to once again borrow the funds needed to meet debt service.

These policies included a fixed exchange rate regime to provide an exchange rate anchor to inflation expectations, the deregulation and development of domestic capital and equity markets supported by the creation of private assets through the privatization of state-owned enterprises and other quasi-government activities, the full liberalization of external trade and external capital inflows to allow foreign investment in the newly liberated capital markets, the removal of controls and restrictions over domestic financial institutions and the liberalization of domestic interest rates to be set by international markets, and the use of tight monetary policy and restrictive fiscal policy to reduce domestic demand and fight inflation.

In some countries such as Mexico, Argentina, and Brazil, the return of capital inflows created policy space and success in providing for a rapid elimination of inflation. The policies were also accompanied by a rise in domestic purchasing power and in domestic consumption, which led to a recovery in domestic growth rates.

However, the success has hidden within it some unanticipated and unintended consequences. The increasing capital inflows led to an increase in external debt, much of it denominated in foreign currency; the recovery in domestic consumption with open domestic markets led to an increasing commercial account deficit. Because capital inflows often exceeded the financing requirements for the rising external deficit, the result was an overvaluation of exchange rate, sometime in nominal but in all cases real terms. Tight domestic monetary policy created large international interest rate differentials that supported the capital inflows and also led to large incentives to borrow in foreign currency at lower interest rates that led to currency mismatch in financial and non-financial sector balance sheets. The rising level of debt, with high interest rates, led to a rising debt service that increased domestic fiscal deficits and produced financial sector weakness. Eventually, for capital inflows reversed and produced financial sector and exchange rate crisis, that eliminated any increase in policy space and once again reduced policy space to zero.

Thus developing countries faced a new policy conflict. Inflation would not have been reduced without the existence of the exchange rate anchor and the return of capital inflows in quantities sufficient to prevent external deficit from creating an exchange rate crisis. But, capital inflows financed increased domestic consumption, not investment, whereas the high interest rates that were required to sustain them and currency overvaluation that they produced reduced the competitiveness of domestic producers. Solving the policy conflict to combine growth and price stability became hostage to the willingness of international investors to continue to maintain their investments. Or, As Keynes had already noted, monetary policy had become the hostage of international capital markets.

This loss of policy control that resulted from the very success of the economic policies that accompanied the Brady Plan[5] thus led to domestic monetary policy being determined by foreign investors as domestic interest rates had to be sufficiently high to ensure the capital inflows needed to meet debt service and the commercial deficit. Nominal fiscal balances went out of control as they came to be increasingly determined by the level of interest rates required by foreign investors. The overvaluation of real exchange rate, the liberalization of domestic markets, and high interest rates made it increasingly difficult for domestic producers to restructure to meet international competition. Finally, the external balance came to be driven increasingly by debt service and thus less responsive to traditional policy measures such as reduced domestic demand. All of these factors can be seen in the experiences of the major Latin American economies, which applied these structural adjustment policies as part of their Brady Plan exit from the debt crisis of the 1980s (UNCTAD, 1998).

Resolving the policy conflict – the Mexican experience

In Mexico licensing and other controls and restrictions on imports were substituted by tariffs starting around the time of the mid-1985 devaluation, followed by a series of sharp reductions in tariffs starting in 1987 leading to a rapid increase in imports.[6] At the same time regulations on foreign direct investment were liberalized, and by 1989 authorization became nearly automatic.[7] The new Salinas government proceeded with the privatization of state-owned enterprises (small- and medium-sized enterprises had already been wound up or sold starting in 1983), deregulation of the banking system, and the liberalization of domestic financial markets. Tight monetary policy produced large interest rate differentials that allowed the deregulated banks to fund sharply increased domestic lending with foreign borrowing, whereas international investors produced boom conditions in domestic equity and bond markets and a sharp real appreciation of exchange rates. The foreign inflows led to a return of rising external indebtedness that the introduction of the Brady Plan had reduced at the same time as it bolstered central bank foreign exchange reserves.[8] At the same time, the wild expansion of bank lending – largely designed to beef up balance sheets to attract foreign partners – led to a sharp increase in non-performing assets[9] in conditions of substantial currency mismatch for domestic financial and non-financial borrowers and rising overvaluation of the currency. The introduction of the North American Free Trade Agreement (NAFTA) at the same time as a new government was taking office in conditions of domestic political unrest led to a sharp exit of institutional investors in peso-denominated domestic assets. The reports of $29 billion of dollar-indexed short-term Tesobonos dwarfed the existing foreign exchange reserves that had fallen from a peak of around $25 billion in 1993 to around a fifth of that amount. The risk was not just the collapse of the exchange rate; it was of convertibility itself. The resulting Tequila Crisis led to a collapse of the domestic banking system, which has now come to be majority controlled by external financial institutions.

The Argentine experience

Argentina went through a similar experience with the exception of a fixed peg to the US dollar through a currency board arrangement as its exchange rate anchor. Although this prevented nominal appreciation, it aggravated real appreciation of the exchange rate. Trade liberalization started in the late 1980s with unilateral reductions of tariffs, that is, without any reciprocal concessions from its trading partners, but under unconditional most favoured nation (MFN). The currency board was instituted in 1991 on the grounds that this would bring about reductions in interest rates because the peso was as reliable as the dollar. However, although inflation did decline to near zero in around two years, large interest rate differentials prevailed, leading to large capital inflows and substantial real appreciation of exchange rates. At the same time all state-owned enterprises were privatized, and all state controls were eliminated. The decline in debt that had occurred by the end of the 1990s was reversed and despite the elimination of the losses from state-owned industry from the government's balance sheet (indeed it had benefited substantially from the receipts from privatization), and fiscal deficits soon returned. Hit by contagion from the crisis in Mexico and under pressure from the IMF to reduce fiscal deficits, the new De La Rua government continued policies of fiscal austerity[10] that plunged the economy into an ever-deepening recession.[11] As receipts fell more rapidly than the government could introduce expenditure cuts, international investors eventually lost confidence in the government, and the policy tricks introduced by Cavallo, called back to his former post of minister of finance, were unable to stem a capital reversal, which produced bankruptcy of the banking and pension systems, a collapse of the currency board, and the largest sovereign default in history.[12]

The Brazilian experience

Brazil started its experience of trade liberalization started under the Collor government in the late 1980s. After a long series of adjustment plans, in 1994 the Real Plan provided for a new "real" value of the domestic currency and a fixed exchange rate.[13] The sharp decline in the rate of inflation produced an increase in domestic purchasing power and an increase in domestic consumption at the same time as it produced first a nominal and then a real appreciation in the exchange rate. Domestic monetary and fiscal policy remained highly restrictive in support of the Real Plan, leading to large interest rate differentials that led to high capital inflows, rising external debt, and rising fiscal deficits. Capital inflows continued in the face of a rising internal and external deficit, as an election approached at the end of 1998. An IMF support loan provided the external reserves necessary to reassure foreign investors that the exchange regime would be maintained, but after the elections, a foreign exchange crisis brought depreciation in January 1999 that allowed a loosening of the restrictive policies and some recovery in growth. In difference from the other two countries, the banking system emerged unscathed; in fact it earned substantial profits speculating on the depreciation.

This marks a significant difference between Brazil and Mexico and Argentina, on the one hand, and the Asian countries after the 1997 crisis, on the other. This is for two reasons. First, Brazil employed a restructuring of the financial system as part of the Real Plan. Through the Proer and Proes programs,[14] the government committed around 11% of GDP to close insolvent private and state-owned banks and restructure the balance sheets of those remaining.[15] In addition, after the restructuring the central bank, the central government offered exchange rates, and interest rates linked debt, which became the major investment in the banks' portfolios, thus insulating them from both the risk of monetary policy to defend the exchange rate and the impact of the devaluation when it finally occurred. Indeed, because there was a widespread expectation that the exchange rate was being defended for electoral purposes – in the campaign for the November 1998 election the sitting president ran on a platform that presented the defense of the exchange rate as protection against the return of hyperinflation – banks engaged in extensive hedging and speculative positions in derivatives markets that allowed them to earn record profits after the devaluation in January.

The illusion of creating domestic policy space through foreign borrowing

Thus, throughout Latin America, increased external capital flows were used to emerge from the crisis of the 1980s and provide the policy space to combine growth with price stability. However, none of them were sustainable and led to capital account crises.

How did this happen? The simple answer is that the Fleming-Mundell solution has an inherent flaw, just as the position put forward by Viner had an implicit assumption. The Fleming-Mundell analysis is a flow analysis dealing only with the short term. It ignores the impact of capital inflows on debt stock and the increase in the debt stock on debt service.[16] Further, there is no analysis of impact of the high interest rates required to insure the capital inflows on the amount of debt service on the increasing debt stock – and thus no analysis of impact of rising debt service on current account balance and no analysis of rising debt stock on risk premium on external borrowing and thus on the interest rates that have to be paid on foreign lending. Simply, it assumes that capital flows can be maintained indefinitely, irrespective of the size of the accumulated debt and the interest rates to be paid on this debt. The result is that the idea that an externally financed policy space was a short-term illusion simply delayed the problems caused by the inherent policy conflict.

Keynes had already warned about the false illusion of national policy autonomy financed by external borrowing. As he had noted, a single international monetary standard requires the central bank to relinquish control over domestic interest rates and implies a uniform rate of interest across countries. In the case of developed countries, this was probably the case. In the case of developing countries, there is no tendency toward uniformity, large interest differential remains, but so does the loss of national policy autonomy. Indeed, this position is much the worse because it creates the factors noted here caused by persistent international interest rate differentials.

Any attempt to use interest rates to offset domestic fluctuations in investment would create interest rate differentials and international capital flows that would eventually undermine the country's commitment to the international standard. To resolve this policy conflict, Keynes suggests the control of net capital flows – the foreign capital balance.[17]

Keynes's proposals

Long-term capital flow controls

As remedy to the loss of national policy autonomy, in Chapter 36 of the *Treatise*, Keynes recommends formal controls over long-term capital flows. He notes that most countries have always had registration requirements for capital issues in their own markets and that these could be expanded internationally. He also suggests a tax on purchase of foreign securities not listed in the UK market of 10%.

Supported by short-term controls

But, long-term controls have to be supported by short-term controls. To influence short-term flows, he recommends a dual rate structure that differentiates between financial flows and trade finance, given preference to the latter. He also recommends a more flexible exchange rate structure through variation in the central bank's bid and offer rates within the gold points.

Keynes also recommends the active use of intervention in the forward market, a suggestion that was first made in the *Tract on Monetary Reform* to influence short-term interest rates on short-term capital transactions. Keynes's conclusion is that the central bank should use bank rate, the forward rate, and flexibility in its bid and offer rates to influence short-term flows.

The ideal international financial system

However, Keynes's implicit acceptance of a gold standard system is predicated on the fact that the UK had by that time already decided to return to the gold standard. Nonetheless, he notes that in his view, an ideal system would be one with flexible exchange rates. From the time of the *Tract on Monetary Reform*, Keynes argued that a flexible exchange rate system was preferable to a fixed rate system as long as there was a forward foreign exchange market in which traders could cover their exchange risks.

This is basically the same position that was incorporated in the proposal for the clearing union and the position that he took to the Bretton Woods negotiations in 1944.[18]

Implications of this analysis for current financial globalization

The most important point of Keynes's analysis of these issues for current conditions is his implicit acceptance of the position that dominated pre-war thinking on these issues: external capital flows determine domestic conditions and trade flows rather than the other way around.

In Keynes's words from the *Treatise on Money*,

> The belief in an extreme mobility of international lending and a policy of unmitigated laissez-faire toward foreign loans has been based on too simple a view of the causal relations between foreign lending and foreign investment. Because net foreign lending and net foreign investment must always exactly balance, it is been assumed that no serious problem presents itself. Since lending and investment must be equal, an increase of lending must cause an increase of investment, and a decrease of lending must cause a decrease of investment; indeed, the argument sometimes goes further, and – instead of being limited to net foreign lending – even maintains that the making of an individual foreign loan has in itself the effect of increasing our exports.
>
> All this, however, neglects the painful, and perhaps violent, reactions of the mechanism which has to be brought into play in order to force net foreign lending and net foreign investment into equality. . . . I do not know why this should not be considered obvious. If English investors, not liking the outlook at home, fearing labor disputes or nervous about a change of government, begin to buy more American securities than before, why should it be supposed that this will be naturally balanced by increased British exports? For, of course, it will not. It will, in the first instance, set up a serious instability of the domestic credit system – the ultimate working out of which it is difficult or impossible to predict. Or, if American investors take a fancy to British ordinary shares, is this going, in any direct way, to decrease British exports?
>
> (Keynes, 1930, pp. 335–6)

Will flexible exchange rates produce policy space?

Many developing countries introduced flexibility in exchange rates after the financial crises that followed their successful stabilization policies. Many have now introduced inflation targeting and primary surplus targets as substitutes for the fixed exchange rate policy anchor. Also, a number have managed to create commercial and capital account surpluses. Yet, their debt stocks remain high and nominal deficits are not being reduced, because of the persistence of high interest rate differentials, while growth rates remain low. This would all suggest that Keynes's original recommendation still holds and that some form of management of the foreign balance is still required.

Conclusion

We can thus conclude that in a global economy of financial liberalization, preserving policy space in developing countries will require the following:

- Flexible exchange rates: in all of the cases of financial crisis following financial liberalization in Latin America, the destabilizing capital flows result from either an implicit or explicit exchange rate guarantee. Indeed, in most cases, the opening of domestic markets to international capital flows produced inflows that more than offset the increasing external financing needs and thus created either real or nominal appreciation of the currency. Foreign investors or domestic financial institutions thus had a double advantage – a large positive interest rate differential that could be exploited by borrowing abroad at low rates and investing domestically at high rates plus the exchange rate appreciation that multiplied these already high returns.
- Thus avoiding these destabilizing arbitrage flows will require some form of management to prevent overvaluation and a one-way bet that supports the returns on foreign borrowing that naturally exists from the interest rate differential.
- Controls over capital flows to allow management of interest rates and exchange rates: as long as developing countries use domestic restrictions on monetary or fiscal policy, they will suffer an interest policy determined by interest rate differential. To prevent capital flows being driven by this differential, which has no impact on domestic interest rates or investment, will require some sort of control over international capital flows.
- Restricting issue of foreign-denominated debt by both the public and the private sector to ensure the effective management of foreign capital inflows: because a major source of the speculative flows comes from the ability to raise funds in foreign currency – whether speculative or used to finance domestic productive activity creating a currency mismatch for non-financial corporations – eliminating the source will require controls over the ability of domestic financial and non-financial corporations to borrow in foreign currency. This means strengthening the domestic financial sector. Unfortunately, this will not be easy because the policies followed by

governments to ensure the sale of government debt mean that banks can maximize profits by lending to government rather than to the private sector. Statistics suggest that post-financial crisis Latin American financial institutions no longer lend to the non-financial sector. To the extent that foreign banks have been granted increased access as a means of restructuring after crises, there lending has tended to be for consumer and mortgage lending, again leaving the business sector without sources of finance.

Finally, the pressure on most countries to deregulate the financial system has led to the elimination of national development banks, which in the past had provided lending to industry.[19]

Notes

1 For a summary of the results of these debates, see Harcourt (1971). It is interesting that despite the fact that these conclusions have now been accepted by all sides in the debates, they have been ignored in the development literature and in most of the modern macro-economic literature.
2 See the official report of the Comisión Especial de la Cámara de Diputados, República Argentina (2005).
3 See Guimarães (2002), de Paula (2002), and de Paula and Alves Jr (2007).
4 The original papers were developed by both economists when they were working for the IMF and were published virtually simultaneously. See Fleming (1962), and Mundell (1962).
5 In fact they closely resemble what came to be codified as "Washington Consensus" policies of structural adjustment but with the exception of the exchange rate anchor and financial liberalization – two aspects that were crucial to their success. See, for example, Kregel (1999).
6 See Kate (1990).
7 See Guillén (1995).
8 See Mantey (1998).
9 See Correa (1996).
10 For a revealing discussion of the views of the fund in this period, see the book of interviews with Claudio Loser, who was responsible for fund policy in Latin America at the time in Tenembaum (2004).
11 See, for example, Cafiero and Llorens (2002) and Sevares (2002).
12 A review of Argentine policy leading up to the crisis is available in Kregel (2003).
13 For a detailed comparison of the plans proposed prior to 1994, see Modenesi (2005, pp. 290–5).
14 See Maia (1999) for more information on the details of these programs.
15 See Sáinz and Calcagno (1999), who note that this restructuring was a major source of the increased government indebtedness after the Real Plan but also prevented the collapse of the system after the devaluation of 1999.
16 A more extensive analytical criticism of this approach may be found in Kregel (2007).
17 In Chapter 2 of *A Tract on Monetary Reform* (Keynes, 1923) had already recommended a capital levy on bondholders as the most appropriate method for dealing with the "progressive and catastrophic inflations" in Central and Eastern Europe, and in 1924 he had recommended capital controls as a way of reducing deflationary pressure due to the return to gold. See Skidelsky (2000, p. 191).
18 See, for example, the discussion in Skidelsky (2000, p. 191).
19 Brazil remains the exception in this regard, although a number of Latin American countries are considering resurrecting national development banks.

References

Cafiero, M. and J. Llorens (2002) *La Argentina Robada – El corralito, los bancos y el vaciamento del system financiero argentine*, Buenos Aires: Ediciones Macchi.

Comisión Especial de la Cámara de Diputados, República Argentina (2005) *Fuga de Divisas en la Argentina: Informe Final*, Buenos Aires: Comisión Latinoamérica de Ciencias Sociales (Clacso) and Siglo XXI.

Correa, E. (1996) "Cartera vencida y salida de la Crisis Bancaria," in A. Girón and E. Correa, eds., *Crisis Bancaria y Carteras Vencidas*, México: UAM-IIEc-UNAM-La Jornada.

de Paula, L.F. (2002) "Expansion Strategies of European Banks to Brazil and Their Impacts on the Brazilian Banking Sector," *Latin American Business Review*, Vol. 3, No. 4, pp. 59–91.

de Paula, L.F. and A.J. Alves Jr. (January 2007) "The Determinants and Effects of Foreign Bank Entry in Argentina and Brazil: A Comparative Analysis," *Investigación Económica*, Vol. LXVI, No. 259, pp. 65–104.

Fleming, M. (1962) "Domestic Financial Policy Under Fixed and Under Floating Exchange Rates," *IMF Staff Papers*, Vol. 9, pp. 369–79.

Guillén, H. (1995) "El Consenso de Washington en México," in Jose Luis Calza, ed., *Problemas Macroeconomicos de México*, Vol. 1, Mexico City: Serie Economia UAM Azcapotzalco.

Guimarães, P. (2002) "How Does Foreign Entry Affect Domestic Banking Market? The Brazilian Case," *Latin American Business Review*, Vol. 3, No. 4, pp. 121–40.

Harcourt, G.C. (1971) *Some Cambridge Controversies in the Theory of Capital*, Cambridge: Cambridge University Press.

Kate, A.K. (1990) "La aperture commercial de Mexico – experiencias y lecciones," in Eduardo Gitli, ed., *Estudios sobre el sector external Mexicano*, Mexico City: Serie Economia UAM Azcapotzalco.

Keynes, John Maynard (1923) *A Tract on Monetary Reform (Collected Writings*, Vol. IV), London: Macmillan.

——— (1930) *A Treatise on Money*, Vol. II, London: Macmillan.

Kregel, J.M. (July 1999) "Alternative to the Brazilian Crisis," *Revista de Economia Política – Brazilian Journal of Political Economy*, Vol. 19, No. 3(75), pp. 23–38.

——— (January 2003) "An Alternative View of the Argentine Crisis: Structural Flaws in Structural Adjustment Policy," *Investigación Económica*, No. 243, pp. 15–49.

——— (2007) "Keynes, Globalisation and 'National Policy Space'," Forthcoming in a book edited by João Sicsú, Carlos Vidotto e João Saboia Commemorating the 70th Anniversary of the General Theory, to be published by Editora Campus-Elsevier.

Maia, G. (1999) "Restructuring the Banking System – The Case of Brazil," Bank for International Settlement, www.bis.org/publ/plcy06b.pdf

Mantey, G. (1998) "Efectos de la liberalización financiera en la deuda pública de México," in Alicia Giron and Eugenia Correa, eds., *Crisis Financiera: Mercado sin Fronteras*, Mexico City: UNAM-IIE, DGAPA, Ediciones Caballito.

Modenesi, A.M. (2005) *Regimes Monetários – Teoria e a Experiência do Real*, Tambore: Editoria Manole.

Mundell, R. (1962) "The Appropriate Use of Monetary and Fiscal Policy Under Fixed Exchange Rates," *IMF Staff Papers*, Vol. 9, pp. 70–9.

Sáinz, P. and A. Calcagno (1999) "La economía brasileña ante el Plan Real y su crisis," Temas de Coyuntura, No. 4, CEPAL, Santiago de Chile, July.

Sevares, J. (2002) *Por qué Cayó La Argentina*, Buenos Aires: Grupo Normal.

Skidelsky, R. (2000) *John Maynard Keynes: Fighting for Freedom, 1937–1946*, London: Penguin.

Summers, L. (1998) "US Government Press Release, 2286, March 9, 1998: 'Deputy Secretary Summers Remarks Before the International Monetary Fund'," www.ustreas.gov/press/releases/rr2286.htm

Tenembaum, E. (2004) *Enemigos*, Buenos Aires: Grupo Norma.

Tonveronachi, M. (January 2006) "The Role of Foreign Banks in Emerging Countries: The Case of Argentina, 1993–2000," *Investigación Económica*, Vol. LXV, No. 255, pp. 97–107.

UNCTAD (1998) "Trade and Development Report, Chapter III, Section B: 'Anatomy of the Crises in the Post-Bretton Woods Period for a Discussion of the Similarity in These Crises From the Southern Cone Crisis of the Early 1990s to the Asian Crises of 1997–8'".

Viner, J. (April 1947) "International Finance in the Postwar World," *Journal of Political Economy*, Vol. 55, pp. 97–107.

Williams, J. and F. Williams (2007) "Does Ownership Explain Bank Mergers and Acquisitions? The Case of Domestic Banks and Foreign Banks in Brazil," this volume.

13 Emerging markets and the international financial architecture

A blueprint for reform[1,2]

Recent emerging market critiques of the international financial architecture

The developed world's policy response to the recent financial crisis has produced a growing chorus of criticism of the international financial system by emerging market government officials. The former Brazilian finance minister has complained of the currency wars generated by the extraordinary monetary policies introduced by developed country central banks in response to the Great Recession (Wheatley and Garnham 2010). Criticism was equally sharp when a possible reversal of these policies was intimated and the resulting "taper tantrum" in May 2013 produced sharp volatility in exchange rates and capital flows to emerging market economies (Wheatley 2014).

The new Indian central bank governor has joined in this criticism of the policies of developed country central banks, faulting them for failing to take into account the impact of their policies on emerging markets and calling for increased policy coordination and cooperation (Goyal 2014, Spicer 2014). Seeking a larger international role for the Chinese currency, Chinese officials have also called into question the dominant role of the US dollar—echoing a criticism of the "exorbitant privilege" first launched by French President de Gaulle in the 1960s.[3] And even before its current difficulties in managing the impact of the decline in oil prices on the ruble exchange rate, Russia joined China as a proponent of replacing the dollar with the SDR—the International Monetary Fund's Special Drawing Rights (China Briefing 2010, Reuters Factbox 2009, Oliver 2009, Zhou 2009).

These criticisms of the international financial architecture are not new—indeed, they reappear after every international financial crisis—and neither is the proposed solution: increased policy coordination, replacing the dollar with an international reserve currency, and the creation of regional or emerging-market-governed institutions to replace the US-dominated International Monetary Fund (IMF). Yet there has been little real modification of the Bretton Woods system aside from the unilateral decision of the United States in 1970 to abrogate its commitment under the IMF Articles of Agreement to support a fixed dollar-gold parity.

Not only have these proposals for reform gained little support in the past, they are unlikely to remedy the faults decried by emerging market economies. Indeed, they may make conditions facing these economies worse. This paper provides a discussion of why these reform proposals are of little benefit to the objective of an international financial architecture supportive of developing countries. It suggests that several of the alternatives rejected in the pre–Bretton Woods discussion could provide a basis for a more stable financial system suitable to the needs of emerging market economies. If emerging markets are to achieve their objective of joining the ranks of industrialized, developed countries, they must use their economic and political influence to support radical change in the international financial system.

The chimera of increased policy coordination

In the aftermath of the US decision to break the dollar-gold parity and the collapse of the Smithsonian Agreements to preserve fixed exchange rates, virtually the only role that remained for the IMF was policy coordination to ensure exchange rate stability. Initially carried out through policy conditionality on program lending and Article IV assessments, it has now been extended to consider more systemic interconnections of national monetary and fiscal policies in the form of what is called the "Spillover Report," which seeks to identify the cross-border impact of members' economic policies (IMF 2014). But it is instructive that the attempts to charge the IMF with increased power to impose policy coordination have produced meager results, and even skepticism, among IMF staff (Blanchard, Ostry, and Ghosh 2013). It is instructive that even the modest attempts to adjust emerging market quotas and governance in the Fund, agreed to after the 1997 Asian crisis, have yet to be approved. Indeed, the major fora for coordination are now in the G-20 and the Financial Stability Forum, both also dominated by US policy preferences.

Even more important, there is little historical evidence that policy coordination is in any way beneficial to the stability of the international system. The best-known example of monetary policy coordination was the support provided by the governor of the Federal Reserve Bank of New York to ease the return of the pound sterling to the gold standard in the 1920s. The Fed, in response to the postwar slump in the early 1920s, supported market conditions favorable to the British objective, but the same support after the return to gold in the presence of a run-up in US securities prices is widely believed to have provided the basis for the euphoria in equity markets that led to the September 1929 market break.[4] And the collateral damage of this policy was an increasing flow of short-term funds to Germany that exacerbated the problem of finding an equitable solution to inter-Allied debts and German reparations.[5]

More recently, international cooperation provided the bulwark for the measures taken to resolve the dollar's overvaluation and then precipitous decline in the aftermath of the Plaza and Louvre agreements. According to Toyoo Gyohten, the failure of these coordination efforts was the main cause of the October 19,

1987, equity market break known as Black Monday.[6] Subsequently, the need to allow the United States to lower rates without further depreciation of the dollar led to interest rate reductions by the Bank of Japan in the presence of a rampant equity and property bubble, which precipitated the break in the Japanese market at the end of 1989 that produced a 25-year stagnation and the birth of the zero-interest-rate policies now lamented by emerging market economies.

A clear problem facing coordination that is cited by both Gyohten and Paul Volcker is the fact that coordination has been predominantly in monetary policy, absent fiscal policy coordination: "Whatever its economic merits, the flexible use of fiscal policy is politically difficult. This difficulty is what limits so sharply the potential for the international coordination of economic policies" (Volcker, in Volcker and Gyohten 1992, 292). These difficulties seem only to have increased in the current response to financial crisis.

Unfortunately, while policy coordination appears to have been more the rule than the exception in the past, it does not have a record of producing positive results, and there is little evidence that attempts to consider the impact of domestic monetary policies on other countries can ever be devised in such a way as to provide mutually beneficial results.

An international reserve currency

Since Robert Triffin's devastating critique of the Bretton Woods dollar-gold standard (Triffin 1960), the problems of using a national currency as the international reserve currency in a stable exchange rate system have been well known. But rather than providing an innovative solution to this problem, the current proposals to replace the dollar with an international reserve currency appear to be based on the belief that this could provide a system of implicit policy coordination similar to that which was supposed to have ruled under the freely convertible international gold standard. If each country were responsible for maintaining the gold content of its domestic currency unit, there would be no need for explicit international coordination; it would be imposed by the market adjustment of trade flows to changes in relative gold prices for traded and non-traded goods. However, it is difficult to see how an independent international currency would perform differently from the actual operation of the gold standard. Indeed, the Bretton Woods system was an attempt to escape the instability of the British return to the gold standard in the 1920s.

Keynes's critique of international standards

As Keynes pointed out, the international coordination provided under the gold standard was neither equitable nor stabilizing: "The main cause of failure . . . of the freely convertible international metallic standard," he wrote, was "that it throws the main burden of adjustment on the country which is in the *debtor* position on the international balance of payments" (Keynes 1980, 27). "It has been an inherent characteristic of the automatic international metallic currency . . . to force adjustments in the direction most disruptive of social order, and to throw the burden on the countries least able to support it, making the poor poorer" (29).

Indeed, the historical performance of the gold standard confirms this assessment. When debtor countries are faced with adjustment via credit restriction and declining domestic prices, the pressure on the financial system leads to a suspension of the gold standard, while creditor countries resist the expansion of credit and rising prices by limiting convertibility and implementing counterinflationary policies.[7] Thus, while Keynes's insistence on symmetric adjustment is often explained by a desire to allow the UK to implement policies to maximize employment and prevent systemic deficiency of global demand, it has a more fundamental explanation related to the destabilizing nature of a system based on an international standard. As Keynes observed,

> The main effect of [any international standard] is to secure *uniformity* of movement in different countries—everyone must conform to the average behaviour of everyone else. . . . The disadvantage is that it hampers each central bank in tackling its own national problems.
>
> (Keynes 1971b, 255–6)

Thus, Keynes identified the existence of a freely convertible international standard, rather than the asymmetric adjustment, as the constraint on national policy autonomy.

In addition, Keynes noted "a further defect" in the supposed automatic coordination of adjustment under the freely convertible international standard: "The remittance and acceptance of overseas capital funds for refugee, speculative or investment purposes" (1980, 30). And in contrast to earlier periods,[8] "capital funds flowed from countries of which the balance of trade was adverse into countries where it was favourable. This became, in the end, the major cause of instability" (31). His conclusion was that since "we have no security against a repetition of this after the present war . . . nothing is more certain than that the movement of capital funds must be regulated" (31).

This observation reprises Keynes's view of the variable speeds of adjustment of financial and real variables:

> It is, therefore, a serious question whether it is right to adopt an international standard, which will allow an extreme mobility and sensitiveness of foreign lending, whilst the remaining elements of the economic complex remain exceedingly rigid. If it were as easy to put wages up and down as it is to put bank rate up and down, well and good. But this is not the actual situation. A change in international financial conditions or in the wind and weather of speculative sentiment may alter the volume of foreign lending, if nothing is done to counteract it, by tens of millions in a few weeks. Yet there is no possibility of rapidly altering the balance of imports and exports to correspond.
>
> (1971b, 300)

Indeed, a characteristic of the post-Smithsonian, Bretton Woods system has been the tendency for international capital to flow from debtor to creditor countries. This was first seen in Europe as speculative funds flowed to Germany, forcing repeated exchange rate adjustments, and in the global economy in the negative net flows of financial resources from developing to developed countries in the 1980s. Just as members of the euro area have not been spared financial instability with the single "interregional standard" replacing the deutsche mark, emerging market countries are not likely to find a remedy to their complaints if the dollar is replaced with the SDR or an international reserve currency.

Regional/peer group arrangements

The most innovative proposals from emerging market countries have involved the creation of regional or peer group financing institutions such as the BRICS bank, the Bank of the South, and the Asian Infrastructure Investment Bank, as well as the introduction of currency swap arrangements between emerging market countries to reduce dependence on the dollar for purposes of bilateral settlement. These arrangements do not seem to escape the problems faced by the IMF in promoting coordination, aside from reducing the number of participants and ostensibly eliminating the US role. However, most of the lending arrangements include an IMF program of conditionality at some level, and thus do not escape the indirect influence of the United States. In addition, they do not solve the problem of the reference or reserve currency to be used in such institutions. And those that propose a common currency unit, such as the Bank of the South, do not resolve the problems that Keynes identified regarding the convertible international standard, or those that have been observed within the euro area in terms of providing a common, but nonoptimal, policy mix for all countries involved. Indeed, replacing the dollar with another national currency unit or an independent international unit does not eliminate the problems of emerging market economies with the operation of the IMF. A more radical solution is required—a solution that was initially discussed in the 1940s but eventually rejected because of US resistance.

The road to radical international reform not taken

As Keynes noted in his proposals for postwar international monetary reform, the fact that

> the problem of maintaining equilibrium in the balance of payments between countries has never been solved, since methods of barter gave way to the use of money and bills of exchange . . . [,] has been a major cause of impoverishment and social discontent and even of wars and revolutions.
>
> (1980, 21)

His proposals for the post–World War II financial system sought a solution to the problem by avoiding the difficulties caused by the Treaty of Versailles, represented in his first popular book, *The Economic Consequences of the Peace* (1919). Indeed, it is difficult to understand any of the discussion of postwar international finance without reference to the financial problems of the Treaty of Versailles and the Dawes and Young Committees in dealing with German reparations and the debts of the Allies to the United States.

The problems caused by German reparations payments generated two fundamental principles: (1) that reparations could only be achieved through net exports of goods and services, not by fiscal surpluses and financial transfers; and (2) that this could only be achieved if the recipient country were willing to open its domestic markets and accept an external deficit. The formulation of proposals for the postwar system was dominated by the need to make sure that the absence of these two conditions, which had led to volatile international capital flows and exchange rates, should not be repeated.

As Keynes's thinking evolved, a third fundamental principle gained ascendancy, which Keynes called "the banking principle," and which he defined as "the necessary equality of debits and credits, of assets and liabilities. If no credits can be removed outside the banking system but only transferred within it, the Bank *itself* can never be in difficulties" (1980, 44). But this principle did not refer to credit creation via the creation of bank deposits. It was motivated by an application of his theory of liquidity preference and effective demand. He faulted the gold standard because saving by creditor countries in the form of holding gold stocks reduced global liquidity, and thus the ability to finance global demand.

The banking principle eventually became the centerpiece of Keynes's proposals for a clearing union in which credits were automatically made available to debtor countries to spend. This was of great advantage to the UK, since it meant that the financing of imports required for reconstruction would be automatically available without the need to accumulate dollar balances through export sales (or by borrowing from the United States). On the other hand, the States viewed it as an unlimited commitment to finance European reconstruction, making the proposal anathema to US negotiators.[9]

One of the initial solutions to the reparations problem that is relevant to the concerns of emerging markets, because it took the role of developing countries into account, was proposed by Hjalmar Schacht to Owen Young during the Committee of Experts meeting in Paris in 1929: an international "Clearing House" or International Settlements Bank (see Lüke 1985). The idea behind the plan was to resolve the difficulty faced by German industry in producing for export, due to the loss of raw materials from its former colonies, and the difficulty in penetrating the export markets of its creditors. The clearinghouse was to make loans to developing countries in support of the provision of raw materials to Germany and to create markets in these countries for German exports. Schacht notes that his objective was

> to take decisive action to strengthen German export trade in order to achieve a surplus. . . . The economic history of the past decades had furnished convincing proof that loans should be used first and foremost to help the under-developed countries to make full use of their raw materials and

gradually to become industrialized. Before the war the European capital markets had supplied the funds in connection with loans for the economic advancement of the under-developed South American and Balkan States and many other overseas territories. England, France, Germany, etc., had not been in need of foreign loans: on the contrary they had been creditors and suppliers of capital to under-developed countries. Germany was now an impoverished country and no longer able to make loans to others. If the Allies really wished to help her to meet her reparations liabilities they should grant loans to the under-developed countries, and thereby put the latter in a position where they would be able to purchase their industrial equipment in Germany. No useful purpose would be served by allowing Germany to compete in existing world markets against other European industrial states as she had hitherto done.

(Schacht 1955, 247–8)

This objective was never realized, but the proposal formed the basis for the Bank for International Settlements, with the reduced objective of managing reparations payments.[10]

The reform plans that were discussed in the early 1940s were built on another of Schacht's schemes: the "New Plan," based on bilateral "Clearing Accounts." As economics minister, he applied the "very simple principle that Germany must refrain from buying more than she could pay for, in order to prevent an accumulation of foreign debt which would make a proper trade balance still more difficult to establish in the future" (Schacht 1949, 80). Given that the creditor countries' "system of import quotas had closed markets to German goods," Schacht sought

to find countries which would be willing to sell their goods not against payment in their own currency, but against . . . German goods. . . . The best solution was the establishment of "clearing accounts." Foreign countries selling goods to us would have the amount of our purchases credited to their account in German currency, and with this they could then buy anything they wanted in Germany.

(1949, 80–1)

Since Germany was in bilateral deficit with most countries, this led to "blocked credit balances"[11] of Reichsmarks, or what were called "Sperrmarks," that could only be used for specific types of payments—either to foreign exporters or bondholders, leading to a demand for German exports to release them. As Johan Beyen notes,

[creditor] governments had to square the account with whatever Germany was prepared to deliver; and they were inclined to do so because the German purchases solved their unemployment problem. There may be some exaggeration in the story that the Balkan countries had to buy mouthorgans none of its inhabitants cared to play on, or aspirin in quantities that could have poisoned the whole populations . . . clearing agreements enabled the German government to "modulate" its imports and exports and to adapt its international trade to its needs for rearmament.

(Beyen 1951, 106–7)

Thus, it was not Schacht's 1929 clearinghouse plan, but his system of bilateral clearing agreements that provided the blueprint for both the Keynes and White plans for a stable international financial architecture. Keynes expressed these initial ideas for the postwar system in these terms: "The virtue of free trade depends on [it] being carried on by means of what is, in effect, *barter*. After the last war *laissez-faire* in foreign exchange led to chaos" (1980, 8). He noted in this regard that it was Schacht who provided

the germs of a good technical idea. This idea was to [discard] the use of a currency having international validity and substitute for it what amounted to barter, not indeed between individuals, but between different economic units. In this way he was able to return to the essential character and the original purpose of trade whilst discarding the apparatus which had been supposed to facilitate, but was in fact strangling, it.

(23)

But Keynes assured his critics that this "does not mean that there would be direct barter of goods against goods, but that the one trading transaction must necessarily find its counterpart in another trading transaction sooner or later" (18).

Keynes's proposal was based on the simple idea that financial stability was predicated on a balance between imports and exports, with any divergence from balance providing automatic financing of the debit countries by the creditor countries via a global clearinghouse or settlement system for trade and payments on current account. This eliminated national currency payments for imports and exports; countries received credits or debits in a notional unit of account fixed to the national currency. Since the unit of account could not be traded, bought, or sold, it would not be an international reserve currency. The implication was that there would be no need for a market for "foreign" currency or reserve balances, and thus no impact of volatile exchange rates on relative prices of international goods, or tradable and nontradable goods. In addition, the automatic creation of credit meant that the UK would not be constrained by its nonexistent gold reserves or its nonexistent dollar balances in financing its reconstruction needs for imports.[12]

Since the credits with the clearinghouse could only be used to offset debits by buying imports, and if not used for this purpose they would eventually be extinguished, the burden of adjustment was shared equally: credit generated by surpluses had to be used to buy imports from the countries with debit balances. Alternatively, they could be used to purchase foreign assets—foreign direct or portfolio investment—but the size of these purchases would be strictly limited by the size of the surplus country's credit balance with the clearinghouse. Once a limit on the size of multilateral debits and credits was agreed upon for each country—its "quota"—penalties, in the form of interest charges, exchange rate adjustment, forfeiture, or exclusion from clearing, would be applied and the outstanding balances would automatically be reduced. Although Keynes's initial proposals did not take developing countries into account, the subsequent drafts suggest that the interest charges on the credit and debit balances generated could be provided as additional credits to support the clearing accounts of developing ("backward") countries (1980, 120).

Another advantage that Keynes claimed for his plan was that it was multilateral in nature, by contrast with Schacht's bilateral clearing agreements. It also avoided the problem of blocked balances and multiple exchange rates for different types of balances and different countries, which had been prevalent within the exchanges under the bilateral agreements. Both of these attributes were considered to be primary objectives of any postwar arrangement and were also present in the US proposal and expressly included in the Final Act of the Bretton Woods agreements.

Keynes was not alone in proposing the "clearing" solution

Keynes was not alone in proposing a "clearing" bank as the basis for reform of the international system in the 1940s.[13] A similar scheme, more closely linked to the then-current system of trade bills as settlement under the gold standard, appeared in an anonymously published pamphlet, "A Twentieth Century Economic System," thought to have been penned by William Francis Forbes-Sempill, 19th Lord Sempill.[14] It argued that

> it is necessary to establish a system of international trade under which the problem will be fairly and squarely placed on the shoulders of each nation, as to how it proposes to take payment for its exports: if it does not take payment in the form of imports, it will merely have made a present of its exports. The matter will then be one for settlement, not as between nations, but within each nation as between the exporting industries, which will wish to continue to export, and the new industries, which will be faced by the dilemma of seeing their best customers, the export industries, ruined, or allowing imports in to pay for those exports. . . . The United States has already shown the way to the new system in the Lease-Lend Act. She has there accepted the principle that nations can only pay for goods and services with goods and services.
>
> (Economic Reform Club 1941, 29–30)

The proposal called for the creation of an "international exchange" or "clearing bank" that would deal in foreign exchange trade bills issued to finance trade in goods and services. For example, a US exporter who draws an exchange bill on the UK importer creates a claim on the UK, which he discounts at his local bank for dollars. The exporter's bank then discounts the bill with the US

Exchange Control Agency against the proof of shipment of the goods. The US Control Agency thus holds a sterling claim that could be sold to a US importer who has a bill drawn against him by a UK exporter. It is thus the US importer who pays dollars to the US exporter in place of the UK importer. A similar offset occurs when the UK importer honors the bill by paying in sterling at his local bank, which receives a sterling credit with UK Exchange Control, which in turn now has a dollar claim available for sale to a UK importer. Since all transactions are between domestic residents in the same domestic currency, "international trade would . . . be done by a system of contra account" (Economic Reform Club 1941, 32). The proposal notes that in this way the confrontation is between importers and exporters in the same country—rather than a competition among countries over their trade balances—and as such a benefit to global peace.[15]

This is in fact the way trade was financed under the gold standard, through the use of sterling bills in London, with the exception that imbalances were adjusted by means of the flow of short-term finance bills between the two countries.[16] When an imbalance became so large that it caused a movement in the exchange rate beyond the costs of shipping gold—the gold points—then gold would be physically transferred and the exchange rate would return toward par.

However, in this system, the exchange agencies would agree to hold credit balances up to a specified level, eliminating the need for short-term financing. It reproduces Keynes's objective of symmetric adjustment between creditors and debtors by proposing that "the importing country [i.e., net debtor] would be entitled to cancel the credit, under a Statute of Limitations, if it were not used within seven years" (Economic Reform Club 1941, 33). The system becomes multilateral when the national exchange control agencies of all countries hold accounts in an international exchange clearing bank where credits can be exchanged at fixed notional exchange rates with national currencies against third countries. In both systems, the creation of credit for debtor countries is automatic, due to the clearing arrangements, and thus independent of exchange and capital markets. Each has the advantage of automatically providing the postwar credits needed by deficit countries, without the need to acquire gold or other means of payment.

Both of these proposals are grounded in the belief that imports can only be paid with exports and that international financial stability requires constraining current account imbalances within clear limits, which by extension places similar limits on the degree of capital account accommodation of deficits and the buildup of a country's external indebtedness. In practice, imbalances are limited by the administrative and monetary sanctions placed on the size of debit and credit balances through multilateral negotiation by members of the clearinghouse. National currencies are maintained and national policy autonomy is preserved within the limits of the permitted divergence from external balance. Exchange rate levels and adjustments are also determined by multilateral negotiation within the clearinghouse, compatible with external equilibrium. Keynes's plan uses a notional unit of account—bancor—but it is not necessary, as the same result could be achieved by setting notional bilateral exchange rates in a multilateral clearing system, as in the Sempill proposal. The schemes thus provide an improvement on the Schachtian approach by eliminating managed bilateral trade, multiple exchange rates, and currency manipulation. Indeed, in his maiden speech to the House of Lords, Keynes cited the multilateral nature of these schemes as their basic contribution.

Similarities between the clearing and stabilization plans

At this level, it is understandable that Keynes could consider the US proposals for a stabilization fund as broadly similar to his own, for they were based on the same two principles outlined above and a belief in the importance of external balance, and included similar limitations on the size of the imbalance, given by access to the gold tranche and additional conditional Fund lending subject to multilateral consultation.[17] Although asymmetric adjustment was not formally included, Article VII on scarce currencies provided that Fund shortages of a currency (e.g., a dollar shortage, representing an excessive US credit balance), would trigger limitations on the ability to finance dollar imports and thus permitted discrimination against US exports to force adjustment (although Keynes was skeptical that it would ever be invoked).

Differences between clearing banks and stabilization funds

However, there were two basic differences that caused a radical change in Keynes's thinking about financial system reform. The first was the realpolitik realization that US cooperation was required, and that the United States would not accept his clearing union proposal. This meant that the third principle of Keynes's approach—the banking principle—would be abandoned. There would be no automatic financing of the British needs for reconstruction via clearing credits from the United States, making the loan negotiations with the US necessary. In place of automatically granted credit would be decisions by the Fund that eventually produced conditionality on access above the gold tranche, leading the UK to seek greater autonomy, in particular over exchange rate adjustments. It also meant that the Fund could not be used for the pressing problems of European reconstruction, which would be taken over by the Bank (and explains Keynes's sudden interest in formulating that institution). There was thus no need for speed in initiating Fund operations, accepting a point that John Williams (1949) had stressed in his "Key" currency proposals (although there was a need to have ratification before political interest waned). Nonetheless, Keynes was willing to work to improve the US scheme in the belief that it was important to take action to restore multilateral clearing, and US participation was crucial to this objective.

And a fundamental difference: "I didn't see that coming"

However, the greatest difference, and one that Keynes would surely have resisted, emerged only in the last minutes of the Bretton Woods negotiations and appeared unnoticed until the specifics of the Final Act were distributed: the role of the dollar at the center of the system. There is no mention of the role of the dollar in either the White Plan or the Joint Ministerial Statement. Yet, according to Armand Van Dormael,

> Putting the dollar next to gold at the centre of the postwar monetary system had been uppermost in Harry White's mind ever since he started thinking about the subject. . . . In September 1943 Keynes told White that the United Kingdom did not contemplate going on to a gold or a dollar standard. . . . Whenever the matter was brought up, he categorically rejected the idea that the dollar should be given a special status.[18]
>
> (Van Dormael 1978, 200–1)

Hence the major and crucial difference between the Final Act and the radical proposals of Keynes and Sempill was the presence of a national currency as the reserve in support of exchange rate stability, and thus as the method of control-ling excessive external imbalances. What Robert Triffin was to identify as the Achilles heel of the postwar international financial architecture was adopted without discussion of its implications. Its importance is in how it changes the way limits and sanctions are imposed on payments imbalances. In the Keynes and Sempill proposals, it is the tax or interest charge on the credit and debit bal-ances, and multilateral negotiation over additional remedies, such as exchange rate adjustment, when limits are breached. In the final Bretton Woods system, the limits on imbalances are given by the ability to preserve par value for the national currency and, given the concentration of gold in the United States, on the country's ability to generate dollar reserves. Beyond this limit, there was an automatic extension in the form of the ability to draw the gold tranche, but after that it was given by the conditionality attached by Fund staff to additional program lending. This approach was thus predicated on the expansion of dollar reserves in the rest of the system, which required the United States to become a serial debtor and, as Triffin noted, would reduce its ability to preserve the dollar value of gold. This system preserved market-determined exchange rates, and the speculative activity concerning possible parity adjustment, through what were described as the "gnomes of Zurich" but were simply short-term capital flows taking what was a one-way bet on parity adjustments.

Again, Keynes proved to be correct about the destabilizing role of asymmetric adjustment (he was sanguine about the dollar short, believing that it would soon disappear, making the "scarce currency" clause irrelevant), for this also proved to be the downfall of the dollar-gold system. When the United States was faced with a loss of its gold reserves below the level required to redeem outstanding foreign dollar claims at the Bretton Woods parity, it executed a series of administrative measures, such as interest equalization and operation twist, instead of internal adjustment. When these measures failed, and in the presence of the refusal of Germany and others to revalue, the United States simply exited the system—which is, of course, precisely what happened under the gold standard: the deficit country would just suspend convertibility when the adjustment burden became too great.

Bretton Woods loses control of external balances

After the breakdown of the Smithsonian Agreement and the introduction of flexible exchange rates, the rise of private capital flows in international markets brought Keynes's third element of instability to the fore, and private capital flows came to dwarf the resources available to the IMF. And it soon re-created the problem of international indebtedness. But the real problem was that in a flexible rate system there was no longer any mechanism to limit external imbalances. Capital tended to flow into the debtor countries without limit, in the presence of perverse incentives for interest arbitrage. Countries that attempted to respond to external imbalance by tightening monetary policy to reduce the level of activity were met by flows of interest rate arbitrage funds, which caused the currency to appreciate even in the presence of deteriorating external balances. The only limit on this process then became the expectations of speculators, with capital reversal generating a financial crisis, which then imposed external adjustment. The system that was chosen in order to avoid the automatic creation of credit via the banking principle produced a system with no limits on either imbalances or on global credit creation—or rather, the limit on the size of imbalances was set by the point at which investors realized that they were financing their own debt service (in what was clearly a Ponzi scheme)—and a capital flow reversal resulted in a financial crisis. The IMF was reduced to the role of credit collector, called in to impose policies that would ensure a sufficiently large negative net flow of resources to repay private lenders, at the expense of domestic growth an employment.

It is this boom-bust cycle of capital flows and exchange rate volatility that emerging markets find debilitating. But it should be evident that a substitution of the dollar with an international reserve currency is not the appropriate solution for emerging market economies, as this would merely restore the gold standard and revive the concerns about the governance of global liquidity creation. Indeed, it might make it worse, for a common currency would eliminate even the uncertainty on speculative flows that was created by the spread of the gold points. The experience of the European Union provides a picture of the difficulties that would be faced by the attempt to create a global currency.[19]

The Clearinghouse proposals meet the problems of emerging market economies

Given the historical experience of the negotiations and the performance of the structure launched at Bretton Woods, it would seem obvious that the aspects that emerging market economies find objectionable cannot be fixed by means of the policy proposals they have put forward. It is the structure that has to be changed, and the structure of the Keynes-Sempill proposals would seem to meet the criticisms more directly.

Under these more radical proposals, there can be no currency wars, no wall of money, and no interest rate arbitrage. Foreign investment by any country is limited by its global current account position. Indeed, there would be no need for discussion over the efficacy of capital controls, or whether they should be on inflows or outflows or monitored by the creditor country central bank or the debtor country central bank. As Keynes had envisaged in his original proposal, "international capital movements would be restricted so that they would only be allowed in the event of the country from which capital was moving having a favourable balance with the country to which they were being remitted" (1980, 16–7). Capital flows would extinguish foreign credits in the same way as imports, and thus would only be "allowed when they were feasible without upsetting the existing equilibrium" on external account (17).

Thus, replacing the dollar with a nonnational currency or the SDR will not eliminate the problems facing emerging markets; nor will increased multilateral cooperation, even if that could be achieved. The creation of financial institutions governed by regional or other restricted groupings does create the most important possibility, but not in the form in which they are currently being discussed. The current proposals are primarily designed to escape the inadequate governance of the IMF and the World Bank and the dominance of the United States in both the theory and practices of these institutions. In addition, as noted above, they usually take the IMF as their template and at some level of financial commitment impose IMF program conditionality.

There is no reason why these institutions cannot be created on the template of the Keynes-Sempill clearing unions, building on the swap agreements that many countries have already agreed to on a bilateral basis. Thus, the creation of a common currency for the members of the Bank of the South may not be the most sensible proposal, but the creation of a regional clearing union with a notional unit of account would provide a remedy to the problems faced by these countries. Indeed, Keynes had already considered this as a possibility:

> One view of the post-war world which I find sympathetic and attractive and fruitful of good consequences is that we should encourage *small* political and cultural units, combined into larger, and more or less closely knit, economic units. . . . Therefore I would encourage customs unions and customs preferences covering groups of political and geographical units, and also currency unions, railway unions and the like. Thus it would be preferable, if it were possible, that the members should, in some cases at least, be groups of countries rather than separate units.
>
> (1980, 55)

Thus, the currently proposed financial institutions could be cast in the form of clearing unions.

Indeed, there is already a historical precedent for the operation of a regional clearing union in the European Payments Union, which played an integral part in the restoration of intra-European trade and payments to complement the Marshall Plan.[20] This might provide a better template for the emerging markets initiatives than the IMF.

But they do not necessarily meet the needs of developingcountries in general

Aside from Latin American countries, few developing countries were present at Bretton Woods. India was still represented by Great Britain and the Chinese presence was apparently a question of American political expediency. Indeed, in the discussions of the clearing union there was virtually no consideration of developing countries. This was primarily because the focus was on postwar reconstruction finance. It was only in the discussion of the collateral issues of commercial policy and commodity support schemes that development questions emerged—and they were quickly separated from the financial discussions because they were considered a threat to rapid approval of the international financial reforms.[21]

Only Schacht's original proposal for a clearing union directly concerned developing countries; but, as noted above, this was mainly about financing German inputs of primary materials and providing a market for German exports, rather than laying out a positive development agenda. The other proposal that took developing country concerns into account, if only generally, was John H. Williams's assessment of the postwar proposals; namely, that their "fundamental requirement is the maintenance of an even [external] balance, with only temporary fluctuations from it" (Williams 1949, 158) and that this presumes the same principle as the gold standard, which was "based on the principle of interaction between homogenous countries of approximately equal size" (173).

Recognizing that different countries might require different currency schemes, Williams included only the major "key" currencies in his proposal. He raised the question of whether "the world needs a single, uniform system or a combination of different systems by consideration of the diversity of countries, and in particular the differences in their proportions of home and foreign trade" (189). This line of reasoning leads directly to the needs of countries with different export compositions and the problems faced by countries with primarily commodity dependence that were to be raised by Raúl Prebisch, Hans Singer, Gunnar Myrdal, and others. For these countries may require sustained periods of external deficit (foreign finance of industrialization) or external surplus (export-led development), which is directly contrary to the basic principle of equilibrium external balance as the key to international financial stability. The same is true of multiple exchange rates, which many economists have suggested may play a crucial role in building a more balanced, productive structure in developing countries (e.g., Kaldor 1965, Diamond 1978) but which are expressly excluded under Bretton Woods because of the experience of German rearmament.

Keynes's clearing union approach is just as deficient in this respect, as the stabilization fund and some special measures would have to be included to allow for developing countries to have relatively larger debit (or credit) balances and to eliminate the sanctions on such balances, since they would be the result of a successful development policy. Otherwise, countries that have used either import substitution or export-led growth strategies that are too successful could find themselves facing additional charges and pressure to rein in or adjust their successful policies in order to keep their external accounts within acceptable ranges.

These special measures might include exemption on the size of balances and remission of the interest charges for developed country creditors and developing country debtors. Alternatively, the Bank could have been fashioned as a more development-centered institution and made an integral part of the IMF. Or, more simply, an alternative clearing union institution for developing countries could have been proposed. Clearly, a balanced external account may be the most appropriate objective for the international financial stability of developed countries, but it certainly need not be so for developing countries. Indeed, multilateral institutions and the United Nations have consistently argued for the transfer of resources from developed to developing countries in magnitudes of 0.7 percent of developed country GDP, which would presumably generate interest charges on the resulting deficits and surpluses for the donor and recipient countries (see, by way of comparison, Kregel 2015).

Stable exchange rates and monetary sovereignty

From the point of view of the current difficulties facing emerging market economies, the basic advantage of the clearing union schemes is that there is no need for an international reserve currency, no market exchange rates or exchange rate volatility, and no parity to be defended. Notional exchange rates can be adjusted to support development policy, and there is no need to restrict domestic activity to meet foreign claims. Indeed, there is no need for an international lender or bank, since debt balances can be managed within the clearing union. The external adjustment occurs by creating an incentive for export surplus countries to find outlets to spend their credits, which may be in support of developing countries. The system thus supports global demand. Since all payments and debts are expressed in national currency, independence in national policy actions and policy space are preserved. In modern terminology, countries retain monetary sovereignty within the constraint of external balance, which should correspond to full utilization of domestic resources.

Such a system would reflect Keynes's broader vision of the appropriate role for international financial flows:

> I sympathize, therefore, with those who would minimize, rather than with those who would maximise, economic entanglement between nations. Ideas, knowledge, science, hospitality, travel—these are the things which should of their nature be international. But let goods be homespun whenever it is reasonably and conveniently possible; and, above all, let finance be primarily national.
>
> (Keynes 1982, 236)

Notes

1 Elaboration of a panel presentation at the Jornadas Monetarias y Bancarias of the Banco Central de la Republica Argentina, Buenos Aires, November 18, 2014.
2 kregel@levy.org

3 "The present monetary system consists in the exorbitant privilege enjoyed by the United States of being able to cover is balance of payments deficit with its own dollars" (February 4, 1965).

4 "With reference to the meeting promoted by Montagu Norman, and arranged by Benjamin Strong, including Hjalmar Schacht and Charles Rist (representing Émile Moreau), to coordinate policy in support of sterling, Stephen Clarke notes that "the basic instrument, as in 1924, was an easing of monetary policy which, in the light of the boom of the next two years and of the October 1929 crash, was to become one of the most controversial actions in the history of the Federal Reserve System" (Clarke 1967, 124).

5 Schacht explains that "it had not been possible to comply with the demands of the Dawes Plan and pay the reparations debts out of export surplus. Not once in the course of the past five years had we achieved such a surplus. Rather, we had met all payments of reparations out of the loans made to us by other countries during those years, a system which could not possibly be continued for any length of time. The interest would increase our indebtedness year by year and the loans themselves would not always be forthcoming" (1955, 248).

6 "The crash drew forth a multitude of explanations, but I am convinced that one fundamental cause was the failure to achieve real results in coordinating the macroeconomic policies of the seven major economic powers" (Toyoo Gyohten, in Volcker and Gyohten 1992, 268).

7 The various measures used by central banks to manage the "automatic" gold standard adjustment process are detailed in Bloomfield (1959).

8 "During the nineteenth century and up to 1914 the flow of capital funds had been directed from the creditor to the debtor countries, which broadly corresponded to the older and the newer countries, and served at the same time to keep the balance of international payments in equilibrium and to develop resources in undeveloped lands" (Keynes 1980, 30). This is an assessment very similar to that of Raúl Prebisch concerning the impact of international capital flows on Latin American development in the 19th century.

9 Indeed, the private bankers' criticism of the plan was that it was bad banking, since the lending was automatic with no due diligence or credit assessment!

10 The scheme was an early representation of a special purpose vehicle owned by the major central banks and capitalized with a special issue of five billion gold marks of German discount bonds to support the granting of book credits to central banks, governments, and other guaranteed borrowers to promote lending to developing countries. Since the loans "were only to be granted in the form of book credits, . . . repayments would be made either from another account with the same institution or in cash, and . . . the central banks would be able to utilise the credits they obtained as cover for their respective currencies. Thus, the German obligations were to be used as a basis for international credit expansion, making it possible to mobilise the claims on Germany up to an amount of 10 billion Gold Marks . . . promptly and without any transfer difficulties, since the transfer could only be effected by transfer from one account to another" (Lüke 1985, 73). Since Germany could not qualify for lending, "the American delegation saw in it a device . . . to expose Germany's neighbour and creditor countries to inflation," and thus the plan was never implemented.

11 Without this background it is difficult to understand the amount of space given in the US proposal to such balances, and the concern of the UK for resolution of the sterling balances with its Commonwealth partners in any postwar scheme.

12 Note that while Schacht's 1929 clearinghouse proposal was to create financing and demand for its exports, Keynes's clearinghouse was to create sources of financing for its clear need for reconstruction imports in the face of lost export markets and overseas assets. Just as the Allies were unwilling to open their markets to German exports in World War I, the United States was unwilling to provide what was represented as an unlimited credit for UK imports; the US proposal thus required smaller upfront collateral commitments to join the scheme.

13 A note in volume 25 of Keynes's *Collected Works* (1980, 21, n. 5) indicates that Keynes received a draft plan for a clearing union arrangement written by E. F. Schumacher, but that there is no indication that it had any influence on the development of Keynes's ideas.

14 Published by the Economic Reform Club with a preface dated August 1941, the pamphlet was issued in at least three editions totaling 16,000 copies from November 1941 through June 1942. Keynes's initial clearing union drafts date from December 1940. The contents of the pamphlet were presented by Lord Sempill in a House of Lords debate (Sempill 1941) and in subsequent debates on the issue of postwar planning (Parl. Deb., H.L. [5th ser.] [1942] 115–78; [1943] 102–9). A negative review of the document in the Australian *Social Crediter* (1943) indicates Sempill was the author. Economic Reform Club members were linked to anticommunist, fascist, and anti-Semitic groups. Sempill, a close confidant of Churchill, was later confirmed as a spy for the Japanese and credited with providing support and incitement for the attack on Pearl Harbor.

15 This reflects Keynes's use of "units" in describing Schacht's plan, which pitted interests of exporters against debt holders. Here it is the interests of importers and exporters.

16 Keynes provides a description of this system in the last chapter of the *Tract on Monetary Reform* (1971a), where he notes that it would be compromised by the suspension of the gold standard and suggests the creation of forward markets to provide banks with the exchange rate hedging previously provided by the gold points.

17 From Keynes's maiden speech to the House of Lords (1943): "Most critics, in my judgment, have overstated the differences between the two plans, plans which are born of the same climate of opinion and which have identical purpose."

18 This crucial change in the proposals "was made on 6 July, at the 2.30 p.m. meeting of Committee 2" in an "alternative, submitted by the American delegate, [which] provided that 'The par value of the currency of each member shall be expressed in terms of gold, *as a common denominator, or in terms of a gold-convertible currency unit of the weight and fineness in effect on July 1, 1944.'* . . . There was no further discussion, and the alternative was approved. . . . The second move was made a week later. . . . Harry White was chairman. . . . One of the points to be discussed was the date on which countries joining the Fund should make their initial contribution of gold and gold-convertible exchange. This was a minor point, and, since the 'delegations did not have time to consider the matter, the Committee agreed to refer this question directly to your Commission'. The Indian delegate asked for a definition of gold-convertible currency, which had been discussed, and of which Keynes had said it did not exist. The question as put related to the gold-convertible contributions only, and not to the par value of currencies. Robertson, against Keynes's instructions, but as the responsible British delegate, suggested that the words 'gold and gold-convertible currency' be replaced by 'net official holdings of gold and U.S. dollars', and remarked that this would involve several changes elsewhere. This was White's opportunity. Using his authority as chairman, he referred the matter to a special committee, which took it out of any further discussion. . . . The change from 'gold' to 'gold and US dollars' was lost in the ninety-six page document the chairmen of the delegations would sign a few days later. Whether or not any of them noticed it, or understood its implications, it seems that none of them expressed any reservations about it. Keynes would not find out until later, when he studied the Final Act" (Van Dormael 1978, 201–3).

19 Keynes's proposal is often presented as the creation of a "global currency," but his proposed "bancor" was a notional unit of account and could not be spent by private individuals or used as the basis for private bank credit creation; indeed, it was not essential to the principle of net clearing. After it was clear that it was unacceptable to the United States, Keynes eventually supported the "monetisation" of the US proposal for "unitas" to facilitate government acquisition of currencies outside the Fund. It was his attempt to move the stabilization fund closer to his clearing union. (See Keynes 1980, 342; Skidelsky 2001, 316.)

20 See Kaplan and Schleiminger (1989) for a political and analytical description of the operation of what was in integral part of the restoration of multilateral trade and payments in

Europe. It is somewhat ironic, given the inability of the Bretton Woods Fund scheme to operate in the immediate aftermath of the war, that a scheme similar to Keynes's should in fact be adopted, although subject to the constraints of the postwar economic conditions.

21 The British postwar planning was comprehensive: in addition to Keynes's currency plan, there was a proposal for a "commod" to stabilize primary materials prices, a commercial union (largely the work of James Meade), and an international investment board and development corporation. The latter was apparently the result of a 1941 proposal by Luther Gulick and Alvin Hansen, advising the State Department on postwar reforms, and is mentioned in Keynes's drafts of the clearing union. However, given the antipathy between the US Treasury and the State Department, once the former had started work, it consistently excluded the latter from the development of reforms.

References

Beyen, J.W. 1951. *Money in a Maelstrom*. London: Macmillan.

Blanchard, O., J.D. Ostry, and A.R. Ghosh. 2013. "International Policy Coordination: The Loch Ness Monster." iMFdirect, December 15.

Bloomfield, A. 1959. *Monetary Policy under the International Gold Standard: 1880–1914*. New York: Federal Reserve Bank of New York.

China Briefing. 2010. "Chinese Yuan Seeks Further Internationalization and Less Reliance on U.S. Dollar." December 9.

Clarke, S.V.O. 1967. *Central Bank Cooperation 1924–31*. New York: Federal Reserve Bank of New York.

Diamand, M. 1978. "Towards a Change in the Paradigm of Development Through the Experience of Developing Countries." *Journal of Development Economics* 5 (78): 19–53.

Economic Reform Club (attributed to Lord Sempill). 1941. "A Twentieth Century Economic System." London: Economic Reform Club.

Goyal, K. 2014. "Rajan Warns of Policy Breakdown as Emerging Markets Fall." *Bloomberg Business*, January 31.

IMF (International Monetary Fund). 2014. "2014 Spillover Report: IMF Multilateral Policy Issues Report." IMF Policy Paper. Washington, D.C.: IMF. July 29.

Kaldor, N. 1965. "Dual Exchange Rates and Economic Development." Reprinted in *Essays on Economic Policy*, Vol. 2. New York: W. W. Norton.

Kaplan, J.J., and G. Schleiminger. 1989. *The European Payments Union: Financial Diplomacy in the 1950s*. New York: Clarendon Press.

Keynes, John Maynard.1943. International Clearing Union. 28 Parl. Deb., H.L. (5th ser.) (1943) 527–37.

———. 1971a. *The Collected Writings of John Maynard Keynes*. Edited by D. E. Moggridge. Vol. 4, *A Tract on Monetary Reform*. London: Macmillan.

———. 1971b. *The Collected Writings of John Maynard Keynes*. Edited by D. E. Moggridge. Vol. 6, *A Treatise on Money, Vol. Two: The Applied Theory of Money*. London: Macmillan.

———. 1980. *The Collected Writings of John Maynard Keynes*. Edited by D. E. Moggridge. Vol. 25. *Activities 1940–1944. Shaping the Post-war World: The Clearing Union*. London: Macmillan.

———. 1982. *The Collected Writings of John Maynard Keynes*. Edited by D. E. Moggridge. Vol. 21, *Activities 1931–1939: World Crises and Policies in Britain and America*. London: Macmillan.

Kregel, J. 2015. "Cognitive Dissonance: Post-war Economic Development Strategies and Bretton Woods International Financial Stability." In M. Damill, M. Rapetti, and G. Rozenwurcell, eds. *Macroeconomics and Development*. New York: Columbia University Press.

Lüke, R. 1985. "The Schacht and Keynes Plans." *BNL Quarterly Review* 38 (152): 65–76.

Oliver, L. 2009. "SDR vs the Dollar: China and Russia Want SDRs." *Euromoney*, April 1. www.euromoney.com/Article/2172502/SDR-vs-the-Dollar-China-and-Russia-want-SDRs.html.

Reuters Factbox. 2009. "The Appeal of the IMF's Special Drawing Rights." March 24.

Schacht, H. 1949. *Account Settled.* Translated by Edward Fitzgerald. London: Weidenfield & Nicolson.

———. 1955. *My First Seventy-Six Years.* Translated by Diana Pyke. London: Wingate.

Sempill, The Lord. 1941. The Atlantic Charter: Economic Security. Parl. Deb., H.L. (5th ser.) (1941) 45–64.

Skidelsky, R. 2001. *John Maynard Keynes, Vol. 3: Fighting for Freedom, 1937–1946.* New York: Viking.

The Social Crediter. 1943. "From Week to Week." January 2.

Spicer, J. 2014. "Cool Reception for India Central Banker Urging Global Cooperation." Reuters, April 10.

Triffin, R. 1960. *Gold and the Dollar Crisis: The Future of Convertibility.* New Haven: Yale University Press.

Van Dormael, A. 1978. *The Bretton Woods Conference: Birth of a Monetary System.* New York: Holmes and Meier.

Volcker, P., and T. Gyohten. 1992. *Changing Fortunes: The World's Money and the Threat to American Leadership.* New York: Times Books.

Wheatley, J. 2014. "Brazil Achieves a Hollow Victory in 'Currency Wars." *Financial Times,* November 17.

Wheatley, J., and P. Garnham. 2010. "Brazil in 'Currency War' Alert." *Financial Times,* September 27.

Williams, J.H. 1949. *Post-war Monetary Plans and Other Essays.* Oxford: Basil Blackwell.

Zhou, X. 2009. "Reform the International Monetary System." Basel: Bank for International Settlements. March 23.

Part IV
Financial stability as a chimera

14 Using Minsky to simplify financial regulation[1]

Introduction

Some two years after the adoption of the Dodd-Frank Act, its implementation is still far from complete. And despite the fact that one of the major objectives of the legislation was to remove the threat that banks that are "too big to fail" (TBTF) would require a taxpayer bailout, the financial system has become even more concentrated and the largest banks even larger. According to the president of the Federal Reserve Bank of Dallas, "Dodd-Frank . . . may actually perpetuate an already dangerous trend of increasing bank industry concentration" (Fisher 2012, 1). Indeed, the top five financial conglomerates now account for over 50 percent of total industry assets, and three of them are over or near the 10 percent limit on the share of national deposits set by the 1994 Riegle-Neal Act liberalizing branch banking (see the figures presented in Rosenblum 2012).

And as recovery from the deep recession caused by the 2008 financial crisis seems more visible, and most financial institutions have recovered sufficiently to repay the financial support that they received under the Troubled Asset Relief Program, the specific rules that will be promulgated by government regulatory agencies and are required to make Dodd-Frank operational are facing increasing resistance from the financial services industry. Due to staff and funding shortages in regulatory agencies and the sheer number of regulations to be finalized, most will not be approved or implemented on the timetable required by the legislation.

Support for this resistance and additional delays have come from the judicial system. A ruling by the D.C. Circuit Court of Appeals (in *Business Roundtable v. Securities and Exchange Commission, No. 10–1305*[2]) has vacated a Securities and Exchange Commission (SEC) rule because its analysis of the costs of the regulation was not sufficiently extensive. A second suit has been brought against the Commodity Futures Trading Commission's (CFTC) rule on derivatives position limits.[3] A recent report suggests that a large majority of the rule proposals currently under discussion do not meet the court's requirements on impact assessment and could be successfully challenged (see CCMR 2012).

This goes beyond more specific industry complaints about particular regulations, such as the definition of a swaps trader or proprietary trading, and suggests that the Dodd-Frank legislation may be too extensive, too complicated, and too concerned about eliminating specific past abuses to ever be completed by regulators, implemented by supervisors, or respected by bank compliance executives. Indeed, it has been represented as a veritable paradise for regulatory arbitrage.

The result has been a call for a more fundamental review of the framework of financial system legislation. Some have even suggested a return to a regulatory framework closer to Glass-Steagall's separation of institutions by function. Last year's presentation to this conference (Levy Institute 2011) called specifically for a review of the 1999 "Act to enhance competition in the financial services industry by providing a prudential framework for the affiliation of banks, securities firms, insurance companies, and other financial service providers, and for other purposes," better known as the Gramm-Leach-Bliley (GLB) Act, which has been one of the main causes of the creation of financial conglomerates that are "too big to fail." Allowing the creation of financial holding companies to deal with the full range of financial services made them not only much larger but also much more complex, and thus more difficult to regulate and supervise.

As Hyman Minsky noted in his review of possible post-Glass-Steagall regulatory reform, one little-appreciated benefit of the 1933 Act was that "the scope of permissible activities by a depository institution was to be limited to what examiners and supervisors could readily understand. . . . it was not so much the differences and riskiness as it was the ease of understanding the operations that led to the separation of investment and commercial banking" (Minsky 1995a, 5). In other words, Glass-Steagall's limits on the size and activities of financial institutions would enable supervisors, examiners, and regulators to understand the institutions' operations. While Dodd-Frank seeks to limit government bailouts of large financial institutions, its "Orderly Liquidation Authority" gives preference to the use of Federal Deposit Insurance Corporation (FDIC) resolution procedures for merging failed institutions with larger ones on the presumption that larger institutions have a better ability to absorb new deposits and a lower likelihood of failure. But this is precisely what has led to the creation of a smaller number of larger and larger institutions, many of which surpass the Riegle-Neal limitations placed on the share of deposits that an institution absorbing a resolved bank's depositors may hold.[4] And this will only make the resulting system more difficult to regulate and the job of the supervisors monitoring compliance that much more difficult.

The Federal Reserve Bank of Dallas (Rosenblum 2012) has proposed that the most effective way to simplify supervision of the financial system is to break up the large, complex financial institutions. But this proposal deals only with the size of financial institutions; it does not indicate what the structure of the smaller institutions should be. Creating a greater number of smaller, independent financial holding companies would not necessarily simplify supervision if these companies were still dealing in multiple types of complex, interconnected financing activities involving structured lending instruments. Simply making institutions smaller need not make them safer and more stable, if they are permitted the same range of activities involving the same types of financial instruments. And in the absence of effective antitrust legislation,[5] breaking up the larger institutions would in all likelihood simply engender another process of concentration by merger and acquisition similar to that seen after the suspension of branching restrictions.[6]

In his consideration of possible post–Glass-Steagall configurations of the financial system, Minsky suggested that the simplicity and transparency inherent in Glass-Steagall could be preserved within a bank holding company structure by restricting the assets and liabilities of the separate subsidiaries. In a number of documents prepared for the mid-1990s discussions on reforming Glass-Steagall, Minsky proposed, "One or more subsidiaries of a post Glass-Steagall bank holding company will have monetary liabilities. These subsidiary institutions will enjoy protections from the central bank and treasury which guarantee that their monetary liabilities will not fall to a discount from their face value. . . . In exchange for this protection the assets they can own will be restricted. A representative post Glass Steagall bank holding company will have specialized financial subsidiaries which include not only a combination of commercial, investment and merchant banking subsidiaries but also a sampling of more specialized financial institutions such as credit card operations, payment operations, finance companies and the brokering and underwriting of insurance. Each subsidiary will have a dedicated equity, which protects the holders of the liabilities of the subsidiary" (Minsky 1995c, 3).

The implications of such a system are that, "once the distinction between the payments and financing operations of banks is recognized, it follows that post Glass Steagall banking firms will be structured as bank holding companies in which the payments subsidiary is clearly separated from the financing subsidiaries. In exchange for this protection the assets of the payments subsidiary will be limited to government debt and interest earning accounts at the Federal Reserve: the assets of the payments banks will not include business and household liabilities" (10–11). Thus, the "holding company structure of post Glass Steagall banking [would] quite naturally lead to 100% money" (12), as was proposed by Henry Simons (1934) and Irving Fisher (1935) in the 1930s and by James Tobin (1987) and Robert Litan (1987) in the 1980s.

In this approach, a single subsidiary would be dedicated to the provision of deposit-taking transactions services, while other subsidiaries would provide investment and merchant banking services. If all subsidiaries were sufficiently and separately capitalized, there could be no problem of "bailing out" the speculative activities to save the payments systems, there would be no possibility of using customer deposits for proprietary trading and speculation, and with appropriate balance sheet restrictions on the transactions subsidiary, the moral hazard created by deposit insurance could even be eliminated.

The "vision" of the economic system

It is clear that Minsky meant for this proposal to be a means by which a possible post–Glass-Steagall reform could best provide what he considered the basic objectives of the financial system—to support the capital development of the economy and to provide a safe and secure payment system—because in such a reformed system "the payments and the financing of the capital development of the economy functions will therefor[e] be separated in a post Glass Steagall banking structure" (Minsky 1995c, 8).

But such a proposal implied a method of providing for the system's "capital development" that differed radically from what had been the basis for the economic system up to that point. For Minsky, the capital development of the system meant more than just the gross accumulation of capital stock or the growth of national income, but rather a broader interpretation of the advancement of the economy, including maximizing the level of employment and an equitable distribution of income. Building on Joseph Schumpeter's *Theory of Economic Development* (1934), Minsky proposed an explanation of more or less sustained capitalist expansion in the 19th and 20th centuries, interrupted by periodic crises in which the production interdependencies and financing arrangements and conventions would break down, leaving in their place conditions for renewed expansion. In such a system, equilibrium would be maintained, not by market-based price adjustment, but by a new configuration of productive and financial relations.

He also took from Schumpeter the idea that it was the logic of capitalist expansion that would produce these disruptions. While any economic or political system could suffer from random, external shocks or political upheaval, it would be impossible, by assumption of their nature, either to explain them or to provide a means of countering them unless they could be foreseen. In general, such shocks would only disturb existing relations that could be reestablished in a recovery. In Minsky's view, however, the endogenous disruptions would change the underlying finance and growth dynamic of the system, with a transformed economy emerging to resume its expansionary path. This was not a theory of business cycles, but of Schumpeterian economic development; of continuous, evolutionary change driven by the generation of financial instability through the very mechanisms used by the financial system to support the capital development of the economy.

The importance of this innovative process led Minsky to the view that it "needs to be understood now that development financing involves taking risks. . . . The need is for a regulatory and supervising authority for the financial system that accepts that financing development opens the system to losses that have the potential for adversely affecting the safety and security of the economy's payment facilities. To allow for this possibility the regulators need to try to insulate the payments system from the consequences of such losses. The problem therefore is to provide for protection of the payments system from the consequences of the losses which may ensue from development financing." As a result, Minsky characterized the role of the financial system as servant to two mutually conflicted masters: "any capitalist banking and financing system" is "drawn between two masters" that it "needs to serve: one master requires assurance that the financing needed for the capital development of the economy will be forthcoming and the second master requires assurance that a safe and secure payments mechanism will be provided" (Minsky 1994, 10–11).

Minsky's adaptation of the Simons/Fisher proposal may thus be seen as an attempt to ensure financial stability by separating financial institutions by function, or "master," so that each would serve only one master. Banks that provide payment services can be made perfectly safe and secure by requiring 100 percent reserves in government currency and coin or other risk-free government liabilities.[7] The financing of the capital development of the economy would then take place via retained earnings of corporations or by means of investors' conscriptions committed to financing specific private business activities. Organized and supervised as an investment "trust," such an institution would have a 100 percent ratio of capital to assets and thus should not be considered a threat to the financial stability of the economic system.

In such a perfectly separated, dual system there would be neither a deposit-credit multiplier, nor leverage, nor creation of liquidity. It would reflect the idea that the financial system should operate so as to create Friedrich Hayek's idea of "neutral" money, in which all investment decisions are the consequence of the voluntary savings decisions of individuals. The Wicksellian alternative formulation of this condition is the equality of the nominal rate of interest and the "real" rate of return on investment. In this approach, there are no "monetary" disturbances to equilibrium in the "real" economy, as savings determine loanable funds that limit investment. A financial system that was regulated via a 100 percent reserve requirement on deposits and a 100 percent ratio of capital to assets for investment trusts would then appear to resolve the conflicting objectives noted by Minsky. One institution would provide the safe and secure means of payment, while another would provide for the financing of the real capital development of the economy by intermediating and investing private savings.

But such a system could neither ensure the stability of the real economy nor assure stability of the capital financing institutions, since the real investments chosen could still fail to produce the anticipated rate of return, and sectoral over-investment and financial bubbles could still exist if there were herding behavior by the investment advisers of the trusts that produced procyclical financing behavior. There would always be a risk of investors calling on the government to save them from financial ruin.[8]

Narrow banking and a "monetary production economy"

For Minsky and Schumpeter, such a "narrow banking" system could not be considered a modern "capitalist" system; it would be akin to what John Maynard Keynes defined as a "real wage," as opposed to a "monetary production," economy. In a monetary economy, it is the role of the financial sector to ensure the financing of the acquisition and control of capital assets by increasing the liquidity of the liabilities of the business sector.

But more important, such a system would create a problem in a dimension other than what is now called "macroprudential" regulation. The liabilities of the financial system would be composed of household savings allocated to investment fund shares financing real investments, to the holding of deposits in the narrow banks backed by government debt or currency and coin, and to holding government-issued coin and currency. Business sector savings would be allocated to retained earnings financing, deposits in narrow banks, or government issues of currency and coin. This would mean that total private saving would exceed investment by the private sector's holdings of narrow bank deposits and government currency, creating a tendency toward deflation or recession. Price and/or output stability would then require an exogenous addition to demand to offset this imbalance, such as might be provided by government expenditures financed by the issue of either currency or government bonds, if such issues were held as reserves for the narrow banks or the direct discounting of business sector liabilities. Alternatively, the central bank could engage in the direct financing of public or private sector investment expenditures. The "macroprudential" stability of the financial system would then require the application of what Abba Lerner (1943) called "functional finance." The size of the deficit creating the additional government means of payment required for macroprudential stability would be determined by the private sector holdings of narrow bank deposits and currency, adjusted for the current account position.

Thus, what Minsky believed was the major factor stabilizing the postwar Glass-Steagall system—the existence of a "Big Government" deficit providing a floor under private sector incomes—would be even more important in a narrow banking system holding company structure than it was under Glass-Steagall. Indeed, Minsky's use of the Keynes-Kalecki profits equation was meant to show that it is primarily the generation of corporate income that results from investment expenditures that allows current profits to cover the cash flows associated with the liabilities issued to finance investment. It is the level of business investment and government net expenditure that generate the cash flow that validates the corporate liabilities and produces the real source of financial stability in the system.

In the absence of a large government sector to support incomes, debts could not be validated in a narrow bank holding company structure. But, even more important, it would be impossible in such a system for banks to act as the handmaiden to innovation and creative destruction by providing entrepreneurs the purchasing power necessary for them to appropriate the assets required for their innovative investments. In the absence of private sector "liquidity" creation, the central bank would have to provide financing for private sector investment trust liabilities, or a government development bank could finance innovation through the issue of debt monetized by the central bank. To meet the requirements of the "two masters," such a system would have to combine Keynes's idea of the "socialisation of investment" with the "socialisation" of the transactions and payments system. This suggests that in order to satisfy Minksy's "two masters" the real problem that must be solved lies in the way that regulation governs the provision of liquidity in the financial system.

The "two masters" are Siamese twins

In the modern capitalist system that Minsky analyzed in his financial fragility hypothesis, two different types of financial institutions provide the liquidity required for the financing of Schumpeterian creative destruction. The control of real assets by productive enterprises can be financed through the issue by a financial institution of liabilities that can be used as a means of payment in lieu of the coin and currency issued by the government. This is what is commonly known as "deposit creation," and it has traditionally been provided by what in the Glass-Steagall regulatory system were called "commercial" banks. Alternatively, productive enterprises can issue securities through the services of financial institutions that provide liquidity by acting as primary and secondary market-makers offering to buy and sell the securities at announced bid-ask spreads and in standard amounts. These have traditionally been known as "investment" or merchant banks.

Minsky considered deposit creation the basic activity of banks. He defined it as the "acceptance function": "Banking is not money lending; to lend, a money lender must have money. The fundamental banking activity is accepting, that is, guaranteeing that some party is creditworthy. A bank, by accepting a debt instrument, agrees to make specified payments if the debtor will not or cannot. . . . A bank loan is equivalent to a bank's buying a note that it has accepted" (Minsky 2008 [1986], 256). Thus, for Minsky the basic activity of a bank is not the safe-keeping of depositors' coin and currency, nor is it the investment of depositors' funds because of an informational advantage. Rather, a bank's basic activity is the creation of its own liabilities, which are used to acquire the liabilities of productive enterprises that it has "accepted"—that is, whose payment it has guaranteed. A narrow bank on this definition is not a bank, but simply a safe house or piggy bank for government issues of coin and currency.

Why banks are unique liquidity creators

Minsky noted that a bank's liabilities have to be viewed as embodying more of Keynes's liquidity premium than their assets (the liabilities that they accept and hold as assets in their loan books) if they are to earn income from a positive net interest spread, or "carry" (Ibid., 277). This "credit enhancement" function allows banks to increase the liquidity of the liabilities they accept and thus increase liquidity of the whole system. Banks effectively turn the liabilities that stand behind fixed real capital assets into currency means of payment.

The successful operation of this basic function of banking thus depends crucially on the liquidity of bank liabilities, and this depends crucially on the assurance that bank liabilities can always be used as an equivalent means of payment that the borrower can use to acquire control over real goods, services, and capital assets. This means that bank liabilities have to be considered as a perfect substitute for government issued coin and currency.[9]

It is to ensure this substitutability that banks also issue their liabilities in exchange for government coin and currency of the public. That is, they offer a transaction or payments service to clients. These deposit liabilities are a simple borrowing operation that provides no credit enhancement or liquidity creation. Bank balance sheets thus contain two different, yet identical, promises to pay the holder currency and coin. One is backed by a liability, the promise of a productive business operation to pay; the other is (partially) backed by an asset, the customer's deposited coin and currency. The first function increases system liquidity because it increases the liquidity of the issuer of the liability; the second does not, since the depositor exchanges one type of means of payment for what is a guaranteed equivalent. These promises are treated as equivalent because they are both liabilities of the bank and carry the bank's pledge to exchange them on sight for coin or currency on an equal basis. Since both of these deposit liabilities are the basis of the payments system and serve as a store of existing value for individuals, the essential function of the financial system in creating the liquidity required for financing the capital development of the economy is inevitably joined with the provision of the means of payment. The "two masters" must of necessity cohabit in a single institution. The conflict between them cannot be solved through separation.

The second type of liquidity generation is the activity of financial institutions in providing for the primary distribution and secondary trading of the equity and fixed-income liabilities issued by firms to finance the capital development of the economy. It is this function that Keynes highlighted: "[T]he liquidity of investment markets often facilitates, though it sometimes impedes, the course of new investment. For the fact that each individual investor flatters himself that his commitment is 'liquid' (though this cannot be true for all investors collectively) calms his nerves and makes him much more willing to run a risk. If individual purchases of investments were rendered illiquid, this might seriously impede new investment. . . . So long as it is open to the individual to employ his wealth in hoarding or lending money, the alternative of purchasing actual capital assets cannot be rendered sufficiently attractive . . . except by organising markets wherein these assets can be easily realised for money" (Keynes 1936, 160–1).

In a primary distribution such as a "bought deal," the underwriting financial institution provides a guarantee of the price the issuer will receive for the liabilities and thus the amount of funds to be raised by the issue. The underwriter will buy for its own balance sheet any securities that cannot be sold to the public at the guaranteed price. The underwriter thereby guarantees that he will be able to exchange the issuer's liability for coin and currency or a deposit account held in a bank by the purchaser, or by transferring a deposit of his own. Thus, if the issue is not fully sold, the underwriter will have to get a bank to either "accept" the unsold securities as collateral against the issue of a demand deposit that the underwriter transfers to the issuer or use its own deposits. In either case, the transaction requires the participation and transfer of bank liabilities and the potential access to bank liquidity to ensure the guarantee of liquidity. The "acceptance" function of the underwriter is thus directly dependent on being able to sell the securities to the public or to convince a bank to "accept" them in exchange for a transactions deposit.

The same thing is true for the operation of financial institutions in providing liquidity in the secondary securities markets. For example, the broker-dealers who operate in providing liquidity to the secondary markets as officially designated "specialists" or "dealers" quote bid-ask prices on stocks and hold inventories that fluctuate as they act as net buyer or seller in providing for an "orderly market." These inventories of assets are financed via "call" loans, financed by banks' "acceptance" of the specialist's inventory as collateral. Thus, in general, the liquidity that is provided in the primary and secondary capital markets is directly or indirectly dependent on the liquidity generated by the "acceptance" function of deposit-issuing banks.

In engaging in this creation of liquidity for the capital development of the economy, the banks are always "short" government-issued coin and currency (in practice, central bank reserves). To cover this potential short position, Minsky noted that banks "make financing commitments because they can operate in financial markets to acquire funds as needed; to so operate they hold assets that are negotiable in markets and hold credit lines at other banks. The normal functioning of our enterprise system depends upon a large array of commitments to finance, which do not show up as actual funds lent or borrowed, and money markets that provide connections among financial institutions" (Minsky 2008 [1986], 256).

Since this market-support mechanism to acquire funds as needed is not fail-safe, central banks provide banks with access to reserves through the discount window, where the central bank "accepts" the assets held by the bank in exchange for government means of payment. This means that the ultimate source of liquidity in the system is the central bank "acceptance" function known as "lender of last resort."

Along with the clear recognition of this function in the Banking Act of 1935, an additional mechanism was introduced to ensure the liquidity of bank liabilities: a federal deposit insurance guarantee financed via an assessment of the size of a bank's deposit liabilities that creates a trust fund to be used to provide coin and currency to the depositors of a bank that fails to meet its commitments. It has usually been the case that the depositors of a failed bank have their insured credits transferred to a solvent bank that absorbs the failing bank, rather than being directly reimbursed by the insurance fund for the insured value of their deposits. But, as Minsky observed, it is neither the existence nor the size of the trust fund that provides the liquidity guarantee for the deposits. Ultimately, it is the willingness of the central bank to create reserves against this government agency guarantee. Thus, it is always the central bank in its role as lender of last resort that provides the ultimate source of liquidity for the banks that are regulated and insured. And it is these banks that provide the ultimate liquidity to the rest of the financial system, which in normal times does not have access to the central bank.

Creators of "fictitious" liquidity: shadow "banks"

Minsky (2008 [1986]) noted that "[o]ur complex financial structure consists of a variety of institutions that lever on owners' equity and normally make on the carry, that is, borrowing at a lower rate than their assets can earn" (277). Which is to say, there are institutions that engage in the same type of activity as banks but without the ability to borrow coin and currency from the general public, and thus without the ability to offer their own insured liabilities as a substitute means of payment. Since they cannot provide payments services, their fundamental activity is borrowing and lending to one another, thus increasing what Minsky called "financial layering"; that is, the issue of financial liabilities to acquire the liabilities of other financial institutions.

The liquidity of a liability issued by any nonbank financial institution will then be determined by its ability to finance it—that is, to borrow in order to hold the liability—and this will ultimately depend on access to the liquidity of a deposit-creating bank. In a consolidated view of the financial system, every liability in the nonbank financial system, as well as the short-term liabilities of the nonbank nonfinancial system, are all ultimately dependent on the liquidity created by the deposit-taking, insured banks. This means that a failure to meet a payment commitment by any institution in the financial system will have an impact on all the others in the system, and will ultimately depend on the liquidity provided by the banking system.

For Minsky, a condition of "financial distress" will occur when any individual financial institution "cannot meet its obligations on its balance sheet liabilities." This may evolve into a "financial crisis" when "a very significant subset of the economy is in financial distress" and "'a slight disturbance' in money flows creates such widespread financial distress that financial crisis is threatened" and financial fragility is transformed into "financial instability." At each stage in the evolution toward instability, financial intermediaries become more reliant on other financial institutions, and ultimately banks, to refinance their liabilities. As Minsky noted, "A key to the generation of financial crisis is whether the holders of marketable securities who have large scale debts outstanding can refinance or must liquidate their positions when they need cash" (Minsky 1964, 266). "The worst thing that could happen to the solvency of any financial institution is a forced sale of its assets in order to acquire cash. Imagine what would happen to asset values, if there were a need to liquidate government bond positions by the government bond dealers or if the sales finance companies were suddenly to try to sell their portfolios of consumer installment paper on some market. In order to prevent this type of forced liquidation of assets, the financial intermediaries protect themselves by having alternative financing sources, i.e., by having 'de facto' lenders of last resort. These de facto lenders of last resort ultimately must have access to the Federal Reserve System in times of potential crisis" (Minsky 1964, 376).

It is for this reason that Minsky proposed more active use of the discount window, and recommended that financial institutions always be "in the bank"—that is, borrowing from the window—because this provides direct information to the central bank about the assets the bank holds as its cushion of safety. He also recommended that the window be open to all financial and nonfinancial institutions since their condition ultimately depends on the insured, regulated banks. It would thus be more efficient to provide the funding directly, rather than indirectly through the banks and the banks to their clients. Indeed, this is precisely what the Federal Reserve was forced to do in order to stem the collapse of liquidity in the recent crisis.

Regulators discover Minsky

The recent Bank for International Settlements Committee on the Global Financial System report on global liquidity (CGFS 2011) clearly reflects this view of liquidity in the financial system. It notes the basic difference between what it calls "official" liquidity, provided by the central bank, and private liquidity, provided by private financial institutions who "provide market liquidity to securities markets, for instance through market-making activity, or provide funding liquidity through, for example, interbank lending. The conditions under which these intermediaries can fund their balance sheets, in turn, depend on the willingness of other private sector participants to provide funding or market liquidity" (4). The report distinguishes between market liquidity, "the ability to trade an asset or financial instrument at short notice with little impact on its price," and funding liquidity, "the ability to raise cash either via the sale of an asset (sometimes called balance sheet liquidity) or by borrowing." "This interdependence underlines the endogenous character of private liquidity. At the macroeconomic level, private liquidity is thus closely related to monetary liquidity or funding conditions, as reflected in various monetary and credit aggregates or measures of the cost of funding. The creation and destruction of private liquidity is closely related to leveraging and deleveraging by private institutions. Depending on their ability or willingness to take risks and provide maturity or currency transformation services, financial institutions can both dampen or amplify monetary stimuli provided by central banks or provide stimuli of their own. . . . This gives rise to a pronounced state dependency of private global liquidity. In the extreme, general uncertainty about the viability of banks and other financial institutions can lead to a drying-up of private funding, and the private, endogenous component of global liquidity disappears altogether" (4–5).

The means of creation of "fictitious" liquidity

Minsky's proposal for the "post Glass Steagall" holding company system not only eliminates the creation of liquidity from the transactions function of the system, but also does so for the subsidiaries financing the system's capital development. But the post–Glass-Steagall system that emerged after the 1999 GLB Act evolved in a very different way. It not only preserved the creation of liquidity by the deposit-taking subsidiaries of the holding companies, but also validated a plethora of diverse structures that were introduced to provide additional liquidity into the system as a result of the competition between commercial and investment banks. Dodd-Frank is simply an additional step in the process described by Minsky in which a bailout of the financial institution validates the practices that originally created the difficulties.[10]

Indeed, the recent crisis can be described as the collapse of "fictitious" liquidity created by these structures, the failure of the banking sector to provide sufficient liquidity to prevent the onset of a "debt deflation" (what Minsky defined as the ultimate attempt to access liquidity by "selling position to make position"—that is, selling assets in order to redeem liabilities), and finally, the inability of the Federal Reserve to intervene sufficiently quickly to ensure the provision of liquidity for the non-bank financial institutions which could not find support from the insured banks.

There were three particular stages in the evolution of these nonbank liquidity-creating structures that are important for understanding the recent financial crisis. The first was the rapid expansion in the number and variety of institutions that "lever on owners' equity" and their introduction of innovations that allowed them to earn more than the simple carry or net interest spread. The second was the rapid increase in the use of this liquidity to fund increased financial layering in the financial sector. The third was the increase in the use of liquidity to lend against positions whose return was determined by an expected change in prices (i.e., capital gains) rather than the production of income, but which had virtually no corresponding over-the-counter (OTC) or organized market to determine prices.

This tendency toward the increase in fictitious system liquidity emerged in the 1980s as noninsured, nonregulated financial institutions encroached on the protected deposit business of commercial banks and the commercial banks sought to protect their earnings by developing nonregulated sources of liquidity generation. The most emblematic of these alternative sources of liquidity is the money market mutual fund (MMMF), which issues shares with a fixed net present value of one dollar to finance the purchase of short-term commercial paper, thus providing the equivalent of a sight deposit in a regulated, insured commercial bank. It is a clone of a bank, and operates outside the regulatory regime governing banks. It provides the same transformation of illiquid business debt into a substitute for coin and currency, and can offer better returns and lower lending costs because of the lack of regulation. However, the liquidity so created is fictitious, since it depends on the ability of commercial firms to meet their payments on commercial paper, yet the fund shares are priced as if they were more liquid than insured bank deposits. The problem with the MMMF is that, in contrast to a commercial bank that can create deposits that are a substitute for coin and currency by granting a commercial loan, a mutual fund cannot automatically fund commercial paper by lending to the firm. It has to sell a mutual fund share to the general public in exchange for a sight deposit on an insured bank, or for coin and currency. It cannot engage in the acceptance function that Minsky considers the foundation of the system of financing capital development. A mutual fund share cannot buy a trip on the subway.

Largely in response to the introduction of capital requirements, in the late 1980s regulated, insured banks created "arm's-length" structured investment vehicles (SIVs) to reduce the assets held on balance sheets and to increase their return on equity. An SIV purchases structured assets or mortgages from the originating banks and finances them through the issue of short-term asset-backed commercial paper and some medium-term equity notes. The SIV earns the interest spread between the short-term paper issued to fund the acquisition of the long-term structured assets, augmented by leverage created from over-selling the commercial paper. Just as in the case of the MMMF, the SIV cannot create the funding of its assets; it must sell its paper to the public in exchange for a sight deposit or coin and currency. At their peak, the asset-backed commercial paper issued by SIVs accounted for a third of the total asset-backed commercial paper market.

The shifting of assets from regulated, insured banks' balance sheets thus pro-vided a benefit by reducing their capital requirements and increasing their fee incomes above the net interest margins. It also created an increase in fictitious system liquidity, since an SIV has no line of credit with the originating bank (as is the case with the issue of generic commercial paper) and no access to the central bank in the case of a runoff in its commercial paper as investors decline to roll over their investments (the equivalent of a deposit "drain" for a bank). In case of distress an SIV will be forced to sell its assets. The liquidity created by the SIVs was thus fictitious. After arguing that that they were not formally committed to backing the commercial paper issued by the SIVs that they had created, managed, and administered, the banks eventually admitted a de facto responsibility and took the assets back onto their balance sheets, thus confirming Minsky's rule that liquidity in the system is always dependent on deposit banks. It is important to note that while the majority of assets in SIVs were collateralized mortgage assets, they were originally created to allow collateralization of the banks' credit card receivables, auto loans, student loans, and so forth, all of which were subject to the same increasing fragility as the mortgage-backed assets.

Another source of fictitious liquidity and a popular method of moving assets off balance sheets to increase income was asset securitization. This involves the creation of a formally independent special purpose entity—like an investment trust—that issues liabilities, usually fixed interest, whose proceeds are used to acquire fixed-income assets. The assets purchased from the originating bank are used as collateral for the liabilities issued to fund them. Various combina-tions of income from the assets can be structured to create different levels of risk associated with the different class, or "tranche," of liability. The aim is to create, through tranching, a structure in which the assets produce a higher return than paid on the liabilities. But, as Minsky observed, that should mean that the liabili-ties have a higher liquidity premium than the assets. Liquidity is thus created by ensuring that a large proportion of the liabilities has a higher credit rating than the assets that support them. This is achieved by "credit enhancement"; that is, by "overcollateralization" (the value of the assets is greater than the liabilities issued), by the purchase of credit default swap (CDS) protection, or by purchasing a guarantee from a monoline insurer that is sufficient to convince a nationally recognized statistical rating organization to provide the majority of the liabilities with an investment-grade rating, allowing pension funds, insurance companies, and trusts to purchase liabilities backed by assets that they would not be permitted to buy directly because their creditworthiness is too low. Here, the liquidity is provided by placing assets into a structure that transforms them into more liquid liabilities. Unlike the SIV, there is little maturity transformation in this process; rather, income is generated by transforming illiquid, higher-yielding assets into liquid, low-yielding assets. Again, this is fictitious liquidity, since it depends on the performance of the underlying assets or the conditions of the entities that provide the credit enhancement. Since both the issuers of CDSs and the monoline insurers provisioned against the risk represented by the investment-grade rating of the liabilities rather than the much higher risk of the underlying assets, these guarantees were insufficient to ensure the liquidity of the liabilities.[11]

Derivatives, whether of the plain-vanilla variety or embodied in structured lending vehicles, also provide fictitious liquidity, since they provide the possibility of creating the equivalent of ownership exposure to an asset with only a minimum margin payment. Thus, instead of borrowing from a bank to invest in an asset, it is possible to take a long position by buying an OTC or exchange-traded derivative with only a small margin payment on top of the option premium. Regulated commercial banks were originally allowed to deal in derivatives on government securities since their intermediation was permitted by Glass-Steagall. But the Office of the Comptroller of the Currency, in a series of administrative rulings, eventually opened the way to dealings in derivatives on all types of assets, providing for the creation and dominance of insured banks in OTC derivatives dealing (see Kregel 2010).

Another mechanism central to the recent crisis was the so-called "section 20" exemption that allowed banks to create "security affiliates" to deal in securities if income from these activities did not constitute their "principal" source of revenue (see Kregel 2010). Since banks were permitted to deal in government securities under Glass-Steagall, the principal source of income took the form of running a matched-book repurchase business that created little risk, and could be grossed up to produce any desired revenue to "cover" the income generated from securities trading. This allowed banks to engage in what would become proprietary trading, and, more important, created the "repo" market, in which an investor without capital could take a position in an asset that was funded by the use of the asset as collateral. The only financial commitment was to find the funds to cover the small or nonexistent "haircut" applied to the value of the asset in determining how much would be lent against it. Since such contracts were overnight or extremely short term, they again augmented the liquidity of long-term, less liquid assets. (It is worth noting that the repo market had been a persistent source of fraudulent activity and regulatory difficulty over many years prior to the recent crisis.[12])

All of these innovative structures greatly increased the ability of the system to create and finance the holding of, and speculation in, new types of exotic financial assets. For this reason, they are often described as constituting a "shadow" banking system, but they were not banks and they did not create "liquidity" in the same way as a regulated bank—that is, through the guarantee of provision of means of payment. This fictitious liquidity depended more on particular movements in the prices of the assets and the ability to sell them as required than on their ability to produce income. When these price anticipations were not realized, it was impossible to generate liquidity through the sale of underlying assets without creating declines in prices that produced loss and potential insolvency. Indeed, most of these assets were long term, with no formal or informal markets or market makers. Not only were there no markets in which to sell them, there were no market makers or prices to value the assets. Their very existence and value depended on fictitious liquidity, and when it disappeared, so did their value. Ultimately, the liquidity required to support these assets depended on their acceptance by insured banks. If banks were not willing to provide it, then it had to be provided by the central bank if an outright debt deflation was to be avoided.

In the recent crisis, the fact that many bank holding companies were also involved in the creation of this "shadow" liquidity severely limited the ability of their banking subsidiaries to provide liquidity support, since to do so would have required increasing borrowing from depositors rather than accepting the liabilities of another unit in the holding. A single institution cannot provide accommodation to itself, since it would just be transferring losses from one unit to another, jeopardizing its ability to attract customer "core" deposits.

Liquidity was not used to provide for the capital development of the economy

The basic difficulty caused by the recent explosion of fictitious liquidity is that it was used primarily to finance the acquisition of financial assets that did not represent real capital assets or the expected future income from real assets but rather an anticipated appreciation in the price of the assets—an appreciation that was driven by the increase in fictitious liquidity. The stability of these positions was again dependent on a particular pattern of price change. And many in the industry recognized these structures as implicit "Ponzi" schemes (see McCulley 2007). When these anticipated price movements were not realized, many of the structures in which margins were linked to the value of the position generated an increased demand for accommodation for a position whose value was declining. Thus, the demand for liquidity increased with a decline in the value of the position and the decline in the amount of fictitious liquidity it could provide. The fact that there were no markets to provide evaluations of the worth of the positions made it more difficult to assess risks, leading to an often inappropriate increase in haircuts and margin calls, and reducing liquidity at precisely the moment the structures required additional liquidity to remain viable.

In simple terms, the shadow system created liquidity to fund holdings of financial assets and to generate incomes from trading assets in order to exploit price differences, rather than to generate income and employment. As Minsky pointed out, a borrower's balance sheet represents a flow dimension that is crucial to its stability: the balance between the financing costs of the liabilities relative to the income generated by the assets. For a business firm, this is business income from output, employment, and the sale of output. For a financial institution financing the firm, its income is derivative of the firm's income. However, most of the lending in the recent crisis was lending by one financial institution to another in order to finance their holdings of financial assets and income generated by simple price volatility. This is "financial layering" within the system and represents the increased financial fragility that was generated by this creation of "fictitious" liquidity.

What is wrong with current regulatory proposals?

The basic error in the current regulatory approach embodied in Dodd–Frank is that it does very little to limit the creation of fictitious liquidity or to redirect the creation of that liquidity to the financing of the capital development of the system.[13] Dodd–Frank seeks to limit the exposure of government to the consequences of another collapse of regulated, insured institutions, requiring the latter to hold higher levels of equity capital in order to meet the losses created by a debt deflation caused by a reversal in anticipated prices. But capital is meant to be a reserve to ensure solvency of the institutions, and the insolvencies that were avoided in the recent crisis were created by excessive liquidity creation. The ability to create liquidity depends on the financing institution engaging in the acceptance function. Only a regulated bank offering insured deposits can do this. Avoiding another crisis will thus depend on limiting the means of "fictitious" liquidity creation noted above.

As Minsky's proposal above suggests, the way to make banks truly safe is for every subsidiary of the bank holding company to carry a 100 percent reserve ratio and a 100 percent capital ratio. But no amount of capital can substitute for the creation of the liquidity required for the capital development of the system. This is particularly true for nonbank investment trust structures that are implicitly 100 capitalized.

One way to do it would be to modify Minsky's proposal by placing limitations not only on the assets and liabilities of the subsidiaries but also on the number and functions of the subsidiaries of a financial holding company. Holding companies providing transaction services, a store of value, or financing (for housing, consumers, or short-term business financing of commercial paper) would then be limited to activities closely related to liquidity creation. A separate group of holding companies, with the appropriate related sets of activities, would provide underwriting and capital market services for the financing of productive investment. The aim would be to limit each type of holding company to a range of activities that are sufficiently linked to their core function, and to ensure that each company were small enough to be effectively managed and supervised (see Kregel 2008).

As proposed in last year's Levy Institute report (Levy Institute, 2011), some of the difficulties created by Dodd-Frank are due to the attempt to introduce Glass–Steagall–type provisions into the 1999 GLB Act without revisiting its main provisions relating to the revision of the 1956 Bank Holding Company Act. A realistic attempt to preclude "too big to fail" banks would seem to require revision of GLB.

But such a revision would be both time-consuming and difficult in the present political environment. A more expeditious method of reform that could replace Dodd-Frank would be to ask if there were any reason why the fictitious-liquidity structures that have grown up in the process of deregulation are necessary to the operation of the economy. Indeed, most of the liquidity-creating structures mentioned above were generated by the restrictions on activity caused by the segmentation of financial functions and competition between commercial and investment banks. Since the GLB Act eliminated any such distinction, the justification for most of these structures loses cogency.

For example, is there any reason why MMMFs should exist independent of banks? They could be eliminated by a simple ruling reversing the original court decision that commercial paper was a security and thus could not be operated by commercial banks under Glass–Steagall. Under GLB, there is no reason for them to exist, and they could be transformed into regulated, insured institutions by a simple decision of the Financial Stability Oversight Council.

There is also no reason why securitization should exist in its present form. Indeed, if these structures were regulated like other financial institutions and subject to transparency and reporting, they would in all probability not be viable (see Kregel 2010). As suggested by Lew Ranieri (1996), one of the innovators in securitization, there are some assets that should not and cannot be successfully securitized. Thus, the assets that are permitted in securitized structures should be subject to regulation. It is instructive that government-sponsored enterprises oversaw the securitization of "conforming" mortgage assets without difficulty as long as they met the strict conditions for inclusion. It thus follows that some securitized structures cannot be effectively risk rated, and credit ratings should not be permitted as an indication of their suitability for certain portfolios.

Repurchase agreements should be regulated so that they do not fund speculative financial institutions, such as proprietary trading desks or hedge funds. The supposed need for collateralized deposits of large size could be easily met by extending deposit insurance to all deposits. Repos have been the source of fraud and instability throughout their history, even when they were primarily restricted to risk-free government securities. They could simply be reclassified as loans and regulated as such.

Derivatives have become an integral part of the modern financial system, and hardly any position is undertaken or financing instrument created without the inclusion of a derivatives position. The problem is that while they disperse risk and provide hedging, they often hide the true risk to the purchaser. Trading on regulated exchanges will not change the lack of transparency concerning risk exposure. The problem could be reduced if derivatives positions were fully margined.

These measures would not guarantee system stability, as new mechanisms of fictitious liquidity would quickly be invented. But they could be easily introduced by simply reversing the regulatory and legal decisions that allowed them to come into existence, primarily in order to provide for a more level playing field between commercial and investment banks. The level playing field was secured by the GLB Act, which rendered these measures outdated and unnecessary. They should have been repealed when the act was approved or, better, by revision of the act itself. Either approach would provide a degree of regulatory control over fictitious liquidity creation and thus stem the reflexive impact of its collapse on asset prices. This would also require financial institutions to seek other forms of income; among them, lending to support the capital development of the economy.

All of these decisions are within the remit of existing regulatory agencies or the FSOC and could be implemented rapidly and without the delays surrounding the implementation of Dodd-Frank.

Addendum: the conundrum of regulation

Much of the innovation that has occurred in the Glass-Steagall system was part of an attempt by regulated banks to increase their return on equity. And much of the deregulation in the financial system was introduced in order to allow commercial banks to augment their income and compete with less regulated investment banks. Indeed, some foresaw this problem as leading to the disappearance of commercial banking (see Kregel 1997). Ironically, it is the investment banks that have disappeared as a result of GLB.

For any financial institution, its return on equity is determined by the return on assets multiplied by the ratio of assets to bank equity, better known as leverage. The problem that commercial banks faced was the decline in the share of system assets that were being financed by bank liquidity, along with the decline in net margins on this business. Thus, deregulation provided a way to increase leverage, but the creation of bank holding companies that could use this increased leverage to improve system liquidity and thus inflate the amount of income produced led to greater financial fragility and eventual collapse. An increase in capital ratios does nothing to increase the returns to traditional liquidity creation by means of acceptance lending. Rather, it will simply lead to an increase in leverage or to greater consolidation, as banks seek to improve their bottom line by raising the price of services. An alternative, which Minsky suggested, is for banks to access the central bank directly for reserves to hedge their short cash positions resulting from deposit creation. This would preclude the need for offering retail deposits as the base mechanism for generating reserves.

The conundrum of regulation is to find a way to allow banks to concentrate on financing the capital development of the economy through liquidity creation while at the same time providing secure transactions services, with the combination earning rates of return on capital that are competitive with other forms of capital investment. Increasing the amount of capital required and thus the income that must be earned would appear to be a sure incentive to innovate in the direction of higher leverage and fictitious liquidity, or to charge more for the provision of transactions services.

Finally, macroprudential regulation has to recognize the importance, first noted by Marriner Eccles, of the impact of the employment rate and the government budget on the level of liquidity and the solvency of financial institutions. As Minsky continually emphasized, the success of the Glass-Steagall system was due as much to the existence of Big Government as a complement to the lender-of-last-resort function of the central bank as it was to the restrictions placed on the assets that deposit-taking institutions could hold.

Notes

1 Prepared with the support of Ford Foundation grant no. 1080–1003–1 on Financial Stability and Global and National (Re)regulation in Light of the Sub-prime Crisis.
2 "On July 22, 2011, the U.S. Court of Appeals for the District of Columbia (the 'D.C. Circuit') found that the Securities and Exchange Commission ('SEC') acted arbitrarily and capriciously in adopting proxy voting rules, Rule 14a-11. Although the SEC's adopting release devoted 60 pages to a cost-benefit analysis of this rule, the D.C. Circuit vacated Rule 14a-11 on the basis that the SEC 'failed adequately to consider [Rule 14a-11's] effect upon efficiency, competition, and capital formation.' . . . In reaching this conclusion, the court sharply criticized the SEC's efforts, at one point calling them 'unutterably mindless'" (Kini and Proctor 2011, 1).
3 On December 2, 2011, the International Swaps and Derivatives Association, Inc., and the Securities Industry and Financial Markets Association filed "a legal challenge to the Commodity Futures Trading Commission's (CFTC) final rules that limit the positions that investors may own in certain commodities. . . . [T]he Associations contend that the CFTC's decision-making process in enacting the Rule was procedurally flawed. Among other deficiencies, the CFTC adopted the Rule without making findings as to the necessity and appropriateness of the position limits, as required by statute. Furthermore, the CFTC failed to conduct any meaningful cost-benefit analysis and lacked a reasoned basis for its rule" (*Futures Magazine* 2011).
4 Indeed, a number of influential District Federal Reserve presidents have argued that existing FDIC authority would have been sufficient to deal with the resolution of the larger financial institutions during the crisis; see, for example, Hoenig (2009) and Fisher (2010). Well before the crisis, Feldman and Stern (2005) proposed that FDIC resolution could be used to prevent this process, but this provision was not included in Dodd-Frank.
5 The existing antitrust legislation was written for a segmented system such as Glass-Steagall and has never been revised to deal with the problems of size and competitiveness created by GLB. See Kregel (2009).
6 The history of deregulation in the United States has been to provide an initial period of increased entry and competition, only to be followed by increased bankruptcies and consolidation, restoring industry concentration to even higher levels. The airline industry is exemplary of this trend, which was also followed in telecommunications, energy, transport, etc.
7 But such proposals are not new. The National Banking Act was based on government liabilities backing the issue of national banknotes. In any event, it did not provide the promised guarantee of stability, primarily because of the variability of the securities' value.

Minsky's proposal would provide for a government guarantee to support the mark-to-market value of the assets; see Kregel 1996.

8 Aside from the theoretical difficulties in formulating the correspondence of real and money rates (see Myrdal 1939) or neutral money (see Sraffa 1932).

9 It is for this reason that banks are often characterized as "public-private" partnerships.

10 "Every time the Fed protects a financial instrument it legitimizes the use of this instrument to finance activity; it thus prepares the way for the next expansion of liquidity and the next financial crisis" (Minsky 2008 [1986], 106).

11 It is telling that the SEC appears to have believed that the rating of securities by rating agencies provided an assessment of their "liquidity": "securities that were rated investment grade by a credit rating agency of national repute, typically were more liquid and less volatile in price than securities that were not so highly rated" (Adelson 2007).

12 This list is not exhaustive. For example, rehypothecation of collateral and securities lending in prime brokerage accounts also augment system liquidity at no cost or at only a small haircut on value.

13 One of the greatest deficiencies in the new Bank for International Settlements regulations on liquidity is that they set liquidity requirements for financial institutions rather than limiting the financial institutions that create liquidity. The former are specious for as Keynes reminded, there is no such thing as system liquidity, while it is possible to restrict the operation of institutions that provide liquidity. It is also likely that they will distort the prices of the assets that satisfy this requirement as usually happens with any division between regulatory and nonregulatory assets.

References

Adelson, M. 2007. Testimony before the Subcommittee on Capital Markets, Insurance, and Government Sponsored Enterprises of the House Committee on Financial Services. *The Role of Credit Rating Agencies in the Structured Finance Market.* 110th Congress, 1st sess., September 27. Washington D.C.: US Government Printing Office.

Committee on the Global Financial System (CGFS). 2011. "Global Liquidity—Concept, Measurement and Policy Implications." CGFS Papers No. 45. Basel: Bank for International Settlements. November.

Committee on Capital Markets Regulation (CCMR). 2012. "CCMR Warns that Inadequate Cost-benefit Analysis Opens Dodd-Frank Rulemaking to Challenge and Delay." Media Advisory. Cambridge, Mass.: CCMR. March 7.

Futures Magazine. 2011. "ISDA, SIFMA Sue CFTC Over Position Limits." December 5.

Feldman, R. J., and G. H. Stern. 2005. "Addressing TBTF When Banks Merge: A Proposal. Bank Mergers Provide Unique Opportunities for TBTF Policy Reform." *The Region.* The Federal Reserve Bank of Minneapolis. September 1.

Fisher, I. 1935. *100% Money.* New York: Adelphi.

Fisher, R. 2010. "Financial Reform or Financial Dementia?" Remarks at the SW Graduate School of Banking 53rd Annual Keynote Address and Banquet, Dallas, Texas, June 3, 2010.

———. 2012, "Letter from the President." Annual Report. Federal Reserve Bank of Dallas. March 27.

Hayek, F. 1931. *Prices and Production.* London: Routledge and Kegan Paul.

Hoenig, T. M. 2009. Testimony before the Joint Economic Committee, United States Congress. *Too Big to Fail or Too Big to Save? Examining the Systemic Threats of Large Financial Institutions.* 111th Congress, 1st sess., April 21. Washington, D.C.: US Government Printing Office.

Kini, S. M., and S. E. Proctor. 2011. *"Business Roundtable*: Damming the Flow of Dodd-Frank Rulemaking?" *Banking Law Committee Journal.* Chicago, Ill.: ABA. November.

Keynes, John Maynard 1936. *The General Theory of Employment, Interest and Money*. London: Macmillan.

Kregel, J. 1996. *Origini e Sviluppo dei Mercati Finanziari*. Arezzo, Italy: Banca Popolare dell'Etruria e del Lazio / Studi e Ricerche.

———. 1997. *The Past and Future of Banks*. Rome: Ente Einaudi.

———. 2008. *Will the Paulson Bailout Produce the Basis for Another Minsky Moment?* Policy Note 2008/5. Annandale-on-Hudson, N.Y.: Levy Economics Institute of Bard College. October.

———. 2009. *Observations on the Problem of "Too Big to Fail/Save/Resolve."* Policy Note 2009/11. Annandale-on-Hudson, N.Y.: Levy Economics Institute of Bard College. December.

———. 2010. "Can a Return to Glass-Steagall Provide Financial Stability in the U.S. Financial System?" *PSL Quarterly Review* 63(252): 39–76. Originally published as *No Going Back: Why We Cannot Restore Glass-Steagall's Segregation of Banking and Finance*. Public Policy Brief No. 107. Annandale-on-Hudson, N.Y.: Levy Economics Institute of Bard College. February.

Lerner, A. 1943. "Functional Finance and the Federal Debt," *Social Research* 10 (February 1943): 38–51

Levy Economics Institute of Bard College (Levy Institute). 2011. *Minsky on the Reregulation and Restructuring of the Financial System: Will Dodd-Frank Prevent "It" from Happening Again?* Research Project Report. Annandale-on-Hudson, N.Y.: Levy Institute. April.

Litan, R. 1987. *What Should Banks Do?* Washington, D.C.: The Brookings Institution.

McCulley, P. 2007. "Teton Reflections." *Global Central Bank Focus*. Newport Beach, Calif.: Pimco. September 5.

Minsky, H. P. 1964. "Financial Crisis, Financial Systems, and the Performance of the Economy." In *Commission on Money and Credit*, ed. *Private Capital Markets*, 173–380. Englewood Cliffs, N.J.: Prentice-Hall.

———. 1994. "Outline for Issues in Bank Regulation and Supervision." Paper 73. Hyman P. Minsky Archive. Levy Economics Institute of Bard College, Annandale-on-Hudson, N.Y. (hereafter, Minsky Archive).

———. 1995a. "Reforming Banking in 1995: Repeal of the Glass Steagall Act, Some Basic Issues." Paper 59. Minsky Archive.

———. 1995b. "Would Repeal of the Glass Steagall Act Benefit the US Economy." Paper 60. Minsky Archive.

———. 1995c. "Would Universal Banking Benefit the US Economy." Paper 51. Minsky Archive.

———. 2008 (1986). *Stabilizing an Unstable Economy*. New York: McGraw-Hill.

Myrdal, G. 1939. *Monetary Equilibrium*. Reprint. New York: Augustus M. Kelley, Bookseller, 1965.

Ranieri, L. S. 1996. "The Origins of Securitization, Sources of Its Growth, and Its Future Potential." In L. T. Kendall and M. J. Fishman, eds. *A Primer on Securitization*, 31–43. Cambridge, Mass: MIT Press.

Rosenblum, H. 2012. "Choosing the Road to Prosperity: Why We Must End Too Big to Fail – Now." Annual Report. Dallas Federal Reserve Bank. March 27.

Simons, H. C. 1934. "A Positive Program for Laissez Faire: Some Proposals for a Liberal Economic Policy." Reprinted in *Economic Policy for a Free Society*, 40–77. Chicago: University of Chicago Press, 1948.

Sraffa, P. 1932. "Dr. Hayek on Money and Capital." *Economic Journal* 42 (March): 42–53.

Tobin, J. 1987. "The Case for Preserving Regulatory Distinctions." In *Restructuring the Financial System*, 167–83. Kansas City: Federal Reserve Bank of Kansas City.

Related Levy Institute Publications

Working Paper No. 523 | December 2007 "The Natural Instability of Financial Markets"

Public Policy Brief No. 93 | January 2008 *Minsky's Cushions of Safety: Systemic Risk and the Crisis in the US Subprime Mortgage Market*

Working Paper No. 533 | April 2008 "Changes in the US Financial System and the Subprime Crisis"

Working Paper No. 543 | September 2008 "Macroeconomics Meets Hyman P. Minsky: The Financial Theory of Investment"

Working Paper No. 547 | October 2008 "Minsky and Economic Policy: 'Keynesian' All Over Again?"

Policy Note 2008/4 | October 2008 *A Simple Proposal to Resolve the Disruption of Counterparty Risk in Short-Term Credit Markets*

Policy Note 2008/5 | October 2008 *Will the Paulson Bailout Produce the Basis for Another Minsky Moment?*

Public Policy Brief No. 99 | March 2009 *The Return of Big Government: Policy Advice for President Obama*

Working Paper No. 557 | March 2009 "Background Considerations to a Regulation of the US Financial System: Third Time a Charm? Or Strike Three?"

Working Paper No. 558 | April 2009 "Managing the Impact of Volatility in International Capital Markets in an Uncertain World"

Working Paper No. 560 | April 2009 "The Social and Economic Importance of Full Employment"

Public Policy Brief No. 100 | April 2009 *It's That "Vision" Thing: Why the Bailouts Aren't Working, and Why a New Financial System Is Needed*

Working Paper Nos. 573.1–2 | August 2009 "Securitization, Deregulation, Economic Stability, and Financial Crisis, Parts I–II"

Working Paper Nos. 574.1–4 | August 2009 "A Critical Assessment of Seven Reports on Financial Reform: A Minskyan Perspective, Parts I–IV"

Public Policy Brief No. 103 | August 2009 *Financial and Monetary Issues as the Crisis Unfolds*

Working Paper No. 578 | September 2009 "Money Manager Capitalism and the Global Financial Crisis"

Working Paper No. 580 | October 2009 "An Alternative View of Finance, Saving, Deficits, and Liquidity"

Public Policy Brief No. 105 | October 2009 *It Isn't Working: Time for More Radical Policies*

Poilcy Note 2009/9 | October 2009 *Banks Running Wild: The Subversion of Insurance by "Life Settlements" and Credit Default Swaps*

Policy Note 2009/11 | December 2009 *Observations on the Problem of 'Too Big to Fail/Save/Resolve"*

Public Policy Brief No. 107 | January 2010 *No Going Back: Why We Cannot Restore Glass-Steagall's Segregation of Banking and Finance*

Working Paper No. 585 | February 2010 "Is Reregulation of the Financial System an Oxymoron?"

Working Paper No. 586 | February 2010 "Is This the Minsky Moment for Reform of Financial Regulation?"

Working Paper No. 587 | February 2010 "The Global Financial Crisis and the Shift to Shadow Banking"

One-Pager No. 2 | May 2010 *Reforms Without Politicians: What We Can Do Today to Straighten Out financial Markets*

One-Pager No. 3 | May 2010 *"The Spectre of Banking"*

Working Paper No. 602 | June 2010 "Fiscal Responsibility: What Exactly Does It Mean?"

Working Paper No. 605 | June 2010 "Detecting Ponzi Finance: A Revolutionary Approach to the Measure of Financial Fragility"

Working Paper No. 612 | August 2010 "What Do Banks Do? What Should Banks Do?"

Public Policy Brief No. 115 | September 2010 *What Should Banks Do? A Minskyan Analysis*

Working Paper No. 637 | November 2010 "Financial Stability, Regulatory Buffers, and Economic Growth: Some Postrecession Regulatory Implications"

One-Pager No. 6 | November 2010 *Minsky's View of Capitalism and Banking in America*

Working Paper No. 645 | December 2010 "Quantitative Easing and Proposals for Reform of Monetary Policy Operations"

Working Paper No. 653 | March 2011 "Financial Keynesianism and Market Instability" "

Working Paper No. 654 | March 2011 "Measuring Macroprudential Risk: Financial Fragility Indexes"

Working Paper No. 655 | March 2011 "A Minskyan Road to Financial Reform"

Working Paper No. 659 | March 2011 "Minsky Crisis"

Working Paper No. 661 | March 2011 "Minsky's Money Manager Capitalism and the Global Financial Crisis"

Working Paper No. 662 | March 2011 "The Financial Crisis Viewed from the Perspective of the 'Social Costs' Theory"

Public Policy Brief No. 117 | April 2011 *It's Time to Rein in the Fed*

Research Project Report | April 2011 *Minsky on the Reregulation and Restructuring of the Financial System: Will Dodd-Frank Prevent "It" from Happening Again?*

Presentation | September 2011 "On the Political Economy of the German Position in the European Debt Crisis"

Working Paper No. 698 | December 2011 "$29,000,000,000,000: A Detailed Look at the Fed's Bailout by Funding Facility and Recipient"

One-Pager No. 23 | December 2011 *$29,000,000,000,000: A Detailed Look at the Fed's Bailout of the Financial System*

Working Paper No. 709 | February 2012 "Too Big to Fail: Motives, Countermeasures, and the Dodd-Frank Response"

Public Policy Brief No. 123 | April 2012 *A Detailed Look at the Fed's Crisis Response by Funding Facility and Recipient*

15 Minsky and dynamic macroprudential regulation

Preface

In the context of current debates about the proper form of prudential regulation and proposals for the imposition of liquidity and capital ratios, Senior Scholar Jan Kregel examines Hyman Minsky's work as a consultant to government agencies exploring financial regulatory reform in the 1960s. As Kregel explains, this often-overlooked early work, a precursor to Minsky's "financial instability hypothesis" (FIH), serves as yet another useful guide to explaining why regulation and supervision in the lead-up to the 2008 financial crisis were flawed—and why the approach to reregulation after the crisis has been incomplete.

In connection with a discussion of Minsky's proposals for a new bank examination procedure, first formulated in the 1960s, Kregel describes Minsky's broader contribution as articulating a framework for "dynamic macroprudential regulation." He begins by contrasting Minsky's framework with a common approach to prudential regulation in which it is the idiosyncratic features of individual financial institutions that are the central target of examination and supervision—by contrast with an approach that would address interactions between individual institutions and the financial system as a whole. The former, idiosyncratic focus, Kregel notes, has been adorned with the label "*micro*prudential" regulation.

Although policymakers and regulators in the post-2008 era have now expanded their focus to include what is called *macro*prudential regulation, the approach such regulatory proposals often take leaves them vulnerable to the same criticisms Minsky leveled against "micro" regulation in the 1960s. Kregel explains that most macro regulatory proposals suffer from a sin of omission: they are not informed by a theory of endogenous financial instability—a theory that explains the tendency of the financial system to generate crises as a result of its "normal" functioning. This is precisely what Minsky provided with his FIH. Simply recognizing that the economy exhibits cyclical behavior and that financial crises can occur is not sufficient, Kregel emphasizes. Without a theory of the causes of systemic crises, proposals for reregulation will remain preoccupied with mere idiosyncrasies—only now, instead of dwelling on the particulars of individual financial institutions, regulation will be unhelpfully focused on the peculiarities of recent crises; thus the unfortunate tendency of many reform proposals to aim at "preventing the last crisis."

As Kregel demonstrates, this broader framework informed Minsky's 1960s proposal, in the context of his contribution to a Federal Reserve study, for new bank examination procedures. His "cash-flow-based" approach to examination would assess bank liquidity, not as an "innate attribute of an asset," as Minsky put it, but in the context of the balance sheet of the institution, the markets for the assets it holds, and the unstable, cyclical behavior of the economy and financial markets. The new procedures would take into account the emergence of huge banks and their linkages with the "fringe" of the financial system, as well as ongoing changes in financial practices.

The latter aspect, Kregel points out, is crucial to Minsky's dynamic approach to regulation and supervision. Regulation must be designed to be responsive to changes in financial market practices and institutions, as well as to economic conditions and monetary policies. From this perspective, the challenge for reform is not just the proper formulation and implementation of specific rules, but the development of an approach that is sensitive to the potential of actors in the financial system to adapt and innovate, creating new practices that threaten the stability of the system in ways that may not become apparent until the next crisis hits. Financial regulation and examination procedures need to be constantly reassessed in order to avoid becoming obsolete. And in that sense, as Minsky recognized, "the quest to get money and finance right may be a never ending struggle."

Dimitri B. Papadimitriou, *President*
April 2014

If regulation is to remain effective, it must be reassessed frequently and made consistent with evolving market and financial structures.

—Hyman Minsky and Claudia Campbell,
"Getting Off the Back of a Tiger"

Financial regulation, theory, and institutions

Many financial market professionals and some academics have noted the importance of Hyman Minsky's financial instability hypothesis (FIH) for understanding the recent financial crisis as a "Minsky moment." However, the regulatory reforms introduced after the 2008 financial crisis have not given the same attention to his work on regulatory reform in the 1960s as a consultant to various government agencies. This is unfortunate, for the early work on regulatory reform laid the groundwork for the FIH and served as an equally cogent basis for regulation aimed at enhancing the stability of an unstable financial system. There are two important features of Minsky's approach to financial regulation that distinguish it from the current approach. The first is the necessity of an underlying theory to provide the background for regulatory proposals. The second is the need to assess the impact of regulation in light of current economic conditions, ongoing changes in financial institutions, and likely monetary policy measures. Minsky's FIH provided the basis for what were the first proposals of what is now called "macro" prudential regulation. In addition, he proposed a new examination structure to capture the elements of this dynamic approach to macroprudential regulation.

Regulation without theory

As should be well known by now, the FIH was Minsky's attempt to fill a void in traditional Keynesian or neoclassical general equilibrium theory: namely, the lack of any formal theoretical background in which to couch the discussion of prudential regulation. As Minsky was fond of pointing out, the bedrock of mainstream theory is a system of self-adjusting equilibrium that provides little scope for the discussion of a systemic crisis, since, in this theory, one could not occur. It was thus extremely difficult to formulate prudential regulations to respond to a financial crisis if one could only occur as the result of random, external shocks, or what Alan Greenspan would consider idiosyncratic, nonrational (fraudulent) behavior. The only basis for regulation would be to concentrate on the eradication of the disruptive behavior of bad actors or mismanaged financial institutions. From this initial presumption, the formulation of regulations and supervisory procedures[1] required the assessment of the activities of individual banks—without any reference to their relations with other institutions or the overall environment in which they functioned. It was this sort of supervision that, in the early 1980s, led to the failure to identify the building risks in Penn Square Bank, Continental Illinois, and Seattle First, among others, and drew attention to the problem of banks that are "too big to fail."[2] It is exemplary of this approach that the problems of these institutions had been caused by an out-of-control Oklahoma banker and a Continental Illinois loan officer on the take. This idiosyncratic approach to bank regulation is now given credibility with the name "microprudential" regulation, because it only deals with the actions and conditions of a single institution, ignoring any impact that its activities may have on the rest of the financial system, or vice versa.

From this perspective, the major objective of bank examination has been to identify the deficient or fraudulent operations of an individual bank:

> Examinations are used to collect on-the-spot information that will indicate the current financial condition of a bank and its compliance with applicable laws and regulations. . . . All phases of a bank's operations are covered in an examination,[3] and special reviews are made of trust activities, electronic data processing operations, and compliance with consumer protection laws. An examination thus provides a comprehensive picture of a bank's operations and financial performance. Bank exams, though, do not serve as audits. Examiners confine themselves to evaluating only the activities and

bank records that are necessary to judge a bank's condition and regulatory compliance. Generally, the scope of an examination is limited to the bank's records and does not include verifying all of the bank's asset and liability account balances.

(Sprong 2000, 116–7)

As Minsky noted, in a conference paper coauthored with Claudia Campbell,

The instability of banks and other financial institutions is usually described in term of runs and defaults at particular institutions without a clear explanation of why such strong asset substitution quite suddenly becomes the rule of the day. When conceived in terms of bank runs and defaults, a particular bank fails because of its own, idiosyncratic attributes. Its management has been incompetent or committed fraud. Such a failure may have repercussions on other banking institutions, in that for a time financial markets fail to work normally. This creates transitory refinancing problems for otherwise solvent banks. . . . Idiosyncratic failures can trigger an epidemic of bank failures, imparting an adverse "depression-creating" shock to the economy.

(Minsky and Campbell 1987, 254–5)

As usual after cases of severe disruption, regulations are adapted to prevent the occurrence of crises that have already occurred. Although the importance of such interactions in creating systemic shocks was recognized in the collapse of Continental Illinois, and again after the savings and loan crisis of the late 1980s—and became impossible to ignore after the "Lehman moment"—these events produced only modest changes in examination procedures.

For example, the savings and loan crisis of the 1980s produced a shift in approach toward a more "risk"-based bank examination system:

the banking agencies began developing a new supervisory framework in the mid-1990s. The key element in the new framework is bank examinations that focus more closely on the areas of greatest risk to a particular bank. This risk-focused examination process requires examiners to first perform a risk assessment of a bank before beginning any on-site supervisory activities. Risk assessments involve identifying the significant activities of a bank, determining the risks inherent in these activities, and undertaking a preliminary assessment of the processes a bank has in place to identify, measure, monitor, and control these risks. Examiners then use a bank's risk assessment to direct their examination efforts toward the areas of greatest risk to the institution. For banks with sound risk-management processes, examiners can rely more heavily on a bank's own internal risk assessments rather than having to perform extensive supervisory tests.

(Sprong 2000, 117)

And although the chairman of the Federal Deposit Insurance Corporation (FDIC) at the time claimed that the changes "do not reflect a fundamental change in the FDIC's traditional approach to risk assessment," she nonetheless noted that they were

> working to "bridge the gap" that currently separates the "macro" perspective of economics and market trends from the "micro" perspective of bank examinations in ways that will translate data into guidance that examiners can use in assessing and monitoring risks in institutions with differing levels and types of risk exposure. . . . The result will be a more effective and accurate assessment of an institution's ability to manage its risks within a structured framework, which will enhance safety and soundness.
>
> (Helfer 1996)

But it is clear that this approach to combining micro- and macroprudential regulation still placed the emphasis on the examination of the individual institution, rather than on systemic impacts on the entire financial system. The current approach to regulation in the aftermath of the subprime crisis has been a similar call for a more systemic approach to financial regulation, now baptized "macroprudential" regulation, to provide a supplement to "microprudential" regulation. However, the same criticism that Minsky leveled against the formulation of the "micro" regulation of the 1960s applies today to the "macro" prudential approach, since it is lacking any underlying theoretical framework of the causes of systemic crises that would support formulation of regulations to prevent them. It pretends to provide regulation to deal with systemic issues without any clearly articulated theory of the causes of systemic crises or the cyclical behavior of the financial system. In particular, while most macro policy regulation proposals recognize the existence of cyclical behavior in the economy and recommend measures to deal with it, they provide little explanation of why it occurs.[4] If a comprehensive theory of how endogenous fragility develops is absent, the simple recognition that macro conditions will impact financial performance cannot prevent concentration on the idiosyncratic aspects of recent crises.

Regulation with theory

In Minsky's view, any macroprudential regulation would require "a more complete description of the instability of an 'economy with banking'" (Minsky and Campbell 1987, 255). Such an approach

> needs to look behind the runs and analyze the structure of balance sheets, payment commitments and position-making activities. Position-making for a bank consists of the transactions undertaken to bring the cash position to the level required by regulation or bank management. In the position-making view, bank failures do not arise simply because of incompetent or corrupt management. They occur mainly because of the interdependence

of payment commitments and position–making transactions across institutions and units.

(255)

Since Minsky's FIH approach was built on developing Keynes's "foundations of an investment theory of business cycles and a financial theory of investment in a capitalist economy" (Minsky 1994a, 2), it started by providing the explanation of the cyclical behavior and the systemic interactions that provide the basis for the formulation of macroprudential regulation.

Minsky's early work on regulation dealt not only with regulatory issues, but also with the appropriate type of bank examination from the standpoint of the FIH. Already in 1966,[5] on the basis of his contribution to the Federal Reserve study on the discount mechanism (Minsky 1972a), he had started to outline his ideas for what he called a "cash-flow" based bank examination procedure:

> The suggested examination and analysis of a commercial bank or other depository institution is based upon the view that liquidity is not an innate attribute of an asset but rather that liquidity is a time related characteristic of an ongoing, continuing economic institution.
>
> (Minsky 1967, 1)

The background from the Fed study is that

> basic to the idea of liquidity as an attribute of an institution is the ability of the unit to fulfill its payment commitments. Any statement about a unit's liquidity, therefore depends upon estimating how its normal activities will generate both cash and payments, as well as the conditions under which its assets (including its ability to borrow as an "honorary" asset) can be transformed into cash. . . . Any statement about the liquidity of an institution depends upon assumptions about the behavior of the economy and financial markets. As the assumptions are changed, the estimate of the liquidity of the institutions will vary.
>
> (Minsky 1967, 2)

This is later described as "position liquidity" and "market liquidity," representing the "dual vulnerability [that] emerges wherever cash flows from operations are insufficient to meet financial commitments" (Minsky 1975a, 4). He thus spells out the objective of macroprudential regulation and the inability of traditional regulation to identify systemic risks.

The revised proposal is described as follows:

> The aim . . . was to use the examination process to generate information on both the liquidity and solvency of particular institutions but also on threats, if any, to the stability of financial markets; this information was to be forward-looking and to be such that the implications of alternative

economic and policy scenarios could be investigated. In particular, the examination procedure was designed to focus upon the actual (past) and potential (near-term future) position-making operations of a bank, so that the Federal Reserve authorities would be aware of actual or threatened financial fragility.

(Minsky 1975b, 150)[6]

In support of this approach, Minsky also made recommendations on revising the flow of funds accounts to make macro assessment of financial fragility more transparent (Minsky 1962).

In a series of notes updating his initial 1967 proposal, he points out how institutional changes, in the form of the emergence of "giant multi-billion dollar banks" and "fringe banking institutions and markets," should be a focal point in updating the initial 1967 proposal, and should "enable the authorities to get a better handle on the operations" of these large banks and their linkages to "non-bank financial institutions and various short term financial markets" (Minsky 1975a, 1–2).

However, despite regulators' interest in and recognition of the importance of this "systemic" macro approach, it has yet to produce substantial changes in how supervision and examination are carried out in practice. Indeed, the FDIC has recently recognized its relevance, as well as its scarce implementation:

> Examiner observations indicate that many banks have established only rudimentary liquidity policies and contingency funding plans as part of the overall asset/liability management function. Monitoring ratios are often limited to a static analysis that depicts a point-in-time snapshot of the liquidity position. Comprehensive cash flow analyses that identify sources and uses of funds are rare. For example, a recent review of a multibillion dollar institution revealed that the sources-and-uses report tracked wholesale funding sources but did not incorporate retail cash flows. In many cases, contingency planning policies lack procedures based on bank-specific stress events, are not regularly updated to reflect current market conditions, and are not tested to ensure the accuracy of the assumptions.
>
> (FDIC 2008)

Dynamic macroprudential regulation

But Minsky's "new" approach to examination was not only to recognize the cyclical nature of the interactions generated by financing relations within the economic system, but also to take a much broader approach to regulation that might be called "dynamic" macroprudential regulation. This is the basis for the second innovative aspect of Minsky's approach to regulation:

> The supervisory and regulating structure for banking and finance that is in place not only reflects institutional features of the economy stretching back

over at least 150 years, it also reflects the understanding, i.e. the economic theory, of how our type of economy works that ruled at the time when the bits and pieces of this structure was first put in place.

(Minsky 1994b, 6)

Indeed, this was one of the advantages of Minsky's proposed cash-flow approach:

The perspective underlying the suggestions was of a dynamic, evolving set of financial institutions and relations. All too often, it seems as if the Federal Reserve authorities have been surprised by changes in financial practices. One aim in the design of the examination system was to establish a regular reporting procedure which would force the authorities to be aware of institutional changes that were ongoing, and which furthermore forced the authorities to inquire into how the ongoing developments can be expected to affect the stability of the financial system.

(Minsky 1975b, 150)

In a subsequent note, Minsky gave the following as an example:

One byproduct of the cash flow examination procedure will be more precise knowledge of the relations between the examined institutions and fringe banks. Such a clarification will enable the Federal Reserve to better know what is emerging in financial relations and to be better prepared for contingencies that might dominate as the determinants of its behavior.

(Minsky 1975a, 2)

That is, macroprudential regulation and examination, for Minsky, must not only reflect current and expected economic conditions but also be institution- and theory-specific, which is why Minsky has always insisted that it must be frequently reassessed in relation to the changes taking place in the financial system. In addition, such examination was intended to force central bank policymakers to become aware of the impact of their policy actions on the stability of financial institutions in the context of the ongoing institutional and operational changes in the financial system—something that was clearly lacking in the Fed's analysis of the recent crisis, which has now been revealed to have ignored the mechanics of subprime mortgage securitization and the role of credit default swaps in the interrelationships between banks and other (fringe or shadow) institutions operating in these markets.

Thus, one of the advantages of the use of Minsky's approach to regulation, in which the FIH serves as the basis for macroprudential regulations, is that it

explains why regulatory structures eventually become obsolete or perverse. The normal, profit-seeking activities of agents lead to innovation in order to create new sources of profits; innovations can be in products, processes or finance. The search for profits also drives agents to avoid, evade and adapt to the structure of regulation and intervention put in place to constrain incoherence. In time this undermines the effectiveness of a regime of intervention that "stabilizes the unstable system." Therefore if regulation is to remain effective, it must be reassessed frequently and made consistent with evolving market and financial structures.

(Minsky and Campbell 1988, 6)

Minsky stressed the point that "as the monetary system, the financial system and the economy are always in the process of adapting to changing circumstances, the quest to get money and finance right may be a never ending struggle," because what is an appropriate structure at one time is not appropriate at another (Minsky 1994b, 4).

> Throughout our history the reaction to some "unpleasant events" in banking or finance has been to reform the structure of banking and finance, as well as the structure of government chartering, regulation and supervision of financial institutions. Our predecessors were not fools: They knew the institutions of their time well enough so that when legislation changed institutions, the new structure succeeded in correcting the malfunctioning, for at least the time being. Such a new structure of payments and financing was apt enough, so that a "better" performance of the economy followed. However, the perennial quest for the profits that successful innovators earn energizes entrepreneurs. New financial and banking institutions and new financing patterns for business, households and government units emerge and their users prosper. Over time the initially apt pattern of regulation and supervision becomes increasingly inept: the inherited structure of regulation and the supervision first becomes not quite right and later becomes perverse. A cumulative effect of the institutional and usage changes that occur is that the institutions which are supposed to contain the endogenous disequilibrating forces of our economy lose much of their power to do so.
>
> (4–5)

From this point of view, the greatest error committed in the run-up to the recent crisis was to allow a major change in the institutional structure of the financial system in the 1999 Financial Services Modernization Act without any accompanying changes in the regulatory or supervisory structure. If Dodd-Frank is an attempt to remedy this error, it will by definition be inadequate to the conditions that prevail when it is finally fully implemented.

Regulatory instability

Minsky provided an example of his approach in comments made on the 1980s proposals for reform after the collapse of the savings and loan banks and the insolvency of the FSLIC. He noted that a basic difficulty in any insurance is the risk of moral hazard, but that it was difficult to understand how the problems of moral hazard and increased risk transference only appeared to threaten the survival of the FSLIC system after some 40 years of successful operation. The answer, he countered, was to be found in the institutional and policy changes in which the system operated. In particular, he and Campbell noted "the shift in position-making from trading in liquid assets in the 1960s to transactions in liabilities in the 1970s," as well as "the decrease in the margins of safety used to cushion fluctuations in cash flows" (Minsky and Campbell 1987, 255). As a result of these changes, they observed,

> payment commitments have become more closely coordinated with pay-ment receipts so that small changes in conditions can cause a large increase for units (households and businesses who are indebted to banks and banks that are indebted to depositors) to acquire cash by selling assets that may have thin markets.
>
> (255)

This leads to a need to sell assets to acquire liquidity, which causes a decline in asset prices and a "process that leads to a deep depression" (255). But the change in institutional operations was accompanied by a change in central bank operating procedures from interest rate management to money supply manage-ment, which made the issue of 30-year, fixed-rate assets, which had been safe assets, inherently risky. Minsky and Campbell thus argued that "the problems today are the result of competition for profits that has transformed an initially robust financial structure into a fragile system and in so doing made obsolete the structure of deposit insurance established 50 years ago" (Minsky and Campbell 1988, 7). It was the changed institutions, changed theory, and changed monetary policy that produced increased financial fragility and made deposit insurance untenable in the presence of systemic crises. "Whenever bank failures are due to idiosyncratic behavior," Minsky and Campbell wrote, "actuarial estimates of the probability of payoffs are possible. In such cases the insurance model is applicable and the proposed reforms of the structure of deposit insurance could be beneficial" (Minsky and Campbell 1987, 255). But "a system-wide decline in asset values cannot be contained by a guarantee or bailout of some restricted class of deposits or institutions. If instabilities that can generate large, system-wide losses of output, employment, and asset values are to be contained, more than deposit insurance is needed" (256). The conclusion, which is just as relevant today, was that

> The introduction, in today's environment[,] of risk-adjusted premiums or capital requirements and greater public disclosure of problem institutions, [which] are among the proposals to reform deposit insurance, would make it more, not less, likely that insurance payoffs will be required. In addi-tion, these reforms would increase system instability. A stability-enhancing response would be for Congress to accept that it has an open-ended,

contingent liability and to set in place a well-funded, institutional structure to fulfill its obligations.

(253)

Finally, Minsky and Campbell noted that

> the Federal insurance agencies do not administer deposit insurance as insurance for depositors but as a mechanism to insure the safety and soundness of the U.S. banking system. One of their goals is to prevent bank failures. . . . Recent innovations in the securitization of assets and the globalization of finance have introduced risks of financial dislocations that are only peripherally related to those the authorities are set up to handle.

(258–9)

The solution Minsky proposed to the problems faced by deposit insurance and the stability of the system in general was for the government to accept full responsibility, not only for insured deposits but also for the stability of the financial system. Deposit insurance, as insurance, was an outmoded and inefficient means of systemic macroprudential regulation in the presence of systemic instability and of banks being too big to fail. Indeed, this inadequacy has been one of the major elements of the growth of big banks, as the FDIC is only able to resolve smaller banks without depleting the insurance fund by having them assumed by larger banks.

Regulatory responses

As a possible alternative to the government assuming the contingent liability for the deposit liabilities of all banks, Minsky suggested the creation of a permanent government investment bank along the lines of the Reconstruction Finance Corporation (Minsky 1994a, 11). This would be desirable in an economy facing solvency crises and in which the question of "whether the structure of the Federal Reserve System that created district Reserve Banks to process eligible paper and to create thereby the reserve base for commercial banks is an apt structure for a Central Bank that operates by way of open market operations has never been faced" (8)—by which Minsky meant a Federal Reserve that "was not able to take an equity position in an otherwise bankrupt bank" and thus "unable to contain [an] insolvency crisis" (6). Which is precisely what the Fed and Treasury were forced to do through their exceptional policies supporting financial institutions that were too big to fail and that the federal deposit insurance system could not resolve.

Minsky made a number of proposals besides the government investment bank and government acceptance of the contingent liabilities on insured deposits. One alternative would be for the government to assume direct responsibility for the payments system. The government maintains a constitutional monopoly over the issue of notes and coin, and at one time supported the transfer function through postal money orders. Many other countries, particularly in Europe, maintained postal savings banks until the wave of deregulation and demutualization encouraged their sale to private equity institutions. Indeed, after the creation of the Federal Reserve System, District Federal Reserve Bank notes were the liability of the federal government. It would have been straightforward to allow the District Federal Reserve Banks to issue deposit liabilities to private individuals.

Another alternative would be a return to the approach of the National Banking System, in which the national bank-note liabilities of the national associations were backed by government securities, and require private bank deposit liabilities be reserved by full collateralization with government securities. Although this is the system that failed to allow a sufficiently elastic currency in the 1907 crisis and produced the decision to found a central bank to serve as a central reserve pool, it was given new form after the Fed was, in its turn, unable to stem the 1930s crisis.

The response took the form of the 1930s proposals of Henry Simons ([1934] 1948), Irving Fisher (1935), and "A Program for Monetary Reform" (by a group of experts including Fisher and Paul Douglas [Douglas et. al 1939])— and, more recently, proposals by James Tobin (1987), Robert Litan (1987), and Ronnie Phillips (1995)—for a 100 percent reserved banking system. Minsky considered that such a structure could provide, in place of deposit insurance, a substitute for government assumption of the contingent liability on all bank deposit liabilities:

> One aspect of the 100 percent money schemes was that debt financing of businesses and households was to be divorced from the payments and default free assets systems. This can be accomplished by making contingent value assets the standard for the indirect holding by households of paper that finances business and household debts. . . . Banks, through their loan officer function, are specialists in making loans on the basis of their "hard reading" of private information, which they obtain in the process of deciding whether and on what terms to accommodate a potential borrowing client. As a substitute for bank lending such loans can be the province of special mutual funds which break down the flow of funds from business and household financing into tranches, such that there is a fixed income portion with a relative fixed market value and a variable income and market value portion. These funds would be so structured that the variable income portion would have a high expected return but would also absorb the first say 10 percent of losses due to nonperforming assets: interest rate risk could be finessed by making all credits floating rate credits. . . . We are now in a position to realize the dual setup of 100 percent money: financing the capital development by contingent valued liabilities and a money supply based upon a portfolio of government bonds held by an authority responsible for the payments scheme.
>
> (Minsky 1994a, 12–3)

Thus Minsky envisaged securitization of the loans to households and businesses to provide both fixed and equity-type investment opportunities.

In recommendations for the reform of the Glass-Steagall Act, Minsky built on this approach in a proposal for a bank holding company structure that preserved the benefits of simplicity and transparency inherent in the New Deal legislation. The proposal would restrict the permissible assets and liabilities of the various independently capitalized subsidiaries:

> One such subsidiary can be a narrow bank which has transaction balances as liabilities and government debt as its assets. This narrow bank does not need deposit insurance . . . Because of the nature of its portfolio and the government's commitment to reprice bonds so that they never fall to a sharp discount deposit insurance is redundant. There is no need for a limit to the amount of the transaction balance that is guaranteed not to fall to a discount from its nominal value.
>
> (Minsky 1995, 18–9)

Thus the narrow bank would eliminate the negative influence of moral hazard and make the full government guarantee of all deposits unnecessary.

> Another subsidiary could be [a] business loan fund which uses only short term Certificates of Deposit to fund its activities. These certificates of deposits will be protected by assigned equity. A government insurance fund for 80 percent of the face value of the liabilities will be part of the package. . . . The narrow bank and the short term business financing subsidiary will carry on the transaction and short term business financing banking functions.
>
> (19)

The government guarantee would be transferred from the transactions business of the bank to its short-term financing of business, with the deposit certificates carrying a guarantee. The insurance takes the place of reserves against these liabilities to encourage households to hold them rather than the 100 percent deposits. Indeed, it is now common to encourage governments to engage in public-private partnerships to support specific investment projects, with the government carrying contingent liability for returns. Minsky's proposal provides a similar mechanism that could be used to direct funding toward productive business investments rather than financial speculation. In addition, the holding company would have another subsidiary that would

> carry on the investment banking function. Insurance subsidiaries can carry out the underwriting and sales of insurance products. The merchant banking operation will be financed by own capital as well as commercial paper and certificates of deposit. Because of the high risk these activities will be financed to a larger extent than the other functions by capital: special

liabilities of this subsidiary may well carry some equity kicker. The creation of large denomination "participation deposits" to finance merchant banking activities which carries some of the pains even as it shares in the gains from merchant banking activities.

(19–20)

The most important implication of this proposal, as Minsky seems to have admitted, would be that in such a segregated, dual system there would be neither a deposit–credit multiplier, nor leverage, nor private creation of liquidity. As Fisher had noted in his original proposal, "new loan funds would come out of savings, but no longer out of thin air" (1935, 91). A similar observation was made by Neil Wallace, who interpreted "the narrow banking proposal as one requiring the banking system to be liquid without any reliance on liabilities subordinate to deposits," and concluded that "the narrow banking proposal eliminates the banking system" (Wallace 1996, 7–8).

These proposals would thus require a "substitute for bank lending" in a capitalist system, since they eliminate the creation of liquidity normally associated with the role of the banking system in accepting the illiquid liabilities of the business sector used for financing day-to-day operations. The question is whether the capitalist system could function on this basis (see Kregel 2012).

As Fisher pointed out in his 100 percent proposal, this would not mean that financing would cease, only that it would be limited to the rollover or repayment of existing credits. In essence, the approach would institutionalize the "loanable funds" theory in which saving determines investment.

In this system, the only way additional liquidity could be created to provide increased financing for business investment is if the government ran a fiscal deficit. Bonds issued to cover the deficit would be deposited in the narrow bank subsidiary against credits that could be transferred to private individuals in payment for goods and services or to purchase certificates of deposit or securitized assets, providing for an increase in available investment financing. Instead of being governed by the decisions of banks to extend credit, or the private sector to increase saving, investment finance would then be determined by the position of the government budget and the direction of investment as determined by the extent of the insurance of the liabilities of different types of investment funds.

Indeed, a government deficit would be necessary, for in its absence the system would be deflationary and create an additional problem for "macroprudential" regulation. Alternatively, the central bank could engage in the direct financing of public or private sector investment expenditures. The "macroprudential" stability of the financial system would then require the application of what Abba Lerner called "functional finance." The size of the deficit creating the additional government means of payment required for macroprudential stability would be determined by the private sector holdings of narrow bank deposits and currency, adjusted for the current account position.

In the absence of a government sector deficit to support incomes, liabilities used to finance investment could not be validated in a narrow bank holding company structure. But, even more important, it would be impossible in such a system for banks to act as the Schumpeterian handmaiden to innovation and creative destruction by providing entrepreneurs the purchasing power necessary for them to appropriate the assets required for their innovative investments. In the absence of private sector "liquidity" creation, the central bank would have to provide financing for private sector investment trust liabilities, or a national development bank could finance innovation through the issue of debt monetized by the central bank. Were Minsky alive today, he would probably agree that the current institutional and political structures are not equipped to recognize the role of fiscal deficits in the successful operation of a narrow banking system intended to obviate the need for macroprudential regulation.

If it is not politically or economically feasible to produce a change in the structure of the financial system that separates the means of payment function from the need to finance the production of output and creation of employment, then Minsky's FIH provides another alternative approach to macroprudential regulation. If the cause of a crisis is systemic, and if it occurs endogenously via a process of tendential declines in the cushions of safety composed of liquid assets available to meet the non-validation of debts, then macroprudential regulation must be designed to counter these tendencies. In particular, these tendencies will produce rising ratios of assets to bank equity. The current approach relies on setting specific ratios of liquidity in the form of gross leverage ratios and gross as well as risk-weighted capital requirements. But from Minsky's point of view, it is pointless to place limits on these variables; rather, one must seek regulations capable of dampening the forces that determine them. In particular, it is important in this context to recall his view that liquidity is a property of an institution determined by its "position" assets, the markets in which they are traded, and the current changes in economic policy and institutions.

In an early paper on "money," Minsky identified the market incentives that will drive banks to the creation of assets and new methods of increasing assets in order to compete for market capital with nonfinancial institutions. He starts from the fact that, in comparison to other nonfinancial institutions,

> banks are highly levered organizations: banks borrow $12 for every $1 of capital. . . . If for example a bank makes 1 percent net income after taxes on its total assets, and if it is levered to the extent the average indicates, then it would make 13.2 percent on its book value. Banks usually have a conservative dividend policy, so that a representative bank might pay about 1/3 of their earnings as dividends. This means that the book value of a representative bank would grow at 8.8 percent per year by way of retained earnings. If the banks that retain earnings are to do as well on their new capital as they have done on their old capital, they will need to lever their retained earrings by the same factor of 13 through borrowings. Thus banks, in their profit seeking activities, will endeavor to have their deposits and other debts grow at the same rate as their book value: only in this way can their total assets grow at the same rate as their owners' investment. The observed 13 to

1 asset/book value ratio is the result of offsetting pressures upon the banks. The regulatory authorities, mainly by way of their examination procedures, press banks to have "adequate capital": i. e. to hold the ratio of assets to book value down. The drive for profits makes banks work at evading this constraint: i.e. banks want to increase this leverage ratio.

(Minsky 1972b, 5–6)

Thus the kind of macroprudential limits that are to be placed on gross leverage and the size of bank capital may, on the one hand, give banks a larger margin to absorb loss without facing insolvency; but they will also act as a sharp incentive to find ways to increase leverage and reduce capital requirements through innovation.

Minsky returned to this theme in a 1977 article, again emphasizing that

banks are profit maximizing organizations. Their return on the book value of owners' equity equals the return per dollar of assets times their assets per dollar of book value; i.e., $P/B = (P/A) (A/B)$ where P is profits, B is the book value of owners equity, and A is assets. Given this profit identity, bank management endeavors to increase profits per dollar of assets and assets per dollar of equity.

[. . .]

Our banks are corporations. The market price of their publicly traded shares, like the shares of other companies, is positively related to the expected rate of growth of earnings. If the level, rate of growth, and assuredness of bank earnings are high enough, then the market valuation of the bank's shares will exceed the book value of owners' equity. To first raise the ratio of market price to book and then sustain a favorable growth in the market price of shares require a high rate of growth in expected earnings per share. Because of stock ownership and stock options, management of a bank that is organized as a corporation has a private interest in ever higher share prices—in having the market value of the owner's interest rise relative to the book value of owner's interest. . . . As will become evident in what follows, banking as a generic phenomenon is destabilizing, but corporate banking, especially corporate banking in which management is largely divorced from ownership, is particularly destabilizing.

Earnings minus dividends divided by book value is the rate of growth of book value through retained earnings. If assets grow as fast as book value and if the profit rate on assets remains unchanged, then earnings, dividends, and the book value of equity can grow at the same rate. . . .

If management can sustain earnings per dollar of assets even as the assets per dollar of book value increases, they can raise the price of their shares. . . . The incentive for bank management to raise the asset/book value ratio, if it can be transformed into an increase in the rate of growth of assets and earnings, is strong. In fact, it will pay for a bank to increase the asset/book value ratio even if it results in some attenuation of the earnings/assets ratio. . . . Over the post-war era, bank management has been ingenious in developing reserve-economizing liabilities, so that the growth of bank assets has exceeded not only the growth objectives of the Federal Reserve but also the growth of bank equity. . . . In a world with corporate, growth oriented banking and a fragile financial structure, the Federal Reserve is forced into accommodating the banking system's demand for reserves. The banking process determines the volume of bank liabilities outstanding, and the Federal Reserve is forced to supply sufficient reserves to sustain these liabilities.

Banks have also been ingenious in developing techniques for financing business and financial institutions. These include the developing of covert bank liabilities, such as lines of credit and bank guarantees of financing.

(Minsky 1977, 17–9)

While this was written in 1976, it takes little to adapt it to the recent crisis, in which innovations produced substantial increases in profitability along with rising leverage and declining liquidity ratios. But it also suggests that setting particular macroprudential minima for the two ratios Minsky identified in the bank profit equation may nonetheless produce global asset growth that exceeds the rate of growth of national income and lead to increasing pressure to innovate, increased layering, and financial fragility.

Some additional implications of this analysis have been drawn in a series of papers by Mario Tonveronachi that builds on existing macroprudential proposals and minimum capital requirements to show that, "looking at national banking systems, there should be some close relation between the growth of bank assets and the growth of nominal GDP. This means that fixing the leverage ratio on stability grounds could equally result in allowing bank assets to outgrow GDP or to constrain its growth" (Tonveronachi 2013, 381). Tonveronachi's conclusion is that it would be more appropriate to invert the process and use target ratios for total-asset-growth-to-GDP to determine the appropriate national ratios of liquidity and capital. Thus, rather than placing limits on individual banks and applying uniform ratios across very diverse financial systems with divergent results, the ratio of total asset growth should be tailored to the institutional and policy characteristics of each country. The same procedure could be applied to individual banks on the basis of a cash-flow examination procedure recommended by Minsky. Setting values for A in the above formula for bank earnings would thus lead to concentration on the return to assets and creditworthiness, which was characteristic of traditional originate-and-hold banking.

While the imposition of minimum liquidity and capital ratios is an improvement over the prior risk-based approach, such target ratios are not macroprudential regulations in Minsky's sense. Similarly, stress tests of banks' capital positions are applied to banks individually, rather than in a systemic interaction. Neither approach to macroprudential regulation takes into account the dynamic macro factors that impact the bank's position-making assets and liabilities and the secondary markets in which they trade, or the ongoing institutional and policy changes that are a natural part of the economic system.

Minsky was fond of quoting, in relation to bank regulation, the remark of the great University of Chicago economist Henry C. Simons that "banking is a pervasive phenomenon, not something to be dealt with merely by legislation directed at what we call banks" (Simons [1936] 1948, 172). This suggests that, as Minsky put it, "a fundamental flaw exists in an economy with capitalist financial institutions, for no matter how ingenious and perceptive Central Bankers may be, the speculative and innovative elements of capitalism will eventually lead to financial usages and relations that are conducive to instability" (Minsky 1977, 22).

Notes

1 It is usual to distinguish between banking regulation, defined as the governmental framework of laws and rules under which banks are given license to operate, and supervision, defined as the monitoring of financial conditions at banks under the jurisdiction of governmental agencies and the ongoing enforcement of banking regulation and policies. However, since they are clearly related, they are often analyzed as being equivalent.
2 In its review of the collapse of Continental Illinois the FDIC notes:

> It is not surprising that few observers recognized the problems inherent in Continental's rapid growth; most indicators of the bank's financial condition were good, and some were outstanding. . . . There were, however, two aspects of Continental's financial profile that, with the benefit of hindsight, were indicators of the increased risk the bank took on during its growth period. First, Continental's loans-to-assets ratio increased dramatically . . . by taking more than the average risks in selected areas. One of the most significant of those areas was the energy sector, where Continental had a long history and the bank could claim a great deal of expertise. . . . Continental's lending involvement with three of the largest corporate bankruptcies of 1982 helped turn perceptions of the bank increasingly negative. Such perceptions were reinforced by the advent of the less-developed-country (LDC) debt crisis brought on by Mexico's default in August 1982; Continental had significant LDC exposure.
>
> (FDIC 1997, 238–41)

Thus the rapid growth in the bank's assets and its loans-to-assets ratio were aggravated by the impact on its borrowers of two macroeconomic factors: a change in monetary policy after the appointment of Paul Volcker and a change in oil prices—factors that Minsky insists should be a major part of the macroprudential supervisory process.
3 These areas of bank examination are usually summarized under the acronym CAMELs, signifying capital adequacy, asset quality, management, earnings, liquidity, and sensitivity to market risk. The final *s* was added in the 1990s response to the savings and loan crisis. Banks are rated on a scale of 1 to 5, best to worst.
4 Avinash Persaud notes the

> growing consensus around three ideas: Capital requirements need to have a countercyclical element in order to . . . "dampen rather than amplify the financial and economic cycle" by "requiring buffers of resources to be built up in good times." There should be greater emphasis on rules rather than supervisory discretion to counterbalance the political pressures on supervisors. And these rules should include leverage limits and liquidity buffers.
>
> (Persaud 2009, 4)

5 Indeed, an August 1966 letter from Minsky to FDIC Director of the Division of Research and Statistics Raymond Hengren suggests that he had been contacted by the FDIC to develop "new examination procedures" based on

the time series of cash flows to the institution that is generated by the institution's portfolio . . . costs of money and costs of operation. . . . from today's cash flow from portfolio and today's operating costs and costs of money, today's profits can be derived. This is not enough. What is needed, in order to evaluate the prospects of the institution, is a time series of cash flows to the organization, costs and profits.

A subsequent letter dated 20 October mentions an attached memo presenting Minsky's suggestions on how the procedure might be designed and implemented. Apparently, nothing came of this contact. (The letters and the memo are available in the Minsky Archive [Minsky 1966]). However, his 1975 notes (1975a) on the 1967 proposal suggest that it had been produced at the request of the Federal Reserve, again with no evidence of a follow-up.
6 Phillips (1997) provides an analysis of "the differences in the typical bank examination form and the Minsky form."

References

Douglas, P. H., et al. 1939. "A Program for Monetary Reform," available at faculty.chicago-booth.edu/amir.sufi/research/MonetaryReform_1939.pdf.
FDIC (Federal Deposit Insurance Corporation). 1997. *History of the Eighties—Lessons for the Future, Volume 1: An Examination of the Banking Crises of the 1980s and Early 1990s*, chap. 7. Washington, D.C.: FDIC.
———. 2008. "The Changing Liquidity Landscape." *Supervisory Insights* 5, no. 2 (Winter).
Fisher, I. 1935. *100% Money*. New York: Adelphi.
Helfer, R. 1996. Oral Statement by Ricki Helfer, Chairman, Federal Deposit Insurance Corporation, Before the Committee on Banking and Financial Services, U.S. House of Representatives, 104th Cong., March 13.
Kregel, J. A. 2012. *Minsky and the Narrow Banking Proposal*. Public Policy Brief No. 125. Annandale-on-Hudson, N.Y.: Levy Economics Institute of Bard College. August.
Litan, R. E. 1987. *What Should Banks Do?* Washington, D.C.: Brookings Institution Press.
Minsky, H. P. 1962. "Flow of Funds and Cash Flows." Paper 354. Hyman P. Minsky Archive, Levy Economics Institute of Bard College, Annandale-on-Hudson, N.Y. (hereafter, Minsky Archive).
———. 1966. "Cash Flow Examination Procedures for Banks." Paper 134. Minsky Archive. (See additional files.)
———. 1967. "Suggestions for a Cash Flow Oriented Bank Examination." Paper 175. Minsky Archive.
———. 1972a. "Financial Instability Revisited: the Economics of Disaster." In Reappraisal of the Federal Reserve Discount Mechanism, vol. 3, 95–137. Washington, D.C.: Board of Governors of the Federal Reserve System.
———. 1972b. "A Perspective on 'Money'." Paper 100. Minsky Archive.
———. 1975a. "Notes on: Suggestions for a Cash Flow Oriented Bank Examination." A document prepared for the Board of Governors of the Federal Reserve System in the summer of 1967. Paper 176. Minsky Archive.
———. 1975b. "Suggestions for a Cash Flow–Oriented Bank Examination." In *Proceedings of a Conference on Bank Structure and Competition*. Chicago: Federal Reserve Bank of Chicago.
———. 1977. "Banking and a Fragile Financial Environment." *Journal of Portfolio Management* 3, no. 4 (Summer).
———. 1994a. "Financial Instability and the Decline (?) of Banking: Public Policy Implications." Paper 88. Minsky Archive.

————. 1994b. "Regulation and Supervision." Paper 443. Minsky Archive.

————. 1995. "Reforming Banking in 1995: Repeal of the Glass Steagall Act, Some Basic Issues." Paper 59. Minsky Archive.

Minsky, H. P., and C. Campbell. 1987. "How to Get Off the Back of a Tiger, or, Do Initial Conditions Constrain Deposit Insurance Reform?" In *Merging Commercial and Investment Banking—Risks, Benefits, Challenges: Proceedings, A Conference on Bank Structure and Competition*, 252–66. Chicago: Federal Reserve Bank of Chicago.

————. 1988. "Getting off the Back of a Tiger: The Deposit Insurance Crisis in the United States." Working Paper No. 121. Department of Economics, Washington University. February.

Persaud, A. 2009. "Macro-Prudential Regulation." *ECMI Commentary* 25, no. 4 (August).

Phillips, R. J. 1995. *Narrow Banking Reconsidered: The Functional Approach to Financial Reform.* Public Policy Brief No. 17. Annandale-on-Hudson, N.Y.: Jerome Levy Economics Institute of Bard College. January.

————. 1997. "Rethinking Bank Examinations: A Minsky Approach." *Journal of Economic Issues* 31, no. 2 (June).

Simons, H. C. (1934) 1948. "A Positive Program for Laissez Faire: Some Proposals for a Liberal Economic Policy." Reprinted in H. C. Simons, *Economic Policy for a Free Society*, 40–77. Chicago: University of Chicago Press.

————. (1936) 1948. "Rules versus Authorities in Monetary Policy." Reprinted in H. C. Simons, *Economic Policy for a Free Society*, 160–83. Chicago: University of Chicago Press. First published in *Journal of Political Economy* 44 (February).

Sprong, K. 2000. *Banking Regulation: Its Purposes, Implementation, and Effects.* 5th ed. Kansas City: Federal Reserve Bank of Kansas City.

Tobin, J. 1987. "The Case for Preserving Regulatory Distinctions." In *Restructuring the Financial System*, 167–83. Kansas City: Federal Reserve Bank of Kansas City.

Tonveronachi, M. 2013. "De-globalising Bank Regulation." *PSL Quarterly Review* 66, no. 267 (December).

Wallace, N. 1996. "Narrow Banking Meets the Diamond-Dybvig Model." *Federal Reserve Bank of Minneapolis Quarterly Review* 20, no. 1 (Winter).

Index

Page numbers in **bold** indicate a table on the corresponding page.